Advance Praise for LIVE YOUR JOY and Bonnie St. John

"Without realizing you've learned anything, you'll close this book, stronger, more resilient, and more energized to take charge of your life…and LIVE YOUR JOY!"

—Lynette Lewis, author of *Climbing the Ladder in Stilettos*

"LIVE YOUR JOY isn't just a onetime must-read; it's an every-day should-read that will keep the joy flowing in and through you to everyone you meet."

—Kathi Macias, author of *Beyond Me:
Living a You-First Life in a Me-First World*

"LIVE YOUR JOY is a funny and inspiring collection of modern-day parables, a guide for finding joy in a hectic twenty-first century world."

—Spencer Sherman, author of *The Cure for Money Madness*

"Bonnie St. John is a warrior-sister who truly exemplifies the power of communicating with God."

—Paula White, Pastor of the Church Without Walls

"Bonnie St. John's story is simply gripping…from a small child losing her leg at age five, to a silver medal in downhill racing at the Winter Olympics, to Harvard, to the White House… Bonnie is an extraordinary example of courage and inspiration."

—Amy Dorn Kopelan, author of *I Didn't See It Coming*

"Bonnie's hard work and determination are an inspiration to all and reflect the best of the American Spirit."

—George W. Bush, 43rd President of the United States of America

Live *Your* Joy

Bonnie St. John

FaithWords

NEW YORK   BOSTON   NASHVILLE

FaithWords
Hachette Book Group
237 Park Avenue
New York, NY 10017

www.faithwords.com

Printed in the United States of America

First Edition: April 2009
10   9   8   7   6   5   4   3

FaithWords is a division of Hachette Book Group, Inc.
The FaithWords name and logo are trademarks of Hachette Book Group, Inc.

The publisher is not responsible for websites (or their content) that are not owned by the publisher.

Library of Congress Cataloging-in-Publication Data

St. John, Bonnie.
    Live your joy / Bonnie St. John.—1st ed.
        p. cm.
    ISBN 978-0-446-57925-4
    1. Joy—Religious aspects—Christianity.   2. Christian life.   3. Joy.
I. Title.

BV4647.J68S7 2009
248.4—dc22

                                              2008037864

To God who is my strength in all things.
And to Darcy, my daughter, who brings me endless joy.

Contents

Contents

Introduction

When people meet me they often ask, "How can I have the kind of joy that you do? You were abused as a child; you went through numerous surgeries to have your leg amputated; you've been divorced; you're a single mom. Yet you radiate joy.... How is that possible?"

The reality is, I am not "Little Miss Sunshine" every minute of every day. Once I got started writing about joy, I immediately found myself stressed out. *What if I really don't know anything about joy at all?* I worried. How's that for irony?

I constantly struggle with living joy. Very much so. I gained ten pounds two years ago that I haven't been able to take off, so I obsess about that. There are times when I worry a lot about what other people think of me, even though I know I should rise above that kind of pettiness. I have a long history of debilitating traumas that I have to keep in check and continuously work at healing. Yesterday, I hated the way my hair looked. Truth be told, my moods tend to fluctuate with my trips to the hair salon. I feel great for days afterward, because my hair looks fabulous. As it gets more unruly, I get moodier and crabbier until I finally put a siren on my head and deliver my hair emergency to Veronica, my Dominican stylist. And voilà! I am much more pleasant to be around. Most women's moods depend on their menstrual cycles. Mine depend on my hair cycles.

So I began to realize, the struggling to overcome my own ups and downs *is* the answer! Joy, you see, isn't a destination. I don't ever feel like I get to a place where I can say, "I'm the joy expert. Every day I have joy all day long." It isn't like that. It's an ongoing dance for me. I have to work at it. Joy builds gradually over time, and the process never stops. I can honestly say that I am more joyful this year than I was last year, and I hope I will learn how to be even more joyful next year.

When I try to define *joy*, my sense is that it's very different from something like happiness or pleasure. Pleasure is immediate, like feeling the wind rushing through my hair when I'm skiing, or watching a glorious sunset glisten on the horizon. Happiness, to me, is more about whether my overall life is going the way I want: I like my job, my daughter's health is good, I am in love and feel loved, so I feel happy. Those sensations come from the *outside* in.

Joy, on the other hand, comes from the *inside* out. It feels like a flowing grace that pours out from me into the world. It is a feeling of goodness, a sense of well-being through thick and thin. It is hope, confidence, friendship, positivity, and faith all wrapped into one. When I truly feel joy, it intensifies my pleasure and happiness. A woman in one of my workshops described it as "a silent smile." Don't you love that? It is something that happens deep inside you and truly belongs to you. Joy, or the lack of it, permeates every aspect of your life. When you're joyful, the grass is greener. Colors are brighter. Food tastes better.

That building on the corner has an amazing detail around the doorway that you never noticed before. People seem friendlier, challenges are less daunting, and life just plain feels better.

Now, don't get me wrong. I don't mean to imply that in order to live a joyful life you have to be flying on cloud nine all the time in some sort of blissful stupor. No. Joy can be found in increments, in phases. Think of joy as a reservoir. Sometimes it's full; sometimes it's pretty empty. But when the reservoir is empty, you work at filling it back up, and, hopefully, over time you learn to minimize the low points and get better at raising the levels back to where you'd like them to be.

Even when you're in a situation where people are treating you badly or things aren't going your way, you can still dip into your reservoir and bring joy to the situation. You can be the source of your own joy. When I am around a person who is cranky, nasty, or rude, I always think to myself, *I only have to take this for now. That poor guy has to be around his own crabbiness every waking moment of his life!* Inside myself, I get that "silent smile" because I am the only person I have to be around all the time. That crabby person is not in charge of my joy. I am.

You can always raise the level of your joy reservoir because it's coming from *inside* you. And that is such an amazing feeling! When you learn how to create joy in your life, you stop being a slave to what is happening in the world, and you become the master of your own destiny and emotions.

When my mother died last year, it was more painful than I ever imagined. But even during the week of her funeral, there were times when I could still make other people laugh. Or I could express love for my sister and my brother and bring us closer together. Friends surrounded me like a loving cocoon.

In these moments, joy comes to your rescue—if you let it. When you look around, you'll often be surprised at the places in which joy can be found. You just have to open yourself up to it and be willing to accept and appreciate its power.

Writing about joy for this book has helped me a lot. There were days when I sat down to write in a foul mood for whatever reason—whether I'd had a falling-out with a good friend, a business setback, or a family upset—and the last thing I felt like discussing was joy. On those days, the writing turned me around and brought me back to being the source of my joy. Again and again I proved to myself...this works!

I had fun with the process. For research, I had conversations with friends about how to get an immediate injection of joy—anytime, anywhere. We tested our ideas...and it worked for them, too! Throughout the process of reflecting on my own life experiences, I felt even more empowered to live my joy regardless of the crazy things life dished out. Whether I'm facing something as minor as getting splashed with mud on a newly dry-cleaned trench coat or as major as the sudden death of my mother, I know I can move forward with love and laughter, no matter what.

In this book, I'll be sharing with you a series of experiences along this perpetual joy journey. Some of the stories are from my own life, others were told to me by friends, but all of them involve ways to find joy each and every day—no matter how unlikely that may seem. Each chapter holds a piece of the puzzle I have put together in order to understand how to live my joy. As you read, embrace each notion and begin to apply it in your life—to fill up your reservoir. As you do, you will find you are better able to truly become your own source of joy.

Live *Your* Joy

CHAPTER ONE

Right Now...

Choose Joy

The Visitor

Living in New York City, you get all kinds of houseguests. People come in from out of town, and, mindful of the exorbitant costs associated with a hotel room in our delightful village, you always invite them to stay with you in your home. If you don't live in the city, you may have some grand, Hollywood-ized idea of what a New York City apartment is like—sweeping staircases leading to a second floor, soaring ceilings, elevator doors that open into a grand foyer...Forget it. The average apartment in Manhattan is smaller than most people's kitchens. Every square inch of space is maximized to the hilt. In my first NYC apartment, the kitchen was in the living room, you had to fold up the dining room table to watch television, and you could sit on the toilet to brush your teeth. I once had an estimate done to have the whole place carpeted, and it came out to be less than a lunch at McDonald's.

It was in this phone booth (anybody remember phone booths?) of a home that I found myself faced with an entirely unwelcome visitor. He was this huge, hulking, unkempt man with greasy hair and brown teeth who had rudely plopped himself down, rather like Jabba the Hutt, into my favorite leather easy chair. His clothes had a decidedly tacky style—sort of like the tattered, ersatz top-hat-and-tails of a traveling carnival barker. I could smell the stink of his breath as I sat on the sofa across the room (which meant our knees were practically touching). As he spoke, he wildly gesticulated his arms—wafting waves of putrid body odor all over my Lilliputian living room—and all over me.

We were, as always, arguing. And as usual, he was winning. The familiar frustration of this interplay bubbled up inside me to a fever pitch. I became consumed by it. Nothing else seemed important but this maddening battle of words and feelings. Suddenly, I remembered: this was *my* house! That was *my* beautiful chair his filthy butt was defiling. How dare he treat me that way! Here, of all places! I mustered the strength to ask him to leave.

He left without any objections and I found I almost missed him. That's odd, I thought. I so hate having him around, but the peace and quiet I experience when he leaves is a bit unnerving.

A few minutes later he knocked on the door. I hesitated for a moment, but before I even realized what I was doing I had invited him back in. "I'm hungry," he bellowed.

As he lumbered toward the kitchen, he hocked up a big, gooey mouthful of snot and spat on my polished hardwood floor. I thought I was going to vomit. Instead, I choked back my disgust and began to fix him a sandwich. I thought if I gave him some lunch he'd leave me alone.

"Pickles?" I asked.

He bent over, pointed his enormous fanny in my direction, and let out an earthshaking fart that, I'm pretty sure, indicated he wasn't interested in pickles.

As he ate the sandwich, he insulted the clothes I was wearing, told me I was fatter than the last time he saw me, that my hair looked like a rat's nest, and that my next project at work would probably fail. I felt perfectly awful around him, but for some insane reason—like rubbernecking an accident on the freeway—I couldn't stop listening and ingesting his diatribe. As if that wasn't enough, in a blur of astonishingly bad judgment, I once again offered to let him sleep on my sofa.

Sound absurd? Yes, of course it is. "Mr. Smelly," as I like to call him, isn't a real person at all. For me he is a symbol, a metaphor for the way I sometimes treat myself in my own personal space between my ears: my mind.

Inside our heads we all have our own Mr. Smellys. Shabby, mean, irritable interlopers that we not only let in, but we entertain, feed, and allow to take refuge in the already cramped chambers of our mental homes. Choosing joy is often about clearing out the clutter and making space for the thoughts, memories, and beliefs that lift us up; and, by doing so, bumping aside the ones that pull us down. It sounds so simple, yet I certainly know how easy it is to focus on the things that irritate me—often to the complete exclusion of anything that brings me joy. The irritants demand our attention—joy doesn't. We are forced to consciously pay attention to Mr. Smelly's invasions. The trick is to have the strength and courage to triumph over them.

I once asked a therapist friend of mine, "Have you noticed any patterns? Of all the people you talk to in your practice, what are the most common causes of pain and suffering? Disabilities? Divorce?"

As a motivational speaker, coach, and inspirational author, I was interested in which problems were the most universal. I will never forget his answer: "Relationships are the source of our most intense misery. While relationships can bring us the greatest joy, they can, and do, cause us our greatest agony."

That answer seems right to me. My struggles to keep my life, my thoughts, and my words joyful are most often defeated by what is happening in the relationships I care about.

Most recently I found myself profoundly affected by a situation with a distant cousin (which is how I refer to any family member I'm not exactly sure how I'm related to) who I felt was being abusive toward her three young sons. She lives a couple of hours away from me, but I would hear a story about something she had done to her children and feel absolutely sick (like the time she spent $20,000 on cosmetic surgery and then ended up getting her car repossessed because she couldn't pay the bills). Of course, she coerced her ex-husband or latest boyfriend into bailing her out of these situations by using her children as a lever. She routinely enlisted the boys as a weapon in her long and tumultuous divorce by creating painful dramas designed to make the kids suffer and then blaming their father. Each time I would hear about her latest form of selfishly acting out, I felt so bad for the children that it would haunt me for days. Sometimes these stories dredged up memories from my own difficult childhood with an abusive stepfather and an emotional, unpredictable mother, causing me to relive my own traumas.

I tried to help in small ways. When I could, I took the boys out for an afternoon. We would play in the park, laughing and swinging on the jungle gym, or spend time in a diner just coloring pictures and talking. Their little faces always lit up at the prospect of escaping the lunacy of their home life for a while. Still, they would rush to their mother's defense at the drop of a hat because they had been taught she was a helpless victim. Instead of having a mother who took care of them, they tried to take care of her. I started to realize that their mother probably had a serious alcohol problem. I felt so powerless to do anything. I talked with other family members about trying to get the kids away from her, but since she dresses nicely and is very good at manipulating everyone around her (especially men), we were advised that the attempt would most likely fail and leave the kids even more traumatized.

Thinking about those boys was like a steamroller crushing my joy. I knew that. But I also felt guilty not thinking about them. Would that mean I was a callous, uncaring person? How could I, in good, loving conscience, simply ignore this kind of abuse? Especially since my own abuse had been ignored when I was their age.

I obsessed about what was happening to the boys. I would find myself staring off into space when I was supposed to be putting on my makeup. In the bathtub I would catch myself dwelling on whether they would end up having a string of bad relationships because of what they were going through now. I spent hours trying to think of conversations I could have with them when they were old enough to understand and start healing. I knew these internal monologues of mine were useless, but there they were, like Mr. Smelly, stuck in my world, monopolizing my thoughts. Sure, I could kick him out for a while, but minutes later I would be shocked to find him back, making himself comfortable in my house all over again.

I prayed for help to be more at peace and to turn the situation over to God. I realized that the inordinate amount of time I was spending worrying about a situation I couldn't fix not only was stealing my joy, my energy, and my attention, it was siphoning off my focus on my own child. I reminded myself to focus on the job God gave me, which was to be a good mother to Darcy. As a busy parent, I never have as much time as I would like to spend really thinking about my wonderful daughter and connecting with her on physical, spiritual, and emotional levels. How ridiculous to pour out such tremendous amounts of energy on children I *can't* parent when I could put all that attention on the one child I *can* parent!

I began to wage a battle against the disturbing thoughts of my cousin and her family with thoughts of love and joy for my own daughter. One day, when I caught myself dwelling on all the damage a selfish, destructive, alcoholic parent can do, I instead just chose to close my eyes and conjure up the memory of Darcy's last swim meet.

It was a crisp fall day in New York. From my taxi I could see the trees of Central Park adorned with the brilliant hues of autumn. I'm always struck by the majesty of nature at this time of year. The meet was an "away" match at Trinity, a school on the Upper West Side. I found a place on the bleachers with the other parents and watched the kids nonchalantly dallying around the edge of the pool, waiting for their turn to hit the water. I talked to a Trinity mom on my left, laughing when we got splashed by the lane closest to our feet. I saw Darcy walking up to the edge of the pool, in her red uniform swimsuit, preparing for her race. My goodness, when did she get so big? That helpless little bundle I used to carry around was now intensely focused on the competition before her. This was Darcy's first year in competitive swimming, and she was determined to give it her all. She stepped up onto the block in a line with three other girls. She started out too afraid to dive off the blocks and had insisted on starting in the water. But here she was one month later, diving off with the others.

So it's to be a relay. Oh, good, this is her favorite event.

Bang! The starter gun fired and she dove into the lane. Yikes, she was the first one out! She needed to set the pace for the whole relay team! My heart jumped into my throat, which was a bit dangerous since I was screaming with all my might to cheer her on. You see, we parents think our kids can actually hear us shouting even though they are underwater. Oh, just let us have our fantasy.

Was that a flip turn? From the girl who refused to ever put her face in the water? Wow. They really do grow up in the blink of an eye. There she was, pumping her arms like pistons. I watched her head turn to grab a quick breath with the regularity of a machine. I was lost in a tidal wave of memories and emotions.

Wait a second; she's in the lead. She's in the lead! My baby is winning! Go, Darcy!

It still gives me a shiver just to think about it. I don't remember if her team won the relay, or even if her school emerged victorious over Trinity. All I remember was the look of fierce determination on her face during the race, and then the ear-to-ear smile she flashed me when it was over.

"Did you see that, Mom?" I sure did.

At the end of the meet I asked the coach if I could ride the bus back to school (I wanted to save the taxi fare back to the East Side). "Of course!" he said. "Ride with us!"

What I wasn't prepared for was how excited Darcy got about me participating in her life this way.

"Really? You're going to ride on the bus with us? That's so *great*!" she said. "C'mon. You have to have the whole experience."

She took my hand and pulled me toward the locker room. "Look. You can see behind the scenes."

I felt embarrassed about going with her, but I was so glad that she wanted me to come. She wanted her friends to meet me, and she wanted me to see into her life, too. "Look, everybody! My *mom* is in the locker room!"

She laughed and went off to use the bathroom, leaving me near the crowd of seventh graders who were changing, talking, and laughing. The hot topic today was the upcoming puberty classes at school (aka Sex Ed).

"I have to be in a discussion group with *Ryan*! Can you believe that? I am going to be soooo embarrassed."

"It's worse for me; there are only two girls in my group—the rest are all boys, like Martin, Jeremy and...ewwww...*Justin*!"

Darcy came back to rescue me and we headed for the bus. She negotiated where her friends would sit, since I was disrupting the usual arrangements. She proudly sat next to me on the hard green school-bus seats near the front. I was so thrilled that my thirteen-year-old still liked having me around and wasn't (yet) trying to pretend she didn't know me in front of her friends.

This was a moment I will cherish forever. I believe Darcy will, too. For the rest of my life, I can have that feeling, that memory, that thrill at any time, in any place. Those moments are burned into my heart forever. Take *that*, Mr. Smelly!

The Joy of Waffles

A woman I know named Michelle told me a story about waffles. Not about eating them, although that's part of it. Remember, even though scarfing down a big batch of Belgian waffles, slathered in strawberry goo and topped with a mountain of whipped cream, is true happiness in my book, in the book you're reading we're dealing with joy; a deeper, more ultimately satisfying emotion. Even when it comes to waffles.

Michelle has two nephews she just adores—and they adore their aunt Michelle. She often has them over to her home for sleepovers when her sister is traveling. One of their favorite pastimes is to snuggle up on the couch with a big bowl of popcorn and watch movies together. Being ages six and three and being boys, the sillier the movie, the better. Their favorite is that classic tale of knights in shining armor, fairy-tale princesses, dragon slayings, and other such noble goofing around: *Shrek*. For those of you who haven't seen the movie or read the book by William Steig, the story is a very clever send-up of the old "prince rescues a princess, they fall in love, and live happily ever after" saga. The prince, in this case, is an unlikely hero in that he's a great, green ogre (voiced by Mike Myers in one of his best performances) named Shrek. His comic sidekick is a talking donkey (brilliantly portrayed by Eddie Murphy) who tags along helping/bothering the big green guy with some of the most delightful comic banter since Abbott and Costello.

Here's where the waffles come in. In one of the early scenes, despite Shrek's objections, Donkey convinces his new buddy to let him spend a night at his house. He excitedly goes on and on about how they're going to "stay up late, swap manly stories...and in the morning, I'm gonna make *waffles*!"

Murphy's hysterically funny delivery of this line became an iconic moment in this hugely successful film, and lives near and dear to almost everyone who sees it—particularly Michelle's nephews. Not only do they love this line that makes them giggle whenever they hear it, they love to eat waffles. So, what do you think Auntie Michelle makes for them every time they visit? You got it. Before they arrive, Michelle gleefully goes shopping and tries to find the creamiest whipped cream, their favorite choices of toppings, and the tastiest batter. Just thinking about their little faces around the breakfast table brings her an overwhelming sense of joy.

Michelle's entire persona lit up when she told me this story. That's the way joy works. It can wash over you like a wave. The catalyst comes from anywhere—a look from a loved one, a memory that pops into your head, a smell, a taste, a piece of music, and, yes, even waffles!

There's No Place Like Home

Joy is sneaky. It loves to play "hide-and-seek" with you. Some days it feels like I have absolutely no joy in my life whatsoever. It's just gone. I'm empty. Kaput. My life seems out of control; the walls are closing in; I have no escape. And everything, *everything* bothers me. Whenever I feel this way, I try to remember to take a moment to stop and really, truly look around. When I pay attention, I soon find that little rascal joy, in some form or another, has been there hiding all along. That's a great feeling. I just want to grin, ear to ear, like a child winning a game. All-ee, All-ee, oxen free!

For a real "eye-opening" experience, I like to do this exercise actors use to sharpen their awareness skills: for two hours (or however long I can stay focused), I walk through my life and say nothing, think nothing, but *notice* everything. It's amazing. I see things that I pass by every day in a whole new light. Was the drawer handle on the desk always that shape? When did that tree start to lean to the left? The colors in this carpet are amazing!

Stop. Look. Listen. I'm always surprised by how different life is when you widely open your eyes.

Karen's eyes were closed. She had come so far from her childhood of poverty in Trinidad. Now a successful mother and businesswoman, she seemed to *have* it all—but she couldn't *feel* it. Here's her story:

> When I was twelve years old, it was my responsibility once a
> month to walk the six miles down hot, dusty roads to where our

landlord lived and pay the rent. And of course, I walked back. I was the oldest so they trusted me to carry the money.

During that long walk each month, I worried a lot. I worried because we were always late with the rent. The landlord was always angry with my family and me when I finally got there. As I sheepishly handed over the envelope full of cash, I expected him to yell at me and tell me we would be thrown out on the street the next day. The anxiety of this experience still haunts me.

I also felt sad as I passed all the other houses along the way. I knew most of the families who lived in them. I had been inside many to visit friends from school or church. Every house was bigger than ours. You could barely call where I grew up a "house" since it only had two and a half rooms. There was a living room with a sort of half room attached to it, which was a galley-style kitchen. In the one and only bedroom, I slept with my sister, my grandmother, my father, and my mother. Five people in one bedroom. Having space for oneself, not to mention any kind of privacy, was simply not possible. And we couldn't even afford to own this tiny home.

My mother, determined to make a better life for us, left Trinidad to work as a domestic in the faraway United States. For four years she worked and saved so she could have enough money to reunite our family. I missed her so much it hurt. She finally brought my sister and me over to America after I turned fifteen. I finished school and went to college in the U.S. I am so humbled by my mother's sacrifice.

Many years later, in my early thirties, I remember seeing my dream house for the first time. My mother and I were driving around looking at the beautiful houses in one of the expensive neighborhoods in Potomac, Maryland. We saw a sign for an open house and decided to take a look, just for fun.

Stepping into the foyer of the house, it took my breath away. The house must have been over 6,000 square feet. It had windows looking out onto a vista of trees and grass, with neat rows of flowers in beds lining the back patio. Everything was perfect about it. I remember thinking I would change nothing in the way it was designed. It felt like it was my house. I loved it with a painful, unrequited longing that ached in my heart. I stood there and wept, feeling that I would never be able to own anything like that. Such divine luxury seemed impossibly out of my grasp.

Fast-forward another fifteen years. I had not only worked hard in my job at the postal service and risen to a managerial level, but I had also built a flourishing practice as a real-estate agent on the side. I had saved and invested wisely. Now, here I was, looking to buy a home for myself, my three sons, and my mother! I did it. I really could afford not just any house, but a really nice home — the kind I always dreamed of. I planned to have it custom-built, just for us.

I had put a deposit down with a builder who showed me a beautiful model home. It had a room over the garage with a separate entrance where my mother could have some privacy while my three boys filled the rest of the house with noise and activity. I wanted the builder to add a kitchen in the room for my mother. I also wanted a full bath downstairs so that she could move into the den if the stairs ever became too difficult for her. There were a number of other modifications I wanted in order to make the house just right for my family and me.

But the builder was not being very accommodating. Everything I wanted was going to be a custom quote — meaning expensive — and he was dragging his feet. The housing market was booming so he acted like he didn't need me or my money.

I decided to take a look at another builder's model and talk to them about my options. When I described what I needed, the sales rep told me I would have to go to the Potomac area to see a model home fitting my description. Potomac! The same area where I had seen my dream house so many years ago! I drove an hour and a half to get there with my heart in my throat, wondering if this would be the one.

The moment I walked in the door, I felt it. There was nothing I would change. It felt like my home. The apartment over the garage already had the full kitchen. There was a full bath on the ground floor in addition to the half bath for guests. A private deck with an expansive view extended from the master bedroom, invited me to sit in peace and enjoy my home. It was 8,000 square feet of my own personal kingdom. I wept again, knowing I could finally provide safety, comfort, and luxury for my family. It felt so good. The whole thing went so easily. Within nine months we were all moved in. We were living the dream. The little girl from Trinidad no longer had to fear the wrath of the landlord!

But slowly, life took over. I would come home and rush past the windows with the spectacular views to check my BlackBerrys. That's right, two BlackBerrys: one for my job at the postal service and the other for my real-estate business. I would ignore the vast stainless-steel kitchen with the custom countertops in order to sit at the computer and pound out listings of houses for clients. I would avoid the beautiful deck off the master bedroom in favor of adding to my ever-growing, never-ending "to do" list.

Now, I already know I am a positive thinker. You don't get from a two-room house in Trinidad to an 8,000-square-foot house in the United States without being a positive thinker. But the concept of taking time to stop and think about something that brings you joy is very different from the concept of thinking positive. I wasn't taking any time away from the driven, forthright professional I had become. And I was miserable.

Karen and I were talking one day and this story just came spilling out. I felt that she was engulfed in that awful, blind state of mind where you get all caught up in things like paying your mortgage, paying your electric bills, paying your insurance...but not paying attention. Karen is a very religious person, and she never lost faith or forgot to be thankful for what she had. She was just stuck in a place where she couldn't enjoy the things she was thankful for. As we chatted, it occurred to me that maybe the best thing for her to do was wake up and smell the firewood.

I gave her a simple task. I asked her to just sit alone in her house. No BlackBerrys. No phones. No bills. Just sit there quietly and focus on being *aware* of her home.

I lit a fire in the living room fireplace and curled up on the sofa, sitting still and looking around the room. I let myself remember how I felt when I first walked into the model. How I fantasized about where the furniture would go. How I had dreamed my whole life about having a sofa in a living room just like this. All mine. All to myself. I thought about how much I loved being able to come home to my castle. How proud I was to call this house my home. I walked outside, stood on my manicured front lawn, and gazed up at that glorious structure and thought, I live here. This is my house. It belongs to me.

17

As I felt the warmth and joy of those thoughts run through my body, it was like a weight had been lifted off my shoulders. I went inside, and the first thing I saw was a set of mirrors I had bought to go over the sofa. They were just leaning against the wall — another chore I had pushed aside. I found the hammer and nails and hung them up. I was nurturing my dream.

Over the next few weeks, I made a conscious effort to appreciate my house and everything it represents. I smiled as I prepared dinner for my children in my grand kitchen. I looked at my mother, happily going about her day in the lap of luxury I had provided for her — after all she had provided for me. I sat out on my master deck — master of my domain. Day after day, my joy overflowed — just because I made space for it in my life.

I was in a situation similar to Karen's right after my divorce. I wanted to find a dream home for my daughter and me in which to pick up the pieces of our lives and start over. Because of the sexual abuse in my childhood, I had become very good at shutting down my emotions and living life mainly from logic. In the past, every time I moved into a new place to live, the choices were all about logical considerations such as the distance to work, the number of bedrooms, the monthly cost, etc. I didn't even think to consider what the place felt like. My brain just didn't go there.

Not this time, I thought. In the healing process, a huge part of the work centered around reclaiming my emotions. I was learning to care about how I felt—to care about myself at a deep, visceral level. So when it came time to find a more-permanent residence, I drove all over San Diego looking for a place to live that *felt* good. It was a completely alien concept to me, but I forced myself to give it a chance.

I wanted something rural, so I drove north and toured some of the highly-sought-after homes in rapidly growing areas like Vista, Escondido, and Carlsbad. Mild weather, access to beaches, and small-town atmosphere made these communities a real draw, especially for retirees from across the country. But looking out over this promised, brochurelike paradise, the strangest thing happened. I found the dry, arid conditions too bleak. An easy-care cactus garden surrounded by hardy, drought-resistant shrubs made other people feel good but, I discovered, not me. Even though I knew from my research that these were very desirable locations, I heard myself saying they just didn't *feel* right. And, more important, I listened to those feelings and acted on them. Wow! What a concept!

After I looked at a bunch of alternative locations, though, my shoulders sagged in defeat and disappointment. I just wasn't finding that "feel-good" place. It was getting dark. Being a longtime ski racer, I would have loved to move to Colorado or Montana, I thought. But I couldn't. I wasn't going to take my daughter that far away from her father. This whole idea of caring how I felt was just starting to feel like a big failure. It was much easier to be purely practical.

"I have an idea," said Valerie, my trusty real-estate agent. "If you are willing to go a little farther outside the city."

We drove in her car forty-five miles east of the city on Highway 8. As the road wound through barren mountain-scapes, we climbed up, up, up to 4,000 feet above sea level, and then dropped suddenly into a small, lush evergreen valley. Nestled in the foothills of the Laguna Mountains, on the edge of a national forest preserve, was a little town only three blocks long, with no traffic lights, aptly named Pine Valley. By now it was completely dark and I could hardly see anything. The town had already folded up its sidewalks, leaving only the diner and gas station still open.

Valerie parked in front of the old, fifties-themed diner. I opened the car door and felt the crisp, thin mountain air rush into my lungs. Even in the dark I could see majestic conifers towering over the charming village. I smelled a wood fire in a fireplace nearby, and years of cozy, snowy, blissful images rushed through my brain. I knew I was home. We came back a week later and looked at five houses for sale (there were only five houses for sale in Pine Valley) that were all more affordable than our tiny condo in the city.

I chose an old four-bedroom house with a charming, cottage-style exterior of stonework and wood that was formerly the carriage house for the mansion next door. Originally, it was a two-car garage with an apartment above it. When it was changed into a separate house, it became a lovely, rambling space with rooms that grew off one another and wound around like a labyrinth. The garage was converted into the kitchen and dining room space, a living room with a big black woodstove was added on one side, and three more bedrooms grew out of a long hallway toward the back. My master bedroom was the only room upstairs. It was huge—over 400 square feet—with a walk-in closet and a view of the surrounding mountains. I could also look out over my lawn, and the eight great pine trees I later gave names: the stately "Grandfather" tree, the elegant "Lovely Lady" tree, and the "Twins."

The Twins were a great big, double-trunked edifice that majestically rose out of the ground—reminding me of the pillars at Stonehenge.

Okay. So there I was in paradise, but I still had a lot of healing to do. All my life I had been busy doing, doing, doing: working hard in high school to earn a scholarship for college; training to win Olympic medals; studying at Harvard to finish fast (three years, not four); and then struggling through the overwhelming process of winning a Rhodes scholarship. I never really learned to just play and enjoy life. I just drove myself mercilessly with no regard for my own comfort. So many years of this kind of self-abuse don't just melt away when you sit under a few pine trees—no matter how good they smell.

As a single mom, I started every morning busily getting my daughter ready for her day—bath, breakfast, clothes. I walked her to school and rushed back home to try to cram a full day of work—preparing for speeches, marketing, publicity, and writing articles—into the half-day Darcy spent in kindergarten. I was sure I couldn't take time out for myself because this brief, few hours was the only time I was guaranteed not to be interrupted by my five-year-old.

Too soon, it was time to pick her up, make lunch, read to her, or go out in the garden looking for bugs. I would spend an hour or so with her and then give her an activity to do while I put in a few more hours of work. As anyone who has ever worked at home with a little one knows, it isn't easy to concentrate. Your child will suddenly demand your attention for a simple hug, or for a more urgent need like choking on something she shouldn't have put in her mouth. You stay on alert. That makes everything doubly tiring.

After an hour or two of work (or however much time I was able to steal), I would knock off for dinner and get in more Darcy time with a game or movie. After I read a story and put her to bed, I went back to work until I fell asleep across my desk, exhausted.

I knew that I was luckier than most single moms. I could support the two of us while working from home. I got to walk her to school. Even being able to put off a lot of work until she was asleep and spend quality time with her throughout the day was a privilege. It was a great life. So why did I still feel like a workaholic, constantly rushing from dawn to dusk? Where was the joy? I was breathing the fresh air, but I wasn't tasting it. I was tossing wood on the fire, but just for the heat it provided. I was rushing past the glorious pine trees I had longed for in my search for a good-feeling home. Had I really learned anything about caring for myself?

One day, sitting at the cherry Queen Anne desk my mother had given me (the beauty of which was completely obscured by my professional sprawl), I was earnestly churning out my critical "to do" list: set up interviews to prep for next three speeches, pay bills, organize quarterly sales tax info, etc., etc. I had lived my whole life enslaved to agendas like this that never seemed to end. But it occurred to me that these perpetual lists never include an entry like "Stop and feel joy," do they? *Hmm*, I thought. *Why not?*

I pulled out a clean piece of paper, wrote in big letters "To Feel" across the top, and began to make the most unusual list of my life:

1. Feel like a kid in summer camp: Breathe in the fresh air while walking to school. Slow down and pick up pinecones. Make a collection.

2. Feel close to God: Sit on the lawn and pray under the shelter of majestic, thirty-foot-tall pine trees.

3. Feel in love with nature: Look out the kitchen window and watch the sunset paint the mountains pink.

4. Feel happy: Play your favorite music while you work.

5. Feel snug: Build a fire in the woodstove — enjoy the flicker of the flames and the smell of the burning wood.

6. Feel wonder: Look at the sky at night — more stars than you can ever see in the city.

7. Feel comfy: Put on both woolly slippers — even if you only have one foot!

As that clever, culinary character Emeril Lagasse would say, *Bam!* There it was. My own personal outline to remind myself to take in everything I took for granted. There were so many easy little things I could do and feel — things that took little or no extra time. My problem, I discovered, wasn't time; it was that these "feeling" items never made it onto my list. Why try to change my nature? I realized I am the kind of person who has to write things down. Once I did, all those lovely, joy-generating items became a priority.

Just click your heels three times, Dorothy. Kansas was there all along.

CHAPTER TWO

Confidence...

Joy's Main Muscle

The World According to Mickey Mouse

Zooming along the freeway in my brand-new, red Ford Escort, I scarcely even noticed the beautiful, sunny day in San Diego. It was always sunny and beautiful, so what's the big deal? My thoughts focused on the meeting ahead of me in less than an hour. After a month of preparation, networking, and follow-up, I had landed a major appointment with the executive VP in charge of the local headquarters of a major national bank. As a sales rep for IBM, I was ready to step up to bat and hit a home run.

Joining IBM was my first job after obtaining my M. Litt. (British master's degree) in economics at Oxford. I was pretty full of myself—Harvard grad, Rhodes scholar, Oxford grad—and I was determined to do a great job. I had spent a year in "sales training"; alternating between two-week classroom programs in Atlanta and being a gofer for various sales reps back home in the San Diego office. Now, I finally had a real assignment of my own: selling imaging systems.

Today, we can have scanners for an extra twenty bucks on practically every brand of home or business copier on the market, but back in the early '90s, the ability to take a document and reproduce it into your computer was a big deal. At IBM, the imaging systems we sold were more sophisticated than most of our competitors'. Rather than just a computer for scanning in old files to archive, our systems could transform the flow of work between people and allow groups of people to handle documents, such as loan approvals or insurance claims, without ever touching any paper. Really cool stuff. But the revolutionary aspects of this kind of capability were often lost on folks used to doing things the way they'd always been done. To sell our systems, I had to get to senior management and walk them through understanding how we could transform their organizational efficiency while at the same time significantly cutting costs.

I pulled my sporty little vehicle (I had splurged for the high-performance package with the chrome wheels, the sport suspension, and the spoiler on the back) into a disabled parking spot directly in front of my IBM office. Just because I walk really well with my prosthetic leg doesn't mean I didn't earn the right to that parking spot the hard way. You cut your leg off if you want it!

In the lobby, Richard Delaney (my very own gofer from the training pool) was there waiting for me. He looked as bright-eyed and bushy-tailed as I had in my first few months.

"Would you like me to drive?" he asked.

"No, we'll take my car," I answered, smiling. This was my first new car, and, as you may have surmised, I was darned proud of it.

I felt happy to be taking the newest member of our sales team along with me to show him the ropes. I felt the meeting would go well because I had developed a wonderful relationship with George Shasta at the San Diego headquarters for Big Bank. We met at a Rotary Club event where I was speaking to high school students and we hit it off immediately. Later, I had taken him and his wife out for dinner. Since then I had tailored my Big Bank proposal with his input every step of the way.

However, if I said closing the biggest deal of my career so far didn't scare me down to my five little toenails, I'd be lying. My heart raced. But since I knew I'd planned and worked hard for this, my sweaty palms were also a sign of excitement and antici- pation. Even though I was nervous, I felt sure that the meeting would be easy and enjoyable.

As we drove to their offices a few miles away, I briefed Rich- ard on the situation at Big Bank. They were in the process of downsizing their loan-processing staff and needed a system like ours to keep the work flowing. I answered Richard's questions and then asked him about his training classes in Atlanta.

"It was so hot there during my last class in August, we stuck the lawn chairs in the pool and studied that way," he told me. I laughed, remembering the long hours spent poring over the specifics of technology systems and preparing team sales presentations.

We pulled into the parking lot with the huge, monolithic Big Bank tower looming over us. I remembered from my days on Wall Street how important it was for financial institutions to spend a fortune creating headquarters that were grand and imposing. Something about inspiring confidence. I picked up my briefcase from the backseat and led Richard through the tall glass front doors and into the slick marble lobby protected by a bank of security guards. After passing muster with the sen- try, we rode the elevator to the top floor and gave our names to the receptionist. She made a phone call and said warmly, "Have a seat. He'll be right with you."

Though we were right on time, it was a few minutes before George's assistant, Gail, came out to get us from the reception area.

"Hi, Bonnie," she said. "It's so nice to meet you after talking on the phone so many times."

"It's great to meet you, too!" I said, shaking her hand. It's always funny to me that I don't realize I have a preconceived notion of how someone I have spoken to only on the phone will look—until I meet them and they don't look at all like what I expected. That was truly the case with Gail. "Has your daughter recovered from the flu?" I asked this statuesque blonde whom I had pegged more as a chubby brunette from her warm voice and easy humor.

"She's back to climbing the walls and bouncing off the furniture!" Her dark eyes sparkled when she mentioned her six-year-old daughter.

"I have some bad news, though. George was called out to the national office at the last minute. Late yesterday evening he had to jump on the red-eye flight. Instead of rescheduling, he asked Tom McIntire to meet with you. Tom is George's deputy, his right-hand man, and would be one of the decision makers on a project like this. Let me show you to his office."

So much for the best-laid plans of mice and men! I mused to myself. *So much for an easy ride. Now I have to be ready for anything. Absolutely anything.*

Richard followed me to a large corner office with a sprawling view over the city, complete with a strip of sparkling blue ocean beyond.

Tom stood as we entered, extending his hand. "So glad to meet you. Coffee? Gail, can you get us some coffee? Thanks."

I introduced Richard and myself and launched into the meeting. We spent the first twenty minutes or so getting to know each other, which didn't surprise me since we had never met before. He seemed really excited to find out I had gone to Harvard and won the Rhodes scholarship and he asked a lot of questions about that.

Eventually, when I felt the timing was right, I pulled out my laptop and walked Tom through the presentation I had developed for Big Bank. I had interviewed a number of key people in the loan department to understand the idiosyncrasies of their processes, as well as integrating key data on the volumes of loans, documents, and other factors. I was able to deftly answer all his questions about a transition to the new system and the bottom-line impacts.

As we prepared to leave, I handed him three bound, printed copies of the presentation and felt as though I were blowing the smoke off the end of my pistol. He said he would have to wait for final approval from George, but I felt confident that we had a deal.

Once Richard and I were back in the car and heading to the IBM office I asked, "So, what did you think?" And prepared to bask in his acclamation of my well-prepared pitch.

"I couldn't believe it," Richard exclaimed. "He was so...so rude to you!"

Whoa? What was that? I inadvertently stepped on the brake too hard, jerking us both forward and almost throwing the car off the road.

"What do you mean?" I asked as I reacquired my focus and pulled my snazzy red zinger back onto the freeway.

"Well, when we went in, he reached to shake my hand first

even though you were closer. And then he grilled you on your background. My gosh, Bonnie, he actually asked you what you scored on the SATs!" Richard looked pale from shock and disbelief.

"Tom's whole tone was glacial to you at first. I think it was when he found out you were a ski racer that he started to warm up to you. You got him talking about his son's baseball team, and that thawed the air a little more. Even so, during your presentation he grilled you like a shrimp on a barbie. I have only been going on sales calls with reps for a few months, but I have never seen anyone act like that. It didn't seem friendly to me at all."

"Well, Richard," I replied, still perplexed from his observations, "I'd never met him before today. He may have been taken aback because George dropped this meeting on him at the last minute. He may have another friend whom he would rather give the contract to instead of us. You never know, do you?" Reaching for an easy image reference, I said, "You've got to play it as it lies." A golf metaphor? Yikes! I've never played golf in my life.

For Richard's benefit I behaved as the wise, experienced sales rep and gave him my sage advice. But inside, I felt as stupefied as he did. I had not at all noticed that Tom was giving me an unusually hard time.

I dropped Richard off at the IBM Building and drove to one of my favorite coffee-shop hangouts nearby. I wanted to think.

Poking at the foam on my latte, I ran through the meeting as Richard had described it. Sure, there was some resistance at first, but I met it with a sense of humor, good posture, and a willingness to explain my qualifications. I knew I had performed well. Nothing felt terribly unusual about that.

Then it hit me. It *wasn't* unusual for people to underestimate me or question my abilities. It happened all the time—and I dealt with it all the time. Most of the people I met with as a sales rep, oddly enough, didn't look like me. They tended to be male. They tended to be white. And they tended to be tall. I once read that leaders of corporations were on average taller than the national average for men. Being five foot two meant that I walked into meetings at tie-clip level.

There I was, trying to be taken seriously and sell software, but having the aura and presence of Mickey Mouse: shorter, darker, and cuter than everyone else in the room! It wasn't that anyone was trying to make me *feel* small. I *was* small.

Yet, I had strengthened my confidence muscle so much that a meeting like the one with Tom didn't even cause me to break a sweat. I had not let the stares of kids on the playground define me as disabled; I became an Olympic athlete. I had not let growing up on the poor side of town define me as being worth less than the kids I went to school with in La Jolla; I graduated with honors from Harvard and Oxford. What was it that allowed me to take situations that looked impossibly difficult and cut through them?

Confidence.

It took confidence to keep skiing after falling down all over the mountain. It took confidence to keep studying and excel in school. And it took confidence for me to walk into a hostile corner office with optimism and energy.

That kind of confidence is a fundamental building block of true joy. You live either from the outside in—waiting for others to make you happy—or from the inside out—making your own joy. Confidence, to me, is that exact moment when either you choose to give in to the pressures around you, or you choose to take the world with you where you want to go. When was the last time you faced a fork in the road and went the way that took all your belief in yourself?

In the animated movie *Anastasia*, the lead character is released from an orphanage at age eighteen and told to walk three miles to a fish factory where she was promised a job. Soon she comes upon the classic fork in the road. Anastasia agonizes at the decision before her. Should she go where she was told, take her place in the factory line, and resign herself to the life she was told to expect? Or should she take the other road, less traveled, leading to St. Petersburg, defiantly believing that she is worth more and can expect a better future? Of course she takes the road that requires courage—and, as Robert Frost so aptly said, that made all the difference.

Today, almost two decades after my stint at IBM, I motivate employees of every level, profession, and industry and still draw on those early experiences of transforming reality in an instant with confidence. Even if you are not a one-legged black woman, even if you are not short, even if you are not cute, you will sooner or later find yourself in a situation where you are not accorded the respect you want and deserve. Whether it's your employer, your client, your significant other, or even your kids, you will need confidence to stand your ground.

Nietzsche said, "That which does not kill us makes us stronger." (Actually what Nietzsche said was, "Was mich nicht umbringt, macht mich stärker," but why quibble.) When I find myself in a little over my head, I get this little silent smile. When I feel uncomfortable in that way, I relish the opportunity to build my muscles and push against so-called "reality."

For one of the world's most beloved innovators, Walt Disney, "reality" was getting turned down for loans more than a hundred times when he sought funding for his theme-park idea. He didn't give up. He didn't cave in. His confidence muscle built an empire of happiness and joy on three continents, spanning many generations. And there is nothing "Mickey Mouse" about that.

This Is a Job For...

Superman always ducked into a nearby telephone booth (anybody still remember telephone booths?) when he wanted to make the quick transformation from mild-mannered Clark Kent to the caped, crusading crime fighter and savior of the world in blue tights. When I needed to make the transformation from frazzled, desperate, work-at-home mother of a two-year-old to elegant, inspirational keynote speaker, I always ducked into "Tangles."

Tangles, as you may have surmised, is a hair salon. It is located in the heart of tony La Jolla, California, an idyllic beach community situated just north of San Diego, along one of the most picturesque stretches of the Pacific coastline. La Jolla rivals its better-known northern neighbors like Malibu, Beverly Hills, and Santa Barbara for high-style, beachy California living. Before moving to small-town Pine Valley, my daughter, Darcy, her father, and I were living near there in a condo—albeit far from the multimillion-dollar "mcmansions" that dotted the cliffs near the village. I looked at this occasional visit to an upscale, bourgeois establishment like Tangles as one of the few little perks of femininity I allowed myself at this time. I also knew I couldn't be very successful as a corporate speaker if I showed up with my hair looking like I had just stuck my finger into a light socket.

"Bonnie, looooove!" cooed my stylist, Freddy, one of those really tall men who took up a lot of space in the room, not just because of his physical size, but also because of his diva personality.

"You look like you have been working so hard!"

He meant I looked like something the cat dragged in, which I did. In this neighborhood, most women wore designer sweat suits to walk the dog with Chanel sunglasses—on the dog. As a part-time writer and full-time mom, I specialized in taking frumpy to a new level. After swimming with my daughter that morning, my hair was so frizzy that I just plopped a baseball cap on it and made it go away. I wore my typical "mom" uniform of workout shorts, a plain T-shirt, and my "sports leg." I have two prosthetic legs: the cosmetically covered, pretty, shapely leg I wear with suits (Darcy dubbed this one the "Barbie" leg); and this other one, with all the titanium and hydraulics showing, that looks like something out of *The Terminator*. Not exactly the typical look for this particular slice of Southern California.

"Come…sit down," said Freddy, eyeing the overwhelming challenge before him. "Let me work my magic on you. Where are you going this time?"

"Memphis. I am giving a speech for FedEx," I answered him as I pulled off the baseball cap, revealing the wild, matted mess on my head. "I don't think they're expecting Buckwheat!"

We both howled as I opened my bag of activities for Darcy. I always set her up in the waiting area with books to look at and crayons to color with. I chose a nice spot for her to spread out where I could clearly keep an eye on her from Freddy's fancy swivel chair.

After the wash and conditioner, I detoured over to check on Darcy.

"Wow, these are beautiful!" I said as I looked at the pictures she had produced. Darcy has a vivid imagination, and her pictures were not simply stick people and houses and boats, but flying horses, wicked witches, and mythical beasts. I pulled out some of the toys the salon owner kept in a big basket to give her something new to do while I went back to Freddy. I knew it was going to be a while, and I wanted Darcy to have plenty of entertainment.

In those days, my hair was set on hard rollers and I sat under a dryer for forty-five minutes. This onerous procedure smoothed out my kinky, frizzy African-American hair into shimmering curls that would last for days through airports, hotels, and business dinners. Today, there are many more acceptable African-American hairstyles for businesswomen that involve a natural look. Back in the 1990s, however, natural black hair was a business liability. So, Freddy rolled and pinned and pinned and rolled, all the while alternating between brag-ging about famous clients he'd "done" and dishing the dirt about his love life — which was an elaborately Byzantine soap opera just waiting for the cameras to roll.

By the time he put me under the hair dryer, I was looking forward to three-quarters of an hour of peace and quiet. For me, the pampering wasn't the wash and set, the head massage, or even the prospect of being made beautiful. Pampering for the mother of a toddler is a few minutes of not washing dishes, pick-ing up clothes, catching spills before they hit the floor, or clean-ing stains off the walls. Having nearly an hour to sit still and not do anything is like a trip to the Golden Door Spa for three days.

I glanced at my baby girl playing happily with her toys and then closed my eyes, leaning into the blissful feeling of my maternal escape. I could vaguely hear Melanie, the owner of the salon, talking to Darcy the way adults who never had kids do, like she was a pet dog.

"What do you have there? Good girl!"

As I began to melt into my chair, I felt little hands on my arm.

"Hi, Mom!"

I had a visitor. How sweet. I took the stuffed walrus she held out to me and began making it talk to her in a funny voice.

"Hi, I am Mr. Tusk. Russ W. Tusk, that is!"

She laughed with that tinkling laugh that always turned me inside out with delight. Talking to the walrus kept her interested for another few minutes before she became bored with Mr. Tusk, and with me as well. She left to investigate the rest of the salon. So much for my restful peace. A hair salon is a veritable minefield for a two-year-old. Visions of electrocution and scissor impalement rushed to my brain. I watched her like a hawk.

She spoke to Freddy, who teased her with funny little sounds while cutting the hair of his next customer. When she'd had enough of that, she ran over to Melanie, who gave her a red gummy fish from the candy dish at the reception desk. I was starting to realize it probably wasn't the first piece of candy Melanie had given her. Darcy was getting pretty wound up. I got out of my chair.

"You have to sit down, honey," I said, meaning she had to go back to the waiting area.

"Let her sit here next to me," Freddy said graciously, wanting to help. He pointed his scissors at the empty stylist chair in the station next to him. I helped her into the chair, got her a few toys, and went back under the dryer.

Just as I settled in, I watched her figuring out how to make the chair swivel by holding on to the counter with her hands and pulling the chair around. Now, we've all been there, haven't we? This little exercise is immensely fun when you are under three feet tall. But no matter how you look at it, it's a disaster waiting to happen. I was feeling pretty uncomfortable and decided to make my move. Before I could get out of my chair I saw her complete a full rotation. Who knew a two-year-old could be that strong?

She ecstatically went two, three times around as I quickly walked toward her. Then, just out of reach, in one of those moments that seem to happen in slow motion, I watched her foot catch on a cord near the chair....

In a hair salon there are so many dangerous things a cord can be attached to—a hot curling iron or an electric trimmer, to name a couple. What's the worst thing you can think of? How about hot melted wax?

The scalding liquid went flying across the room, sending queens and customers diving for cover. I flung myself over to Darcy, terrified she would be covered in molten wax. Melanie was at my side, screaming, "She's okay? She's okay?"

Miraculously, no one, including Darcy, was burned or injured in any way. Actually, my mind completely amplified the gravity of the situation. The result of all this drama was really just a hot, gooey glob that pooled into a bit of a mess on the floor. Thank goodness Melanie was a very understanding person. Despite her sincere lack of concern for the turmoil my offspring had wrought, though, I figured it was probably a good time for the two of us to get the heck out of Dodge. No matter how you looked at it, this whole visit wasn't working. So, I packed up my little bundle of trouble and joy, paid my bill, apologized profusely once again, and we headed out.

We had planned a trip to the aquarium after the salon. Since I took as much responsibility for taking a two-year-old into a hair salon as she did for pulling the cord, I decided to stick to the plan. Besides, this wasn't just any aquarium. It was part of the Scripps Institution of Oceanography, one of the top locations on earth for aquatic research. Connoisseurs of all things aquatic from around the world travel there to gaze at the expansive exhibit space full of exotic species arrayed in breathtaking underwater scenes.

As we pulled into the massive parking lot, Darcy squealed with excitement. This was one of her favorite places. I parked, undid the tangle of belts and buckles we use these days to secure our precious packages in a car, and in doing so, casually caught a glimpse of myself in one of the rearview mirrors. Oh, yeah. The top of my head looked like it could tune in the ball game.

Now, this wasn't entirely an accident. To be sure, I didn't really focus on the curlers when I left the salon—I was in a bit of a rush. But I also subconsciously realized that if I had taken them out, all the time and money I had put into my coif would have been wasted. Not to mention the fact that I'd be wearing my swim hair in Memphis the next day. Of course, I could have left the curlers in and gone home to let my hair air-dry with no one looking. But then we would have missed the aquarium entirely. As a typical, guilt-ridden, working mom who was leaving home the next day on a business trip, I overcompensated by being Supermom. So I left the curlers in *and* took Darcy for her outing. Clearly, I was no ordinary mother.

There I was, strolling into the aquarium with curlers in my hair, a bright blue mechanical leg, and a two-year-old in tow. Bless her heart, Darcy didn't think for a moment there was anything odd about the image her good ol' mom was presenting. There were others, though, not quite so oblivious. I was awash in a sea of eye-rolling glances, sotto voce mutterings, and even some rude pointing and laughing from the younger, less-inhibited patrons.

Years of experience in being stared at in this way kicked in for me. I met their gazes...and simply smiled. It takes a special kind of backbone to do that—to have everyone look at you as though you are strange or crazy (or both!) and to look back with complete confidence.

I know what you are thinking, I mentally told a young woman who couldn't even manage to pull her eyes away politely. *I understand how you feel. But I have a secret strength you'll never understand.* I stood ramrod straight and walked my best runway model walk.

When I turned the corner at the jellyfish tanks and walked into the sea anemone room, I faced a whole new group of gawking tourists and La Jolla moms with their Prada diaper bags. I took a breath. There is always an instant in this sort of exercise when the wall of uncouth curiosity, disdain, and pity hits me full-on, and I want to turn tail and run. It takes both physical and spiritual resiliency to absorb all that negative energy and then laugh about it, smile back, and proceed with rock-hard fearlessness. And it felt amazing.

How is it that it can feel so good to do something so difficult? It was actually exhilarating for me to test myself in this way. I wouldn't want to do it every day, but I realized that it felt like I was exercising a muscle—a confidence muscle. It was a familiar feeling because I had to do it as a child.

In elementary school, my leg was made of wood with round

metal hinges on either side of the knee. When it bent, a big piece of wood stuck out in the middle. I looked like Pinocchio. Everywhere I went people stared. Kids teased me on the playground. I had only two choices: (1) cringe and hide, or (2) learn to meet their insults and gazes without backing down. I knew they didn't understand anything about me or my leg. There were times when I even tried to make other people comfortable by explaining my infirmity and demonstrating how adroit I was at getting around. Other times, I just stayed out of sight. But I eventually learned that the best way to survive was to be myself, be confident, and behave like it was no big deal. My confidence seemed to bleed over onto them. If I wasn't embarrassed, it usually helped other people feel at ease.

To me, utilizing the confidence muscle is crucial for living joy from the inside out. Just as I could choose at the aquarium whether to live according to other people's hostile reality or my own self-esteem, I choose in every moment of my life whether to become consumed by the negative experiences I'm inevitably confronted with or, instead, to reach beyond the superficial and allow my inner joy to bubble to the surface.

There are singular moments in life where you have to stand strong or follow the crowd. Imagine that you were a senior executive at Enron during all the malfeasance at that beleaguered company. Would you have stood up to temptation and said no to millions of dollars? That would be pretty hard to do without confidence. Having a strong confidence muscle gives you a platform of strength from which to live your values from the inside out and not get caught up in "what everyone else is doing." If you have confidence in yourself, what everyone else is doing has much less meaning. You can create your own joy irrespective of the forces around you.

By thinking of confidence as a muscle, it's also easy to think about "working out" that muscle to make it stronger. When we put ourselves in situations that challenge us, we grow. Exercising that muscle may be as simple as going to a movie or to dinner by yourself, if that is outside your comfort zone. It could be trying an activity that you are a little bit nervous about, like Tae Kwon Do or ballroom dancing. At work, you can ask mentors to help you get "stretch" assignments that force you to lead special committees, interact with a different department, or maybe even work in a foreign country. Public speaking tests most people's confidence level. Getting yourself out there in front of a crowd as often as you can (whether it's your business associates, your kid's Little League team, or your favorite community group) is the best way to conquer that fear. Find something, whatever it may be, and give it a try. You'll be surprised at the results.

The key is to build up your muscles *before* you need to do the heavy lifting. It's like an isometric exercise against reality. If the world is pushing you to go one way, push back in another. Then, when you really need to flex that muscle, it will be ready—toned and pumped.

When I need to leap tall buildings in a single bound, having my hair done is nice. But having real confidence is about a lot more than a little extra makeup or a well-tailored suit. Real confidence is the strength that comes from deep within. The good news is, with practice, those tall buildings will shrink below us as we rise above with the style, grace, and strength of Superman...or Superwoman!

CHAPTER THREE

Hope...

Learn the Rules

A Portfolio of Dreams

As I washed the dishes from breakfast one Saturday morning in early 1993, I remember feeling the luxurious expanse of the weekend stretching out before me like a buffet of choices. I had worked hard all week at IBM and was looking forward to some time just for me. I wanted to go to the gym and maybe see a movie. Sure, I needed to go grocery shopping, pick up clothes at the dry cleaners, pay bills, and a few other chores, but I usually put those things off until Sunday so I could have some downtime after the workweek.

What I really wanted to do with my Saturday, I thought to myself, was hole up at Beans, my favorite local coffeehouse, and continue writing the proposal for my first book. I had dreamed of being a published writer since I was in the fourth grade—maybe even before that. I've always loved books. Books kept me company on the playground when I couldn't jump rope with the other girls. Books helped me escape from my abusive stepfather at home. Books opened up worlds, experiences, and adventures far beyond my humble existence in suburban San Diego. To be an author meant reaching out to others and tossing them the lifeline I had grabbed on to so desperately.

Every delicious hour I could steal away and work on my

book proposal meant I was an hour closer to my noble fantasy of becoming a real writer. For me, it was addictive.

Brrrrrring! The phone clattered, rudely snapping me out of my reverie.

"Hello?"

"Hi, Bonnie, it's Sarah."

"Oh, Sarah! Great to hear your voice!" I was so excited to hear from my old friend from college. Sarah Smith is one of my favorite people, not to mention one of the world's great thinkers. "What's up?"

"Well, you know I volunteered in Bill Clinton's campaign. Now that he's been elected, we're looking for people to apply for jobs in the White House. I immediately thought of you. Are you interested?"

There was a beat of silence as her words sank in. This wasn't the usual let's-grab-a-coffee-and-catch-up kind of phone call from an old college chum.

"Wow! Um…Wow! Uh…Thanks for thinking of me." I hoped my mouth wasn't sputtering as much as my brain was. "What kinds of jobs are you talking about?"

"All kinds of things—all policy areas, like domestic, international, economic, environmental, technology. We'll also need people for the advance team, speechwriting, research, and a million other things. The important thing is finding people with brains, character, loyalty, and a strong work ethic."

This was for real. I wasn't dreaming. This wasn't some kind of practical joke my mind was playing on me. And I wasn't getting "punk'd." Ashton Kutcher was only fifteen years old at the time. Too young—even for Demi Moore.

"Is this a trick question? What do I have to do to apply?"

I blurted, never even considering the consequences of such a decision.

"Just fax your résumé to Patricia; I'll give you the number. Better mail it also," Sarah explained casually, as if she asked people to apply for White House jobs every day. Which, at that point, I suppose she did.

"Can you recommend some other people whom you know?" Sarah continued. "We have a lot of positions to fill, and we want good, strong recommendations to find the best people."

"Sure, I can recommend some people. Should I have them call you?"

"No, just tell them to fax and mail their résumés, too."

Sarah and I talked a bit longer about our work, our husbands, and mutual friends before hanging up. The receiver barely hit the cradle before my knee (remember, uno) began to buckle. I quickly found a chair and sat down heavily. *Holy cow.* Me, applying for a job in the White House. I could get to work in the West Wing—way before they made a cool TV show out of it—in the thick of one of the most exciting political environments since the Kennedy family moved in back in the '60s!

The whole idea was thrilling, but I quickly realized it was also pretty darned scary. I liked my job at IBM. I had put a lot of passion into my goals at work, starting two new service programs with special permission from the branch manager, and I was finally making a strong reputation for myself. Did I want to leave that behind? Plus, I was working on my book proposal. You know, save the world, the word *author* after my name, my own Dewey decimal number...Let's not even mention the fact that Washington DC was three thousand miles away from where I was living in Southern California. Not exactly a comfortable commute. I was married, and my husband had a good job he really loved. Where did the White House fit into my plans?

I decided to procrastinate by calling a few friends, as I'd promised Sarah, and proffering them my inside line on jobs in the brand-new Clinton administration.

First I tried Nicholas, a friend who had spent many long nights with me cramming for exams in the government department at Harvard. He wasn't home. Next I called Martha, another member of our college study group.

She picked up after two rings. "Hello?"

"Remember all the courses we took on American government?" I asked. "How would you like to try out the real thing?" I explained the opportunity to her, anxious to get her take on all this.

"Thanks for letting me know. That is so exciting." Martha must have been as shocked as I was.

"I don't know if I can apply, though," she told me. "My husband and I are living here in San Francisco. We'd have to move. I don't think we can do that."

"Yeah, I know what you mean," I responded. "My husband works here in San Diego at one of the best oceanographic institutes in the world. I couldn't ask him to leave either."

"Besides," said Martha, "there will probably be a million people applying. What are the chances?"

Ah. A voice of reason. Of course this whole idea was ridiculous! A silly dream. So impractical, improbable...impossible! To apply, I would need to rewrite my whole résumé, tailoring it specifically for this opportunity. Why bother spending three or four hours on a Saturday working on this when I probably wouldn't be offered a job? And if I did, I wouldn't be able to pick up my life and move out there anyway! Pointless.

"I know. I'm pretty sure I won't do it either," I found myself saying.

After I got off the phone, I struggled with what to do. The last thing I wanted was to give up the bulk of my Saturday, my one day of freedom, and spend it updating my résumé and writing a cover letter. Tomorrow would be filled with errands, laundry, and getting ready for the upcoming week. Besides, a brand-new *Star Trek* series called *Deep Space Nine* was premiering tonight. I really wanted to see that.

But then I thought to myself, *Wait a second!* This wasn't some stint at the local Piggly Wiggly. This was the *White House!* Washington DC! The most powerful place on earth. Serving at the pleasure of the president of the United States! And, more specifically, *this* president, William Jefferson Clinton—a lightning rod for the kind of massive governmental change I yearned for with every fiber of my intellect. There would be laundry and grocery shopping for the rest of my life. I could TiVo *Star Trek*. Well, TiVo hadn't been invented yet, but you get the idea. An opportunity like this came along once in a lifetime. So what if the odds were long? So what if I had other dreams, too? So what if I didn't know how it would work out? All they were asking for was an application, right?

Once again, I was at a crossroads. If I waited to do things until I had all the answers, the parade would be long gone before I made my first move. I could apply, and if I couldn't find solutions for those other problems, I didn't have to go. *Just fill out the application.* I could always respectfully say, "No, thank you...*Mr. President....ARRRRRGH!*"

But if I didn't even apply, I would never have the choice. I would never know what might have been.

When I worked on Wall Street I learned about investing in stocks and bonds. The most basic rule for making money is that you should have a diversified portfolio. You invest in low-risk positions like Treasury bills with a portion of your funds, and then you can put another chunk in a few higher-growth/higher-risk mutual funds with small companies or international stocks. Plus, you should be prudent and invest in all levels of risk in between. The precise way you allocate your assets depends on your appetite for risk.

In the same way that there are basic rules for investing money, there are rules for "How to Hope." I realized that following my dreams meant deciding how to invest my time and my willingness to hope, just like investing money. Applying for the White House job meant diversifying my portfolio: in addition to my day job and my book proposal, adding this long-shot opportunity somehow started to make sense. In terms of allocating my energy and passion appropriately, I was only being asked to invest a few hours in this million-to-one chance. So, why not?

I find that most people hope too much or too little. By investing your time and passion wisely in a wide range of hopes and dreams, you can get a big payoff in terms of living your joy. Foolhardy "dreamers" who completely disregard the viability of their passions are often disappointed and frustrated. Ultra-conservatives who always do only the practical thing can wake up one day feeling that they have wasted their lives. Somewhere in the middle is what works best for me. The porridge isn't too hot or too cold; it's just right.

So I packed up a pad of paper, gathered copies of my outdated résumés, and drove over to Beans to draft my screen-play for *Ms. St. John Goes to Washington*. I would live the fantasy of being on the White House economic team for the next few hours instead of my usual writer fantasy. I did not have to choose one dream over the other in a permanent sense. All I had to do was figure out the best use of a few free hours on a single Saturday.

But, since anything worth doing is most certainly worth doing well, I gave this fantastic notion my best shot. I rewrote my résumé and cover letter carefully, crafting, in my opinion, a nicely compelling treatise on my background, qualifications, and desire to come aboard and join Team Clinton. When it was all cleaned up, spell-checked, and polished, I sent off my mis-sive and waited for the phone to ring.

And waited.

And waited.

After a few weeks, I actually forgot about the whole thing. When you have a full portfolio of dreams, there is plenty to keep you happy and working toward bigger and better joys. I didn't have time to sit around thinking about that one-in-a-million chance of working in the West Wing. Then one day, out of the blue, Alexander Graham Bell's lovely little invention once again treated me to a surprising conversation.

"Bonnie, this is Marion. We'd like to interview you for a job at the National Economic Council—part of the White House staff. Interested?"

After I picked myself up off the floor, I was able to squeeze out the words "Sure. When should I come out for the inter-view?" I tried to make myself sound casual but failed miserably. The hyperventilating probably gave me away.

"Well, I need to set up appointments with the head of the NEC and his two deputies. I will call you back in a couple of days with some times and dates. Okay?"

"Sure," I answered, unable to come up with anything more erudite than a single syllable. The line went dead. Marion was gone.

Uh-oh. I felt like the tide had just shifted. I was no longer embarking on that fantastic exercise in futility, but I had come face-to-face with a real opportunity for a real position: a presidential appointment to a job. My mind raced again.

Good investors take risks, I thought, *but not all risks*. They use the information they have to assess whether the risk is a good bet: a calculated risk. Having a portfolio of dreams means making assessments about what is a good bet for your future.

I weighed what I knew. Those muckety-mucks were going to invest their time, too, and that had to mean a lot. They couldn't interview hundreds of people, only a few. Yes, going to the interview would require a bigger investment, a greater focus, but my odds couldn't be all that bad if I had reached this stage.

Could I overcome all the obstacles? I spent the next few days going over the various logistical hurdles. My husband and I discussed how we could make it all work. The book could wait. My business career would only be enhanced by a stint in the White House. You know, where there's a good, strong, earnest will, there is almost always some sort of a way.

If you look back on your life, sometimes you can whittle down the trajectory of your course to a few defining moments. This was one of those moments for me. I now became focused on landing myself inside the white stone porticoes of 1600 Pennsylvania Avenue.

Marion had said she'd call in a couple of days—meaning two days, as I understood it—but I still hadn't heard from her after four. So I mustered up my newfound determination and dialed the West Wing once again.

"One ringy-dingie," as Lily Tomlin would say. "Two ringy-dingies…three ringy-dingies…" It went on and on.

Finally, after the tenth ringy-dingie, a secretary picked up. I asked for Marion.

"Sure. I will have to go find her. Will you hold?"

What choice did I have? I waited ten minutes. Just as I was about to hang up, she came back on the line.

"Marion didn't pick up? I am sorry. She said she would. Perhaps you should call back later? I will leave your number for her."

I called back in an hour and left my number again. The third time I called that day turned out to be the charm.

"Hi, Bonnie. It's Marion. I am still working on your interview appointments. I will get back to you in a couple of days—can't wait to meet you!"

The next four days were a slo-mo replay of the first go-round. No phone call from Marion. After repeated efforts to track her down, I finally got her on the line after calling every twenty minutes for two hours.

"Well, I think I can fit you into the schedule on Thursday, but I am not sure. Why don't I call you back?" she asked.

"Oh, no!" I probably said with more angst than I meant to. "Today is Tuesday. Unless you call and tell me that the plan has changed, I'll just book a ticket and come out tomorrow. Will that work?"

She agreed.

"Oh, by the way," she added, "the federal government is not

allowed to reimburse any of your expenses for the flight or accommodations. I am sorry about that, but we can't. Is that okay?"

What could I say except, "Sure, that's fine. I will be there first thing on Thursday," in my most cheerful voice.

Remember, in the early nineties, there wasn't anything like cheap deals on Web sites à la Expedia or Orbitz, so I spent the next hour or two phoning various airlines to find a flight. As I put the phone back in its cradle and massaged my sore ear, I faced the reality that the only flight to get me there was a red-eye leaving the next day and arriving Thursday morning... depositing me exhausted and, well, red-eyed, only a few hours before the interviews would start. But wait, it gets better: the price was equivalent to more than half my monthly take-home pay as a sales rep at IBM.

This was starting to feel like being a poor kid from Southern California scraping her way to Olympic medals in ski racing. Wait a second. I'd already done that. *You'll always wonder if you don't try your best....* I sucked up the pain in my bank account and bought the tickets.

After the grueling red-eye flight, I arrived in our nation's capital to find that all my hard-won interviews were canceled because of the funeral for the first black Supreme Court justice, Thurgood Marshall. How's that for irony? But they weren't getting rid of me that easily. I told them I'd camp out in the lobby until they were ready to see me. So there I sat, waiting and watching famous people hurriedly zoom past my not-so-lofty perch by the door: Al Gore, Tipper Gore, Hillary Clinton, and many others. Finally, after much hand-wringing and apologizing, Marion was able to squeeze in my interviews at odd moments during the day.

Being willing to try, to take the shot when you have the chance, to risk a little, but not too much—that's what makes it possible to make your dreams come true. Don't just hope for one thing, or dream of one thing. I have hoped for many things—a whole portfolio of goals—and a few of them have actually come true. Like getting a job in the White House.

In the end, I spent a thrilling eighteen months living and working alongside some of the smartest and most dedicated people I have ever met in my life. Even with all the frustrations and anxieties that kind of grueling existence imposes on one's psyche, I wouldn't trade a second of it for anything.

Many years later, I met a fellow at a convention who seemed very interested in how I managed to actually land my job in Washington.

"I sent in my résumé, too," he offered, vestiges of disappointment still lingering in his voice.

"Well, what happened?" I asked.

"They never called me back."

I shook my head. Linking my arm in his, I said, "Let me explain to you about investment portfolios...portfolios of goals, that is...."

A Vision Isn't Always
What It Looks Like

I have a friend, Jana Stanfield, who is a wonderful, spiritual folksinger. She's recorded a number of CDs, all with a positive, inspirational message. She talks about the fact that her goal as a musician is to give people a "faith-lift." Don't you just love that? Her lyrics are always very clever, and her tunes are just beautiful.

One of my favorites of Jana's songs is called "Every Dog Knows." It's all about her scruffy, lovable dog, Buddy, and his unqualified devotion to her. Regardless of the trials and tribulations of her life, Jana can always count on Buddy to snuggle up to her and kiss her woes away. The song goes on to tell about a time she dressed Buddy up like a refugee from the Westminster Kennel Club—all primped and bedecked with frilly accoutrements—so that she could enter him in a 4-H contest. Buddy, ever the dutiful friend, suffered the humiliation of all this with dignity and aplomb, despite the fact that the contest was a two-hour drive from their home and Buddy—as always—got sick in the car. A mess of matted fur and vomit-coated bows, Buddy still managed to win the blue ribbon because no other dogs showed up that day to compete! It is such a sweet story of pure, unadulterated warmth that it makes me smile every time I hear it. It certainly gives me a "faith-lift"!

A couple of years ago, I had scheduled a speech in Nashville so I called Jana to tell her I'd be in town. She graciously invited me to stay with her—an invitation I happily accepted. She even picked me up at the Nashville Airport in her cute little black PT Cruiser, and ferried me out to her lovely home on the outskirts of "Music City, USA."

On the way, we decided to stop for coffee at a local café. I could tell she had something on her mind. She wasn't her usual jovial self. After we exchanged the customary "catch-up" banter, I poked a little.

"So, what's going on with your life, really?" I inquired, hoping she would let me in to help and then equally hoping I would have some help to offer her.

"I'm just so bad at this vision thing," she confessed. "I've never been able to make goals work. You know, you're so good at it; how do you do it?"

I was floored. Here was this woman who has been so successful. She writes and performs her own music, she started her own record company—back in the days when that was unheard of, particularly for a woman—she has sold more than one hundred thousand CDs, and still she thinks she has problems setting and reaching goals.

She told me the story of her latest CD. After doing the monumental work it takes to write, record, and produce an entire album of songs, she decided a reasonable goal would be to sell at least ten thousand copies in the first six months. So, she marshaled her years of experience in the music industry and put together a release schedule, complete with a detailed advertising-and-marketing plan. She organized tour dates and publicity campaigns. She did affirmations. She wrote positive things. She put notes on her mirror. She meditated. She visualized her goal coming true.

But after doing all this, six months came and went and she had sold only five thousand copies, not the ten thousand she wanted. She thought she had failed. She was wallowing in defeat and self-doubt.

I knew right away that she needed to shift her point of view. Just because we have a vision for how we want things to be doesn't mean they will always work out that way. Sometimes they will, and that's wonderful. Goals are important, but if we doggedly stick to them despite very real circumstances and conditions that affect their outcome, we are setting ourselves up for disappointment. That disappointment, then, translates into feelings of defeat. That's where Jana was. Frustrated and deflated.

Setbacks aren't always the worst things that can happen to us. To the contrary, we often have to take a step backward *in order* to take a step forward. This is the ebb and flow of life. If we always try to bend the world around how we think things *should* be, we'll never get ahead. We need to realize that flexibility is one of our most important assets. Only then can we truly navigate our missions and aspirations. You've heard it a million times: when life deals you lemons—*make lemonade!*

Jana and I talked through a series of adjustments she could make to reset and reevaluate her expectations for the CD. She extended the time periods and set more achievable benchmarks for sales. She refocused her marketing-and-advertising plan to make it more efficient and, hopefully, more effective. As we talked, albeit in very broad strokes, I could tell she was shifting her attitude. I could feel the excitement creeping back into her demeanor. She was returning to her joy.

We left the coffee shop filled with positive, zestful feelings and headed to her house. Crossing the threshold of Jana's warm, charming Tennessee home, I heard the unmistakable clatter of stony toenails vigorously tap-dancing across the tile of the kitchen floor.

"Buddy!" Jana hollered. "Come meet a new friend!"

My heart skipped a beat. I was finally going to get to meet this heroic legend of love and affection in the flesh—or, to be more accurate, in the *fur*. I had often envisioned a picture of Buddy in my head as I listened to the song. Sometimes, depending on my mood, he was a regal golden retriever with a long, flowing mane; sometimes a floppy, cuddly beagle; sometimes just a delightfully bedraggled mutt with huge, adorable brown eyes. But now I was going to get to put a face, and a cold, wet nose, to the name. I felt as though Mel Gibson were about to round the corner. And then, suddenly, in a rush of giddy excitement, through the doorway he bounded, skidding to a stop right in front of me—tail wagging and tongue dripping. To say I was stunned would be an enormous understatement. Buddy was a huge, black, manicured and poofy-trimmed...*poodle!*

"This is Buddy?" I exclaimed, completely unable to cover my astonishment.

"Yeah, I know." Jana smiled, clearly understanding where I was coming from. "I thought the real image wasn't, somehow, right for the song. Not many people know my little secret...."

Buddy jumped up and kissed me all over. It was as though we were destined to fall in love with each other in an instant. He spent the entire weekend by my side whenever we were together. I felt it. I felt the warmth. I felt the devotion. I felt the faith-lift. Buddy's soul was everything I had imagined and more, even if his outward appearance didn't exactly fit my preconceived notion.

Sometimes we just have to ignore the package and take what life deals us for what it is, not what it appears to be. Sometimes a setback is really a gift. And sometimes, despite expectations, our hero isn't a grand and exalted lion, but, rather, a cuddly, drippy, foofy poodle.

Dare to Hope

After my fifth-grade class ended, I walked outside with Irma and Robin. I liked them, and, mostly, they liked me. We had that funny little emotional back-and-forth that ten-year-olds have. Some days they ignored me. Other days they were my best friends. They always seemed to stay loyal to each other, though. They were close neighbors and played together almost every day.

Robin was talking about walking over to Irma's house, but I stayed silent—knowing I couldn't go. Ahead, I saw a van pull up to the curb. It was painted to look like a regular school bus—mustard yellow with "School Children" in black across the top—but everyone knew it was the "handicapped" bus. Darn, it was earlier than usual. I said good-bye to my would-be playmates and hurriedly walked apart from them, hoping that they wouldn't follow me too near the bus or look too closely at the other kids inside. I hated having to be one of the drooling, limping freaks who populated that embarrassing little vehicle, although I was used to it by now. I had my leg amputated when I was five. Before that I could walk only with the help of this massively uncomfortable brace. At least my wooden "Pinocchio" leg was better than that. What I really missed, though, was being part of the group. I would have given anything to be able to pop over to a friend's house after school and "hang out" like the other kids.

"How's my partner in crime today?" The smiling face inside beamed.

I have to admit, I really did like the bus driver. His name was Clyde, so naturally we made Bonnie and Clyde jokes. "What do we do?" He posed, waiting for my reply.

"We rob *banks!*" I retorted, and we exchanged a hearty high five. Good old Clyde. It still makes me smile to think of him.

Lucky for me, we drove straight to my house before dropping anyone else off. Nobody really socialized on that bus, so after my little banter with Clyde I looked out the window at the scenery slipping by, and once again settled into the solitude that was my daily after-school ritual.

I crawled out of the yellow-and-black van right in front of our cozy little stucco house with the neatly trimmed lawn in front. Door-to-door service was one of the perks of being disabled. I walked up the path, always remembering the countless hours I had spent out here pruning bushes, pulling weeds, and sweeping the walks. It wasn't until I was much older that I realized how much our tiny yard meant to my mother, who had grown up in the ghetto in Queens, New York. In her youth, she had never been able to plant flowers, grow a lawn, or hang a swing from the tree in front as we did. For her, it was a miracle. For me, it was a lot of chores and the occasional croquet game—using a beat-up old set of balls and mallets Mom had scrounged at a garage sale.

I let myself in through the unlocked front door. As always, the house was empty. I breathed deeply. I had the whole place to myself for several hours and loved the sense of decadence that unsupervised time afforded me. If I couldn't have a normal social life with my friends, at least I got to do what I wanted here for a while. As the littlest in the family, I rarely won an argument about what to watch on our one and only TV. But for the entire afternoon, it was all mine. No sister to pick on me. No brother for me to follow around and pester. No trying to stay out of Mom's way in case she was in a bad mood or had work for me to do.

As though time itself stretched out infinitely, I was in no hurry. I threw my sweater on the easy chair in the living room and sat down on the ottoman to take off my shoes and socks, which I happily left wherever they landed. When my stepfather was around he would "fine" me for leaving my clothes scattered about. By the time he took five cents here and ten cents there, I often ended up owing him money instead of getting my two-dollar-per-month allowance. He had been gone for some time now, though, and I took a fiendish pleasure in leaving my stuff on the floor.

Before turning on the TV, I took a moment to steal a little snack from the piggy-shaped cookie jar on the kitchen counter. These sorts of treats were rationed out when my mother was home, but when the cat's away...I carefully decapitated the pig's ceramic head and peered inside. Yes! It was still half full—and with Chips Ahoy! My favorite. With no one around to watch, I could eat as many as I wanted. I tried to show some restraint by starting with only two cookies. But I left the jar close to the edge of the counter, knowing I would go back for more.

*Just sit right back and you'll hear a tale, a tale of a fateful trip...that started from this tropic port aboard this tiny ship....*I settled in with my friends Mary Anne, Ginger, the skipper, the professor, the millionaire, his wife...and, of course, Gilligan.

After *Gilligan's Island*, *The Brady Bunch*, and a few other shows (punctuated by several more trips to the cookie jar), I was suddenly shaken out of my sugar-induced TV coma by the sound of Mom's car rolling into the driveway. Oops! I was supposed to be starting dinner.

My sister and brother were scholarship students at an exclusive private school in La Jolla, twenty-five miles north of where we lived. My mother would pick them up every day after work and then fight her way through traffic all the way back home. All three of them came home together at about 6:30 or 7:00 p.m., very tired and very hungry. They had decided one day that, since I got home at 3:30, I should cook dinner and have it waiting for them when they got in.

I jumped off the couch and ran for the kitchen, turning off the TV as I went, knowing that I had only a few minutes before they unloaded all their heavy book bags and Mom's huge satchel of papers to grade. If I was lucky, they'd be finishing some conversation in the car before they got out.

I frantically pulled a pot out from the cabinet under the counters, splashed some water in it, put it on the stove and turned on a flame. I turned on the broiler to heat up. I got a package of spinach out of the freezer, tore it open and threw the contents into the pot, even though the water hadn't boiled yet.

I grabbed a package of steak from the fridge and found a pan for it. I was sliding the steak under the broiler as I heard the key in the lock. I slid my little ladder closer to the fridge and climbed up to reach the Potato Buds instant mashed-potato mix.

I heard my sister going into the room she and I shared, and my brother dumping his stuff in his room as I measured the potato flakes, milk, and butter into another pot.

Whew! So far so good. It really was beginning to look like

I hadn't forgotten dinner after all! A little ingenuity, hustle, and the blissful ignorance of a ten-year-old can sometimes be a magical combination!

My mother came in and set her heavy grading book on the counter that divided the kitchen from where she stood in the dining room. She looked around at my bustling activity.

"Dinner's almost ready," I said brightly, hoping she wouldn't focus on the open cookie jar still poised at the edge of the counter.

"Come and set the table," Mom sang out to my brother and sister. She turned back to me. "I have to call a parent. One of my students won a Shakespeare contest, and she says her mom won't let her go to the state championships." She opened her grade book and took the phone off the hook, preparing to dial.

I put on the oven mitts and bent down to pull out the broiler and turn over the steak.

"Um, Bonnie, look at this," I heard my mom saying. I straightened up and looked over the breakfast bar as she handed me a simple, white, trifold brochure. I thought, *What's this? Did my dinner-making subterfuge fail me and she has written down my punishment already? Had my school issued an early report card and I wasn't up to snuff? Was I being summoned to appear in court by the messy clothing police? What?*

I took a breath and looked down. It was a brochure with a simple silhouette on the cover: a skier, with mountains in the background. But wait; there was something different about this skier. He had only one leg. Just like me! I held this amazing image in my oven mitt and stared at it. I remember it was as if a lightning bolt had struck me.

Skiing? Amputees? It took a while for my mind to wrap around the concept at all. Then I read the simple motto inscribed under the picture: "If I Can Do This, I Can Do Anything." I can do *anything*. Instead of being a kid who wasn't even allowed to walk home from school with her friends, I could *ski*? I could feel the wind in my hair and glide gracefully down a French Alp like the folks I watched on TV or in the movies?

It was as if all the sound in the room was suddenly turned off—I couldn't hear my mom talking on the phone, my sister clanking dishes and silverware, or my brother getting the glasses out of the cupboard behind me.

The hair stood up on the back of my neck. I could ski! I, the poor, one-legged girl, could be *graceful*. In that moment nothing really mattered but the possibility. It felt like I seemed to grow three inches. No...more! I went from feeling like a person of small, limited size to feeling like a person of grand and glorious proportions. Now, I could have thought about how in the world I would actually get to ski, or how much it cost to ski, or that we lived in San Diego where there was no snow, or that black people don't even like the cold. None of that mattered at all. I was liberated.

In that moment, joy was one with the possibility.

"You're burning the steak!" my mom shouted, breaking my reverie as she hung up the phone. I dropped the picture on the counter and bent down to pull the pan from under the broiler. I put the steak on a platter, put the mashed potatoes on the side, and got a serving dish for the spinach.

"Steak, spinach, and mashed potatoes again?" said my brother, Wayne. "Can't you cook anything else?"

"How about pork chops and applesauce tomorrow?" I asked. "With rice and broccoli." Knowing that rice and pork chops took longer, I would have to start cooking earlier tomorrow. But none of this mundane dialogue affected or interested me in the least. I had a vision. I had a dream. I felt joy.

Taking Aim

Over the past year as I've been writing this book, I have been blessed with an extraordinary opportunity. The Shriners Hospitals have invited me to visit and speak at several of their twenty-two children's hospitals all over the country. The Shriners are a wonderful group of people. They have established this vast network of hospitals dedicated to providing state-of-the-art health care for children with disabilities—absolutely free. Yes, you read that right. When a child is treated at a Shriners hospital, there is no bill. Ever. If it weren't for the Shriners, this little black kid from San Diego would have had a very different life. They paid for all my surgeries, all my prosthetics, therapy, etc. until I was eighteen years old. I owe this organization a lot, and I was thrilled and honored to be able to give back to them by touring their facilities and visiting with their patients and staff.

In each city, I scheduled a speech, brought toys for the kids, and signed books for the parents and staff. I met with the patients, sat with them, held their hands, and stood there with my titanium leg proudly showing, a symbol of what was possible for their future.

Sounds amazing, doesn't it? The joy of reaching out and helping others can be one of the deepest, most gratifying endeavors we as humans can experience. The looks on the faces of those kids will just melt your heart. Every moment I spent with these precious beings will live with me forever. To do this was amazing all right, but it was also, for me, a whole lot more. It was one of the hardest things I've ever done in my life.

Walking through the doors of the Shriners Hospital in Los Angeles was like a form of time travel. Instantly, I was transported back nearly four decades to the five-year-old me, in the hospital on Halloween and dressed as a bat, leaping, limping, and flapping my wings as I went trick-or-treating down the corridor of the administrative offices. I watched that silly apparition, wistfully reliving the last days of having my own two feet. As I continued down the hallways, I saw more ghosts of me at various ages: the ten-year-old who came in for another surgery to shorten her stump; the fifteen-year-old back for yet another surgery to have pins removed from her bones. Every vision conjured a lonely, painful, excruciating experience.

I shook off the phantoms of my past and rode the elevator upstairs, where a group of teens and their parents was expecting me. As I walked into the room and looked around at kids in wheelchairs, covered with bandages, or lying in beds on wheels with tubes snaking out of strange equipment, anxiety grabbed at my heart. The first thing I felt was a wave of anguish at the palpable suffering of these kids who should be out causing trouble or getting their first kiss. The second wave that hit me was the memory of so much of my own pain: nights of screaming in my sleep, hours of crying in the physical therapy room, and the endless tedium of being trapped in a hospital bed with no parents, no siblings, and no real friends around to offer any sort of comfort. Layered on top of that were the bitter, embarrassing recollections of my teen years—desperate to fit in and be liked, but haunted by my freakish appearance.

Drowning under these torturous waves of emotion, I nevertheless fought the overwhelming urge to turn around and run out of the room. I had come so far to build a positive self-image, to feel strong and to feel good about my body....Why, oh why, did I have to go back in time to one of the most painful periods of my life?

It was something I had to do. Like a soldier returning to the front lines to drag out the injured, I couldn't leave them behind while I rested in safety. Seeing these kids in bandages, I knew there was a war — a war for their hearts and souls. I had fought my own battles decades ago, but for them the fight was just beginning. The reason I had come back was suddenly clear.

I smiled at the group. They smiled back. I began walking around the room with energy and purpose, showing the kids my Olympic medals and autographing postcards of myself skiing for each one of them. I wore shorts so that my sporty leg could be easily seen and admired. I asked their names, shook hands, hugged, and made contact with each person there. I wanted them to see and feel the future that was waiting for them...a future where dreams could come true. Time travel works both ways.

Sitting in a wheelchair, a dark-haired little girl from Mexico with the sweetest smile looked up into my eyes.

"I had a good friend before my leg got hurt. Now she doesn't like me anymore." Her sadness struck deep in my soul. "What can I do?" Her accent gave the words a rich, lyrical sound that underlined the message.

How could anyone turn their back on this beautifully strong young lady? All at once I felt the anger of injustice as well as the desire to put my arms around her.

"She was never a real friend," I answered. "From now on, you will make better friends who see what's inside you and value the most important things about you."

A glow of optimistic peace and happiness washed over her face. That moment alone made the trip worthwhile. I gave in to the urge to hug her.

I knew there were a lot of hormones in the room...so I talked about dating. "When I was fourteen," I said, "I heard a saying: 'He'll go for anything on two legs.' It meant a boy had standards so low that he would try to kiss every single girl—ugly or pretty, short or tall, mean or nice. But, the saying implied, not if she only had one leg like me. I thought it meant that I was below the standard of even the most indiscriminate person. I thought I would never, ever get a date with anyone!

"But my sister told me not to think that way. She said, 'Because you have one leg, you'll never have to date jerks!' And she was right. Over the years, many men have wanted to take me out to dinner and spend time with me. But they have been the kind of men who are not just looking for a Barbie doll. They wanted to get to know me for who I am."

I spent more than an hour there talking with kids who had been burned, had amputations, suffered from debilitating diseases, and more. I talked about what it was like to learn to walk all over again after my amputation. I told them the story of seeing the picture of an amputee skier for the first time and then getting invited to try skiing by a friend in high school who believed in my ability to do it more than I believed in myself. I answered their questions, listened to their problems, and gave them hope.

Toward the end of my time there, a mother who was seated in the back of the large room put her arm around her thirteen-year-old son, who was badly burned on his face and his arms. She leaned forward and said earnestly, haltingly, because

English was not her first language, "Do you think...do you think my son will ever lead a normal life?"

I paused for a moment. Every fiber of my being resisted the idea of simply saying, "*Yes.*" At first I didn't know why. Of course, that's what this poor, struggling mother wanted to hear. She needed to hear the Olympic athlete tell her, and her son, it was all going to be okay. That he was still "normal"—not hopelessly damaged and therefore relegated to living an inferior life. Then, it just came out of my mouth:

"I hope not," I blurted out. "He should aim higher!"

I paused as the nervous laughter in the room subsided.

"I wish someone had told *me* that sooner. I wasted so much time wishing I could be normal. I wasted so much energy trying to cover up my leg and pretend it wasn't there. Normal is way overrated. Be interesting. Be exciting. Be yourself."

Hoping for a better life didn't mean that I suddenly got to have two legs, find out I had rich parents, or miraculously become a person who was never abused as a child. It didn't mean a fantasy about a world where I had no problems and I blended into the crowd. Hope means stretching yourself, trying new things, and finding out what a better life looks like for you, now, in this world.

No matter what your circumstance, dare to hope. Dare to hope for ridiculous things.

Dare to Aim Higher.

CHAPTER FOUR

Positivity...

Wake Up and Smell the Joy

Beating the Joy Stealers

My cell phone rang for the twentieth time that day, and it was only 10:00 a.m. I glanced at the screen before answering to assess the importance of the caller and whether or not I would let it go to voice mail. It was the hair salon. *Muy importante!* I had to get on a plane for a speech later that day and had been swimming all weekend—not a good combo. (You may have noticed by now that several of my stories take place in a hair salon. I'm a black woman. Deal with it.) I was hoping they were just calling to confirm my appointment for that afternoon. Alas, it was bad news.

"Bonnie, schveetie." It was Clair, the heavily accented owner of the salon. Picture a cross between Zsa Zsa Gabor and Natasha from the old Rocky and Bullwinkle cartoons. "I'm zorry, dahlink, but Gloria is shick and can't do you today."

Yikes! Getting a good hair appointment in New York City at the last minute is harder than being granted an audience with the pope. I'm sure Clair sensed my extreme panic, or maybe she got a clue from the choking sounds I found myself croaking into the receiver. Either way, she came to my rescue immediately.

"Don't vorry, don't vorry," she added. "Herman vill do you. He's brilliant."

Herman had jumped in for the ailing Gloria several times before. Gloria had a tendency to be a bit feeble and canceled appointments often. I found out later that, despite her high cheekbones and beautifully flowing blonde hair, *Gloria* was really *Gary*, a man. But that's a different story....

"No problem, Clair. Herman will be fine. I'll see you at two."

As I hung up the phone, something about all this bothered me. I knew Herman did a nice job on my hair, but I was feeling subtly apprehensive about this disruption to my carefully planned day. I just couldn't quite put my finger on it.

Two o'clock came before I knew it, and there I was at Hair Apparent (not the salon's real name...but it should be, huh?) on the Upper East Side of Manhattan, with Herman striding toward me.

To say that Herman was muscular really doesn't capture the whole picture. He was sculpted from head to toe with a tiny waist, enormous shoulders, and hardly an ounce of fat on his tall, ebony body. He usually wore a uniform of leather pants and shirtless vest, with miles of tightly braided, jet-black locks cascading down his back. I suddenly remembered something that explained the tiny apprehension I had been feeling earlier. Herman was what my friend, Lynette Lewis, would call a classic "Joy Stealer."

Have you ever run into a person who, no matter what is going on around them, always seems to be having a miserable time and insists on sharing it with you? You know: their cup is half empty, there's a hole in the bottom, and the water is dripping on their brand-new shoes! You can be having a perfectly lovely day until you meet up with one of these folks. Within a few minutes, you want to put a bullet in your brain or theirs—it doesn't seem to matter which. Try to avoid these Joy Stealers at all costs. They can suck the life out of you.

As he twirled and tugged on my hair, Herman, as expected, launched into his theft of my blissful psyche. Cutting and kvetching, he told me that his landlord wouldn't fix the plumbing in his building and he was forced to go downstairs and shower at a friend's apartment every day. It sounded very unfair. He complained about a friend who borrowed his motorcycle and got a parking ticket but didn't tell him. I sympathized with his shock and anger. He even talked about Clair giving him the worst clients, the worst space in the room, and expecting him to do all the extra chores like cleaning the bathroom. It was clear that the world was out to get him. I could feel the joy oozing out of my body and puddling in a blob on the hair-covered floor.

I remembered the last time he did my hair. The entire world was being cruel and unjust to him then, too. In fact, I truly felt sorry for him. Not because I was the client and he had to do hair. Not because of what the world did to him. I felt sad because of what he was doing to the world and to himself. It was as though he poured buckets of manure on himself and those around him every hour on the hour, like clockwork. By the end of my last appointment I had felt so buried in the muck of his indignation, suffering, and anger that I wanted to take a bath afterward. It was as though his negative energy actually became styled into my hair and embedded in my skin. I felt like fleeing the chair to protect my precious scalp.

But then I got a better idea. "Herman," I asked, "have you noticed that every story you've told me since I sat down is about someone doing something bad to you? Being unfair? As a favor to me, would you please tell me about one person who has done something nice for you recently? I would really like to hear a more cheerful story."

I hoped this would take him in a positive direction. Maybe he would get a chance to see how good it felt. Maybe he would begin to learn that when you shift your attention toward being positive—even as the world around you seems unfair—you can begin to break the vicious cycle of negativity and, in its place, create a more upward trajectory in your life. But even if it didn't generate any lasting change for Herman, I figured at least it would improve my hour.

So I waited.

He thought.

I waited.

He thought.

I waited some more.

Twenty minutes went by in complete silence. I was surprised, but it was a dramatic improvement over the litany of wrongs and injustices I would have had in store if I hadn't spoken up. I settled into my own thoughts and enjoyed getting my hair done in peace.

Finally, he said, "I know you're right. But...I can't think of anything to say."

I really felt sorry for him. How awful it must be to carry all this baggage around with you all day. Life's tough enough. I remembered a story a friend had e-mailed to me a few days before that I thought might give him something to think about.

"Let me share an old legend with you, then," I began....

One evening an old Cherokee told his grandson about a battle that goes on inside people. He said, "My son, the battle is between two 'wolves' inside us all. One wolf is Evil. It is anger, envy, jealousy, sorrow, regret, greed, arrogance, self-pity, guilt, resentment, inferiority, lies, false pride, superiority, and ego.

"The other wolf is Good. It is joy, peace, love, hope, serenity, humility, kindness, benevolence, empathy, generosity, truth, compassion, and faith."

The grandson thought about it for a minute and then asked his grandfather: "Which wolf wins?"

The old Cherokee simply replied, "The one you feed."

I really don't know if this made a lasting impression on Herman or not, because I changed salons soon after that. They did great hair at Hair Apparent, but the negativity was way too high a price to pay for it. The lesson, though, stuck with me, and I call upon it from time to time when I feel as though I may start to become a Joy Stealer myself. The important thing is to be aware of this tendency and to nip it in the bud when it comes along. When I am really stuck on a rant, I have even resorted to enlisting my friends to stop me from polluting our get-togethers by going on and on about something negative. And it works! My face is red when they call me on it, but boy am I glad. That kind of energy can become overwhelming.

Whatever it takes, just keep reminding yourself to feed the right wolf.

If We Cry at Weddings, Why Not Laugh at Funerals?

On September 11, 2001, an icy chill consumed the souls of every American and every compassionate member of the human race. Tragedy surrounds us every day—automobiles crash, brutal murders defile our cities and towns, crippling diseases attack our society—but this was different. This vile, cowardly, nonsensical act perpetrated by a group of pathetically misguided zealots hit us all with a force rarely experienced in modern civilization. The entire world stopped and felt the pain. Over and over, on every possible venue, we watched the Towers fall, the fireball over the Pentagon, the scorched Pennsylvania field. And we were stunned. We couldn't believe it.

Living in New York, the devastation was even more pronounced. Everyone here knew someone, or at most was one degree of separation away from someone, who died that day. An evil cloud hung over the city—literally and figuratively. People wept in the streets. Fear and panic were everywhere. *What's next? Will they attack again? Should we leave town? Where should we go? Is anywhere safe?* We just put one foot in front of the other and blindly staggered from day to day. It was all we could do to make it through. There was no joy to be found. Anywhere.

Even the media, who are normally detached enough to quickly recover from almost any kind of trauma, had no idea how to handle such a massive catastrophe. They reported the facts, to be sure, but there was a sense of genuine confusion and unease as to what else to do. The latest sex scandal or high-speed car chase seemed so insignificant and unimportant. I was reminded of the old kinescopes I've seen of the great Walter Cronkite, visibly shaken, removing his glasses and shedding a heartfelt, black-and-white tear as he announced the death of President John F. Kennedy on that fateful November day in 1963. The comedians especially—David Letterman, Jay Leno, and the like—were completely at loose ends. How do we go on? When is it okay *not* to talk about this? When is it okay to laugh again? No one wanted to be the first to break the sorrowful, respectful silence. It is in these dire circumstances of adversity that the notion of joy seems the most challenging. But, during these times, it can also be the most surprising. I experienced this feeling of intense grief and the power of joy on a more personal level when tragedy struck my own family one recent New Year's Eve.

That particular Christmas holiday, my family decided to all get together for the first time in five years. In adulthood, my siblings and I have scattered to the wind. My brother, Wayne, lives in North Carolina with his wife and three children; my sister, April, and her husband live in Michigan; my mother lived in San Diego; and Darcy and I live in New York. We all speak on the phone from time to time, and visit one another, but gathering as a group is quite rare. Not by design, mind you, just by circumstance.

We were so glad that we finally pulled off this reunion. The only person missing was Darcy because we had arranged for her to spend Christmas with her father before all this came up. She joined us on the phone, though, and her presence was very much a part of the event.

My brother and his wife hosted our gathering, since it

was hardest for him to travel with his young children. It was a lovely time. The house was a bit crowded, so my mom and I decided to stay together at a nearby motel and commute to Wayne's for the festivities. After the usual Christmas frenzy of the children tearing through miles of brilliantly colored wrapping paper, I really enjoyed escaping to some quiet time with my mother in our Holiday Inn sanctuary. We had gone on a cruise together earlier in the fall, and we were beginning to truly break through some of the baggage we both had built up over the years regarding our relationship. I genuinely enjoyed her company. We laughed like girlfriends on a sleepover as we chatted each other to sleep from across the aisle of the motel room's two beds.

We all spent the next five days gabbing, bonding, laughing, teasing, and just plain being together. On December 27, surrounded by her children and grandchildren, Mom celebrated her sixty-seventh birthday with a beautiful dinner, complete with a special chocolate cheesecake drizzled with "Happy Birthday" in chocolate syrup. Mom always loved chocolate. At the end of the visit, we hugged, kissed, and promised to do this again very soon. No way were we letting another five years pass without being together again.

A few short days later, December 30, I found myself once again in New York unpacking from the trip and preparing to slip back into my life after the respite of the last week. I was looking forward to getting a little writing done before surrendering to more holiday reverie. The phone rang. *Odd*, I thought. I get most of my personal phone calls on my cell phone and this was my business line. I expected that to be quiet at this time of year. I picked it up anyway. Instinct.

"Ms. Bonnie St. John?" the official-sounding woman's voice inquired. "I'm calling from the San Diego police department." Now, I was really curious—and more than a bit apprehensive.

"Yes," I replied tentatively.

"Are you the daughter of Ruby Cremaschi-Schwimmer?" My mother had hyphenated the names of her last two husbands—only one of which I had any fondness for. It always bothered me a bit when I heard her referred to in this way.

"Yes." I could feel the anxiety brewing inside me. *This can't be good.*

Slowly, deliberately, she spoke the words I had been dreading all my life: "I'm sorry to inform you, Ms. St. John, that your mother passed away this morning."

I'm not really sure what happened right after that. Everything just seemed to move in slow motion. There were some more details about a massive heart attack; paramedics rushed to the scene; they did everything they could; we're very sorry...I couldn't hear any of it. I just wanted to get off the phone. I collapsed on my bed. I cried; I shook; I curled up in a ball. I reached out for help. My friends came running to my side. I grieved.

Thankfully, Darcy was still with her father in San Diego. I decided to take some time to compose myself and prepare for breaking the news that her beloved grandma was gone. My first call was to my brother. He simply refused to believe it. "There must be some mistake," he argued. "It's a lie. We just left her yesterday!" My sister, April, was devastated. She and Mom had probably the closest bond of all of us. We all were in shock.

I flew to San Diego the next day. It was surreal. I remember just going through the motions of life in a trancelike state.

When I finally got to my hotel, it was late at night. There was a huge party going on in the lobby, with balloons and music. People were dancing, laughing, and having all kinds of fun. I asked the bellman what was going on.

"It's New Year's Eve," he answered, cocking his head and looking at me as though I might have started celebrating a little too early and a little too hard.

I cracked up laughing. I had forgotten New Year's Eve! A burst of joy shot through my body. Whew. I could laugh. Thank God!

Now the bellman really thought I had lost it. He ushered me to my room with extra care. But I didn't stay inside and mope. I decided to escape downstairs to the rollicking party for a respite from my pain. I even danced—on this wildest of holidays, no one noticed or cared whether I danced and cried at the same time. It was a wonderful release.

The next day we began the daunting task of planning a funeral. Mom had been an educator—from teacher to high school principal—so the lives she had touched were vast in number. Ultimately, more than three hundred people showed up to honor her memory. When my mother married her third husband, she converted to Judaism. Even after his death many years ago, she continued to take her faith seriously and was a devout Jew. Her rabbi presided over the ceremony, which became this amazingly unusual, eclectic mix of Hebrew tradition and black gospel! There will never be anything else like it, I'm sure.

It was a huge undertaking, but people came out of the woodwork to help. A cousin with a video-editing facility created a tribute video that played on a loop at the reception. The gospel choir from Lincoln High School came together to sing—something my mom always said she wanted—even though they had completely disbanded after the school was closed several years prior. Another cousin, a violinist with the San Diego Symphony, played some of Mom's favorite music at the service. The perfect venue, a glorious ballroom replete with ornate architecture, beautiful gardens, and the ability to house and feed a crowd of this size affordably, became available at the last minute. My brother, sister, and I were enveloped in a cocoon of love, warmth, and, despite the circumstances, joy.

This amazed me. All this joy around such a terrible, sudden tragedy. Our loss was supplanted by the celebration of my mother's life. We reconnected with relatives we hadn't seen or even heard from in years. My siblings and I bonded in a way I never thought we could. We pored over old photo albums long since packed away. We happily recounted wonderful memories. We struggled over the obituary, the details of the service, the feelings we all had—bad *and* good—of life as the children of Ruby Lee Page-St. John-Cremaschi-Schwimmer. We all came together in honor of our mother.

Wayne and his family were staying in Mom's condo by the beach, where we all met each day. Her passing had been so sudden that every time the phone rang we had to deliver the sad news to yet another unsuspecting friend—and Mom had lots of friends. One day as Wayne was coming down the stairs from the second floor to answer one of these calls, he noticed his son, Roman (age six), had beat him to the punch and picked up the receiver.

"She's dead, she's dead, she's dead!" Roman exclaimed as he slammed down the phone and nonchalantly resumed playing with one of the treasures he'd uncovered in Grandma's garage.

"Um, Roman, who was on the phone?" his father nervously queried.

"How should I know?" he replied, with the matter-of-fact directness only a six-year-old can muster.

At first we were upset and tried to "fix" the problem. I dialed star 69 to no avail. Suddenly, realizing there was nothing any of us could do, my brother started to giggle. I caught the bug and laughed, too. Soon my sister was laughing with us. It was funny—Roman was just telling the truth on the phone in a way that made sense to him. All the tension and gloom burst, and we laughed until tears ran down our faces.

I can only imagine the reaction of that poor caller. We'll never know who it was.

A few days later, it came time to perform the last ceremony of this poignantly exhausting episode in our lives. One of my mother's few clear instructions regarding her death was that she wanted to be cremated. Now, this was a challenge, since cremation is strictly forbidden in Jewish tradition. A heartfelt session with the rabbi as to the many lucid and compelling reasons for this position had left us with understanding, but still resolved to carrying out her wish—a decision that almost cost us the ability to have her rabbi and good friend preside over the service. Another little complication was that she had requested her ashes be strewn over a beloved place that held many fond memories for her: the rose garden in Balboa Park.

It turns out that, at least in California, it is illegal to scatter human remains *anywhere* but at sea. The director of the funeral home very politely informed us that a public park was clearly out of the question. Once again, even in death, nothing about Mom was easy. We decided to ignore his warnings and perform this ritual anyway—albeit at dusk. Perhaps the cover of darkness would make the whole enterprise a little less conspicuous and, therefore, less prone to action from any kind of law enforcement. Visions of all of us getting thrown in the pokey were vivid in our imaginations. Well, at least in mine.

So there we were, on a freezing cold, dark January evening. Present were April and her husband, Michael; Wayne and his wife, Mary, and their three children, Savanna, Sierra, and Roman; my ex-husband, Grant (who had steadfastly loved and cared for my mother even long after our divorce), and his wife, Noelle; Darcy, and me; plus Lily, Matthew, and Samantha, Mom's grandchildren by marriage—a surreptitious band of mourners skulking around the San Diego park system one step ahead of the local authorities.

You may conjure a lovely image of the Balboa Park rose garden, which, at most times of the year, is exquisite, a veritable jewel in the crown of the gorgeously picturesque Southern California landscape. In early January, however, even in San Diego, roses are dormant. All our pathetic little flashlights could illuminate was a woefully parched collection of brown, thorny sticks dangerously protruding through the soil.

Undaunted, though, we diligently and reverently carried out our task. We said a prayer, reflected on our dear Ruby once more, and set out to fulfill her final wish. The vessel holding her remains, tightly wrapped in a box, was surprisingly large. We each had a small paper cup, which we filled and carried throughout various parts of the garden, praying and sprinkling as we went, memories flooding our minds, hearts, and souls. I remember Darcy holding my hand. It was very loving and very peaceful. Well, mostly peaceful.

"*MOM!*" The pious silence was suddenly broken by Wayne's six-year-old son, Roman. "Is there any more Grandma left? I want to put her over here."

"No fair!" chimed in Savanna (age eight). "Roman already got more Grandma than I did!"

"I want more Grandma, too," yelled Sierra (also six), not to be outdone. And a rush ensued for the last bits of gray dust.

Out of the mouths of babes! We all smiled, even chuckled. But more important, we all experienced an infusion of pure joy. Not only were we smiling, but Mom was smiling down upon us as well.

CHAPTER FIVE

Authenticity...

Get Your *Joy*

Should-ing All Over Myself

Have you ever seen one of those posters of a gorgeous beach scene with two Adirondack chairs parked lazily just a few feet from a perfectly blue sea, waves gently crashing, pristine white sand beckoning you to sink your toes into its warm, pillow-soft surface? I usually see that poster when I'm rushing through an airport. I look for only a moment, but when I do I can hear the sounds of the ocean lapping up on the shore, and I can smell the salt air. In that moment, I am convinced that if I could simply transport myself there, I would immediately feel joy. I would relax, unwind, and be in a state of bliss. Mission accomplished, Madison Avenue!

So when my friend Ann let me use her place in the Hamptons for a week one summer to work on my last book, I thought I had hit the lottery. My daughter was off with her father in California, meaning I was flying solo. I became consumed by the idyllic notion of the reclusive writer surrounded by a background of expansive sea vistas, a sound track of cool ocean breezes wafting the faintest echoes of distant seagulls, a half-filled glass of white wine off to my side, sweatily awaiting the occasional sip. I conjured the ghosts of Ernest Hemingway churning out his exquisite prose while lounging among the low-rise, whitewashed villas along the Costa Del Sol, and Graham

Greene clacking away on an ancient Smith Corona amid the crystal-blue grottos of Capri. *This is it*, I thought. As fast as I could, I rented a little blue Honda Civic, bid a fond farewell to the sweltering milieu of New York City in July, and sped off down the Long Island Expressway in search of my poetic mecca.

Ann's house was not like the famous mansions in the Hamptons, with butlers and miles of manicured lawns like you see on *Lifestyles of the Rich and Famous*, but I liked it much better. She and her husband, Ron, had years before bought a lovely property with a tiny, 800-square-foot summer cottage and torn it down to build in its place a structure about three times that size — which by local standards is still very modest — but built to their own, exacting standards. It is their dream house, and they did an exquisite job designing and decorating it.

The house was surrounded by grass on all sides, with lovely shrubs and trees. Immediately I felt the lush, green garden soothe my soul. Gone in an instant was the constant din of honking horns, crashing garbage trucks, and wailing sirens I had become far too used to in the city. The soft ground almost felt odd under my feet (well, foot) after the constant bashing I had become accustomed to from the rock-hard NYC pavement. Living in the city you sometimes forget how nature — real trees that are not imprisoned by foot-high wrought-iron fences — can affect you. To simply stroll in this garden or sit under a shady tree was the absolute antidote to my world of high-rise glass and steel.

When Ann designed the house, she insisted on the Mediterranean notion of "bringing the outdoors in." French doors formed the entire front wall of the living room and could be left open in the evening to allow the fresh, cool ocean air to flow through the house. Above the French doors was more glass, all the way to the A-framed ceiling, giving the glorious feeling that the garden was merely an extension of the living room. Off the kitchen, a screened porch with cozy, floral-cushioned white wicker chairs provided a charming multi-purpose space—family room, dining room, or, as it became instantly clear, the perfect place for me to plug in my laptop and embark on my literary journey.

On my first evening there, Ann took all of us to the beach—me, Ron, and another couple. Along with beach chairs and towels, she packed up a lovely gourmet picnic with the finest cheeses, hummus, fancy crackers, chilled blush wine, and other delicious delicacies. Ann's spread was even more luxurious than the picture in the airport.

If you haven't figured it out by now, Ann is my Martha Stewart friend—she designed and decorated the charming home at the beach as well as her gorgeous apartment on Central Park West, can throw an exquisite dinner party, and is the consummate hostess. Knowing that I am mentally deficient in this arena, when I moved into my last apartment she graciously showed me, step-by-step, how to do basic things like pick paint colors. Once, she even let me tag along with her to pick wallpaper for one of her bathrooms in the city—a process that proved to be far too advanced for my abilities. I was in awe of the way she clearly and efficiently cast aside pattern after pattern, color after color, finally arriving at the perfect swatch, which, of course, translated beautifully into the quintessential wall covering for that particular space. Every time I squat myself in that lovely little room, I remember the whole process and feel, once again, astonished by her ability. For my part, I think I'm destined to just stick with paint.

Our outing to the beach was well scripted. As heavily laden as we were, it was necessary to drive, rather than walk, the half-mile to the beach. We unloaded our goodies, trudged through the sand, and set up camp. The next few hours passed pleasantly as the sun disappeared over the horizon while we relaxed, chatted, and noshed.

After the weekend was over, everyone else returned to the city, leaving me alone in the house for five days of writing. I shopped for healthy food at the local grocery store and put myself on a low-fat, high-protein regimen with a daily dose of jumping rope. I set up my laptop in my designated, screened-in retreat off the kitchen where I could refill my teacup in a few short steps and enjoy the atmosphere of being outdoors while still having an outlet and a table for my computer. I settled in and happily began tapping away at my keyboard.

One day while I was writing I received a call on my cell phone. "Hello, my name is Karen Kangers. I work in the office of Mrs. Barbara Bush. Are you available to speak with her now?"

Over the last twelve months I had repeatedly requested an interview with the former first lady, and current first mother, for the book I was writing. I had gone through the formal channels, but I had also pulled every back-channel string I could think of—contacting everyone I knew who knew her or had anything to do with anyone who might know her. At first I had garnered a few positive indications, but then dead silence for six months. Now, suddenly, out of the blue, a "Yes!"

"Wonderful," I answered while mentally running through my options as quickly as possible. I needed to set up my tape recorder, find a blank tape, find a plug, Yikes! Had I known this was coming, I would have spent hours researching, thinking of questions, and planning the interview in detail. Too late now.

"Can I call back in five minutes when I get myself set up?" I begged, hoping to stall for a moment to compose myself before speaking to one of the most influential women of the century.

"Sure," said Karen.

It turns out, as it usually does, that all my panic was completely unfounded. Mrs. Bush was kind, gracious, and modest—an absolute pleasure to speak with. I often find that when I get myself all worked up about something, it turns out to be not nearly so onerous as my mind made it seem. Sure, she was only the second woman in history to be married to one president and give birth to another (the first was Abigail Adams), but Barbara Bush goes through life day by day, just like the rest of us. She wakes, has her coffee, cooks, prays, visits with friends, and chats on the phone with nosy writers like me all the time. Easy.

By the end of my week in the Hamptons, I had made significant progress on my book. I was healthier, happier, and feeling genuinely refreshed and restored. After overcoming the abuse in my childhood, working to pull myself up through education, and struggling as a single mom, here I was, at long last, living my dream of being a real author. And it was sweet.

But, I realized, after that first night on the beach with Ann and her guests, I had not gone to the beach again—not once. Even though it was only a half-mile away, I didn't go. No Adirondack chairs. No pristine, sun-drenched sand between my toes. No saltwater-frizzed hair. Nada. I thought about it once or twice. But then...*Naaaah.*

With one leg, I can't walk very well in sand. Imagine having no real ankle to deal with the uneven ground. I can't get my artificial foot wet; so walking in the surf with pants rolled up is only a fantasy (a fantasy I will live out one day with an old leg ready for the scrap heap). Besides, I don't like getting too hot and sweaty in the sun. I really hate getting sand all over myself and my stuff, too.

Each time I thought about going down there, it seemed a lot less attractive than simply staying in my lush garden, in my spa environment. For the full five days, I didn't see another human being. I didn't go to restaurants, I didn't go to town, and I didn't go to the beach. For five whole days, I didn't have to worry about my hair, my wardrobe, or what anyone else thought of me. While that is not the way most people carry on in the famous Hamptons, for me it was bliss.

The picture of the Adirondack chairs on the beach originally drew me in, but actually sitting on the beach wasn't my real joy. This realization was like a whack on the side of the head for me. So many times I had agreed to take beach vacations with friends or family, thinking that because it was what they wanted (or at least what they thought they wanted), it was what I wanted, too. When I had the chance to truly listen to my feelings, the beach receded in importance.

It is so easy for me to buy into the brochure, to buy into what everyone else wants, to feel I *should* want it, too. Even now, I feel guilty writing that the beach isn't my thing, as though I am an ungrateful wretch. I can hear that voice in my head: *There are children starving in Africa! You should go to the beach and like it!* As if my choice of luxury would have any impact on them anyway.

A friend of mine became a TV news reporter in her early

twenties. She had succeeded in an extremely competitive field, doing something most people would think of as a really "cool" job. But it wasn't her joy. She wanted something else for her life. She wrestled with the idea of quitting this job that she knew she *should* be grateful to have in order to try and possibly fail in another—sort of a bird-in-the-hand-versus-one-in-the-bush choice.

One day she woke up with clarity. *I'm taking up space in someone else's dream!* she thought.

It was a dream job, but not *her* dream job.

Having the courage to listen to my feelings, and to honor them, is extremely difficult for me. I know that is a legacy in part of the sexual abuse in my childhood, which taught me in the harshest, most visceral way that my feelings would not be respected. Many men and women I know have some other reason why they buy into wanting what everyone else wants, even if it leaves them empty and undernourished like a four-course meal of cotton candy. An alcoholic parent or spouse, having little money, being an immigrant, being physically abused, being abandoned, emotional neglect—there are so many roads to this place.

The way out for me has not been a quick helicopter ride, but more like a long, winding junket aboard trains, buses, taxicabs, and even on foot. For example, last night, my daughter and I stopped off at the grocery store while walking home from school.

"Should we have stir-fry or pasta?" I asked.

We debated the relative merits of each—which was easier to cook, which was healthier, and so on. Then suddenly she said, "But which one do *you* want?"

It was only then that I realized I hadn't asked myself.

The way out is a road paved with remembering to ask myself that question every day, in all things, big and small. This doesn't mean leading a narcissistic life of doing only what you want all the time. No. It means constantly being aware of what you want and feel. Only then can you make choices that are right for you. My choice may be to do what someone else wants in order to help make them feel good. There's nothing wrong with that at all, as long as I recognize that I am making that choice for that reason. Being a "pleaser" is so ingrained into my psyche that I have to constantly check myself against falling into that morass of ignoring my feelings. I move forward on this road when I learn to stop the chatter in my brain about what I *should* do or *should* want long enough to hear a genuine answer to the question of what I *do* want.

It is important to note that there are certain people, too, who help me bring to light what I want—maybe even more than I can on my own. Making time to be around people who love me as much as they love themselves is a result of more of my hard-won wisdom. Darcy and my best girlfriends, for example, will listen to me and my needs in a way that is like water on a parched plant. I grow when they listen to me. Their love helps me become more who I am. I become more capable of feeling joy. Real joy. *My* real joy.

CHAPTER SIX

Humility...

Be Helpable

Listen to Your Mother

Ken Kragen was a master "star maker" during the high-flying '70s and '80s in the entertainment business. Ken is responsible for taking singers like Kenny Rogers, Lionel Richie, Travis Tritt, and Trisha Yearwood from being complete unknowns to mega fame and fortune as recording artists and movie and television stars. I found myself reading his book, *Life Is a Contact Sport* (William Morrow, 1994), not so much because I was smart enough to seek his advice, but more because my mom made me do it. At age thirty-four, my mother couldn't *really* make me do anything. But moms have their ways, don't they?

I had put it off with the "I'm too busy excuse" for as long as I could until finally I reached that point—you are probably familiar with this—where it actually becomes easier to open the book for a few minutes than to have to face up to my mom, yet again, and have to make excuses.

Funny how the tables turn. As a kid I asked and asked until I got what I wanted by exhausting her resistance. As an adult, it works the other way around.

So there I was, putting in the minimum obligatory time on this book my mom made me read, when it hit me out of the blue. In life, there are certain moments, certain conversations, and certain people that change everything. This was one of those rare "lightbulb" moments.

My mom, you have to understand, was a big country-music fan. What she wanted me to read in the book was a memo Kragen wrote to Trisha Yearwood when he agreed to represent her, outlining several key changes he wanted her to make in order to set herself on the road to stardom.

The first item on the list was: *Get into the very best possible physical shape through proper eating and regular exercise.* He suggested that she take a nutritionist/trainer on the road with her. Basically, he was telling Trisha—in the nicest possible way—that she was a little too chubby to be a superstar and needed to drop a few pounds. At first I thought my mother was trying to subtly tell me I had to lose some weight. She was always after my sister and me to lose weight, stand up straighter, and go to the hair salon more often (that one really sank in with me!). I figured she was using Kragen to augment her normal, well-wishing-mother diatribe.

But I continued to read Kragen's memo to Trisha anyway. It was the fourth item that really caught my eye:

A successful career is really a result of the collective efforts of a great number of people (record promotion men and women, salespeople, booking agents, publicists, managers, lawyers, business managers, promoters and their substantial staffs). All of these people have various priorities in their lives and an important part of our job is to keep you at or near the top of their lists. One of the best ways to do that is through regular, imaginative, and personalized "Thank yous."

The other items on the list dealt with looking good, producing a great next album, making her concerts more exciting, getting better photos, and other kinds of things you would expect. But this note really jumped out at me. It wasn't enough to look good, work hard, and be talented. If you didn't receive the help of an epic cast of thousands, you wouldn't make it to the top.

The difference, I realized, between superstars and those people we all know who have talent, work hard, and yet never make it to the highest levels, is very simply *how much help they get*. He who gets the most help wins!

What Kragen was telling Trisha, and what he preached throughout the entire book, was to cultivate help from others. This resonated so strongly with me that I even coined a new term for it: being "helpable."

I had spent my whole life thinking that my life was all about striving to be strong and ruggedly independent. With my disability, the idea was to move from crutches to walking freely. As I grew up, my goal was to be financially independent of my mom—to take care of myself. As a woman working in corporate America, I had to prove that I was as good as, or better than, the Y chromosome in the next cubicle. Help, I had been taught, was something you asked for when you were weak, in trouble, or incapable. The goal was always to be strong and unassailable.

Or was it?

I began to notice all the little ways I stopped other people from helping me. When my daughter asked, "Mom, do you want help with the dishes?" my usual response was, "No, honey, you have a lot of homework. I'm fine."

So I practiced in the mirror: "Yes, I'd love to have your help in the kitchen," until it felt like a more natural response.

I began to let men open doors for me and carry heavy packages—literally lightening my load. Beyond accepting more help, I forced myself to actually ask for it: a ride to the airport from a friend, hiring someone to help with cleaning once a week, and even joining Jenny Craig for help in losing a few extra pounds (for you, Mom!).

At work, I took to heart Kragen's message about thank-yous. I hired a massage therapist to spend the day at the agency that booked all my speeches. She gave ten-minute massages to every employee who signed up! Since they work the phones trapped at a desk all day, it was the perfect gift. They enjoyed it so much that the owners of the company decided to make it a monthly ritual!

This "helpable" thing, I realized, not only allows you to be more successful, it brings a tremendous amount of joy into the world. Kragen himself went far beyond making money for country-music singers; he mobilized his contacts to create "We Are the World," a song recorded by a large group of famous artists—including Stevie Wonder, Lionel Richie, Bruce Springsteen, Michael Jackson, Dionne Warwick, Cyndi Lauper, and Diana Ross—and raised millions of dollars to fight famine in Ethiopia and other parts of Africa. A few years later he was helpable enough to create "Hands Across America," a single moment in which five and a half million Americans formed a 4,152-mile human chain across the United States to raise money for hunger and homelessness in America. Being helpable gives you far more power to help others. When helpable, you can be bigger than yourself.

After everything I'd learned there was still one area of my life where the philosophy was difficult to apply. It was still hard for me to take advice from my mother, even though she was right about Kragen's book. It made a tremendous difference and gave me another important building block for expanding my joy. You'd think I would never again resist one of her suggestions. Hmm. You'd think. Maybe...maybe I was going to need some *help* to be more *helpable* where my mom was concerned. Don't we all?

Little Man

Beverly frequently travels for work. It is hard for her, since she has a five-year-old son, Tyler, whom she has to leave with her mom when she is away. A few weeks ago she had a trip scheduled to North Carolina. It was just for a few days, so she was able to pack everything she needed in one carry-on rolling suitcase. Even though it was just one bag, it was still pretty heavy.

As was the habit, on the morning of the travel day Beverly's mom came to her house to pick up Tyler for his visit with Grandma.

"Mom, can you drop me off at work?" Beverly asked. "I'm going to be leaving from there, and I'd prefer to keep my car at home."

Beverly's mom happily agreed, and the three of them drove off to Beverly's office.

Tyler was pretty comfortable with this arrangement since he really enjoyed his vacations with his grandmother. Beverly could always tell, though, that he also had pangs of missing her. When they got to Beverly's office, Tyler jumped out of the car.

"Mommy, you need some help," said Tyler, grabbing the suitcase she had pulled out of the backseat.

"Thank you, honey, but I can carry it," Beverly told him, looking down at his little face and already starting to miss him.

"No, I'm going to help you."

His voice was firm, as though he were the parent and there was no room for argument. He pushed his mother aside and began to drag the suitcase toward the security desk in Beverly's big office building. The physics of all this was extraordinary, since the bag was taller, and probably weighed more, than his pint-sized, five-year-old body. He got to the security desk, huffing a bit, but undaunted in his mission. The security guard was amused, but respected what was obviously going on.

"What can I do for you, young man?"

"I'm helping my mom," replied Tyler in his most adult voice.

"Well, carry on!"

The look on Tyler's face made Beverly just melt. It was a combination of fierce determination and sheer pride. He lugged that heavy suitcase onto the elevator, past the receptionist, down the maze of hallways, and all the way to Beverly's office.

"Okay, Mom, you have a good trip and I'll see you when you get back," Tyler declared. And with that, he turned on his heel and started heading back downstairs to his grandmother, his tiny stature filled with confidence and strength.

Beverly called out to her little man, "Well, wait for me. I'm going to walk you back downstairs."

"I know the way, Mommy. I'll be fine."

And away he went; creating one of the most joyful memories any mother could ever ask for.

Sometimes, letting other people help you isn't because you *need* it. Letting people help you is a way of bonding with them, connecting with them, and creating a sense of goodwill.

Most of us get a jolt of joy from helping others, but we forget that we can give that same gift of joy by letting others help us. If you are like me, you hate to bother anyone. Yet we may be depriving our friends, family, and coworkers of feeling capable, needed, and appreciated when we act like an island with uninviting shores.

I remember having coffee once at a French teahouse with a major political fund-raiser. He had helped me to set up my interview with Barbara Bush for my last book. I was astounded when he casually explained how he likes to ask for small favors or a bit of information from people on a regular (but not annoying) basis. This was one of his strategies for keeping in touch.

I had always thought I was supposed to jealously guard my contacts and wait for one big thing I needed rather than pestering them and wasting their time on little things. I am sure this kind of communication is a delicate ballet and he understands the subtleties better than I ever will. But the whole idea that being more helpable could expand and deepen my relationships in the professional world was a whack on the side of the head for me.

Being helpable is not the same as being vulnerable. You don't have to bare your soul, appear helpless, or show weakness in any way. Instead, allowing yourself to be open to letting others get close to you and care about you lets them feel the joy of being bigger, gracious people. Think about little Tyler delivering his mother's suitcase. It *literally* made him feel like a bigger man.

CHAPTER SEVEN

Friendship...

Connect with People

It Doesn't Take a Rhodes Scholar...

A Rhodes scholarship is one of the most prestigious academic awards in the world. Established in 1902 under the terms and conditions of the last will and testament of Cecil John Rhodes, founder of the De Beers diamond cartel, the scholarship was designed to select future leaders in the English-speaking countries of the world. To "win a Rhodes," applicants must not only exhibit flawless academic achievement but also demonstrate the promise of an ability to "fight the world's fight"—and most do. The list of Rhodes scholars reads as a veritable "who's who" of corporate and governmental leaders around the globe.

The competition is fierce. Each year, thousands of applicants vie for these coveted positions, which number less than one hundred per year, with only thirty-two from the United States. A winner receives a full two-year scholarship to Mr. Rhodes's alma mater, the venerable University of Oxford in England, plus a generous monthly stipend, which effectively removes all financial burdens of postgraduate study at one of the world's leading academic institutions. Pretty darn good deal.

In the United States, eight to ten scholars in each of sixteen regions are selected for the grueling, final interviews based on bulky applications including transcripts, a heap of recommendations, and an essay. If you are selected, the rest of the process occurs in less than twenty-four hours. First, all the candidates go to a cocktail party, which sounds fun but is really to allow the committee of former Rhodes scholars to see whether you slop your drink on yourself or in any way offend other civilized people. It turns out that looking suave and comfortable, being easy to talk with, and knowing how to dress help your chances to be selected as a future world leader. The next day, candidates all wait together in one sweltering, anxious room sweating all day long as each takes a turn at being grilled by the committee. At the end of this long and torturous period, the committee calls all the candidates together and announces two names—and only two names—as the winners.

"Bah-nny...Sah haint...Jah-han." When the syllables of my name came out of their mouths, I didn't recognize them at first. It was as if the world slowed down and I was caught in some parallel universe.

"Me? Me?" I was truly shocked. The poor little crippled black girl, whom the San Diego Unified School District wanted to send to a "special" school, was granted this illustrious honor? God surely smiled on me that day. I was going to get to trot my little tush through the grand, imposing gates of one of the oldest and most distinguished universities in the world—and it wasn't going to cost me a penny!

You have to understand that before this, I never had enough money to do anything. I like to use the old adage that when I was growing up, we didn't have money left at the end of the month, we had month left at the end of the money! Our family sometimes had to eat canned soups and drink powdered milk for a few days until Mom got her next paycheck because there was nothing left for groceries. I lied about my age to get my first job in fast-food so I had a little spending money in high school. I went through Harvard in three years instead of four because I was afraid that, even with the tuition drastically reduced by a scholarship and my income from bartending, we would run out of money before I graduated. Even when I made it to the Olympics, I had to wear other people's cast-off ski clothes and mismatched gloves that I had gotten out of the lost and found at a ski area (back in those days, Paralympians weren't fully outfitted in sponsor-decorated clothing—just a jacket and sweater). I almost didn't even make it to the Rhodes scholarship interview because I was broke. My mom bought the airline ticket to California for me, but I had no cash in my bank account to pay for a taxi or anything else on the way there. Another candidate insisted on lending me a hundred bucks to make sure I got on the plane. Now, thanks to the generous legacy of an early twentieth-century philanthropist, all my bills would be paid...with a generous salary to boot! For the first time in my whole life, I didn't have to worry about money at all.

Tears filled my eyes as I envisioned my new life ahead. I didn't have to raise money, tend bar, wait tables, or anything! All I had to do was soak up every drop of education this fantastic opportunity could offer. I could join the world-famous Oxford debating society. I could take bike rides in the Cotswolds, some of the most lush, beautiful countryside in all of Great Britain. I planned to paint watercolors, read anything and everything, plant a garden—just plain "Live My Joy" for the next two years.

The British system of higher education is a bit different from what we are familiar with here in the colonies. A University, particularly one the size of Oxford, comprises several "colleges" (Oxford has thirty-eight), all with different reputations, famous professors, and unique atmospheres. As a traditional matriculating student, one would apply to a specific college in order to gain admission. As a "Rhodent," as we were affectionately known by the Brits, all I had to do was pick one. I picked Trinity College. I wish I could say the choice was made because of some driving scholarly appeal. The truth is, I picked it because it was centrally located (I am disabled, remember) and was reputed to have the most beautiful English gardens on the entire campus.

Nine months after that fateful twenty-four hours of judgment, I arrived at Trinity. There it was, dead center in the bustling city on a wide stretch of road, separated by a dividing median, called Broad Street (sort of like the town's "Main Street"). Turning 360 degrees, I was surrounded by historic architecture, some of which dated back to the eleventh century, from the gargoyle-covered stone towers that make up the magnificent Bodleian Library to the elegant dome of the Christopher Wren–designed Sheldonian Theatre. Looking toward my new home, I saw only a massive stone wall, a bit dusty and gray from years of metropolitan grime, topped with an ancient spiky fence designed to strike terror in the heart of anyone thinking of taking a hop over the top—as if that were even possible. The gigantic iron gate, large enough to accommodate an entire coach drawn by a team of horses ferrying the latest noble scion to fulfill his academic destiny, wasn't open. "Open says-a-me," I exclaimed, dramatically flinging my wishes toward the enormous entryway, conjuring visions of horns blaring a fanfare and my name being ceremoniously announced to the anxiously awaiting royal welcoming party. Alas, the reality was a touch less dramatic. I got to schlep my little suitcase through a tiny wooden door I discovered just to the right of the baronial entrance.

However, stepping through that disappointing hatch, I felt like I had walked into paradise. On the other side of that drably fearsome wall, the view instantly opened to an enormously expansive lawn, at least as large as a football field—and as even and trim as a putting green—with elegant yellow-stone buildings, a medieval bell tower, and hydrangeas under every ancient casement window. The grass was, quite literally, greener on the other side of the fence. The shocking change from the crowded, dirty street, bustling with people, into this gloriously serene, hallowed environment, felt like a magic spell suspending the rules of time and space. To step over that threshold is to gain entry to a secret world, a world where the clock stopped centuries ago. There were no cars, no tourists, and...no telephones?

Oxford is the oldest university in the English-speaking world. As you can imagine, it is steeped in tradition. And, being British, everything is allowed to steep a little longer. So, there were several challenges about my new life to which I had to learn to adapt, one of which was communication. Remember, this is 1986: no e-mail, no cell phones. At Harvard, my dorm room had a phone that I shared with my roommates. Not at Oxford. Here, two well-worn pay phones were shared by the *whole college* of more than two hundred students. To communicate we couldn't call, so we sent little paper notes to one another throughout the college and throughout the city using a surprisingly efficient system. Each college had a "porter's lodge," manned twenty-four hours a day, to control the comings and goings through the main gate. Several times a day, the notes were distributed by the "porters" into a series of small cubbyholes in a large wooden structure that vaguely resembled a pigeon coop. Each student had his or her very own little cubby and could retrieve personal notes at will.

I want to take a moment to tell you about the porters. Any British breeding at all would have trained me to politely nod at them and walk on by, going about my business. But I was enthralled by these guys. I have to say, except for a few unusually dedicated New York City doormen, the porters at Oxford are the most helpful people on the planet. Even on my darkest, gloomiest days, their cheerful demeanor could always make me smile. I thought of them like the happy-go-lucky chimney sweeps in *Mary Poppins*. These charming gentlemen were probably the result of generations of the "serving class" in Britain, and they were darned proud of it. Rightly so. People often think of the British as cold, aloof, and eternally constipated, but outside the upper crust, I found my new mates to be extremely warm and wildly funny—when given 'alf a chance.

By my third day, I was truly enjoying life. I was out of bed at five o'clock every morning to row for one of many Trinity College crew teams and was toying with the idea of joining either debate or theater. As often was the case, I ran into Shirley, my round, middle-aged "scout." The scouts were the gaggle of women who cleaned our rooms every day. Again, they were as delightful to me as the porters. Okay, we didn't have phones, but a housekeeper? Not a bad trade.

"Where ya off ta, me duck?" Shirley cheerily chirped.

"I'm off to the Nag's Head Pub on the Turl, for tea and crumpets." I enjoyed saying "crumpets" almost as much as eating them. You just can't get real crumpets here, dripping in butter, like you do there. I was meeting Susan, Terri, and Lisa, three African-American women who would become my buds, my pals, my "peeps" in Oxford, and, later, my lifelong friends.

As I walked by the porter's lodge, about to step out into the modern-day auto traffic crowding onto a street designed for only two horses to pass, a voice called out to me: "Oh, Miss Syn-jen!" Colin, the head porter, teased me by calling me "Synjen" the British version of "St. John," and crooked his finger, beckoning me to step into his giant tollbooth, which stood as the portal between town and gown.

"You have a message, milady," he said with mock solemnity. He was proud as a new papa that I had received my first little paper slip in my very own pigeonhole.

Eagerly I pulled out my note, which was simply handwritten on a folded piece of paper without an envelope. My face fell as I read the brief words.

"What's wrong, luv?" Colin asked, observing my distress.

"It's nothing," I told him as I fought back my tears and tried to cover with a smile.

What usually happens when you think you have it made? The rug has a nasty habit of flying out from under your feet. The note was from my "tutor" (kind of like an adviser here in the States—a professor to whom you report), and it stated that I had been denied admission into my chosen course of study, the M. Litt. (British master's degree) in economics, and instead was enrolled in a PPE (politics/philosophy/economics) under-graduate program. His note concluded by saying, "Meet me at 4:00 p.m. on Thursday. Write an essay on John Stuart Mill. You may find the following three books helpful...."

I tromped through town without even noticing the ancient

spires peeking out from behind red double-decker buses loaded with rubbernecking tourists. How could Oxford do this to me? I had graduated with honors from Harvard in politics, economics, and philosophy! The PPE would be virtually the same degree over again. I would waste two years here and return with no graduate degree!

As I walked, I went through an emotional journey that was by now as familiar as the back of my hand. I let myself feel frightened and helpless for a few minutes and then grabbed myself by the scruff of my neck and asked, *Now what are you going to do?* I brainstormed all the things I could do to change the situation and began to feel confident and strong. By the time I arrived at the Nag's Head Pub, I had formulated a plan to challenge Oxford's decision about what I could study. They might have thought I wasn't good enough for their graduate program, but I became determined to prove them wrong.

I was so happy to see my friends, knowing they would support me.

"Can you believe they are doing this to me?" I told them. "They demoted me from a graduate to an undergrad!"

After listening to my crisis and commiserating, my friends told me their big news.

"Hey, Bonnie," said Terri, "this will cheer you up....We are going to put on a play! We're going to do *Colored Girls!* It's gonna be great."

The groundbreaking literary masterpiece *For Colored Girls Who Have Considered Suicide When the Rainbow Is Enuf,* by Ntozake Shange, is probably the quintessential dramatization of the black woman's experience in modern America, and it is one of my favorite plays. It is structured in the form of twenty "choreopoems" that are set to music, recited, and "danced" into a beautifully stylized depiction of the gut-wrenching stories of seven women known only as the Lady in Red, the Lady in Orange, the Lady in Blue, and so on, each representing a different color of the rainbow. The excitement of a chance to play one of these women alongside my new friends was almost too thrilling to bear.

"Which lady do you want to be?" asked Susan. "I kind of like the Lady in Blue, but we should all discuss who would be the best for each one."

"Oh, no!" said Terri. "You all know I just *have* to be the Lady in Red. I am so perfect for it." She giggled. "And I *do* look good in red." Terri's enthusiasm was, and still is, so easy to get caught up in.

But I felt a million miles away. All my mind was doing was calculating how much time it would take to get involved in this little theatrical undertaking. Hours upon hours of rehearsals. Performances. Commitments that could not be undone... Ahhhhhh! *How can I get involved in this? I have to study. I have to do research. I have to focus. I have to take on Oxford University itself. I don't have time for playing around with my friends!*

I used to engage this pattern of behavior whenever I got my back up against a wall. I call it "declaring martial law" on myself. I just put my head down, blinders on, and doggedly trudge my way through with bullheaded determination. I dropped the crew team, crossed theater and debate off my list, and relegated myself to the library. Lovely, eh? Yeah, it's not pretty. It always seemed like the right thing to do, though. Work hard and you'll succeed — isn't that what we're always taught?

I decided to do everything I could to get what I thought I

needed. I reapplied for the degree program. I began meeting with economics tutors and professors in numerous colleges to find someone who would agree to oversee my research and convince the committee to accept me. I got extra funding from Rhodes House for a private tutor in math and statistics. I continued attending the lectures as if I were accepted. I remember cornering one of the economics professors afterward and asking him, "Do you mind if I sit in on your class? I am reapplying to get into the M. Litt. in econ."

"Oh, no, I don't mind," he answered with a plummy British accent and a warm smile. "But I was a member of the committee that reviewed your earlier application. You won't get in."

Still smiling daggers at me, he turned on his heel and left without waiting for my reply. In the conjugation of human elitism, one first encounters the notion of conceit, beyond that egomania, followed by megalomania, and then, in a class all by themselves, Oxford professors.

I persisted. It took me four years to do the two-year program, but I got my master's in economics. In the end, I won. Or did I?

Now when I look back, I feel quite sick, actually. I finally had the opportunity to enjoy a carefree life, and I threw it away within the first week of school. I could have breezed through the undergraduate curriculum, barely breaking a sweat, while soaking up all that joy-generating atmosphere I had dreamed about since the moment I won the Rhodes. But I didn't know how. Reviewing the course of my life, I can't see one job or one opportunity I would have missed out on if I had done PPE instead of economics. I probably would have even learned *more* without the change, because undergraduates receive more resources and more attention than graduates—the opposite of how it works here in the States. In a peculiar quirk of the Oxford system, I found out I would have even been awarded an MA—a master's degree—in the end, and no one stateside would have known the difference.

As the great American philosopher, John Belushi, so eloquently put it: *"But, nooooooo!"* That would have been too easy. Remember the old commercial for Listerine? "I hate the taste...twice a day!" The message is that you have to keep banging your head against the wall, no matter how much it hurts, because it is good for you. Well, that's exactly where I put myself back then. I couldn't see, or wouldn't *allow* myself to see, any other choice. I was shut down. What I didn't realize was that every time I chose this course of action, I was shooting myself in the foot—and since I only have one, this was a real problem. It's like the advice: "No pain, no gain." Sure, it is important to take the hard road sometimes. But when your thought process degenerates into "More pain *must be* more gain," you may find that you're a tad off-track.

In economics, we study a phenomenon called "the point of diminishing returns." This is the point at which more work actually adds up to less output. You see, more work is not necessarily better work. As a matter of fact, it almost never is. If you work 24-7 all the time, you don't leave yourself any room for the things that make you happy. If you close yourself off from the things that make you happy, you can't possibly be living your joy. If you're not living your joy, your work will eventually begin to suffer. And mine did. I managed to eke out the master's degree in four years, but it was not my best work by any measure. Under so much stress, with so little academic support, I actually felt myself becoming more stupefied day by day.

Even though I shut down emotionally and withdrew into my work, my girlfriends, Susan, Terri, and Lisa, didn't let me get away so easily. They continued to include me in our tradition of Wednesday lunch. They continually dragged me out, sometimes kicking and screaming, to watch the performances of *Colored Girls* (even though they weren't able to convince me to perform), the American-style gospel choir they helped to create, and a whole host of other extracurricular activities I had dismissed as folly. Thank God.

We went through everything together, from boyfriend troubles to academic crises. I will never forget Terri feverishly scratching the bottoms of her feet one late night in her room at St. Hilda's College when she got into a panic about her exams, and all of us surrounding her for support. Or how Susan mobilized a whole team of Rhodes scholars to retype Lisa's thesis overnight from her rough handwritten draft, after the typist she hired damaged the computer file and lost all her work. When I got engaged, Terri threw my bachelorette party: a getaway to the coast for the four of us.

I thought that what got me through my degree program was shutting out life and working myself to the bone. But I was way too emotionally handicapped to realize what was really going on. Looking back all these years later, I see that I could never have survived that academic environment, colder than the bone-chilling dampness of the British climate, nor those professors, more foreboding than the hideous gargoyles hovering over every medieval Oxford building, without the emotional strength, support, and perspective of these extraordinary women. My girl gang. I will never forget what they did for me.

In the end, I can claim victory. I wrestled my way back into the program and completed my M. Litt. in economics. But if I had it to do all over again, I definitely would have played the Lady in Yellow....

Joy Begets Joy

"Welcome to *Live Your Joy*! I'm your host, Bonnie St. John," I said directly into the camera.

When I first began hosting my weekly Web-TV show, I was petrified of speaking directly into the camera. Looking into that cold black hole of a lens just seemed like staring into an abyss to me. They kept telling me to "make friends with the camera." Yeah, right. It looked back at me without any friendship, without any warmth, without any feeling at all. It was weird.

After a while, though, I learned that long plastic-and-glass protrusion wasn't scary at all. I began to see past the hardware, past the hot lights that crowded around me, and into the hearts and minds of the viewers. Just like looking into the faces of the audience at a speech, I spoke to my viewers like they were my best friends. I knew I had something really important to say to them. Something I really needed to tell them about *right now*. It was liberating and very exciting. And never was that feeling so pronounced as it was today, with this guest—one of my favorite people.

"We're talking about women's friendships and how important they are to your health and well-being. My guest is Joy Carol, author of *The Fabric of Friendship: Celebrating the Joys, Mending the Tears in Women's Relationships*." I turned to her and touched her arm. "Thank you so much for joining us!"

"It's my pleasure, Bonnie, to be here with you," Joy answered.

The warmth between us was easy and genuine. I had met the

appropriately named "Joy" through two other dear friends of mine. We were both asked to speak about our books at a fund-raiser for women in Africa. How perfect that we met through women friends. The message in Joy's book had touched me profoundly. During the first half of my life I wasn't able to really "get it" about women's friendships. I associated with and liked spending time with a lot of women, but the whole dynamic was often completely befuddling to me. I made a lot of mistakes.

Now that I was the master of my own Web-TV show, I had the opportunity to use my personal bytes of fame to answer the question I get asked the most: *"Bonnie, you've been abused, divorced, disabled, and much more....How do you stay joyful?"* On the show I interviewed the kind of people who had pushed me to grow up and get past the pain, to move on, to live joy—people with titles like: life coach, therapist, minister, celebrity role model, or simply author. With Joy Carol, who is an author, speaker, counselor, and spiritual director, I planned to help viewers learn to prize friendships as I ultimately had.

"What is the most surprising thing you learned about women's friendships while writing the book?" I asked.

"That real, authentic friendships have been *proven* to make you stay healthier and live longer!" answered my guest with her characteristic way of exuding joy. "Harvard Medical School has done a long research study that shows if you don't have good friendships in your life, the impact on your health is like smoking, drinking too much, or not exercising."

"So I can hang out with my girl gang instead of exercising? That's so much more fun than sweating in the gym!" I said.

"It is fun!" agreed Joy.

"Okay, cut! Let's hold the roll for a second," said the director. "You two are doing fine, but we're getting too much glare off that window." In the background behind us was a panorama of New York City high-rise buildings. "John, do you have some low-density filter to put up there?"

This meant we were going to take a break. Another lesson I learned about TV production is that an amazing amount of time and effort goes into what looks like a simple setting. Hours and hours of lighting, positioning the cameras, pulling cables, and dressing the set are spent preparing for every "take." As a matter of fact, there is a cute little saying my director taught me:

> It's not the time it takes to take the takes that takes the time; it's the time it takes *between* the time it takes to take the takes that takes the time!

While the cameramen dealt with the lighting issues, Javier, our makeup artist, came over to pat us down with powder. Although his muscles bulged everywhere, he had the gentlest touch as he arranged a stray bit of Joy's hair and straightened my clothing where it bunched in an odd way.

"Here you go, honey. That is more slimming for you. You look amazing!" said Javier, who seemed to move around the room with a continuous, smooth Latin beat. Part of the way he makes you *look* beautiful is by always making you *feel* gorgeous. His little pep talks ("Your skin... flawless! Have you lost weight since I saw you? You are my favorite person to work with because you are so fun!") while he applies his art to my face and body leave me positively radiant inside and out.

Doing television would be worth it if only to have Javier do my makeup and put together outfits for me. In my bones, I am much more the skier-mountain girl or the studious nerd than the fashionista. I use the combinations of accessories he puts together long after the taping, plus I get his secret shortcuts to doing a professional-looking makeup job even on my own. Yes, I'm coachable.

While we were waiting, Joy had us cracking up with a story about how her panty hose were falling down as she walked over to the studio from the subway. After trying to keep them up unsuccessfully, she finally let them fall to the ground, took them right off in the street, and tossed them in a trash can as she walked past. She had us all laughing 'til it hurt. Joy was, well, so full of joy.

"Okay, we're clear," said the producer. "Bonnie, do a clap for us."

I clapped my hand in front of the camera. You know, I always try to do what the director tells me to do, but this little maneuver was so odd I finally had to ask him what it was for. In the old days of film production, the picture was photographed onto the film in the camera, but the sound was recorded on a separate tape-based recording device. They used that funny-looking black-and-white-striped "clapper" to synchronize the two by finding the exact frame in the picture where the jaws of the clapper first closed and lining that up with the point on the sound track where the snap was first heard. They then locked the two systems together and they stayed in perfect sync—the sound matching the picture. Nowadays with video, the sound and picture are recorded at the same time on the same device—always in perfect sync. My clapping merely gave the editor a reference point to synchronize the two cameras we were shooting with so he could cut back and forth between them as he put the segment together.

"We've got speed. Whenever you're ready, Bonnie."

I began where we left off. "You didn't say all friendships are healthy, though. You said *real, authentic* friendships. Why is that important?" I asked, leaning forward for the answer.

"People will call anyone a friend. 'You're a friend...and you're a friend.' But meanwhile they really are not our friends if they hurt us, use us, or abuse us. A friend is someone who accepts you for the person you are...knows where you have been...and still gently encourages you to grow."

"How do you find that kind of friendship? I have been in and out of some bloodsucking and manipulative friendships!" I shook my head at the memories.

"Only you know what is real and what is good for you," said Joy. "You'll feel it."

"Maybe that's why I had so much trouble! When I was younger I was so emotionally numb and stunted that I didn't feel much. I just didn't get it about friendships or make them a priority. I only had friendships at work or if other people made all the effort." I said this thinking about my girl friends in Oxford. I had distanced myself with work, but they never really let me go.

"What turned it around for you?" Joy asked me.

"It wasn't enough to just tell myself to do it," I said. "I tried going through the motions. But it wasn't until I did more healing work on myself—therapy, yoga, and prayer—that I could feel whom I wanted to spend time with and also feel the support, love, and joy they gave me. Going through the motions without feeling anything doesn't work for friendship either." Joy nodded her head in understanding. "Are most women good at cultivating friendships?" I asked.

"Bonnie, Phyllis Chesler wrote a book called *Woman's Inhumanity to Woman* about how women are envious, killing one another with competition, backstabbing, and gossiping. Other authors have written about women's friendships' being warm and wonderful and supportive. Both things are true."

"That's what I love about your book. You tell us that good relationships are not automatic; we have to mend the tears, celebrate what's good, and if it can't be fixed, shake the dust off and move on."

"The source of most problems in women's friendships comes down to one thing: a lot of women just don't feel good about themselves. All our lives we are told about what we are doing wrong. Made to feel not good enough. When a woman doesn't value herself or her gender, it is hard to have healthy friendships. Like in your case, you needed to heal the wounds and build your self-esteem."

"What is your advice for cultivating better friendships?"

"In addition to building self-esteem?" Joy began counting off on her fingers. "First, set reasonable boundaries so you don't give too much more than you receive. Second, diversify your friendships—no one person can meet all your needs. Third, have reasonable expectations—most people won't do or be everything you want them to be. Fourth and most important:

Learn to communicate. You need to be honest but not brutally or hurtfully so."

"Thank you, Joy, for helping us better understand how to Live Your Joy by having healthy, authentic friendships! I so appreciate your taking the time to be on the show today." I turned to the camera and smiled.

"Cut!" said the director. "Excellent. Great job, you two! I really loved it."

I turned to Joy. "What I want," I told her, "is to be one of your friends."

"Of course!" she said. "Let's get to know each other better.... We'll see where it takes us."

When she hugged me I felt the warmth and healing energy she radiates even more strongly. *What a woman!* I thought to myself. Being friends with her would make me feel accepted as I am, yet her very presence would also beckon me to grow into a better person. And that, I had just learned, was the definition of a true friend.

An Olympian-Sized Dream

My wipers barely moved fast enough to keep some semblance of vision possible through the windshield of my rented red Volkswagen Rabbit. When snow falls like this, it covers the surface so fast you really have to work at keeping up with it. Even with the mush pushed to the side, it was still difficult to tell whether or not the Salt Lake City street was still beneath me, or if I had irretrievably veered off onto some farmer's cow path. Why was I out here in one of the worst blizzards of the season? I had a mission. I had a noble purpose. But I was scared out of my mind since — at age thirty-six — it was my first time driving in snow.

How, you may wonder, *could you have reached age thirty-six without driving in snow? You were a ski racer, for goodness' sake!* The sad truth is that I could never afford a car when I was ski racing. So when I lived in snowy places, I rode buses or lived in a dorm. I didn't get a car until after I finished college and got married, but then I lived in San Diego for another ten years. I never drove in snow. I hate to admit it, but I was far more afraid of *driving* in snow than skiing on it at seventy miles per hour on one leg!

After all those years of managing to avoid it, what would push me over the brink of my fear and into the driver's seat during a snowstorm? Friendship.

Ben Finley, who had convinced the National Brotherhood of Skiers to fund my racing when he was president of the group, was flying into Salt Lake City to attend the opening ceremonies of the 2002 Paralympics, at which I would be speaking.

Granted, I was saying only a few lines. Most of the opening ceremonies would be filled with stars like Stevie Wonder, Wynonna Judd, and Donny Osmond alongside flashy displays of fireworks, skating shows, and musical performances. Only three athletes were going to speak for a total of ten minutes—and I was so proud to be chosen as one of them.

As president of the NBS nearly twenty years beforehand, Ben had introduced me to all the black ski clubs across the country and asked them to raise money for me even though I was a disabled skier. Those clubs not only gave me money for race entry fees, airplane tickets, and ski clothing, but also often opened their homes to me as I traveled all across the country. I absolutely felt the true spirit of brotherhood, in every sense of the word, from this incredible organization.

When I went to the Paralympics in Innsbruck, Austria, more than thirty-three members of the NBS signed up to go and cheer me on. You can imagine a large crowd of black people in Austria turned a few heads! One of my teammates once commented on my cheering section, saying, "Wow, Bonnie, you sure have a large family!"

Indeed I did.

At only nineteen years of age, I felt so much pressure to win for them that I even wrote a letter to Ben asking if it would be okay if I didn't win. I was only the third-ranked woman amputee skier on the U.S. team—so I wasn't expected to beat my teammates, never mind the international competition. Ben sent a letter back telling me, in no uncertain terms, that they would love and support me no matter what—win or lose. What an amazing thing to say. That letter meant so much to me. It made me feel able to do my best with so much less stress. And, my best turned out to be a silver and two bronze medals!

But at the last minute Ben, my champion, couldn't go to Austria with us. He had suffered a collapsed lung shortly before the event, and the doctors wouldn't agree to any air travel. Despite years of supporting me and my ski racing, he was left out in the cold.

That's why, when I found out I was speaking in the opening ceremonies in Salt Lake, I called and invited him to come. I hadn't seen him in years, but I wanted to share the excitement and hoopla of the Olympics with him—at long last.

"It's like a chance to come and enjoy the Olympics you didn't get to go to in 1984. Come and celebrate with me!" I told him.

He enthusiastically said, "Yes!" So, to pick up this very special person, I got behind the steering wheel and braved the slippery white stuff accumulating on the frozen Utah streets.

Years before the Salt Lake Winter Olympics, I knew I wanted to be there. Since I had competed in 1984, this was the first time the winter Olympics and Paralympics would be in the good ol' U.S. of A. I had this vision of getting a job as a news commentator, renting a big ski house, and inviting all my friends to come and celebrate with me. When I saw and felt this vision in my mind's eye, it was a sense of wanting to live my joy...to be surrounded by friends, family, and loved ones celebrating how far I'd come. I'd spent the two or three years prior doing my intense healing work—reliving my childhood abuse in therapy, praying for hours in nature, doing yoga—and now I was actually able to feel the desire to be surrounded by people who loved me.

To make this dream come true, I made every connection I could think of and told them I wanted to help out in some way in Salt Lake. I volunteered for the U.S. Olympic Committee's mentoring program and gave speeches in Colorado Springs for the youth programs they run at their big training center there. I was asked to give an inspirational speech to the Olympic committee staff in Salt Lake City when Mitt Romney took over after the bribery scandals erupted. I asked for information about who would be running things in Salt Lake and could give me a job. I contacted them, their contacts, and their contacts' contacts. Nothing.

As the Olympics got closer, my hopes and dreams began to fade. One month beforehand, I had no job, no volunteer assignment, and certainly no sports commentator job with NBC (I still didn't even know I would get invited to be in the opening ceremonies for the Paralympics). To make matters worse, the 2002 Olympics in February took place not long after the World Trade Center bombings in September 2001. With the economy in disarray and no one wanting to fly, corporations were cutting way back on the kinds of meetings I was usually hired to speak at. As a single mom with business slowing way down, I was in no position to rent a big chalet and invite all my friends to join me in the snow!

High on my list of very supportive contacts was a fellow named John Naber, the four-time gold medal Olympic swimmer who had served as a network sports commentator many times.

"I'm a summer athlete and I don't have any specific contracts to be in Salt Lake," he told me several weeks beforehand. "But I am going anyway."

"How?" I asked. "Why?"

"I'm going to stay with another Olympian who lives in Salt Lake. I'll be available to help while I'm there. You'd be surprised how it works. If you just come, we'll get tickets to things; we'll meet lots of people. It will all work out. Even though it isn't the summer Olympics, I may get asked to comment on something for TV. Who knows?"

Wow, I thought. *Why not?*

"I know some other people who are sharing an apartment.... I'll give you a name."

Until John said it, it never would have occurred to me to *just go.* Since work was slow, I had the time. I could always fly out of Salt Lake City if something came up, couldn't I? It would have been so easy to go the opposite direction and declare martial law on myself like I did in Oxford: *The economy is down, I have to spend more time marketing! I can't afford this. The sky is falling!* What stopped me was this intense desire to enjoy myself (where did that come from?) at the Olympics.

You see, when I was competing, I didn't get to enjoy the Olympics. I was still in the mode of beating up on myself and caring very little for my own feelings. It was "Verk, verk, verk!" and no play for Bonnie in Austria. Being a spectator in Salt Lake, I could go to the parties, watch the skaters, trade pins in the big tent, and for the first time participate in all the fun that surrounds this spectacular international event. I wanted to go, and I was willing to make a priority out of feeling that joy.

Once I committed to the joy of this experience, lots of good things began to happen. The Shriners Hospital in Salt Lake offered me the use of one of the apartments they have to house parents while their children undergo surgery. In return, I agreed to speak at several of the Olympic events they were hosting—a scheduled stop of the Paralympic Torch at the hospital on its way to the stadium, a meeting of trustees, and of course speaking to the kids in the hospital and their parents.

It quickly became clear to me that I would see lots of my friends even if I didn't have a big chalet to house them. Both of my amputee ski-racer roommates from the Paralympics—Lana and Martha—were coming to the Olympics. Friends and coaches from Burke Mountain Academy in Vermont, where I had trained, were staying in Deer Valley right on the edge of the trails where the Alpine events would be held.

Again, once I committed to going, lots of opportunities to help arose. I was asked to help the USOC with hospitality for sponsors: sitting with corporate execs at a special dinner, handing out tickets for closing ceremonies to parents of the competing athletes, and more. I even convinced a small local station in Arkansas to let me cover a news story for them about a group of kids who raised the money to go and see the Olympics—so my dream of being a sports commentator came true! But the biggest thing of all was being asked to speak in the opening ceremonies for the Paralympics.

In addition to inviting Ben Finley, I flew my mother, Ruby, and my daughter, Darcy, the short distance from San Diego to soak up the excitement and celebrate the Olympic spirit with me.

After picking up Ben at the airport, we drove straight to the Shriners Hospital, which sat high on a hill at the very edge of Salt Lake. As you pull into the large circular driveway in front of the building, you see a row of international flags on the edge of the property where it drops sharply away, creating a breathtaking view of the surrounding snowcapped Wasatch mountain range.

The hospital had set up its own cauldron—a replica of the cauldron that holds the Olympic flame in the stadium throughout the games—which was to be lit in a huge ceremony that day. The Shriners wanted to keep the Olympic spirit visible here at the hospital. I left Ben with my mother and Darcy as I ran up to my room to change into my Olympic jacket and medals before the big event. The snow had stopped, revealing a glorious, crisp winter day.

When I returned, there were children in wheelchairs and on crutches with their parents and friends, nurses and doctors, all crowding around outside the large entryway to the hospital. There was a festive air of anticipation as we waited for the torch runners to be spied coming toward us.

"There they are!"

Word spread like wildfire through the noisy pack of patients, who were pointing and craning their necks to witness the symbolic parade. The flame was carried high in the air by a blind runner who held the torch in one hand and the leash of his guide dog in the other. More uniformed members of the torch-run team ran alongside him as he neared our throng.

It seemed impossible for the hospital's administrator to quiet this multitude, but as the moment neared to ignite the flame, every man, woman, and child held his or her breath, leaving a silence so complete that the sound of the runner's feet could be heard. Man and dog gracefully loped toward the cauldron. They stopped just shy of the structure as one of the patients, a five-year-old girl with dark ringlets and big brown eyes, was wheeled over by her tear-streaked mother. The torchbearer passed the flame to the little girl, and she, with the help of her doctor, touched the flame to the cauldron, igniting a joyous wave of pride and spirit that infused the hearts of everyone present. As that beautiful Olympic flame danced up toward the sky, our ragtag horde of disabled kids, parents, and hospital staff flung off cares about surgeries, illness, and pain to release deafening whoops and cheers that echoed from the very hills surrounding us. It was a moment I'll cherish forever.

Later on this same terrace, I would give a rousing emotional speech about the potential of each and every child to make his or her dreams come true. That night I would ride into the Olympic stadium on a float with Wynonna Judd and two other disabled athletes and speak about my dream to be a skier. Thirty thousand people would scream in response, fireworks would decorate the night sky, and the Paralympics would be officially opened.

But at that moment—as a small child lit our unofficial cauldron and I stood there with my mother, my daughter, and Ben Finley, surrounded by the Shriners who had given me a medical miracle—I felt the Olympic spirit sink more deeply into my bones than it had even when I was competing. Looking at the faces of those close to me as well as the faces of all the disabled kids who were a miracle in process, I felt that anything and everything is truly possible in this world. I felt—I *really* felt it—love, support, and a boundless joy. I knew right then that my dream of winning at the Olympics had finally come true.

CHAPTER EIGHT

Resilience...

Fall Down? Get Up!

Getting Over the Hump

When I pitched the notion of writing a book called *Live Your Joy* to my editor, it was summertime. The grass was green, the sun was shining brightly through the floor-to-ceiling windows in my house, the air had that wonderful, balmy summer smell, and writing about joy just seemed like a really good idea.

I had escaped the sticky August heat of New York City to spend a few weeks in a beautiful log cabin high in the Catskill Mountains of upstate New York, buried in a wooded landscape offering a delicious blend of sturdy, leafy deciduous trees alongside magnificent, piney evergreens. Each morning I did my thirty-minute yoga routine out on the deck overlooking a lush, multicolored valley with two exquisitely symmetrical rolling hills framing the horizon in the distance. With each breath I inhaled crisp, aromatic mountain air. I felt the warm glow of pure, unadulterated sunshine on my skin. I leisurely shopped for organic vegetables and meats at the friendly local grocer for my new cleansing diet. I took long walks in the woods to exercise. I watched birds lazily glide across the dale, buoyed by an elegantly soft cushion of air.

Writing about joy was going to be so easy.

Then suddenly my fantasylike, woodland lifestyle came to an abrupt end. In September, I moved back to New York

City and my twelve-year-old daughter returned from spending the summer with her father in California. The school year started off with a bang: up at 6:30 a.m., rushing the ten blocks to school, and trying to cram in eight hours of work before I had to go back and pick her up at 3:00 p.m. The book tour for my previous publication, *How Strong Women Pray*, was starting in a few weeks, so I had endless "to do" lists filled with travel arrangements, media pitches, and various other details to supervise in the never-ending parade of minutiae involved in promoting a new book. When I watch *Murder, She Wrote*, the old TV series in which Angela Lansbury plays a famous mystery writer, I always chuckle when I see her lovingly escorted from place to place, happy and carefree as a Cape Cod clam, signing books for hundreds of adoring admirers who enthusiastically line up to spend a moment in her presence. Well, that may be how it works for the likes of Stephen King or J. K. Rowling, but for yours truly it's a bit more of a grind. Until I've sold a couple million books, lil' ol' me still has to work very, very hard to set up promotional events and book-signings, get the word out, and fly myself all over the country to launch my baby into the world. Come to think of it, getting a book out *is* a lot like childbirth. Summer was the conception. September began the pregnancy.

I'm not complaining, mind you. This, too, was living my joy, albeit in a more hectic mode. I was so proud of my daughter and treasured the time spent walking her to school and back. But I also loved my work. I looked forward to sharing the stories of prayer from the extraordinary women in the book, like Maya Angelou, Edie Falco, and Barbara Bush, with audiences across the nation. Truly, I was living my dream life. It's just that I had to work a lot harder at it than I did in my summer hideaway up in the woods.

Once we hit "pub date" (the book's birthday), things moved so fast I didn't have any time to even muse about "living my joy," much less write about it. I was in three or four different cities each week. I traveled so much that I was starting to look familiar to the flight attendants. *Weren't you on my three o'clock to Cincinnati last Tuesday?* I spoke sometimes twice a day and was constantly interviewed on TV and radio shows, sometimes by telephone at all hours of day and night: morning drive time, evening talk shows, Sunday morning gospel—anytime, anywhere.

I remember being in the Baltimore airport at one point, talking on the phone to a radio host in Kansas City who was taping me as I sat in the gate area waiting for a flight to Chicago. The interview continued as they called the flight and began boarding. I kept answering questions as everyone else left the boarding area one by one. Finally, I knew I had to get on the plane or the folks waiting for me in Chicago were going to be one keynote speaker short for the party. Juggling my purse, coat, and computer bag, I held the phone to my ear and continued the interview while handing my ticket to the rather unsympathetic flight attendant and trudging down the gangway just in time for the airplane door to close behind me.

My life became a blur of airports, hotels, book events, and TV studios. I missed my daughter terribly, but we both knew all this would last only about six weeks.

I shouldn't make it sound all bad. It was a whole lot better than my last book tour ten years ago. With a book on prayer, I was often in churches speaking and praying with hundreds of people. I was once invited to speak at a conference of more than two hundred women ministers! Being prayed over, being prayed with, and feeling so blessed kept me going with a great deal of positive energy through it all.

Thank goodness, I thought, for the Thanksgiving break to relax after this nonstop, peripatetic lifestyle.

So what did I do? I invited my brother and his wife to join us for the Thanksgiving holiday with my nieces and nephew (twins, age six, plus a seven-year-old). However, since they live in Charlotte, that meant they stayed with me for four days. Those of you who've done this know that having guests for the holidays means far more than just cooking a good turkey dinner—a feat, by the way, in and of itself. I had to deal with sheets on beds, meals, transportation, activities for kids, and more! I had literally signed up to become my own resort. And, in an even more egregious moment of insanity, I offered to take care of all the kids while my brother and his wife took a day off to enjoy a romantic twenty-four hours in New York City without the burdens of parenthood. I knew they didn't get much chance to take time out alone together, and I knew they appreciated my offer to give them this little time alone. All this was done with the best of intentions, but I just didn't factor in how tired I would be by Thanksgiving. So there I was, exhausted out of my mind, driving four kids all around the country for horseback riding, crafts, movies, and endless games of make-believe. I am sure that you, dear reader, would never get yourself in way over your head, way overcommitted, and way past the end of your rope. Would you?

After that so-called vacation, I was actually grateful to go back out on the book tour where I could rest! Suddenly, being alone in a hotel room far away from home sounded blissfully peaceful. The week after Thanksgiving, I squeezed in three more cities with book-signings and media appearances.

But that's not all. Darcy's thirteenth birthday arrived next, in early December, like a light at the end of the tunnel that turns out to be a freight train. I had sworn I would keep her birthday simple, no matter how many fancy bar or bat mitzvah celebrations she was invited to attend. Back in September, I had soberly explained to Darcy that we would keep her party very small and easy this year because we were so busy with the book tour. Kind and loving person that she is, she firmly agreed. It would not be like last year when she invited eight girls to come to our house in costumes representing meticulously accurate queens from around the world and throughout history including Cleopatra, Queen Noor, and Queen Isabella. Prior to the event, each girl received a dossier explaining her character's past, offering tips for clothing choices, and including a few key phrases in her native tongue. The party itself had three acts with props, clues, a full-blown murder mystery, and a trial at which I presided as judge. That, friends, was a major production. *This year,* I thought, shaking my hand at the sky like Scarlett O'Hara, *as God is my witness, it will be simple.*

So, how did I find myself driving a large Chevy Suburban filled with five giggling, screaming, soon-to-be teenagers up to the cabin in the woods for a two-night sleepover? And how did I get talked into another murder mystery, this time with a kidnapping and clues distributed throughout the nearby small town (in the library, the hardware store, the diner, etc.), which was four times *more* complicated than the party last year? Was I truly insane or just mentally helpless?

After thirty-six hours of twelve-year-old girls laughing, dancing, picking on each other, messing up the house, and doing everything *except* sleeping, I felt like I was having an out-of-body experience.

I returned to the city just long enough to pack my suitcase, again, for the next round of interviews, speeches, and book-signings. Zombielike, I smiled, shook hands, and scrawled my name into books that were put in front of me. Over the Christmas break, after Darcy went back to her father, I finally got the chance to lie down—and got really sick for two full weeks. My body simply shut down, declaring itself in a state of rebellion.

In January the book-signing events started up again with a vengeance. One event I had been particularly looking forward to was hosted by my church at a nearby organic café. It felt good to be surrounded by familiar faces, to read from my book and talk about prayer with so many of the warm, friendly people I'm proud to call my friends and fellow parishioners.

The real art of a good book-signing, I've learned, is knowing when to shut up. Since I am used to giving speeches for a living, talking for forty-five minutes to an hour is as easy for me as falling off a log. But at a book-signing, people don't usually want you to yammer on for that long. You read a bit from the book, talk about behind-the-scenes things that happened while writing, and answer questions. After about thirty minutes, the crowd will generally start to get antsy. You see, most people really came just to buy an autographed book, maybe as a gift for Mother's Day or the birthday of a friend. They are always polite enough to patiently listen, but they really want you to get out your Sharpie and start scribbling your John Hancock in a reasonable amount of time. As an author, you have to respect that. You've got to give people time to actually buy the books. After all, that's what you're there for, too.

"Let's take a break," I said.

Another great thing that happens once you stop talking is that people come up and talk to you, and this group was no exception. They told me their stories. I got hugs. I felt loved. Because most of the people were from my church, I was introduced to new friends by old friends. Of course, I also signed books.

As things began to slow down a bit, an elderly woman came over and tugged on my sleeve.

"What about when prayer doesn't work?" she asked.

Her eyes bored into my soul. In them, I could see an endless prairie of a long, hard life—well lived, but well worn. Not deep sorrow or horrendous pain, but simply the wind blowing across a vapid expanse of nothing. Hollow. I looked back at her like a deer caught in the headlights.

"Prayer. Not work?" I stuttered.

"Yes," she continued. "You talk about how wonderful prayer is and connecting to God in conversation. When we come back from break, why don't you talk about what it's like when it isn't working and you can't seem to find God at all?"

I knew from experience that we wouldn't be coming back from break. The event was scheduled for two hours. I waited more than twenty minutes for people to arrive, talked for thirty minutes, and then let people buy their books for another thirty minutes. After an hour and a half, the whole thing was winding down. I didn't think there was any need for me to give another speech. Not only did I reckon my audience was ready to head home for dinner and their favorite TV show, I was getting pretty hungry myself. I figured if I just listened to her now, that would be it. I was humoring her.

"Are you having trouble praying?" I asked. I felt like the gentle angel leaning over to help. In retrospect, I would see that she was like a Dickensian ghost of my own future come to tell me about myself.

"I used to be a pastor," she told me. "For thirteen years. I was one of the first women to become a minister around here. So it was always tough."

She had brightened up, talking about the past. Then she slouched again. "But now I can't pray. I feel nothing." A long pause. "Sometimes, if I just sit by a river I feel good. Is that praying?"

"Yes," I said, a bit perplexed but curiously drawn to her. "I think prayer is a lot like water. There are times when we go to the well, draw the water, and carry it to the crops. But there are also times when just sitting by the river is enough. It is knowing that God's love is flowing before we see it, through our lives and far beyond where we can perceive here on earth."

I said these things wondering if it made any difference to her. We talked for a few more minutes and then I extracted myself from her, as though I could wash my hands of this uncomfortable subject by returning to shaking hands, signing books, and wishing people well.

Just when I thought I could call it quits and make a hasty exit, one of my friends from church came over with the elderly ex-pastor in tow.

"She has a question," my friend told me. "She wants to talk about it."

Of course I knew what her question was, and I didn't want to talk about it. I looked at the clock. The official book-signing was scheduled to last another twenty minutes. My daughter was tired and hungry. I was tired and hungry. I really had thought I could escape talking about this. But I stopped and surrendered to the situation.

"Sure," I said warmly. "Let's talk."

Three of the women from my church, my daughter, the ex-pastor, and I sat down around a small table and began to talk.

"What do you do when you pray and pray but feel only darkness inside?"

Suddenly I realized it was really me that they were talking about. I had become a burned-out shell. Emotionally and spiritually, I was drained. Although I talked about prayer and prayed in large groups, I had lost the time to quietly connect with God. On planes when I tried to pray, I felt nothing. Mostly I just fell asleep.

Why had I pushed myself to the limits and beyond?

I felt that if I did enough publicity, I could get "over the hump." Before the book, I was a minor celebrity: quoted on a Starbucks cup, honored by the president, but most people didn't recognize my name. Pushing hard on the book tour meant I would spend more money and spend more time away from my daughter, but if I got famous enough, I could charge higher speaking fees, pick and choose where to go, and hire more assistants to help. Being "over the hump" as a celebrity meant having an easier life.

Yet, I found myself at the end of the book tour wrung out

like an old, moldy washcloth. Financially, emotionally, spiritually, and mentally, I had given it my all. And I did well: appearances on *The Today Show, The 700 Club; Oprah and Friends* radio, good, steady book sales. I was still getting booked as a speaker, but not as I expected—with tons of offers from which I could pick and choose.

I realized that instead of getting *over* the hump, I had pretty much slammed right into it. I had run at the hump with all my energy, crashed into it really hard, and slid down to where I now found myself, not only exhausted but on a deadline to write about joy, of all things, and feeling completely empty. If there were a needle on my gauge, it would have been so far past the "E" it would have busted, like in one of those old *Road Runner* cartoons. With a *boing* sound effect.

Frequently I was wide awake at 4:00 a.m., already worrying about everything. In addition to the book tour, I was hosting a weekly radio show called *Live Your Joy*, launching a new Web site, and rolling out weekly Web-TV segments. My mind raced: *Who is my next guest? What will we talk about? Why doesn't the e-commerce system provide the right sales tax reports? Where will I find a new Web support team now that my designers have gone out of business? Did I RSVP to the last bar mitzvah Darcy was invited to? Will my dry cleaning come back before my next speaking event? Can I get my hair done in time for the next TV segment?* Often, I just got out of bed and started working on my computer instead of lying there. I was doing a hundred things all at once, with no sign of seeing the top of that eponymous hump anytime soon.

So there I sat at that watershed book-signing, surrounded by these loving women, purportedly to talk about the problems of a burned-out ex-pastor, but what I really saw was a burned-out ex-Bonnie.

I wish I could say those women told me the secret or prayed the right prayer and it all turned around. It wasn't that way. They did give loving support. Each woman talked about a time she had been in that place. They checked in on whether the elderly woman was depressed enough to need to see a professional.

"You can't mess with that," Judy clucked. "Depression is a serious illness. When people try to 'buck up' and cheer themselves out of it, the disease can go untreated for far too long." If she didn't need to seek out a therapist, they counseled patience. They talked about taking extra care of oneself. Eating right. Resting.

"Sometimes you can't chase peace," Elaine said to the pastor. "You just prepare for it, and let it come to you."

Boy, was she right. Putting myself back together took time to rest, to clarify my path and decide what to keep doing and what to let go. It took time. It took patience. It took faith.

Physically, I was exhausted. I had gained ten pounds on tour from a lack of exercise and an abundance of restaurant food. That meant not only that my clothes didn't fit, but also that my artificial leg was beginning to pinch during the day since it was too tight. I didn't feel good or look good.

Eating healthy food and exercising were important, but I felt too tired to do either. It took baby steps to build up to bigger baby steps.

I remember certain moments that felt like breakthroughs, like the day I got up and actually felt like doing my thirty-minute yoga routine. I had amazing energy and clarity all day.

There was also the day I prayed in the sedan all the way to the airport. Although I got distracted and had to keep pulling my attention back, I didn't fall asleep! I prayed for clarity going forward. I must have prayed from the deep desperation I felt because later that day I received a waterfall of clarity. I sat on the plane writing as fast as my pen would go, making a long list of things to *stop* doing. It felt exhilarating!

That wasn't the first time I had to pull myself back from the brink. I had been there during my divorce. I had been there dealing with my sexual-abuse issues. I had been there after my first book tour. I had been there at the end of a three-year relationship that ended badly. I have lots of practice picking myself up again emotionally and spiritually.

Here's some good advice I received recently: Try to stay in your body. Given my history of sexual abuse, I tend to flee from my body under duress. Often called dissociating, this reaction is an actual disconnection from physical sensations. Since emotions are felt in the body, dissociating is a form of self-anesthetic that protects from sadness and anger but also eliminates joy.

I guess that's why yoga can make such a difference—also dancing, massage, or a hot bath. Anything that anchors me, that helps me feel safe in my body, can bring me back to life. By reintegrating myself, getting back to wholeness, I am more able to access my inner wisdom, to listen to God and to pray...and thus to live my joy.

There is joy in the process of picking myself up after being spiritually or emotionally knocked down. It requires tenderness. Tenderness *from* me, *for* me. I had come full circle from beginning to write *Live Your Joy*. At the beginning I had the "spa environment" joy of writing out in the woods while feeling rested, eating healthy, and breathing in the fresh, pine-scented air. Then I had the "hectic working mom" joy of being in New York City, taking care of my daughter, and planning the book tour. That morphed into the "maximum-speed book tour" joy of being able to intensely connect with millions of people, pray with them, and play full-out. Finally I came around to the joy of recuperating. What I learned was that my joy isn't just one speed. It isn't a lifestyle I can optimize or maintain. It is a set of seasons, cycles, and rhythms. Joy isn't just about getting over the hump. There is joy even at the bottom of the hump.

Still, I have to admit, I wouldn't mind seeing how the other side of the hump lives....

CHAPTER NINE

Faith...

Rely on the Rock

Finding Joy at the End of My Rope

By summer of the year 2000, I had become completely disgusted with the fact that my Olympic physique had, seemingly
irretrievably, turned to flab. I had to finally admit that my *I-
just-had-a-baby* excuse didn't work anymore, since Darcy was
now almost six years old. Desperate to find a workable method
for returning my body to something I was happy to walk
around in, I took on the "Body for Life" challenge: a weight-
loss regimen by ex-bodybuilder Bill Phillips.

Over the years I had doggedly forced myself through the
rigors of *The Zone*, *Weight Watchers*, and even *Jenny Craig* for a
time. Unfortunately, as is often the case with these diets, I had
gained back every pound I'd ever lost—and then some. Fortu-
nately, my last attempt had been so long ago that I acquired the
sort of amnesia about this whole process that makes it possible
to feel optimistic yet again. The book *Body for Life*, I rational-
ized, presented more than just another diet plan where you eat
six times a day. I was bound to succeed, I felt, with the fitness
routine, the essence of which is that you work out six days a
week—three days of cardio and three days of weight lifting.

The catch was, I lived in Pine Valley, California. The
boonies. That meant the nearest gym was a leaky closet in
the back of the high school with a few musty, old, outdated

machines…and even that was thirty miles away. To work out six times a week, I was going to have to do it the old-fashioned way: at home.

I bought enough dumbbells, in various sizes, for all the weight lifting I needed to do and let them populate my living room. For the cardio, I decided to go far out of my comfort zone and try running. *It'll get me outdoors in this beautiful countryside*, I argued to myself. *It'll be great.*

In retrospect, I'm convinced the diet-induced fanaticism that drew me to this decision must have constricted the circulation to my brain. I have *always* hated running. For my entire life, I had successfully blamed my poor running performance on the fact that I had only one leg. An ironclad excuse, no? Who could argue? That is, until those amputee track stars with the high-tech, artificial running blades for feet got lots of publicity and proved to everyone that amputees, in fact, can run like the wind. Even though it would be another eight years before Oscar Pistorius, the double-amputee sprinter from South Africa, would be officially granted the right to qualify for the Beijing Olympics against the nondisabled runners, my perfect excuse for not going jogging had been permanently ruined.

So there I was, out on a big green, grassy field in my fancy blue running shorts, stretching to warm up. I looked around at the ring of mountains on the horizon and breathed in the heavenly air. I felt like I could do anything and everything I put my mind to. Luckily, there was still enough oxygen getting to my brain that I knew I couldn't run a whole mile. The plan was to alternate between running for two minutes and walking for two minutes until I got up to twenty minutes. I programmed my trusty digital stopwatch for the timings and set out on the first day of the rest of my return to the ranks of the truly buffed. Even with this easy start-up regimen, I was quickly huffing and puffing like a marathon runner with a two-pack-a-day smoking habit.

My second day of running was even more dramatic. I ended up in the emergency room. In fact, I discovered, I could not do anything and everything I put my mind to—especially when it came to running. Right in the spot where my artificial leg rammed into my thigh every time I landed on it, I had gotten a boil. It rose up underneath my skin: big, red, and tender, making it impossible to wear my leg at all, never mind run. The doctor lanced my boil (that means he cut it open to let all the pus out) and relegated me to crutches for a week while it healed.

You might think that was the end of my running career, but no! I am a persistent little cuss if nothing else. After letting the wound heal, I repeated the experiment: early mornings in the park, running shorts, and stopwatch. Albert Einstein said the definition of insanity is doing the same thing over and over again and expecting a different result. Turns out he was right. Go figure. This time, though, it took three days to achieve: boil and emergency room visit. While under the knife for the second time, I had the clarity to understand that running, for me, was equivalent to cursing myself with a plague of boils and pestilence. It was like a sign from God that I should leave it alone. I don't mess with that.

I turned to jumping rope for my cardio workout. When I jump rope, I take off my artificial leg and hop up and down on my one and only good leg. Hence, no artificial leg banging into my thigh! As part of the *Body for Life* routine, I needed

twenty minutes of cardio, cycling between low and high inten-
sities, rising to higher and higher levels. The regimen I came
up with was to jump a hundred times, stop for a break, then
two hundred times, stop for a break, and, finally, finish with
four hundred jumps. After nearly keeling over with exhaustion,
I would do the whole thing again for a grand total of fourteen
hundred jumps... and zero boils.

It was a great workout.

During that same period in my life, I was also spending a lot
of time learning to pray. I had moved to the countryside to heal
my emotional wounds and recover from my divorce. And for
the first time since childhood, I was attending church regularly
at our local nondenominational services. Prayer had helped me
stay sane and keep on track with my therapy, even as the horrible memories from my childhood began to backwash into my
life like the coke you drank too fast spurting out of your nose.
Prayer helped me deal with the mess. Since my life was really
messy, I prayed all the time.

When the going got tough one morning during my new
jump-rope routine, it was natural, then, for me to pray. During
the set of four hundred, I got so tired I was about to collapse
and fall over. Still trying to keep going, I prayed, "God, give
me strength," a simple prayer. Suddenly, I felt renewed energy
course through my veins and muscles. I was amazed. It worked!
I finished the workout with a renewed sense of vigor that came
from a place deep within my being. A place I felt I had never
tapped before. It felt wonderful.

After that, I always prayed for strength when I got to the
end of what I could stand in my workout. Every time, I felt
this extra power kick in. As the days went by, I began to look

forward to that moment when, at the end of my own ability, I would be able to count on some extra help from God. Rather than dreading the moment my muscles wore out, as I always had in the past, I raced forward in my workout, anticipating that feeling of stepping off the end of the plank and walking on the water.

Soon my new habit affected how I approached daily life. Having this concrete, physical proof every day of the power of prayer and God, I could walk through my challenges outside the gym as well, knowing that when I reached the end of my emotional strength I would find God there for me. Learning to pray and receive this kind of pure strength got me through the long, dark trials of the soul I was experiencing at that time. I believe it was only with the help of my faith that I survived those early days of emotional healing that involved reliving years of abuse as a child during the long hours of therapy.

During the first few years that I began to really pray on a daily basis, I would spend most of the time listening. I would close my eyes and focus on being thankful to God. I basked in the benediction of being in the divine presence and felt grateful for the time to shut out everything else. Once I felt calmness and connection, I asked, "God, what do I need to know today?"

On the majority of days the response was love. I would feel a loving presence rain down on me, surround me, and fill me with a joy beyond anything I knew. Looking back, I am convinced that God needed to teach me what it felt like to love myself every day. I just didn't know. I didn't have the experience of being loved and treasured as a little child.

Being taught to love and value oneself is *the most* fundamental building block for joy. How can you make joy a priority if you don't love yourself? Joy never demands our attention like troubles and woes do. We must choose joy and make time and space for it, or lose it. Jesus felt that having more wine to enjoy a wedding feast was so very important that he performed a miracle to accomplish this feat. We must love ourselves enough to know that we deserve a miracle.

That faith journey—living life with more faith, more prayer, and more love—really changed everything for me. Throughout this book I have shared stories about experiences that were the building blocks I used to pull myself back into finding joy in my life. The final building block I want to share with you is this: everything works better with faith. Remember the old TV commercial for crackers? "Everything tastes better when it sitz onna Ritz!"

For me, all kinds of joy-builders work better when they sitz onna rock…a rock of faith, that is.

God Is My Outrigger

When I began to ski I used special pieces of equipment made for amputees called "outriggers." As the name suggests, outriggers are short, steel forearm crutches modified with small, specially designed ski tips on the ends instead of the rubber stoppers you usually find there. They're kind of a combination of ski poles and crutches. Wikipedia defines the outriggers attached to canoes as something used to "stabilize the inherently unstable," which is a good description of why one-legged skiers need outriggers. Skiing on one leg is *inherently* unstable.

Going down the mountain in those first days and weeks, I leaned on those outriggers like the training wheels I used when first learning to ride a bicycle. Unlike ski poles, I could lean on outriggers for balance and support while I skied—making a sort of tripod with my one leg and two arms—leaving three clear tracks in the snow behind me. It wasn't graceful, but it was stable.

When I first prayed as a child, I leaned on God the way I had leaned on those outriggers. "Fix my life, God!" I begged. I wanted all my problems to go away. I wanted a certain boy to like me. I wanted our family to have more money. I prayed hard. I bargained with God. And, like leaning on the outriggers, it wasn't pretty.

One day while out skiing, I saw Diana Golden, a champion ski racer, fly down the hill on one leg using ordinary ski poles rather than the special outriggers for the disabled. Watching her ski was like being a fish and watching another fish fly through the air. She was the Jonathan Livingston among the rest of us seagulls. I desperately wanted to fly like she did.

I went off on my own and tried to use ski poles just like her. I kept trying, but every time my balance wobbled a bit, my arms got yanked back behind me. See, you can lean on an outrigger and it will ski alongside you. But when you lean on a ski pole for support while you are still moving, it pokes into the snow and your arm stops moving while the rest of your body keeps going forward. It feels like your arm is being ripped off. (I know skiing is an expensive sport, but it shouldn't cost an arm...and a leg—literally!)

Frustrated, I threw down the poles and began to ski with no supports at all. At first, I could manage only to get down the very flat slope of the bunny hill—and only if I didn't turn at all! Again and again I went up and down the hill with nothing in my hands. As it got easier and easier, I could turn back and forth, wave my arms, and virtually dance on my single ski.

I felt like I was defying gravity itself! I tried tight turns. I tried wider, arcing turns. My balance was becoming so strong I went to a steeper hill. Still with no poles, I danced my way down the hill feeling a new sense of balance and freedom.

In the same way that I wanted to use normal ski poles to be cool, I was trying to succeed in the world without the right support. Not by faith and prayer, but by fitting in, looking good, and competing socially. I permed my kinky hair straight, earned money for contacts instead of glasses, and struggled to find my balance in a two-legged world. I was frustrated that no matter how hard I prayed, God didn't wipe out all my problems. I gave up on God and figured I could do better on my own. It was like trying to ski with no poles, no support at all. For that, you need really, really good balance.

After I learned how to ski with nothing in my hands, I turned to using regular ski poles. You see, once I no longer needed them for balance, I could use them without leaning on them. I could pole-plant, turn, and feel graceful. With poles I could ski more aggressively with quicker, snappier turns than I could even with outriggers. It felt good because poles are so much lighter than the clunky outriggers. Plus, I felt more "cool," more normal, being on the same kind of poles all the "normie" skiers used. I loved it!

The coaches with the U.S. Disabled Ski Team, however, felt differently. They knew that amputees could finish more races without falling when they used outriggers instead of poles. And of course, actually finishing the race is pretty important. While Diana Golden was on the team, the coaches fought with her about the ski poles. Sure, you can ski beautifully on one leg with poles, but there is no room for error. The first time a bad ice rut surprises you or you lose your balance just a little bit—whamm!—you're out. Outriggers allow the little mistakes to be forgiven; poles don't.

Once I qualified for the U.S. team, the coaches not only wanted me to race using outriggers, they wanted me to stop skiing with poles at all—cold turkey. I needed to be at one with the outriggers, not treating them like a heavy imposition on my skiing freedom.

I hated it, but I did it. I still wanted to ski upright—not bending over on the outriggers like a tripod. Despite the weight of the outriggers, I held them up off the snow while I skied. Good form required keeping my upper body facing downhill while my ski turned back and forth, so that meant I wasn't keeping each outrigger on one side of my ski. Imagine carrying a weed-whacker in each hand while skiing—it was very difficult! Yet I could ski full-out, take more risks, and not worry as much about falling. On poles, I realized, I was more timid because any little mistake would be fatal. The coaches were right, darn them!

Coming back to prayer and being supported by my faith was a similar experience. Some people may feel that going to church, striving to be obedient to that small voice you hear inside, and not just doing whatever you want to do every day is heavier and more limiting—like skiing with outriggers. The spiritual journey isn't always fun and games. But having that support there when you stumble allows you to go full-out. To live with faith is to be able to risk more for what you believe in and are passionate about. You can rely on more than your own strength and balance.

On the outriggers I began to experiment and push the envelope further. One day, in a sudden epiphany, I realized I could use the weight of the outrigger to my advantage. By stretching out my outer arm during the turn, I could get more centrifugal force with the extra weight and use it to counter my own weight. That meant I could lean farther into the turn and carve harder as I went around.

I began to appreciate the value of outriggers. They were heavier and less graceful in some ways, but in the end, I was a better, faster skier who would win three medals at the Paralympics in 1984. Me and the outriggers were a winning combo.

Early in my life, I started out leaning heavily on my faith. I got angry and frustrated because the leaning I did didn't seem to change anything, so I went off on my own. Certainly, just as I learned more balance and strength from skiing with nothing in my hands, I learned a great deal about my own inner strength by going it alone in life. I learned to find confidence in myself, to laugh at my challenges, to hope, to be positive, to have resilience, and many of the other building blocks necessary for living a truly joyous life.

However, I found that flying solo had its limits. Trying to do everything myself meant controlling everything, feeling stressed with the weight of the world on my shoulders, and holding back for fear of falling. Ultimately, doing everything myself, without faith, was not the most joyous way to live.

I came back to faith and prayer just as I came back to outriggers: for the support. If I never fell down in life, if I never faced nasty emotional surprises, if I never had financial shocks, maybe I wouldn't need that outrigger of faith to keep me upright. But life has big ups and downs. As humans, we get knocked off balance on a regular basis. Remember that definition of an outrigger: something to "stabilize that which is inherently unstable." Faith, I believe, is the stabilizer for the inherent instability of being human.

It wasn't enough to just turn everything over to God and wait for happiness to miraculously show up. Nor did it work to carry all my burdens alone. With God as my outrigger, I was able to step out on faith, use my skills and talents to their limits, and then even push myself a little beyond anything I thought possible. By leaning further into my relationship with God, I move closer to my true, God-given potential. For me, that is the meaning of winning the race...the human race of life.

Stacking all the building blocks for joy—my hard-won wisdom—on a foundation of faith, freed me to live a greater joy that goes past my own understanding. God and me together... quite a combo!

Appendix

Excerpts from
How Strong Women Pray

Bonnie St. John. *How Strong Women Pray*. New York: Hachette Book Group, Inc., 2007.

Introduction

People ask me how I got the idea for *How Strong Women Pray*. Actually, I was praying.

I was sitting on my living-room floor in New York City praying one morning several years ago, as was my routine at the time. I had come to a point in my life where I looked forward to these moments I shared with God at the start of every day. Not because anything was particularly wrong. So often, prayer is relegated to moments of dire need. No, praying for me had become a source of well-being, joy, and faith. As I prayed, I would feel physically strengthened—from good to better than good. I remember appreciating how much I had drawn from prayer over the years. Feeling uplifted in the good times and, in bad times, finding the courage to move forward. I knew that learning how to pray was one of the most important things I had ever done.

Without prayer, I would have collapsed under the weight of the difficulties in my life and failed as a mother. I would not have been able to inspire others to overcome their own obstacles. I am not sure who I would be at all.

Yet, most people who knew me as a strong woman—an inspirational speaker, a one-legged Olympic ski champion, a Rhodes Scholar and former White House official—did not know that prayer was important to me at all. Millions of people knew my life story, yet they had no idea that I prayed, no inkling that prayer made a difference in my life.

I began to wonder how many of the women I looked up to were also privately powered by prayer. So I set out to interview strong women—some well-known, others not—to find out what they knew about relying on prayer in the real world.

What I learned from these incredible women was more sacred, more practical, and more uplifting than anything I could have imagined. I began to wonder if I would be able to put such an ethereal feeling into words. But the words of the women themselves gave me a guide. The concrete details they were able to share about their prayer lives inspired me to try new ways to pray and to focus more on what matters most.

In the pages that follow, I also have shared the ups and downs of my own prayer evolution as the thread that binds the stories of other women together. As a whole, this book is a spiritual quilt of women's lives you can wrap around yourself. Their stories had such a profound impact on me, and on my life in prayer, that I truly feel I am not the same person I was when I began this project. Your life may never be the same again, either, after reading them.

I interviewed women from their twenties to their nineties living in the Northeast, the South, the Midwest and the West. African-American, Asian, Romanian, Rwandan and Caucasian women were included. I spoke to conservatives and liberals. They were athletes, beauty queens, politicians, TV producers, poets, doctors, and, of course, mothers.

Despite their differences, their prayer lives were similar. They prayed anywhere and everywhere: in cars, bathrooms, beds, gyms, planes, and more. They talked to God in normal words, sometimes even out loud.

I've learned that prayer is simply the desire to be closer to God. God is always there for us, reaching out to connect. We are the ones who turn away, get busy, and tune out God. Prayer is what brings us back into alignment—into oneness—with God.

Conversations about prayer are rare. People can go to church together every day and never talk about how they pray. Husbands and wives can pray separately for a lifetime and never share the experience. Even in a prayer group, most people talk about what they are praying about, not how they actually pray.

On the rare occasions we do talk about prayer, it is usually with experts (such as ministers or scholars) who tell us what we should do or what we should feel. They can't help it. It is their job to be teachers. What makes this book a unique and incredibly nurturing experience is hearing real people open up and talk candidly about their prayers.

When you read this book, I believe you will begin to hunger for discussions about prayer, too. As a matter of fact, why don't you, right now, think of a friend or loved one with whom you can start to have this kind of discussion? Contact that person, work out a comfortable time and place to get together, and start talking about prayer! If you like, you can use the exercise I created for my prayer group (see p. 274) or use the discussion guide at www.howstrongwomenpray.com. I can't guess what you will discover about yourselves, but I can predict that you will get closer to God.

In the meantime, sit down and relax. Get a cup of tea or coffee. Get out your journal if you want to write down any of the feelings that might come up for you as you read. Let's go on this journey together to meet twenty-seven extraordinary women who share their innermost feelings about their lives and prayer. The blessings available to us—and through us—are truly without limit.

Marty Evans

Marsha, or "Marty" Evans, is one of only a handful of women ever to attain the honored rank of rear admiral in the navy. After retiring in 1998, she was asked to lead the Girl Scouts of the USA, the largest organization for girls in the world. From there, she went on to head the Red Cross, where she served as president and CEO until 2005.

She is tall, fit, and attractive in a wholesome, girl-next-door kind of way. She is known to be a strong leader, but also a fun person. It's not unusual to see her on the dance floor with young people at the various youth events where she appears.

When she was promoted to an admiral in the navy in the 1990s, it happened to be just after the Tailhook scandal. For her first acting duty as an admiral, she was named to head a special task force created to change the culture and climate of the navy to respect women.

The scandal began when it became public that the navy's Tailhook Convention included many cases of harassing and molesting of women. Things got worse when the Pentagon reported that senior navy officials deliberately undermined their own investigation to avoid bad publicity and ignored the participation of senior officers at Tailhook. President Bill Clinton fired the secretary of the navy and Marty was the woman who was supposed to figure out what to do.

As a brand new admiral, this was her first assignment. For Marty the task felt enormous — overwhelming. The Tailhook scandal was in the media every day, and she was on the hot

seat. The scariest thing of all was that it looked like she probably would fail this challenge. In her twenty-four years in the
navy she had always gotten things done well.

But Marty was the scapegoat—set up with an impossible
task—and expected to fail. She was the woman who would
take the blame for the navy's treatment of women when the
next crisis emerged. No one expected her to turn the ship.

Marty thought to herself "Why me?" She hadn't asked for
this. She was a good officer and could have done so many
other things with her skills. She wondered, "What if I just can't
do this?"

I remember one crisp October day when I walked into
my office at the Pentagon. The office had an exterior view,
which was pretty special in the Pentagon. I walked over to the
blackboard and picked up a piece of chalk. It was an old-fashioned blackboard on a big oak stand, the kind where the board
rotated so you could write on both sides. I started writing, and
the entire framework for a solution came flowing out of my
chalk.

The framework I wrote became the basis for changing the
law to allow women in combat roles. Today the treatment of
women is significantly better: you don't mistreat the members
of your team who you rely on with your life. It had an influence
that was felt far and wide outside the military as well.

It was the answer to several days of particularly intense
prayer. What was remarkable to me was how fully formed the
ideas came out. Suddenly, the whole thing seemed simple.

I asked myself, "Why are women being attacked, denigrated,

and disrespected?" The navy had a law that prevented women from doing many of the jobs they were qualified to do. Suddenly it came to me, since women were not allowed to be on the team and to go into combat, they were not respected.

You can't imagine how hard I prayed through the entire Tailhook experience. When I learned how to pray way back in Sunday school, we were told that you can't just go right into asking for the forty-two things you want. I learned to pray with the acronym ACTS: adoration, confession, thanksgiving, and supplication. That means before you get to supplication, you have to adore God, confess your sins, and give thanks.

But as I led the Task Force, my supplication was way out of balance. I found myself asking for a lot. I really did need help. I didn't know where to start. There was no book, no manual, and no leadership guide to cover this unique situation. I was challenged to my limits. I prayed hard from August to October.

The experience changed me. I learned two things. First, it's a fact that God never gives you more of a burden than you can bear. I had heard those words before, but after that experience I knew it as a fact. Even if your burden may seem too heavy, you'll be given the strength you need to get through.

Second, I learned that life's burdens make us more grateful. I am a Christian, but I learned the Buddhist perspective: the times we have burdens are necessary to make us appreciate the times without burdens.

I have always prayed regularly, but my prayer routine has changed as more pressures crowd out the meditative quality of my prayer. I increasingly need to rejuvenate or restart myself. I need blank space. Regular exercise is the one time when I really do have some success in tuning everything out and getting a mental break.

I find myself praying as I dress after working out in the gym. I go to a gym with very few women. In the locker room I am alone. It's peaceful.

It's a ritual for me. I clear my mind and I pray. If I try to start solving problems too quickly, I mess up the ritual and it doesn't work.

One of my problems is "owning" more issues than I should. Because I came from an alcoholic family, I grew up feeling that if only I could achieve enough I could somehow fix my father.

It's a common problem. In my case, I became hyper-responsible for everything. It's a struggle for me to let go and let others own part of a problem. As a leader it is better for me to tackle the largest, most complex problems and leave the rest to others. But, truth be known, I love the little details. I struggle to step back, see the big picture, and be more strategic.

I think prayer helps me to be a better leader. After consciously clearing my mind, I can see things differently. I am better, not only in my job, but also in my personal relationships. Creating a blank space for forty-five minutes without worrying and having intrusive thoughts allows me to pray on the right things. I can skip one day, but if I skip two, I get more obsessive.

When I pray I reflect on my imperfections. I ask God to perfect the imperfections in me. Organizations reflect the behavior, values and attitude of their leader. As a leader, you get back what you reflect.

So I pray for things like:

Make me the person that others will want to follow.
Make me a good reflection and a model of the best
  qualities.
Help eliminate the flaws in the mirror.
Make my actions and values—both conscious and
  unconscious—worthy of imitation.

Line Dancing with Jesus

Bonnie's Story

I took a deep breath, shut the door of my hotel room, headed toward the elevator, and went down to the conference center adjacent to the hotel.

As I walked I went through a mental checklist: I'm wearing my red, white, and blue Olympic jacket, my Olympic medals, shorts, and sneakers; hair done; makeup done. I began reviewing the speech in my head for the hundredth time.

I had left my job at the White House to start a family with my husband and to become a speaker and author. Having a child and wanting to be at home gave me the courage to follow my dream of inspiring others as a writer and speaker. Telling the story of the one-legged girl from San Diego who becomes a ski racer was something only I could do.

In the two years since I'd left Washington, I was very productive on the home front: our daughter Darcy was one year old. In terms of writing, I had successfully landed a contract for my first book. Developing my reputation as a speaker, however, had proven more difficult than I'd thought.

Even though I had many achievements—ski medals, White House experience—no one wanted to hire me to speak for a big convention unless I could prove I had done it before. I was getting little jobs, speaking for fifty people, one hundred people, and once even one thousand people. I also spoke at a number of big conventions for free—not as the headliner but as one of many presenters for small workshops. I was building my experience and skill as a speaker, but it was slow and hard work.

Grant and I struggled to make ends meet. With a new baby, our expenses were up while money was down with only one salary. Our time, energy, and patience were stretched as tight as our wallets.

As I walked toward the convention center I could feel tension washing throughout my body. This time I was the headliner!

Today I would be keynote speaker for a conference of more than 10,000 people from around the world. My biggest fear was that I would pee in my pants when I got on stage. I was afraid I would stand there and forget my lines, like I did in the church pageant so many years ago.

I went into the meeting room. Holy-moley! It was as big as a football field. The ceiling was so high you almost felt outdoors. I began walking from the back through the dark sea of empty chairs toward the dramatically lit stage. I felt dwarfed.

When I reached the stage I introduced myself to the producer in charge. He brought over the sound tech, who put on my microphone and sent me on stage to test it. When I finished the mic check, I asked, "Where's the bathroom?"

When I gave speeches, I needed quiet time where I could close my eyes. In a crowded convention center, the bathroom was the only place. I shut myself into a stall, sat down and began my ritual of focus to do my best. I used the same mental focus technique that had worked for ski races.

I was terrified. This felt more frightening than exams at Harvard or even racing at the Olympics. At least in skiing and school I felt like I knew what I was doing. I wasn't sure what 10,000 human resource professionals wanted me to say. As I sat there, tense and afraid, trying to go through the steps to focus my mind, suddenly an image of Jesus intruded into my thoughts.

It wasn't just the face of Jesus, it was His whole body. And He wasn't just standing there, He was... He was line dancing?!?!!

As I sat there in the bathroom stall at the convention center, I saw myself line dancing to the country and western Muzak playing through the hotel's sound system. Jesus was kicking up His sandals; His robes were flying as we danced. He smiled at me and His blue eyes laughed.

All my tension melted away. I laughed and relaxed. I felt He came to help me and He gave me exactly what I needed. It was especially striking because I had not thought about Jesus in years.

I went out on stage with confidence and joy. I gave the speech of my life.

As a result, many of the corporations in the audience hired me to speak for years afterward. I used a recorded tape of that speech as my demo for prospective clients. In so many ways, that speech kicked off my current career working as a headliner for major conferences and Fortune 500 clients all over the country. Thank You, Jesus!

My experience of being supported by God through prayer in a critical work situation was similar to Marty Evans being supported by God at work. She, however, had prayed over many months and asked for help. I had been meditating for quite a while to prepare for speeches, but God reached out to me with my vision of Jesus... line dancing!

After that, I began to invite God into my mental preparation for speeches more and more. I had been making quiet time a priority and that is where God found me. By the end of one year, I felt that I worked with God and that God worked through me to inspire people.

To give speeches, I knew I needed God's help. Oddly enough though, I didn't feel I needed God's help in my private life. We struggled with parenting, marriage, and daily life without any thought that God could help. We believed in God, but didn't understand that He could make a difference on a daily basis. That seems incredible to me now, looking back.

For the next two years, my relationship with God grew and grew. But it was strictly a work-based relationship.

Amy Grant

Singer and songwriter Amy Grant lives in Nashville, Tennessee, with her GRAMMY Award-winning country singer husband Vince Gill and their blended family of five children. The pretty brunette with the infectious smile has won numerous accolades for her music. The Dove Award for contemporary album of the year and Artist of the Year, and the GRAMMY Award for best gospel performance. She was the first artist to perform a Christian music song for a GRAMMY broadcast. Her song "Baby, Baby" was the first pop song by a Christian artist to reach the coveted number one spot on *Billboard's* chart.

Amy started writing songs when she was just fifteen. Actively involved in a youth group at a hippy church down on Music Row in Nashville, a lot of the groups' kids lived in public housing. There were drug problems and teen pregnancies during the time she was involved with the group. It was a very different world from where Amy went to school.

She describes her father, a doctor, as a very gentle, quiet man. She was well taken care of and went to a fine girls' school. Amy was drawn to this church "because, there, I felt like all the Bible teaching I had in my very sheltered world just came face-to-face with people having real-life problems," she says.

When she first started writing songs, Amy would sing them for the kids in the youth group at this church. One day, one of the kids said to her "I just get this feeling when you start singing, Amy, that if you would just let God, that He would use you." Amy remembers kneeling down in that circle of kids and asking them "Would you guys pray for me? Pray that whatever God wants to happen in my life I won't get in the way."

That prayer in her teens with the hippy church youth group set her mind in a new way. Rather than wanting to be a star, Amy wanted to feel a sense of purpose with her music. She was willing to let God use her to spread His Word.

She feels what's happened to her career-wise was like the little boy who showed up with five loaves and two fish. You know the story: Jesus prayed and it turned into enough to feed 5,000 with baskets of food left over!

Nowadays, I do pray, but it's not at a specific time with a specific posture. I don't know that I have very many routines in my life period.

The first thing I see in the morning, with my eyes blurry before I put my contacts in, is the coffee pot. The best sound I hear in the morning is the hiss when the water runs all the way through the steamer. My mind is always really fuzzy in the morning so I don't always wake up thinking "Thank You, God, for this day, it's good to be alive."

There have been times in my life when I have been so scattered—running and answering calls and driving carpool—that I would get hours into a day and say: Gosh, I have not even turned my attention on the One who made me! I haven't even prayed for my children yet!

Then one day I found myself in a hole-in-the-wall craft store in Colorado where I saw a charm made of twisted wire wrapped around several objects. As soon as I saw it I thought to myself: This is the answer to my morning! I was determined to use this charm to start the day off right.

So I bought that charm and hung it by the coffee pot on a cabinet knob! When I see it, I say "Oh, right!" and I pray, "God, create in me a clean heart. If your mercies are new every morning, and I believe they are, I need new mercies for this day, and make me right with You so that I can be right with other people."

I have assigned different meanings to each of the things wrapped in the wire, kind of like a hippy rosary, I guess. At the top of the stack is a pale stone heart—that reminds me to pray for a clean heart. Then you go on down and there's a little ivory flower—there I pray for our home to be a safe and loving place where we can all grow. Below that there's a ring with hearts on it, where I pray for my relationship with Vince to be strong and full of love. And at the very end is a little keychain with little miniature keys, which reminds me to pray for each of my kids. I don't have a set thing that I say, but I just tick down the wire.

That might seem really goofy for some people, but I have kind of a "milkweed in the wind" personality. Whatever Type A is...I'm definitely not that.

My favorite place to pray is outside, partly because it's away from anything man-made...away from the clutter of my own life and my to-do list.

If I can just walk outside, I say: Oh, yeah, that tree God made, that sunset, those clouds rushing overhead, the birds in the air. I'm reminded of Scripture: "He knows when a sparrow falls, He knows every hair on your head" (see Matthew 10:29-30).

There are times that I have just danced with joy under a full moon, arms flung out to the stars, just dancing...so glad that nobody could see me, but wanting to say without words: "God, this is how I feel about all the great things that I've experienced in this life." I was running and jumping and twirling! And that is a form of prayer.

Singing can be prayer for me, too. That verse comes to mind, Acts 17:28: "For in him we live and move and have our being" (KJV). So where does prayer stop and start? I know there are times that we're consciously in prayer, especially when we're in need: "Thanks God, I don't know what to do here. Please inspire me. Give me the words to say." That obviously is active praying.

But I think there are times when you see a sunset and it catches your breath. The sky goes from pink to lavender to deep purple and your eyes well up with tears and all you're doing is just chill bumping. I think that's worship, when you acknowledge: "God, You did a great thing when You made this world!"

When I heard about this book, *How Strong Women Pray*, what came to my mind was: strong or stubborn? Strong women can take on everything and try to solve everything. We don't always accept help graciously.

But prayer instantly reorients the frazzled mind. To humble yourself enough to bow your head says, "God, I know You see the whole picture." It puts things in their proper place; that's what prayer does. Whatever view I have is limited by where I am on the continent, where I am in my period cycle, where I am in my life, where I am emotionally. But when you start praying, when you address God, suddenly you're talking to the One who sees it all. Along with that, trust replaces worry.

One night, Vince and I were lying in bed and I said "I just cannot sleep. Can we pray together for the kids?" I had a son and two daughters, Vince had one daughter, and together we had another daughter.

My prayer was simple. We mentioned each one by name and what was going on with them from my perspective. Then, of course, I'm reminded: "God, You see this child. You see this teenager. You created them and You know all their green light zones. You know the things that are going to give them a sense of purpose." When I prayed, I felt my heart stop racing. Praying gave me peace.

The most important thing I've learned about prayer is in my failures. I have learned how deep and wide and high and long the love of Christ is. In the ways that I've let myself down or let other people down, I've realized the absolute healing power of forgiveness.

In Sunday school class we were studying about the life of Peter. Somebody asked, What is the difference between Peter and Judas? As a young child, I would have said, "Judas was a scoundrel who betrayed Jesus."

But what's the difference between the guy that betrayed Him and wound up killing himself and the guy that betrayed Jesus and wound up being the rock on which the church was built? The only difference between those two is that one felt that his sin was too great to be forgiven and the other trusted absolutely the power of love and forgiveness.

God can and does forgive anything. The difference is not what Judas did wrong. It's that Judas gave up. He felt like he had done the unforgivable. But according to Jesus, there is no unforgivable. There's nothing that can separate us from Him, nothing.

"For I am convinced that neither death nor life, neither angels nor demons, neither the present nor the future, nor any powers, neither height nor depth, nor anything else in all creation, will be able to separate us from the love of God that is in Christ Jesus our Lord" (Romans 8:38-39 NIV).

One of the gifts of being forty-five is that I really know that at a gut level. I know that as a result of countless snot cries with my face in the dirt! Times when I have messed up so bad that I know I am so far beyond dropping the ball; I am at real failure. Nobody wants to be there. But that's really where you find Jesus. You find Him in other ways at other times, but He shines the brightest when you think there's no hope.

There's a Bible verse in Hebrews that says, because we have Jesus who knows every temptation that we've known, "Let us hold fast the confession of our hope without wavering, for He who promised is faithful" (Hebrews 10:23 NKJV).

I always think about that verse and say, "Do not be afraid to bow your head because there's not anything that you can think or do that is going to be a shock to God."

On Top of the World

Bonnie's Story

I walked onto the set for NBC's *Today Show* for my guest appearance as a woman who had everything. I wore a red, white, and blue Olympic jacket with my silver and two bronze medals around my neck. I wore shorts to show off my blue, titanium sports leg.

Matt Lauer sat with me on the sofa and asked about each of my achievements: Rhodes scholarship, Harvard degree, White House economic official and, of course, the ski racing. He asked about my husband, Grant, and my three-year-old daughter, Darcy. Under the hot studio lights, I basked in the glow of having it all. As a motivational speaker, I worked from home and had time to spend with my daughter, but also enjoyed the feeling that I was making the world a better place. I had worked and struggled to create a life for myself that included everything I thought I needed to be happy. The five-minute interview ended in what felt like the blink of an eye.

Montel Williams saw me on the *Today Show* and decided to devote an entire hour of his TV show to my story...something he had only done for six people before. Nine million viewers would hear about my story and about my first book, *Succeeding Sane*.

A tremendous opportunity with only one catch: He wanted to focus on the sexual abuse in my childhood. Since I had never talked about it before in public, I wasn't sure what to do. To make me more comfortable, the *Montel Show* sent tapes of similar shows so that I could see that the show would be tastefully done.

The taping was supposed to start in forty-eight hours. A flurry of emotions, phone calls, and arrangements began. Decisions had to be made quickly. Some were easy: Grant and I decided our daughter was not going to appear on a show that focused on abuse. Non-negotiable. Grant, however, decided he would go on the air and be interviewed in order to support me.

Other decisions were harder. The producers asked my mother to appear on the show. I was worried they would try to blame her for what had happened. I knew they would ask all kinds of questions trying to find out one thing: How could you not know what was going on?

My stepfather started his sick hobby with both my sister and me shortly after marrying my mother. I was only two years old and my sister, five. Because he was retired and my mother worked until after 5 p.m., he had free access to us after school before she came home. He stopped molesting my sister when she was six, probably because she was becoming more likely to tell. He didn't leave me alone, though, until four years later when I turned seven. Perhaps he had a harder time stopping with me because there wasn't another girl waiting in line.

Although I had faced steep ski slopes and audiences of 10,000 people, I had never faced up to my feelings about childhood abuse. All of my life I coped with my past by avoiding thinking about it. From the very beginning, my denial was so deep that my brain actually blocked the memories until my stepfather died when I was eighteen. After I remembered, I coped by moving on with my life, just like my mother told me to do.

My sister, on the other hand, coped by expressing her pain and getting help. Besides the support of her close girlfriends, she joined several support groups and went to a therapist. She had encouraged me to do the same, but I waved it away.

"Heck," I thought, "I'm an Olympic ski medalist, Rhodes Scholar, author, and businesswoman. Nothing's wrong with me!"

As the furious preparation for the *Montel Show* began, I called my mother to discuss it. Normally, we all avoided this subject because it was so painful. I had no idea what she thought.

"Mom, they are going to ask you on the show when you first found out about the abuse. What will you say?"

"When I read your book," she answered, as if the answer was perfectly obvious, "*Succeeding Sane.*"

I was shocked. I knew I had told her about it when I was eighteen. I had mentioned it on several occasions since. I knew my sister had mentioned it more often than I did. Now my mother was saying she only found out this year. How could she "forget" all the other times she heard about it?

My mother, who also had been sexually abused as a child, coped, not just by "putting it behind her," but by dissociating or blanking out her abuse memories—and ours—to avoid the pain. I felt sorry for her. I didn't want her to go on the show. They would tear her to pieces. I got the producers to agree to do the show without her.

Grant and I flew to New York and were greeted with a limo to take us to the hotel. In the morning, Grant rushed with me to Lord and Taylor as soon as it opened to find something suitable for me to wear. In fifteen minutes we found a peach silk suit that fit and then raced over to the studio. I turned myself over to the makeup and hair people. I worried constantly about whether I was making a big mistake. Grant was a rock through everything.

As the moment got closer to stepping out on stage, I was a wreck. I could hear the live audience murmuring like an ocean on the other side of the curtain. As my fear rose up higher and higher I found myself repeating Psalm 23... Yea, though I walk through the valley of the shadow of death, I will fear no evil (KJV). It was as though talking about my stepfather, Paul, would somehow make me a helpless, terrified child again.

Once the interview began, it got easier. Montel was kind. He continuously held up my book and encouraged people to buy it. On commercial breaks, he and his staff flipped through my book to reference their favorite parts. I was impressed by how much work they put into telling the story—the skiing, my disability, everything.

They brought out Barbara Warmath as a surprise guest. It was such a joy to see her after so many years! It was so nice of her to come out to support me on the show also.

The hardest thing was seeing this picture of Paul on the screen. They showed it over and over. It was Thanksgiving and he was standing over an enormous, shiny turkey that my mother had cooked. He had a big fork and knife ready to carve. He smiled broadly with the three of us kids around him. My mother must have been taking the picture. It made my stomach queasy every time I had to look at him, smiling.

Near the end of the show, when I realized I had talked about what happened without dying or being destroyed, I felt liberated! At the end of the show, I held up my fist and vowed to reclaim my feelings for myself. Little did I know where that journey would take me.

My sister warned me that talking about the abuse in public would have aftershocks and suggested I seek help. Again, I dismissed her advice. "My life is great," I thought. "Why do I need help?"

But she was right. I found it hard to "just put it behind me and get on with life." Our home, our daughter, and even my husband increasingly made me anxious.

Coming home from preschool with Darcy triggered my memories of being assaulted after preschool while my mother was still at work. The effort of suppressing the memories in that particular situation drained me so much that I fell asleep on the floor as Darcy played. I had no idea why. More often than not, I avoided being home in the afternoons by taking Darcy out to the mall until dinner.

My behavior was typical of people with PTSD (Post Traumatic Stress Disorder). I avoided and suppressed painful memories without even knowing I was doing it. It steadily took a toll on me. Since mothering was new to me, it was hard to know what was "normal stress" for a new mom and what was not. Like all new moms, I just coped the best I could.

Delilah Rene

Delilah Rene is the beloved, husky-voiced, nationally syndicated, radio-show host who has an audience of seven million listeners. Her nighttime radio show, heard across the country, features romantic music, listener requests, and dedications. Callers often pour out their hearts to her.

As the guest speaker at a prayer breakfast, she stepped up to the podium, eyes bright, blond hair shining in the light, strong, sassy and beautiful. Then she began by talking about a well on a farm that she bought. The well was a hole in the ground covered by a three-foot slab of cement, with a three-inch hole where the hand pump attached. Her kids enjoyed pumping the water and playing in it.

The government had informed her that the well was unsafe and must be covered.

"But it is covered," she told them, "with a three-foot slab of concrete. The kids can't fall down a three-inch hole."

They suggested she hire a crew to break up the cement slab so that the well could be filled in and made safe. Furthermore, they warned, the water might be unsafe. She was threatened with fines. Her permits for rebuilding the old farmhouse would not be granted. Inspectors were sent out.

Delilah had the water tested and proved it was safe. She filled out forms. She begged and pleaded. Finally, when nothing worked, she threatened to use her fame on the radio to embarrass the politicians. She got her permit.

Then, Delilah's prayer breakfast speech abruptly changed gears. She began talking about a young girl, Doretta, who was pregnant at fourteen, possibly by a member of her own family. She went into the foster care system, and while moving through various homes, became pregnant again and again. Most of those children were taken away and also put into foster homes until the time when Doretta would reach eighteen. Later, when Doretta was an adult, she was living with five of her six children, as well as her boyfriend, who was the father of the two babies in diapers. He beat Doretta and her eight-year-old boy so badly one day that the neighbors called the police. Delilah described the scene found by the cops: crack, empty pizza boxes, and drugged-up parents.

Then Delilah traced the path of Doretta's kids, the second generation in foster care. She detailed a complaint from a girl of nine that she was being raped by the teenage son of her foster mother, a complaint which was not believed and ignored. Months later, after a school program on "inappropriate touch," the same girl reported being raped that very morning and was taken in a police car to a hospital. After the examination confirmed the rape, she was removed from the foster home...but her sister was left in the same home with the same teenage boy!

Delilah's story traced three of Doretta's kids through seven foster homes. There were rapes of the boys as well as the girls. One was beaten with a lamp cord. Delilah's account was detailed, including names of social workers, dates of placements, and details of the abuse the children lived with at each stage.

The story about the well had seemed shallow. The foster care story seemed overly graphic and painful for a prayer breakfast.

Then Delilah delivered the punch line: "I adopted three of Doretta's children." Delilah, as a single mom, already with four children of her own, adopted three of these extremely troubled kids from foster care.

Why was the government so concerned with my well? They sent inspectors, charged fines, and had rules and standards. Why couldn't they put that energy into protecting my children? Why do our tax dollars go to pay people to be foster parents who routinely rape, beat, and neglect our children?

My children will never be normal. One of my daughters ran away to look for her mother and we found her selling herself on the street two weeks later. When they come from a world where drugs, prostitution, and abuse are normal, how do I teach them to love, to trust, and to have values?

I pray for everything: healing for my children, on a physical level as well as emotionally. I pray for parking places, wisdom, safe driving, safe flights...everything that I need or want, I ask Him for.

I don't have a prayer routine that I follow. I pray when I wake up and I thank God for the day...I pray when I drive. I talk to the Lord out loud, as if He is sitting next to me.

I have never prayed kneeling...well, not often, anyway. My prayers are an extension of my thoughts. No matter where I am or what I am thinking about, I try to invite God into the conversation going on in my head. I try to praise Him in all situations, even when I am angry or frustrated. If I am stuck in traffic, I thank Him and realize He might be protecting me from an accident up ahead or something. I pray when I am happy more than when I am sad or upset. I pray for listeners who call or write and share a tragedy or sad story.

I'm always busy. I have seven kids. I have a career, I have animals. I run a company. I am busy eighteen hours a day, seven days a week.

I used to believe that if I prayed with faith, God would be like a genie in a bottle and grant my prayer, if it was in keeping with His Word. I prayed for my mom to be healed of cancer. I believed she would be. I expected a miracle. She died.

It took me a long time to realize that God is God and He will do what He knows is best, and that I can pray specifically, but I must trust the outcome to Him, even when it is not what I would want.

I used to try to do formal prayers, I used to pray in tongues and groups and churches. Now my prayers are more a part of my life, like breathing. I look at the mountains and I think "God created all of this simply to bless us? Amazing!"

I try to be a good example for my kids in prayer. My son, Zack, at age seven, has some unique challenges. He has mild autism and ADHD, he is high-strung, often a wild boy. But he "gets God." He gets God in the sense that the moment he hurts or has a bad day or sees someone bleeding or senses any problem, he says, "Mom, ask Jesus to fix this." He turns to the Lord first in every difficult situation. I *love* his wonderful faith!

My kids have always attended church and schools within our church, so they have a wonderful understanding of how prayer changes things. Knowing that God will always, a hundred percent of the time, provide all my needs, gives me the freedom to not worry. I always remember Philippians 4:19: "But my God shall supply all your need according to his riches in glory by Christ Jesus" (KJV). If He promises to take care of all my needs, I need not worry about tomorrow or my future, which allows me to use my time and energy to be loving and creative!

Acknowledgments

Writing a book is an arduous task, to say the least, fraught with blind alleys, frustrations, pitfalls, blocks and all sorts of joy-stealing experiences. I am so fortunate to have around me a coterie of wonderful people, who support me, hug me, strengthen me and otherwise contribute to the ultimate joy that this book has brought to me and, I hope, to all who read it.

First and foremost, all the glory goes to God for the positive, nourishing, and uplifting characteristics of this book. I take full credit for any and all of its defects.

My editor, Adrienne Ingrum, has guided me, now for the second time, through the long pregnancy and ultimate birth of this book. Her early insights helped shape the form of every chapter here. Her clear, consistent, unwavering advice, as always, raised the bar of my creative endeavors with every discussion—and there were many. Adrienne is a true person of joy, and her creative talent and spirit are very much a part of the pages herein. I only hope I can work with her again and again and again.

I had the privilege of collaborating with Allen Haines on the entire writing of this book, which made the process itself far more joy-filled than it would have been on my own. We argued in cafes about what went into each chapter, we swapped drafts, and laughed a lot as we scribbled our way from blank page to finished product. His experience in Hollywood and television taught me how to write in a more entertaining and "film-like" way. He is a gifted writer. The book would not be what it is without his major contribution.

I am also very grateful to the enchanting and devoted group of supporters who joined me for a series of teleclasses in early 2008 that kick-started the writing of this book. You know who you are, and my sincere thanks are with you.

Thanks to my friends whose lives appear in the book as part of my journey. Susan, Joy, Terri, Lisa, Jana, Rik and Amy…you have helped me to learn about joy. God bless each of you.

Working with my wonderful publisher on this second book continues to be even better than the fantasy scenarios of being a writer I conjured up as a child. I hear horror stories from other writers about experiences with their publishers, but I have none of that. All the good folks at Hachette/FaithWords support me, believe in what I can do, and are doggedly in it for the long haul. Big thanks specifically to Rolf Zettersten, Harry Helm, Jana Burson, Sara Sper, and Preston Cannon. Without you I could never have the joy I feel as a writer.

Of course, I would never have had the opportunity to work with all these wonderful people if it were not for my agent, Richard Pine. He is always willing to help me be my best in every way. I love his guidance, intelligence, and pure spirit. He makes my dreams come true.

But most of all I owe deep, sincere gratitude to my daughter, Darcy, who not only appears in the book, but had to live with me while writing it. A gifted writer herself, she often read through drafts and helped me to make them better. She is so supportive in every way possible: bucking me up during the writing, sending me her prayers and energy while I am off on book tours, and just laying her head on my shoulder when she knows I need it. From the day she was born, this incredible young woman has taught me so much about joy. Darcy, you are my joy guru!

About the Author

Bonnie St. John is one of the nation's leading inspirational speakers and has been featured on the *Today Show*, CNN, *The 700 Club*, *Good Morning America*, as well as *People* magazine, the *New York Times*, *Essence*, and many others. She has been awarded an honorary doctorate degree for her life's work in motivating others, and was recently honored at the White House for her unique contribution to African-American history.

Despite the amputation of her leg at age five, Bonnie became a silver and bronze medalist in downhill skiing in the 1984 Paralympics at Innsbruck, Austria, making her the first African-American to win Olympic medals in skiing. She went on to graduate from both Harvard and Oxford (as a Rhodes scholar), and was appointed to the White House National Economic Council.

As the president of her own company, Bonnie now focuses on bringing out the best in others through inspirational speaking for corporations and associations as well as writing books and articles. Her books include: *How Strong Women Pray*, *Succeeding Sane*, *Getting Ahead at Work without Leaving Your Family Behind*, and *Money: Fall Down? Get Up!*

Bonnie lives her joy in New York City with her daughter, Darcy.

Please visit her web site, www.bonniestjohn.com, where you can download a copy of a Starbucks Cup with her famous quote, "Winners get up faster," see and hear her Web-TV and radio shows, and find many other joy-building online materials.

Second Drafts
of History

Second Drafts of History

E S S A Y S

Lance Morrow

BASIC
BOOKS

A Member of the Perseus Books Group
New York

Books published by Basic Books are available at special discounts for bulk purchases in the United States by corporations, institutions, and other organizations. For more information, please contact the Special Markets Department at the Perseus Books Group, 11 Cambridge Center, Cambridge MA 02142, or call (617) 252-5298 or (800) 255-1514, or e-mail special.markets@perseusbooks.com.

Designed by Jeff Williams

Library of Congress Cataloging-in-Publication Data

Morrow, Lance.
  Second drafts of history : essays / Lance Morrow.
     p. cm.
  ISBN-13: 978-0-465-04750-5 (alk. paper)
  ISBN-10: 0-465-04750-5 (alk. paper)
  I. Title.

  PN4874.M5865A35 2006
  973.92—dc22

                                                            2005017092

06 07 08 / 10 9 8 7 6 5 4 3 2 1

For Bill Buckley
With deep affection

Contents

PART TWO: PEOPLE

PART THREE: IMAGES

PART FOUR: OUTRAGES

PART FIVE: DILEMMAS

PART SIX: METAPHYSICS

ACKNOWLEDGMENTS

Most of these pieces appeared originally in *Time* magazine or on TIME.com. I am grateful to Jim Kelly, the managing editor of *Time*, for permission to reprint them here.

Over the years, I have had the pleasure of working for a number of superb editors at *Time*, and in addition to Jim Kelly, I would like to thank Ray Cave, Jason McManus, Edward Jamieson, Richard Duncan, Stephen Smith, Walter Isaacson, and Steve Koepp.

The best of them are no longer with us—Henry Grunwald and Ronald Kriss. I remember them with professional admiration and the deepest personal affection.

INTRODUCTION

The fourteenth-century Japanese essayist named Kenko withdrew from the imperial court at Kyoto. He settled in a cottage, became a Zen Buddhist monk, and brushed his thoughts onto scraps of paper that, according to legend, he glued onto the walls of his hermitage. After his death, a friend unpeeled these compositions and published them as *Tsurezuregusa,* or *Essays in Idleness.*

There are 243 of them. Kenko lamented the passing of the old ways. He had a crank's sense of ceremony and tradition. It annoyed him, for example, that Japanese officials had forgotten how to hang a criminal properly. My favorite essay is the one that reads, in its entirety: "Do not hold the antlers of a young deer to your nostrils; there may be insects on the antlers that can crawl up your nose to your brain and kill you."

Kenko—like the great Montaigne two centuries later, the progenitor of the modern essay in the West—drew a self-confident line from his reclusive and hilariously personal eccentricities to the dimension of the universal. For a monk, Kenko was worldly and irritable enough. His compositions were brief, austere, wistful sometimes with the Japanese sense of evanescence. Montaigne, of course, went on forever—disorganized, tedious, charming.

Perhaps Kenko wrote sparingly because he was constrained by the available wall space at his cottage. I am not sure what the proper length for an essay is. Every essay has its natural length. All of Shakespeare's soliloquies are brief, compact essays. *Moby Dick* is perhaps not so much a novel as a series of essays (on the Whiteness of the Whale, on cetology, and so on) hinged together by the lurid melodrama of Ahab and his obsession. What is the Book of Job? A sadistic fable? A morality tale? A poem? A thunderous conundrum? All of those. It is an essay, too, I would say—perhaps above all an essay, if an essay is a way of thinking through difficult and perhaps insoluble problems.

Many of the essays in this volume were written for *Time* over a period of several decades, and their length was usually dictated simply by the magazine's layouts. (Over the years, the size of the accompanying illustration increased, and the space available for words shrank.) Some of the pieces in this collection are almost as brief as Kenko's warning about antlers— although maybe not as instructive. There is something to be said for the energy of compression that space limitations and deadlines produce. The trick is to be—or to sound—calm and authoritative in the midst of haste and turmoil. A good jazz pianist knows how to work even in a noisy club. Conditions are never ideal; you play your music, and try to be heard.

These essays date from the 1980s to the present. Some, like the reports on the 1984 and 1988 presidential campaigns, were written literally on the fly, while I was traveling with candidates from city to city. At a newsmagazine, one wrote with enforced concision and sometimes under the embarrassing necessity of sounding more certain about the subject than one had a right to be. Inevitably, some of the opinions expressed in these essays now seem to me wrong, or half-wrong, or in need of explanation.

In any case, *essayer*—Montaigne's thought when he published his *Essaies*—means "to try": to try to think something through. An essay, honestly done, is the adventure of an idea in your own mind, in a conversation with yourself. The essay records the motions of your thought. That is the reason that a good essay must be honest: There is nothing more transparent than the effort to fake something as unfakeable as brainwork. If it is fake, the fraud is instantly—simultaneously—apparent. That is one reason, I think, that essays (personal, casual essays, not elaborately technical treatises) are easy to judge. They speak to basic, universal instruments in our minds.

Essays of this kind put together the private and the public dimensions of the mind—apply experience to news, past to future.

Italo Calvino once listed the reasons why he loved his adopted city of Turin. He mentioned its people's absence of "romantic froth." He praised their reliance on their own work, their innate diffidence and reserve. He liked their "sure sense of being part of the big world of action, not a closed, provincial world." He admired their "pleasure in liv-ing tempered with irony," and their "rational, clarifying intelligence."

Turin was the ideal city of Calvino's mind, and the virtues that he claimed for the city were the ones that he wished for himself as a writer. I suppose that any writer would like to have the virtues of Calvino's Turin. On the other hand, I grew up in Dwight Eisen-hower's Washington, where no one ever detected a fleck of romantic froth, or irony, either. Washington was the big world of action, of course—capital of the superpower—but it managed also to be a closed provincial place: horizontal, leafy, endearing, willfully banal, covertly venal.

As a young man, I moved to New York, the anti-Washington: bright, jagged, vertical, insomniac, and so cosmopolitan as to be . . . not quite America. It was 1965. I lived in a grimy apartment in a not-yet-gentrified neighborhood of the Upper West Side, one floor down from a Puerto Rican pimp (a friendly neighbor, though given to violent late-night rows with his girlfriend that thumped my ceiling for an hour at a time). In the morning, I would disappear into the pavement under Broadway and ride the subway, rattling and screeching, to midtown. I would ascend with the hordes, out of the moles' hole, into the abrupt and dazzling Oz of Rockefeller Center.

In an airless office on the twenty-fifth floor of the Time-Life Building, I banged away at a Royal manual typewriter, pausing now and then to flip a sharp new pencil end-over-end so that it would stick like a stalactite in the foam-board ceiling, which eventually became dense with pencils, an inverted forest.

From my perch, I looked west toward the Hudson River, where, as I watched, the *Queen Mary* and the *Queen Elizabeth* and the *France* and the *United States* slow-motioned up from the harbor and, fussed about by tugboats, parked at the piers in the West Forties.

I worked as a writer for *Time*—a rewrite man, doing the magazine's People section. The job was tougher than you'd think. Sometimes I stayed at it most of the night and emerged from the Time-Life Building at four in the morning. A prostitute would approach me, and when I ig-nored her, she would jeer, "What's the matter, don't you like girls?"

I hated the People section. The items had to be laboriously machined and polished—sprightly little zircons about Jackie Kennedy and Aristotle Onassis and Richard Burton and Elizabeth Taylor and Anita Ekberg and Sophia Loren and a few dozen other demigods of celebrity. This was Calvino's romantic froth, produced by Reddi-Whip. When the *France* slid out toward the open sea, my heart went with her; my fingers stayed behind at the keyboard and tooled this junk. Little Charles Dickens in the blacking factory was not more miserable than I. At the end of *Time*'s editorial week, on Friday and Saturday evenings, the glossy management of the Luce empire would wheel out carts of good liquor and we would get drunk: the woozy and vaguely desperate conviviality of closing.

After a year, I made good my escape from the People section (which eventually inspired an immensely successful magazine in its own right) and went to writing national news. In the 1970s, *Time*'s managing editor, Henry Grunwald, started a new section called Essay, and I became one of its regular contributors. *Time*'s early essays ran to two pages of the magazine—about 1,800 words. Their content was unbearably earnest and dense, as if the editors thought to reconvene all of Henry Luce's didactic Presbyterian missionary instincts and apply them to the subject at hand—the future of Africa, say. The results were worthy and indigestible—essays over-researched and edited with a trowel, not so much written as accumulated. The essays spoke with the voice of an opinionated encyclopedia—or the voice of Frank Morgan as the Wizard of Oz. It would have been unthinkable to use the first-person singular pronoun. I was not much more than a kid (or so it seems at this distance), and I stood behind a curtain and worked the thunder machine. I rather liked the curtain, the institutional concealment, and although I had always been one of those children given to dispensing precociously grave pronunciamentos, I was not certain that my unadorned first-person singular would be credible.

It has been said that the essay is not a form for the young in any case—that it should be attempted only by writers who have some maturity and experience of life. I think that is true of the personal essay. Those early pieces for *Time* were not personal essays so much as ex-

ercises in the journalism of ideas—or in the tendentious organization
of data.

But Henry Luce's magazine changed as the years went by, and it
ceased attempting to speak with one institutional voice. The two-page
essay became a rarity at *Time*, and the one-pager more an entertainment, a *causerie*. Roger Rosenblatt and I and others writing essays for
Time pulled aside the curtain and wrote more personally, even using
the first-person pronoun. I felt naked the first few times, but eventually I probably became, like many essayists, a kind of exhibitionist.

On the other hand, Montaigne, nothing if not a grownup, wrote
with blithe animation about his defecations and his kidney stones.
That ruthless intimacy was, in fact, part of his immense vernacular
charm, such a relief after centuries of forbidding scholastic formality.

But if you are going to be that ruthlessly intimate, you had better be
Montaigne—who, in any case, could have used a good editor. I think
that on the whole I would be content to be judged by the standard of
what Italo Calvino called the "rational, clarifying intelligence."

PART ONE

Moments

The Fate of the Reckless

July 22, 2002

I WAS ON MY BROTHER'S SAILBOAT, *AEOLUS*, IN SAN FRANCISCO Bay. We left Alameda at midday under a hazy sun and powered down the estuary and then hoisted sail and aimed at Alcatraz. Suddenly, crossing a visible line (the water flat-slack on one side, all agitation on the other), we caught the wind roaring through "the slot" at the Golden Gate Bridge. Now *Aeolus* shot through sparkling air, heeled over among whitecaps, and we watched two windsurfers skimming almost at the speed of the wind itself—their sails transparent membranes: dragonflies.

I stayed for several days. At night, I slept alone aboard the boat in the marina, and woke up rocking to the first swells made by ships passing down the channel at dawn. The wind whined lightly in the rigging and the halyards slapped.

As Ratty told Mole (in *The Wind in the Willows*), there is nothing as wonderful as messing about in boats. There's something about merely being around boats—boats riding at anchor, the forest of masts at a marina gently scissoring as a wake passes through, or boats in motion, sailing or powering or drifting—that soothes the eye and mind in some sweet preconscious way. It's the floating, I suppose—the dreaminess, a kind of amniotic suspension.

On that afternoon sail, going nowhere special, watching the dragon-fly windsurfers, we tacked toward Sausalito and blazed along on the slot wind. But in the middle of this sunny picnic of a day, the radio, which had been emitting idle sailors' chatter, stiffened us up with this:

"SOS! SOS! This is the yacht *Reckless*. SOS! SOS! This is the yacht *Reckless*." (I call the boat *Reckless*, but it had another name, another of those jaunty amateur sailor's adjectives.)

The voice was calm and matter-of-fact, a man's voice. He repeated the same call several times.

A woman's voice came on, responding from the Coast Guard, calm but urgent—identifying herself. Asking for details. Telling the *Reckless* to go to another channel. We dialed to the other channel, too.

Silence. The Coast Guard came on again and asked for more information. Silence.

We sailed on. We came about and pointed west toward Oakland.

Then the same male voice: "SOS, SOS, this is the yacht *Reckless!* SOS, SOS, this is the yacht *Reckless!*"

Still in command. But the voice more urgent. *Houston, we've got a problem.*

Some part of the mind was summoned to rescue, to do something. But we sailed dreamily, briskly on. And merely listened. We had no idea where *Reckless* might be—out in the open ocean, perhaps. On fire, maybe. Was his radio sending but not receiving? Was he sending, and then hurrying out of earshot to deal with whatever the crisis might be—bailing? Dousing flames? I took it on faith that this was not a prank, for the voice was sober and persuasive, and I imagine in any case that the consequences of abusing the distress call must be severe.

The drama vanished, simply and enigmatically. A few more calls . . . and then, unbroken silence. We never learned the fate of the *Reckless*.

We speculated for a time—about hazards to navigation, cargo containers, for example, fallen off ships and floating just below the surface. Maybe *Reckless* got hulled by one of those. The ocean blanks of medieval maps were marked, *Here Be Monsters*. Contemporary maps should say, *Here Be Cargo Containers*.

Coming back up the estuary toward Alameda, we joined a parade of sailboats riding in on bright swollen spinnakers, the sails like the bulging throats of mating frigate birds. Now and then the wind would fluke around and a spinnaker would collapse—a ruined soufflé.

We did not try to join the gaudy parade. We started the engine and dropped the sails, and motored in just as the sun was going down beyond the Golden Gate—out beyond which there remained a question mark, a small, dark blank in our minds.

The Nixon Library

July 30, 1990

A séance on a hot day in Orange County, California. Everything in the cloudless morning seemed like a memory of itself from long ago. Gene Autry stood and waved his white Stetson. Billy Graham and Norman Vincent Peale materialized. Bob Hope shambled slow-motion across the stage like an amiable pink hologram. Four Republican presidents were there, and four First Ladies. The centerpiece, Richard Nixon's career, was laid out in a sort of waxen splendor. Scarcely a trace of the fatal accident showed.

The ceremony to dedicate the Richard Nixon Library and Birthplace was a strange conjuration of the past, subdued and defiant at the same time, like the man himself: an assertion of greatness, a denial of disgrace. Watergate sat inconspicuously in the audience (H. R. Haldeman, Ron Ziegler, Rose Mary Woods, among others from the memorable cast), but only George Bush mentioned the subject in passing. A flock of white doves went blurring over the University of Southern California Trojan marching band. The other presidents praised Nixon as statesman and peacemaker. What seemed like several billion red, white and blue balloons were cut loose and sailed away in the flawless blue.

It was to be Richard Nixon's day of vindication, his ultimate emergence from the "wilderness" that followed Watergate. It had been sixteen years since he flew west to San Clemente in disgrace. He worked long, stubbornly and bravely, to rehabilitate his reputation. He wrote seven books, traveled the world, kept himself on a relentless forward trajectory. He was performing yet again his old miracle of self-resurrection.

The ceremony at the library, however, felt like a culmination. The compound at Yorba Linda is a single-story, pink sandstone museum and library that cost $21 million and looks like a suburban mini-mall. It stands beside the small, white frame house where Nixon was born in 1913. Having consecrated the place—his life from birth through presidency all handsomely compacted there—Nixon completed a circle. As he spoke last week, he seemed a little tired and rambling. It had after all been an exhausting seventy-seven-year circuit from the room where he was born to this ritual of fulfillment. But even in the mellowness of the moment, Nixon still gave off emanations of the film-noir pol that a part of him has always played, the shadow of that something in his character that is remorseless and bruised and unforgetting.

Nixon's has been an astonishing story of ambition and endurance. His fascination derives from some primal quality in him to which Americans have always responded, sometimes with a hatred so fierce as to be nearly inexplicable on rational grounds. The Nixon on view in Yorba Linda is a version carefully controlled by Nixon himself. His is the only president's library built and operated entirely with private funds, except for the Rutherford B. Hayes Library in Fremont, Ohio. The library is Nixon's show. It will contain only a very careful selection of the presidential papers. The original papers are stored in a government archives in Alexandria, Virginia. Nixon has succeeded in blocking the release of 150,000 pages of documents. One can understand why a man who failed to burn the White House tapes that eventually doomed his presidency would in later life grow careful about information and its control.

The Nixon compound is thus more a museum than a serious scholar's archives. The 293-seat theater continuously runs a movie called *Never Give Up: Richard Nixon in the Arena.* A hallway gallery displays thirty of the fifty-six *Time* covers on which Nixon appeared. Exhibits lead visitors through the whole saga with photographs and artifacts, including a hollowed-out pumpkin, microfilm and a Woodstock typewriter (the famous items of evidence that nailed down the case against Alger Hiss), and an old woody station wagon like the one Nixon used for his 1950 race for the Senate against Helen Gahagan Douglas. A 1952 television set plays the "Checkers" speech, the mawkish little masterpiece that saved Nixon's vice-presidential candidacy in 1952.

Another television set plays the 1960 debates against John Kennedy, which may have cost Nixon the election. In a Watergate section, one can listen to three excerpts from the White House tapes and see a montage of the last day in the White House.

One room displays bronze-tone, life-size statues of ten world leaders, including Charles de Gaulle, Konrad Adenauer, Winston Churchill and Mao Zedong. Trying to hurry history's verdict, Nixon has always had a habit of dressing the set with giants, setting the delay timer, and then jumping into the picture himself.

NAPOLEON IN EGYPT

March 22, 2000

It is now two centuries since Napoleon's expedition into Egypt fell apart. It would be a shame if such memorable idiocy were to pass into darkness without a salute. The invasion of Egypt speaks to us today. It is a vindication of the Mel Brooks version of history.

Napoleon was only twenty-nine when he launched the invasion. A bourgeois knockoff of Alexander, the Corsican hoped to conquer Egypt in a quick stroke. Why, exactly? Well . . . to "liberate" it! Then he would proceed in triumph to Paris, depose the directorate, take over France and get on with ingesting the rest of the world. Napoleon was full of ideas.

Almost nothing went well. The Egyptians were not grateful to be liberated. Nelson destroyed the entire French fleet in the Bay of Abukir off Alexandria, leaving Napoleon and his 36,000-man expedition stranded among scorpions and Mamelukes.

Napoleon sulked in Cairo. In France, his wife, Josephine, conducted an appallingly public affair with a young lieutenant named Hippolyte Charles. It was the talk of the army. Napoleon fretted and gnashed his teeth. He sounded curiously helpless. "It's a sad situation," he wrote to his brother, "to have so many conflicting sentiments about a single person in one's heart."

Napoleon consoled himself by taking to bed the wife of one of his young lieutenants in Egypt; he dispatched the poor husband back to France on an "urgent secret mission." Napoleon set up housekeeping with the woman, arranged a quickie divorce for her, but then, some months later, breezily abandoned her by telling her one afternoon that he was off to Alexandria to check the fortifications. She never saw him again.

The Egyptian adventure deteriorated. The people of Cairo rose in general insurrection. Napoleon bombarded al-Azhar, the city's largest mosque, then sacked it and allowed his troops to run amok, killing men, women and children in the streets. The bloom was off the liberation. Napoleon sought glory northward, marching toward Syria. He took Jaffa. Four thousand prisoners, who had been promised their lives, were marched before Napoleon's tent; he asked peevishly, "What am I supposed to do with them?" They were herded to the beach and slaughtered in the surf.

Bonaparte laid siege to Acre but took a pounding and gave it up. Napoleon was the great-grandfather of spin. His official army bulletin proclaimed a great victory. When his secretary protested such a colossal lie, Napoleon said with a smile, "Mon cher, you are a simpleton. You really don't understand a thing."

Napoleon eventually scurried back to France, abandoning the remnants of his army to straggle home as best they could.

But he had managed to construct an entire parallel universe of lies, more real and more politically efficient than the truth. As the historian Alan Schom has written: "On returning to France . . . much to his utter astonishment, the thirty-year-old Napoleon Bonaparte found himself greeted by a madly exuberant French people who knew little of his phenomenal disasters and instead saw only the man who had captured Malta, the Pyramids, and Egypt, the latter-day republican crusader who had taken Cairo from the heathens."

But wait: For all the spectacular folly of the Egyptian campaign, it ended by laying the foundations for extraordinary work in Egyptology, archaeology and related fields. In the course of atrocious glory-hounding, Napoleon, who fancied himself an intellectual, had brought with him the best scholars of France. Their work, including the discovery and decoding of the Rosetta Stone, endures.

How glorious. How weird. Let us end the celebration with a chorus of Cole Porter:

> *If Napoleon at Waterloo-la-la*
> *Had an army of debutantes*
> *To give the British the well known Oo-la-la,*
> *He'd have changed the history of France!*

A COUNTRY STORM

May 28, 2001

LIGHTNING CAME DOWN LIKE A WOLF ON THE FOLD AND BLEW the telephone box off the side of the house just now. Nature has been setting a bad example this weekend.

We were reading, with the dog on the floor between us, curled up upon himself like a chambered nautilus. The air cracked and the room flashed white. Lightning, firing in through the phone line, exploded around us like gas from the stove when the pilot light malfunctions.

Outside, where the lightning bolt had tunneled the air, stray leaves fluttered down from the maple tree, smelling of spent electricity. The leaves looked like the fluttering canary feathers in Sylvester and Tweety cartoons after the cat has gobbled a bird.

Everything's in a violent, cartoonish mood today.

In the attic above me, an animal has died. A carrion smell seeps through the ceiling. A squirrel, maybe. A raccoon? For a week, I heard something scuttling up there—as if to answer the clicking of my computer keyboard, as if the animals were weighing in with a contrary point of view. I assumed, in any case, that a creature that had found its way into the attic would find its way out. Then the scuttling stopped, and in a day or two, the dead smell began. I must go up through the trap door in the ceiling in the hall and see if I can find the corpse.

A merlin has come to pose upon a post outside a kitchen window— dove-colored and innocent, until you look again and see it is no dove, but a merlin, that is, a pigeon-hawk. Yesterday, not far from the post, we found a catbird lying dead on its side, unmarked by struggle or wound. Perhaps it died of cardiac infarction or some other internal disaster, but I suspect the merlin.

Under the porch, we find a handful of motherless baby squirrels, alarmingly whitish and hairless, fetal and fumbling, wizened little old blind men. We put peanut butter out for them, and they eat it for a couple of days, but we have not seen them since Friday.

I thought the merlin had killed the squirrels' mother. But then I saw her lounging around the maple, as if in a housecoat, and decided she's just a lousy mother. Or perhaps it was Mother who perished in the attic. Maybe the cats ate the baby squirrels—delicacies, no doubt, like sushi. The cats, fat as pashas, having yet to shed the opulent fur they acquired in the long cold winter, sit motionless, an hour at a time, under the maple, hoping to pounce on a careless songbird. But the cats will settle for red squirrels, which themselves lie in wait and hope to kill songbirds. We need some law and order around the farm; everyone's little teeth and claws are dripping.

The cats bring offerings, neatly severed red squirrel tails that they lay ceremonially outside the kitchen door, where we feed them. The cats leave the tails for us like tips for the waiter. My wife assembled a collection of a half dozen red squirrel tails, laid out in a row on a shelf in her office. But in the middle of the night, the mice came into the office and carried every one of the tails away.

An albino hawk has come to the valley. I like to watch him presiding over these complexities of the food chain. I see him riding the air currents that curl up from the ridges on either side as the wind flows through the north-south valley. He was born a red-tailed hawk, but colored all white, a relatively rare occurrence but seen sufficiently often to earn the albino a short item in the bird books.

Now the storm is over, and the sun returns. The albino rides the light. At a certain angle, the bird becomes a radiance, a sort of feathered parhelion, a sundog. Yet at the core of the radiance, you make out a dark center, the bird's skeleton and organs—in the way your hand looked to you when you were a child and you shined a flashlight beam through it, and through the translucence of your flesh, saw the dark blur of your bones.

REAGAN AND MRS. LINDBERGH
AT THE FULL MOON

February 8, 2001

A LEMONY FULL MOON RISES ABOVE THE FROZEN RIVER, AND back in the foothills, coyotes whoop in their companionable way: not the mob-noise of a kill tonight, but a moonlit hootenanny, all the skulkers come together to sing barbershop.

They might be so many Washington politicians harmonizing in the silvery light of the president's honeymoon.

Time is elastic; the moon's gravitational pull works on memory, producing distortions and elongations, the slightly demented tugs of the past. Hamlet's father's loose around Elsinore. Doctors say that at the full moon, there is agitation in the psychiatric wards.

Did the full moon have anything to do with a man waving a pistol outside the White House, the one the Secret Service shot in the knee? That was sweet shooting, by the way, only slightly more hurtful than the kind that Roy Rogers, King of the Cowboys, used to do to knock a gun out of the bad guy's hand—immaculate gunplay. Alas, I see that Roy's wife, Dale Evans, has died, having survived into an age of movies that by digital magic turn each screen death into the gaudiest, bloodiest horror.

The news seems agitated. It arrives in surreal and disturbed condition—a notch stranger than its usual agitated banality. The surreal can be hilarious, too. I have before me a headline from the Wednesday business section of the *New York Times*: "Trade Feud on Bananas Not As Clear As It Looks."

Sad news comes in on the full tide. Anne Morrow Lindbergh, a lovely writer, the widow of Charles Lindbergh, dies in her house in Vermont. She slips off and away, having lingered some years already in the kingdom adjacent to death, the region of intermittent blankness where Ronald Reagan took up residence for so long. She was ninety-four. Uncoaxed, the lives of Anne Morrow Lindbergh and Ronald Reagan flash before the eyes of the memory—a cascade of images, quick-cut and all out of sequence, the celebrity American Century tumbling through the mind. It must be the moon.

Ronald Reagan and Anne Morrow Lindbergh were born four years apart, long ago, in a different America, before the flood, and both came over with us into a new millennium, though they were enveloped in fog as we crossed the line. They make me think of Woodie Guthrie's 1930s ballad based on *The Grapes of Wrath:* "We buried Grandpa Joad on the Oklahoma Road, / and Grandma on the California side."

Reagan and Mrs. Lindbergh were the bright side and the dark side of the age of publicity. Mrs. Lindbergh lost her first-born child to the savagery of fame. She hated the jackal press. She felt safe from it only when she was up in the air in a two-seater plane with her husband, cut off from the earth. She thought all celebrity was empty, and cherished her private world.

Reagan was all bright public American presence; some—his enemies, anyway, and sometimes his friends and biographers—suspected that he was, in private, a vacancy. Not a dunce altogether, but an ordinary man who inexplicably became magic when lights and camera switched on.

But I find that with the full moon comes a feeling of disgust at political nastiness of all kinds. If I was ever inclined to think ill of the Clintons, I shall, in the future, try to think of them only as the Roy Rogers and Dale Evans of our time.

Tonight I shall put my wallet in the window before I go to sleep. It's said that if you do that at the time of the full moon, it works even better than Alan Greenspan to ward off recession.

THE SUPERMICE

August 8, 2001

THE MICE IN OUR FARMHOUSE ARE CAN-DO INTELLECTUALS—mice of action. My wife opened a kitchen cabinet the other day and caught two of them using their tiny, humanish hands to unscrew the top from a jar of Skippy 25 percent reduced-fat chunky peanut butter. Two nights later, amazingly, they succeeded, and rewarded themselves with a mouse feast that left the peanut butter half gone and, all around the jar, a triumphant scattering of scats, which look like chocolate sprinkles.

It is only a matter of months before these Darwinian marvels learn to use a can opener, a skill that will lift them to a higher stage of mouse evolution—and to the more civilized pleasures of canned Mexicorn, Bush's baked beans, and solid white, water-packed tuna. In a generation or two, smart young mice will have a system of pulleys that will open the refrigerator door in the middle of the night. God knows how a new infusion of butter, protein-rich cheese, yogurt, red-leaf lettuce, and V-8 juice will invigorate the breed and enlarge its cerebral cortex.

It is hard to be hostile to creatures so charmingly intent, so assiduous, and so eagerly scrambling up the food chain. I guess they would not be cute if they carried bubonic plague. But these being glove-gray country mice that have skittered in from a Tom-and-Jerry cartoon, I root for their innocence and ingenuity. I am even mouse-proud. My mice are smarter than your mice! After the stunt with the Skippy peanut butter jar, I felt as if they had gotten 800s on their SATs. These guys are good.

There was a time in my primitive past when I dealt with mice by setting out the ancient instruments of death—the medieval cheese-baited mouse-whackers that terminate the hungry midnight rodent like the Inquisition nailing a Cathar. In bed, I would hear a trap going off in the middle of the night: THWACK! A little extinction in another part of the house. In the morning, I would dispose of the carnage.

The cats, Bruce and Frankie, are useless—tender, almost Franciscan in their laissez-faire, live-and-let-live mouse-tolerance. See no mouse, hear no mouse, eat no mouse. There seems to be a strange detente, inexplicable in Tom-and-Jerry terms. I think that Bruce and Frankie have nervously acknowledged the evolutionary velocity of the mice and have decided to stand aside, perhaps in the hope of future favors when the mice take over.

Having abandoned mouse-whackers, on Buddhist grounds, and having despaired of the cats as hired assassins, we have resorted to a "Havahart" trap—a small rectangular steel cage, with doors at either end and bait in the middle, that captures the mouse alive. We have caught a mouse on each of the last two nights (baiting with peanut butter, of course). I come into the kitchen and find the little prodigy, eyes bright with terror, scrunched in a corner of the cage, under the flap door. It's possible that part of his unhappiness arises from humiliation at being fooled by such a childishly transparent device. He finally looks at me, however, directly in the face, and I am astonished at a hard, still, appraising look in his eyes, which reminds me of the fixed gaze of a magazine editor I once worked for (a man whose evolution, it must be said, ran rapidly in the other direction, descending toward the rodent stage).

Each morning, I drive a captured mouse a mile down the road and release him near the empty house where the hermit died a few months ago, on the theory the mouse can inconvenience no one there. It disturbs me, however, to think that before long the mice in their growing colony of exile may organize a Restoration, and one day march back down the road to our farmhouse, and, in their thousands, reclaim what is theirs. After the revolution, they will set me to work in their kitchen, fixing them peanut butter sandwiches.

Reagan and Mondale

October 22, 1984

The atrium of the Hyatt Regency in Louisville is a bright interior shaft that rises sixteen stories from the lobby. It makes the inside of the hotel look like a shopping mall with ambitions to become a cathedral. Or, on the night of the presidential debate, like a gala high-rise tenement. Tiers of balconies, one on every floor, overlook the lobby. They were festooned that night with American flags and sheets emblazoned with Republican slogans, and the faithful leaned out over each ledge to cheer Ronald Reagan when he returned from the debate: "Four more years! Four more years!"

Reagan, mounting a stage in the lobby, down at the bottom of this festive well, may have been relieved to be working with a script again. In the soft and almost purring voice that he could direct with such intimacy at a crowd, the president gave a short talk, part inspiration ("Fly as high as you can!"), part politics as manly game ("Come November, we're gonna tell Coach Tax Hike [Walter Mondale] to head for the showers"). The Republicans hollered and whooped. It had been a long night. Ronald and Nancy Reagan made their way to one of the glass elevators that run up one wall of the atrium. The Reagans walked inside and turned and waved through the transparent doors.

And then, an astonishing apparition: The glass capsule abruptly whooshed the Reagans—still waving—skyward, as if it were speeding them back up into the clouds, back into the fleecy, mythic realm from which they had come. A hallucination out of Erich Von Daniken: elevators of the Gods.

Until the debate, the presidential campaign had been a disengaged and ghostly pageant, on either side a kind of somnambulation: Reagan working under a charm, Mondale under some sour malediction. After

Louisville, the campaign began to develop, like a Polaroid picture in one's hand as the images start to come clear.

One sometimes thought that the author of the Mondale curse was Mondale. He seemed to be psychically disconnected from his own passions, to be neutralized by an internal maze of deflectors and scruples. He displayed a genius for undoing his successes. In any case, he had no political traction. People heard not so much the substance of his words as his voice, an instrument that tended to reduce his strongest convictions to a whine. Maybe it was the upper Midwest talking, the boyhood as a Norwegian minister's son. In the vibrations of his voice, like wind through fence wire on a gray day, one heard the coming of a Minnesota winter.

If Mondale seemed at a psychic remove, Reagan worked at a physical remove, not talking to reporters, heading out perhaps twice a week to address rallies of his believers, to congratulate Americans for acting American and to dismiss the opposition—and, indeed, most complexity in the world—as being archaic, depressive and implicitly unmanly.

So the campaign proceeded across the weeks and months with an air of inevitability, of history on cruise control. No one paid a great deal of attention. It was like an argument going on in another part of the house. Reagan was so far ahead, nearly everyone agreed, that he would carry something close to fifty states, maybe even all of them.

It was not merely that Mondale was something of a lusterless and dispiriting alternative to a personally popular sitting president in a period of peace and economic recovery. A more mysterious and complex process was occurring. Americans considered Mondale with a merciless objectivity. But they came to absorb Ronald Reagan in an entirely different and subjective manner. They internalized him. In later months, Reagan found his way onto a different plane of the American mind, a mythic plane. He became not just a politician, not just a president, but very nearly an American apotheosis. The Gipper as Sun King. For some.

A dispassionate witness may say that it was done with mirrors and manipulation, with artfully patriotic rhetoric and Olympic imagery, the Wizard of Oz working the illusion machine. But that does not entirely do credit to the phenomenon. In an extraordinary way, Reagan came in some subconscious realms to be not just the leader of America but the embodiment of it. "America is back," he announced with a bright, triumphant eye. Back from where? Back from Vietnam and Watergate and the sexual revolution and all the other tarnishing historical uncleannesses that deprived America of its virtue and innocence.

Partly by an accident of timing, partly by a simple genius of his being, Reagan managed to return to Americans something extremely precious to them: a sense of their own virtue. Reagan—completely American, uncomplicated, forward-looking, honest, self-deprecating— became American innocence in a seventy-three-year-old body. (The American sense of innocence and virtue does not always strike the world as a shining and benign quality, of course.)

Whatever the reasons, the campaign of 1984 did not stack up as an equitable contest. Reagan's aura purchased him surprising immunities. The polls showed a majority of Americans disagreeing with him on specific issues but planning to vote for him anyway.

Reagan went to Bowling Green State University for a political appearance that looked and sounded like every Big Ten pep rally of the past twenty years compacted into an instant. Reagan's helicopter, deus ex machina again, fluttered down onto the grass outside, visible to the waiting crowd through a great window, and the students erupted in an ear-splitting roar, waving their Greek fraternity letters on placards. RE-BUILDING AN AMERICA THAT ONCE WAS, said one sign. The young seem prone to a kind of aching nostalgia for some American prehistory that they cannot quite define, but sense in Reagan. The chant of "We want Ron!" elided into the Olympic chant, "U.S.A.! U.S.A.!" To some extent, they were merely exuberant kids making noise, but their identification with, their passion for, a seventy-three-year-old president was startling. And so was their equation of the man with the nation he leads. Who would have thought that an aged movie actor would be, for so many of the young, the man for the 1980s?

His critics speak of Reagan scathingly as an empty man, and yet he was a man with, sometimes, a dramatic gift of self-presentation. He conducted himself with a remarkably amiable dignity and sense of discretion, a sort of perfect American gravitas. In Milwaukee one day, after he spoke at the city's Oktoberfest, a small, seraphically lovely little blond girl in a peasant dress came up hesitatingly to give him a bouquet of flowers. Politicians are often oafs around little children, overdoing it. With an exquisite sense of tenderness and courtesy, Reagan took the flowers, bent slightly, talked to the girl, then gently picked her up for a moment. He talked some more, set her down, and, head bobbing slightly, waved the flowers over his head in a gesture that was simultaneously self-deprecating and triumphal.

Many Americans were inclined to be curiously protective of Reagan. Perhaps, after so many failed presidencies since the assassination of John Kennedy—think of Johnson, Nixon, Carter— Americans were eager to see Reagan succeed. Or, at least many Americans were. Many were not. One of the accomplishments of Reagan's campaign was to create a sense not only of inevitability but of unanimity as well. Reagan's managers did this by crafting his campaign not as a political argument but as a traveling ceremony of patriotic inspiration.

A presidential campaign is a phenomenon of surreal trajectories. The plane rises out of the weather, out of the mess and scurry of one campaign stop, and breaks up into pure sunshine. One flies through the blue altitudes, over the abstract, tumbling snowfields of cumulus, then plunges down again, into the weather, into another part of America. The nation ceases to be a geographic continuum. It becomes, instead, a sequence of fragmented locales, discrete and (except for hurriedly noticed details of local color) interchangeable, like particles in Einstein's physics. The gods ascend and descend, with their entourages and motorcades. They sweep to the event and sweep back to the plane and away. It is always touching, a little haunting, to see the people waiting on the access roads for the motorcade to hurry by, waiting for an hour or two in little clusters, holding signs of support or hostility, waiting for a glimpse that lasts a few seconds. The sight is haunting because those people, receding in the distance, always look as if they have just been abandoned there by the roadside.

Time is minutely scheduled, and yet, as experienced, weirdly elastic. Yesterday seems like last month. The memory of everything but the past hour or so vanishes. The campaign, the long march, often goes on in a kind of twilight. There are sudden bright bursts of light and color and balloons and rhetoric, and then the twilight descends again. If one is flying with the White House press, the most reliable thread of continuity is ABC's Sam Donaldson, who prowls buses and planes with the air of an amused and vaguely irate large dog, sleekly alert but inner-directed, snout in the wind, picking up scents, eyes manically abstracted. Every so often he loudly barks out some strange witticism to no one in particular.

The day after the Louisville debate, the White House spinners were hard at work on the press plane, on the buses. The president was heading to Charlotte, North Carolina, for an appearance with Senator Jesse Helms and then to Baltimore. The spinners, a patrol of top White House staff members, had the task of chatting with the press and trying to get a favorable spin on stories. They were working that day at damage control.

The debate was a sudden deflation. One could hear the air rushing into the vacuum. Now Reagan seemed flat and disconcerted and, weirdly, somehow a stranger to himself. In Charlotte, a city that takes pride in having made its busing program a model for the rest of the country, Reagan denounced the practice of busing and was greeted with silence. The Baltimore event was curiously disheveled. Reagan was there to unveil a statue of Christopher Columbus at the Inner Harbor. The crowd was dotted with protesters ("No More Years! No More Years!") and anti-Reagan signs (DEAD MARINES FOR REAGAN). Back on the press bus, Donaldson bellowed to his constituency: "Big Mo ain't here today!"

Louisville, at least for the moment, set certain reversals in motion. Mondale had frequently been the spiritless candidate before. A few days earlier, he had flown to Little Rock, to address a meeting of the Rural Electric Cooperative. Introduced in a not-very-charismatic line as a "long-term friend of rural electrification," Mondale looked out at the crowd with a weary countenance, with his hawk's beak and the hooded eyes that at certain moments give him the look of a middle-aged prince of the House of Saud. Mondale's delivery was dismal. His sentences sounded like great labor, as if his voice were being forced to carry an unwieldy armful of words, staggering toward the door under their weight, and then dropping the last two or three syllables just before he got to the period. Laboring and pleading. A few farmers got up and walked out.

But after Louisville, Mondale was transfigured. His eyes shone. His voice took color. The debate legitimized him as a candidate, gave him plausibility and stature. An extraordinary though usually buried theme of this campaign was manhood. There was a bizarre testosterone factor at work. Reagan was tough. Mondale was a wimp. The debate in some senses reversed that, too. Reagan for the moment seemed weak and lost and old. Mondale, in the eyes of the electorate, was granted his manhood.

So at Pittsburgh a couple of days after the debate, Mondale fired up a huge rally at Market Square. The band played the theme from *Rocky*. Hard-hatted steelworkers cheered him on. His rhetoric even began to swagger, to grow looser and more colloquial. In Cincinnati, he talked about sending criminals to "the slammer." Fighting Fritz.

The campaign was momentarily changed, or at least pitched into the possibility of new possibilities. If Reagan remained the probability, the debate introduced that new shadow of age, the specter of presidential brownouts. On the press bus, one entertained fantasies of an autumn of the Gipper, of Reagan winning in a moment of culminating splendor in 1984, then, over the next four years, fading off to become a merely ceremonial presence, the emeritus of the American dream.

The campaign planes arc back and forth across the landscape. The pilot breaks into a little public-address rhapsody about the brilliant foliage underneath. One afternoon the shadow of the Mondale plane upon the clouds below is surrounded by a brilliant yellow halo. Why? Has Mondale acquired an aura, too? Everywhere in the plane is the little insect click of laptop computers: information in bits and bytes pollinating the nation, a part of nature now.

Land in another city. The motorcade hurtles toward the people yet again. The campaign proceeds. The dreamwork of American power.

The Beauty of Weeds

July 2, 2001

Consider the weeds. Our field has gone rank and knee-deep with Bedstraw and Queen Anne's Lace and Vetch and God knows what other dense rural jungle life, patrolled by overflights of stinging deer flies and creased by deer paths. How do the hawks spot field mice and voles through such dense camouflage?

Their names teem with a secret Shakespearean life. When I browse through field guides to wildflowers and weeds, I feel as if I have rediscovered a rich, hidden vein of the English language—a parallel universe populated by such vivid protagonists as Carrion Flower and Wild Bleeding Heart, as Vipers Bugloss and Crazyweed, as Hog Peanut, Corn Cockle, Tansy Leaf Aster, Showy Orchis, Death Camas, and that damned elusive Scarlet Pimpernel.

The names savor of medicinal witcheries and faery mythologies. Weeds are infinitely more interesting in their way than mere pampered uptown flowers, those sleek, overbred show dogs. You can boil the wild weeds, eat them, put them on wounds. Their names are surrounded by an atmosphere of gossip. What goes on between Pokeweed and Bluebead Lily? The groundlings—or groundhogs—want to know. What conspiratorial dialogue is whispered between Blue Toad Flax and Monkshood? What soliloquies from Trumpet Creeper, from Lady's Thumb, from the grizzled Salt-marsh Fleabane?

The characters are wildly sexual—it is their whole game, what with pistils and stamens and their frank, unblinking, scandalous fertility, and our salacious Italian bees stirring constantly among them, the messengers of love. A soap opera of many seasons goes on and on, starring characters like Blue-bird Violet, Motherwort, Spreading Dogbane, Lady's Thumb, and Spiked Lobelia.

Emerson said, "I am a god in nature, I am a weed by the wall." Right on both counts. The point is that the weed and the god are much the same thing.

I tried to dig a small pond for water lilies, but the shovel blade went an inch down and hit rock. Everywhere I dug, I clanged against rock. I called in a guy with a back hoe, and he harvested boulders for a couple of hours, until we had a hole big enough to be a bull's grave and ringed with enough rocks to build another house. This field has never been cultivated, for good reason, and, if domesticated at all, is meant for sheep. We once thought about tilling it and putting in something organized, like wheat. We gave up the idea.

We opted for the general sexual riot of weeds and wildflowers—for the loquacious Elizabethan catalogue, whose random beauty lives at an opposite end of the universe from the laboratories of the genetically altered, from the sinister utilitarianism toward which, alas, we are flying at the speed of light.

Let a hundred flowers bloom—

Bittersweet Nightshade,
Heal-All,
True Forget-Me-Not,
Blue Vervain,
Spring Larkspur,
Spiderwort,
Monkeyflower,
Dog Violet,
Common Butterwort,
Spurred Butterfly,
Crown Vetch,
Henbit,
Spotted Joe-Pye Weed,
Gray Beardtongue,
Spreading Dogbane,
Live-Forever,

Steeplebush,
Crazyweed,
Woolly Locoweed,
Hairy Vetch,
Lady's Thumb,
Common Speedwell,
Field Milkwort,
Lyon's Turtlehead,
Ragged Robin,
Calypso,
Common Burdock,
Spotted Knapweed,
Hairy Willow Herb,
Purple Saxifrage,
Red Baneberry,
Slender Glasswort,
Toadshade,
Climbing Bittersweet,
Birdsfoot Trefoil,
Moth Mullein,
Smooth False Foxglove,
Showy Rattlebox,
Prince's Plume,
Agrimony,
Squawroot,
Mouse-Ear Hawkweed,
Rattlesnake Weed,
Coltsfoot,
Tickseed Sunflower,
Jerusalem Artichoke,
Sneezeweed,
Swollen Bladderwort,
Clammy Ground Cherry,
Purslane,
Muskflower,

Rough-Fruited Cinquefoil,
Climbing Boneset,
Pearly Everlasting,
Wild Madder,
Bouncing Bet,
Tread-Softly,
Lopseed,
Dodder,
Virgin's Bower,
Smaller Pussytoes.

As the Sermon on the Mount continues: ". . . I say unto you that even Solomon in all his glory was not arrayed like one of these."

ANIMAL FEELINGS

February 15, 2001

Do animals have feelings?

The *New York Times* discussed the subject the other day. Some scientists think animals are capable of primitive emotional life. Some scientists think not.

Fred has been sulking ever since the report appeared. Freddie is a hound of many moods. Now he flattens himself with his jowl-flaps splayed on his little Aladdin's mat under the kitchen table. He will not rouse himself even when a horde of crows appears like Visigoths on the grass outside, an outrage that usually stirs him to a storm of indignant imprecation.

Feelings? Fred is as moody as Rudolph Valentino. His life has the exaggerated theatrical emotionalism of a silent movie.

Some animal behaviorists believe that a character like Fred is motivated only by the hope of the next snack. This is unjust. When I return home, particularly after an absence of more than a day, Fred levitates with chaotic excitement and happiness. He springs into the air on all four legs at once, his tail thrashing, his body performing twists like a high-diver's—an astonishing sight, a midair electricity of vibrating honey-colored fur. When he comes to earth, he trombones his neck and howls out a conversational WOOO-WOOOO-WOOOO! There is no cynical quid pro quo food reward in prospect. He feels elated that I am back. I would be more flattered by this if gregarious Fred—the perfect host, the perfect guest, the dog at ease in any situation—did not stage the same welcome for virtually everyone.

Well, not everyone. Goofball or not, Fred is a discerning judge of people and will not warm to some. Fred has his expertise and his elaborate instruments. He knows the sound of my car half a mile down the road. That much is easy. He also possesses the mysterious dog's fore-knowledge of when I will be back, even an hour or two before I arrive.

It is said that at the moment when Franklin Roosevelt died in Georgia in April 1945, his dog Fala ran headlong through the screen door of the cottage—burst through the wire screening itself—and vanished howling into the woods. He was found a couple of days later on a nearby mountain.

I would not call Fred a rational dog. What he possesses, and lives by, are precisely feelings. He inhabits a universe of polychromatic drama filled with absolutely nothing, as far as I can tell, except emotions (ecstasies, disappointments, depressions, moments of astonishing solicitude and tenderness if the humans are feeling low). And, of course, smells.

The essayist Edward Hoagland, in a splendid piece called "Dogs and the Tug of Life," mentions that the dog's sense of smell is at least a hundred times as keen as a man's. He goes on to become somewhat personal: "The way in which a dog presents his anus and genitals for inspection indicates the hierarchical position that he aspires to, and other dogs who sniff his genitals are apprised of his sexual condition. From his urine they can undoubtedly distinguish age, build, state of sexual activity and general health, even hours after he's passed by."

A dog, in other words, is a journalist.

The Earth Cracks Open

October 30, 1989

IN THE SPRING OF 1872, THE NATURALIST JOHN MUIR WAS asleep in a small cabin in the Yosemite Valley. "At half past two o'clock," he wrote later, "I was awakened by a tremendous earthquake . . . the strange thrilling motion could not be mistaken, and I ran out of my cabin, both glad and frightened, shouting, 'A noble earthquake! A noble earthquake!' feeling sure I was going to learn something."

It would be funny to think he actually uttered those words, that he ran out in the middle of an earthquake looking for sermons in the shaking stones. Muir was alone in the moonlit mountains, in any case, and so he could indulge his charming nineteenth-century awe. When the earth turned in its sleep, it crushed much landscape in the folds. But somehow the event could keep its innocence. If nature does something awful, is it part of the electrical display of God the Father, or merely geography rearranging itself, obeying an impersonal agenda?

When the earth cracks open to dismantle a city, metaphysical questions suggest themselves: A natural wonder of such sinister possibilities shakes a person's confidence in the predictable daily life of the world. What would Muir learn? Does cataclysm have anything to teach? That the earth retains its genius for big surprise? Or is it, as those who are more organized in their superstitions believe, that some profound and punishing principle of disorder and annihilating wrath has been set loose in the world?

Of all natural disasters, the earthquake somehow is the most unnerving. It is the earth talking, after all, and so it speaks with a primal power. Earthquakes in Scripture mean that God has crumpled up the order of the world and cast it down in disgust. "And the foundations of the world do shake," says Isaiah. "The earth is utterly broken down."

Or, agnostically, earthquakes are a wandering, enigmatic fierceness, now and then breaching the surface like Moby Dick.

An earthquake rides on a principle of disintegration—the disintegration not only of architecture and pavements and lives but also of the entire idea of order, of process and human control. "What can one believe quite safe," asked Seneca, "if the world itself is shaken, and its most solid parts totter to their fall . . . and the earth lose its chief characteristic, stability?" The familiar world goes rioting down to rubble. Reality comes to rest at a crazy angle.

The terror lies first in the surprise. An earthquake is a sudden emergency. It is a drama in the theater of the unknown, a cruel improvisation, hidden from one moment to the next, as the future is hidden—as, for that matter, God is hidden. The event does not announce itself as most other disasters do, as a hurricane does, or a flood, or even an erupting volcano, which is after all hard to miss as dangerous geography. A plague too arrives more slowly. That is no consolation, but at least the mind and nerves are prepared. The event proceeds in a logical continuum of developing bad news.

An earthquake is an unannounced convulsion—nature performing a Shakespearean tragedy that begins absurdly in the fifth act: After fifteen seconds, Hamlet and the others lie dying, the stage is covered with blood and debris. For many years, one may have lived on top of the San Andreas fault and made doomy jokes about it; it is like having a violent beast in the basement, knowing that one day it may burst up through the living-room floor. But there is no preparation for the moment. Only certain animals feel premonitory vibrations undetectable to humans. They grow skittish. Horses glare with a wild panicked eye.

Sometimes storms, even hurricanes, can be exhilarating. It is fun to stand on a beach during a histrionic blow. An earthquake is not that kind of thrill. The worst part may be the feeling of helplessness. There is no right thing to do just then, except perhaps to flee the building. There is no knowing where the earth will open next. The wild cracking follows no principle but the terrifyingly random. Denial ("this is not happening") competes with fascination.

A major earthquake lays waste the human sense of scale. When reporters write about earthquakes, they invariably say that cars and other large objects were "tossed around like toys." Architecture collapses upon itself. The human idea of proportion is outraged in the rifting and shearing.

So certainties vanish. The earth liquefies. It becomes as wild as surf. The solid is abruptly fluid. Normally, earth is the refuge, the stability, the foundation of things. The earth should be alive only to grow vegetables and flowers. Now the earth itself becomes a beast, all teeth and gashes and sudden topplings. Reality has turned molten and violent.

Sometimes when the earth cracks open, it produces good stories. In March 1933, Albert Einstein was visiting the Long Beach campus of the University of California. He and his host from the Department of Geology walked through the campus, intently discussing the motions of earthquakes. Suddenly they looked up in puzzlement to see people running out of campus buildings. Einstein and the other scientist had been so busy discussing seismology that they did not notice the earthquake occurring under their feet.

There may be something perversely cathartic about earthquakes. For some time humankind has been in the business of manufacturing its own disasters—wars, acid rain and other pollutions, drugs, a globe aswarm with refugees. Perhaps it is a relief for a moment to be face-to-face with a disaster that humans did not invent, a cataclysm that has at least a sort of innocence of origin in larger powers.

The survivors will proceed like Odysseus and his men, after one of their escapes: "And so we sailed on, aching in our hearts for the companions that we lost, but glad to be alive."

Ruin of a Cat, Ghost of a Dog

December 14, 1992

Sarajevo—A line that turns up in Balkan propaganda catches the spirit of things: People must decide whether they choose "to be the carcass or the vulture."

A fog rises this morning from the carcass of Sarajevo. The city has a clinging, ragged aura. Fog seeps through shattered buildings and seems to puff through the bullet holes in windows.

The vultures sit in the hills. Drunk on slivovitz and nationalism, they fire through the intermittent radiance.

Serb artillery shoots from the slopes on one side of the city, and Muslim shoots from the other. Sometimes both sides throw shells at once. Sometimes they drop them into town. The big shells arrive with a crisp, concussive WHUMP! But sniper fire you hear only at the shooting end—an irregular background noise of flat, hard pops. You look up wildly at the hills and imagine the snipers squinting through crosshairs. You wonder what they may be able to see through the mist. You pause to decode the physics: The sound you hear has been taking its time, traveling a lot more slowly than the bullet itself.

The Renault sedan scurries across the Miljacka River on the little bridge where Gavrilo Princip assassinated the Archduke Franz Ferdinand in 1914. A brainless loop of history: The twentieth century, after all its adventures, has arrived back in Sarajevo again, working on blood feuds and apocalypses. Lessons learned: possibly none.

Along the streets, we catch the haggard, unslept faces of the besieged, a glimpse of their trudging, cringing body English. Shops boarded up. The driver, who is, improbably, a Russian, pitches the Renault along, overrevving and popping the clutch, to the National Library. It is a splendid nineteenth-century Moorish building that has been hammered so often, so heavily, that it is a gutted shell. In a city where more than 17,000 were killed and 110,000 wounded between the spring of 1992, when the siege began, and December of that year, it may be odd to be disturbed by the fate of a building. But to murder a library is metaphysically sinister and wanton. What dies, of course, is more than individual life—the stuff of the civilization, the transmission of past to future, goes up in smoke. It is not an accident.

That is the deeper wiring. We ask the driver about mere electricity. None for seventeen days, he says. Do he and his wife fetch water in buckets from a central supply somewhere?

"My wife does not," he says. "She was killed by a shell sixty-seven days ago." Stunned silence. I cannot see his face. We mutter, "Sorry." The driver hurtles on.

Elie Wiesel arranged this visit to parts of what used to be Yugoslavia. He tells a press conference later that Sarajevo looks to him like "a ghost city, a tragedy formed into a city, like a city in Germany in 1945." He says, "I saw a cat that was a ruin of a cat. I saw a dog that was a ghost of a dog." He says, "I feel the time has come to weep."

I am not moved to weep, but rather to feel anger and disgust. This is not tragedy. The word *tragedy* would give this business too much moral elevation. What has happened in Bosnia is just squalor and barbarism—the filthy work of liars and cynics manipulating tribal prejudices, using atrocity propaganda and old blood feuds to accomplish the unclean political result of "ethnic cleansing." The displacement of a million innocent civilians, turned into refugees, is not a consequence of the war, but precisely the purpose of the war. It has worked.

Wiesel leads his delegation into the palace of Alija Izetbegovic, Muslim president of the shrunken republic of Bosnia-Herzegovina, which is now only an archipelago of besieged fortresses. Wiesel has come to try to project a little of his sanity and decency in the war zone, to hold everyone to a higher standard and possibly to make some of the killers ashamed of what they are doing. In an ornate ceremonial room painted toxic green, Wiesel, wonder rabbi out of Auschwitz, sits side by side with Izetbegovic, whom the nationalist Serbs see as the spearhead of a fundamentalist Muslim state, the nightmare of Islamic conquest drifting up out of the fourteenth century from the Battle of Kosovo, which locked the Serbs into five hundred years of Turkish rule. Gunshots outside. No one even blinks. Part of the mise-en-scène.

An elegant, doleful man named Miroslav Jancic, poet and former diplomat, introduces himself. Sarajevo is a concentration camp, he says in quiet anguish. "How do you eat?" I ask. "Not well," he says. "This shirt used to fit perfectly." He inserts two fingers between his neck and the buttoned white shirt collar. Possibly the worst crime of the war—worse even than the ingenious atrocities that are the specialité de la maison of the Balkans—is the systematic starvation of entire populations by the Serb fighters surrounding cities like Tuzla and Srebrenica and Sarajevo.

In armored personnel carriers supplied by the United Nations Protection Force, we make our way from the besieged to the besiegers. We pass through the lines, through checkpoints and no-man's-lands, to the headquarters of Radovan Karadzic, the Serb nationalist chieftain. Karadzic is a poet and, in civilian life, bizarrely enough, a psychiatrist. A sleek, fattish man with an expensive double-breasted suit, bushy eyebrows and flamboyantly styled long hair. I try to conjure up a psychiatric session with this healer. I see certain Hippocratic problems with a head doctor who would lead his patients not out of murderous fantasies but deeper into them. After you've spent a short time in Bosnia, your mind seems to slip into hallucination.

Karadzic says, with some accuracy, "This is not an ideological war. This is just two close neighbors who hate each other." Then the hallucinations begin. Elie Wiesel asks him why he is besieging Sarajevo.

"We are not besieging Sarajevo." Oh.

Why did the Serbs destroy the National Library?

"We did not destroy the National Library. They did. You can see. It is ruined by fire from the ground floor up. We could not have done this. They removed their books and burned the building."

The drama has several simple, fierce motifs. One is Revenge and Counterrevenge (Newton's third law: For every atrocity there must be an equal and opposite atrocity). A second motif is Complete Denial (We did not do it; they did). Which yields the third theme: Everyone Is a Victim, which means, of course, that everyone is justified in committing any act. We–they. We victim; they did it. The dynamics of rage and outrage reverberate through the mountain forests and down the generations.

Karadzic, the Balkan commando-psychiatrist, explains, "This war is a continuation of World War II—the same families, the same revenge." Everyone agrees about that. After the war, Tito and communism merely suppressed the blood hatreds. Tribal memory and the fierce dynamic of revenge went into a kind of holding pattern for nearly fifty years. With the collapse of communism, all the terrible deeds committed during World War II (and World War I, for that matter) came streaming back, demanding vengeance. The Croats' alliance with Hitler, and the savage enthusiasm of the Croatian ultranationalist organization Ustashi in slaughtering Serbs from 1941 to 1945, created a vast accumulation of hatred and blood debts. A Serb will say, "Croats are a genocide people."

Dusko Zavisic, a young Serb photographer who escaped from Sarajevo, told me that as a boy he was taken to visit the museum at the World War II Croatian concentration camp at Jasenovac. The pictures there of murdered Serbs were so horrifying he could not eat for two days afterward. In the latest war of Croats and Serbs, the Croats destroyed the museum. It was Dusko Zavisic who took the photographs of atrocities in Vukovar last November. He said that for days he was afraid to close his eyes because the afterimages of mutilated bodies and smashed heads would always jump back into the foreground of his mind.

A display of the Vukovar photographs now hangs in the Museum of Applied Art in Belgrade. Applied art indeed. The photos depict slaughters of amazing awfulness, performed with conscienceless ingenuity. Here, for example, we see an instrument that looks like a tuning fork, but with the prongs more widely spaced, about 3½ inches apart. A local trademark is to gouge out both eyes. Hence this handy device. Studies in the Balkan Department of Comparative Atrocity.

The worst part of it is some vibration of horrid pleasure. Too many of these people enjoy killing. It has become a sort of cultural addiction.

In the Museum of Applied Art, five women stand sobbing in front of the photographs of the burned and mutilated Serbian victims of Vukovar. The women's shoulders heave, tears flood their cheeks. They point to the savaged bodies in the pictures: That was a cousin. That was a brother. That was a husband.

The last leaves cling to the trees. It has rained: The water caught in furrows of the fields holds reflected sunset—sweet sky visible through holes in the earth. We cross the Bosna River and head into the mountains. There is a sliver of new moon. It looks somehow covert—like an eyelid, watching.

It is full dark at the Manjaca camp. Here the Serbs hold more than three thousand prisoners, mostly Bosnian Muslims, mostly fighters, we are told. We find one smirking, screwy kid who is a German. He joined the Croatian forces (he is wearing a black Ustashi T-shirt) because he said he wanted an adventure that he could write a book about. The camp commander, Lt. Col. Bozidar Popovic, is a barking, strutting martinet who wields a Mini Maglite as if it were a swagger stick. His voice never drops from a shout. He bellows, "I am a humanist!"

An enormous shed, unheated, dark except for a few short-wicked oil lanterns—smudged night-lights. The hundreds of prisoners sleep close together, in orderly right-angle ranks. They have straw mats and blankets (though how many blankets is a point of argument—the colonel says five, which seems extravagant, and the men say fewer). They keep their possessions in cardboard boxes that they hang from what look like the railings to hold dairy cows as they are milked. The shed smells of cows (an effect both disturbing and distantly wholesome, a smell from childhood). The army insists that the building is an equipment shed.

The small parade of visitors, beaconed by the lights on shoulder-held TV cameras, sweeps in like a surprise midnight political parade. But it is silent—eerie and embarrassed. The prisoners rouse themselves and stare from the shadows with big, wondering eyes. They seem young, with fierce, thick, uncombed hair and raw, cold-roughened faces.

But Popovic is better than he seems. The Serbian camps at Omarska and Trnopolje became notorious earlier in the year. Atrocity stories poured out of them—beatings, torture, murders. Manjaca now seems disciplined, well regulated. The Serbs, of course, would not display it otherwise. The prisoners, out of earshot of their captors, speak well enough of the camp, and even compliment Popovic as strict but fair. Popovic returns, defensively wagging his finger, and says he can disprove all the lies the prisoners have been telling. Elie Wiesel raises his eyebrows: "Actually, Colonel . . . "

"No, no," Popovic barks on. "They say they are innocent! But did they tell you about the lists of Serbian women they kept that they wanted to put into harems?" There it is again, the Muslim horde. Wiesel calms the colonel and pleads for more blankets for the prisoners.

Marshall McLuhan's famous metaphor sees the world as a global village. Actually, it has become a global city, a megalopolis with some rich neighborhoods and many poor neighborhoods and some that are terribly dangerous. Unfortunately, the big city has no police department, and the neighborhoods (the former USSR, the Muslim world, South Africa) are getting more dangerous. Almost everyone agrees it is too late for military intervention in Bosnia. The place makes me think of Yeats's haunting line, "And wondered what was left for massacre to save." The place to intervene, they say, now must be in Kosovo and Macedonia. Everyone talks about the coming winter, about people freezing to death and starving. Everyone talks about a Balkan war.

Caught in the Act of Soliloquy

June 1, 1998

I AM AS SANE AS YOU ARE.

On the other hand, I know it looks a little off when I walk down Sixth Avenue talking to myself or stop, gesticulating, for the light at 48th Street, and make a scathing, irrefutable point to, um, myself. It could be worse—Tourette syndrome, for example. Tourette sounds awful; this just looks crazy—or maybe a third of the way there. People in the street flick me a glance: "Uh-oh."

A friend of mine has a sister who is deaf and talks to herself in sign language, which takes the behavior into a new dimension. When I heard this, I thought, "Aha, there's proof of what I have been saying: Talking to yourself is just a way of thinking things over, of processing ideas through articulation, a sort of audible shadowboxing. The deaf woman turns her brain waves into fast-forward hand dancing. Same thing." As a writer, I talk to myself in order to try out ideas—a rough draft recited to the pigeons—before writing them down. A playwright must speak the lines aloud. What's crazy about that?

Of course, that is putting a high-minded gloss on the behavior, as if the auditorium of one's mind were always resounding to symposia on Wittgenstein or on human rights in Myanmar. Caught me talking to myself? Just another oral presentation of apodictic obiter dicta on the solo stage! Thomas Jefferson dines alone! Shakespeare's soliloquies elevated talking to oneself to the highest art; on the other hand, Hamlet may not have been traveling with a full seabag, either.

In fact, most talking to oneself involves a low order of business— pettiness, self-justification, improvised rants or what the French call *l'esprit d'escalier*, the things that you should have said a moment ago, lines you think of while coming down the stairs. (The British call it "taxi wit," which may prove that the French think faster than the

Brits.) This debased muttering is directed at salesclerks, ticket-writing cops and even would-be muggers: "You know, son, when I was in 'Nam . . . " Talking to oneself is inherently a private act, not meant to be shared, and as such it may be a safety valve for venting the mind's little gases and toxins. Best done silently and/or alone, Emily Post would advise.

Long ago, the humorist Finley Peter Dunne ("Mr. Dooley") described being vice president of the United States as "a sort of disgrace, like writing anonymous letters." Talking to oneself is cousin to that. It seems a Richard Nixon sort of thing to do. If Nixon did not actually talk to himself, he gave the impression that he did. For all his reputation for covertness, Nixon's real problem was his inability to conceal the darkly busy workings of his mind—the wheels turning, the eyes darting. You could almost hear him talking—a subliminal tape—even if the words were not audible. Nixon also had the alarming habit of talking about himself in the third person, which is an inverted variation on talking to oneself. In talking to oneself, one invents an interlocutor; Nixon, speaking of himself in the third person, in effect erased an interlocutor—himself! Consider another variation: Joan of Arc. It was not so much that she talked out loud to herself as that she listened intently to the voices in her head.

Some entrepreneur should organize a service that would pair off people talking to themselves, a buddy system that would allow them to go on with their soliloquies but would let them appear, as they walk down the street, to be conversing with each other. Many marriages go on for years along these lines.

Of course, it is embarrassing to be caught orating to yourself. Here are a few ideas on how to handle it:

- Slide, without transition, into singing softly or humming, as if the soliloquy were simply the spoken part of a musical performance, like an opera. In this way, you give the performance an obscurely higher purpose, as if it were a rehearsal that the bystander was fortunate to overhear.

- Go on talking so volubly to your invisible friend that the over-hearer begins thinking he may be the one who is nuts; this works only if you and your nonexistent friend vanish quickly around a corner.
- A tough but effective trick: Make yourself dematerialize, or make the talking-to-yourself moment vanish, in the way that Jacqueline Kennedy Onassis used to disappear psychically, even when people were looking directly at her. The overhearer should think that somehow he hallucinated the moment. Remember that in the age of television, reality dissolves, moment to moment, into thin air.
- Carry a cell phone in hand at all times, or a pocket tape recorder, and lift it quickly to your mouth at the embarrassing moment.
- Have a dog with you on a leash. Always address your remarks to the dog. (This, of course, raises a different set of questions about your intellectual relationship with the dog.)

THE MILLENNIUM

October 15, 1992

THE MILLENNIUM IS THE COMET THAT CROSSES THE CALENDAR every thousand years. It throws off metaphysical sparks. It promises a new age, or an apocalypse. It is a magic trick that time performs, extracting a millisecond from its eternal flatness and then, poised on that transitional instant, projecting a sort of hologram that teems with the summarized life of the thousand years just passed and with visions of the thousand now to come.

The millennium year 2000 is counted from the birth of Jesus Christ in Bethlehem of Judea, in the year (so the Bible says) when Caesar Augustus decreed that a census of the world be taken. A millennial year has thus occurred only once before: fifty generations ago, in the year 1000, on what was a very different, more primitive planet earth. So this millennium has a strange, cosmic prestige, a quality of the almost unprecedented. The world approaches it in states of giddiness, expectation and, consciously or unconsciously, a certain anxiety. The millennium looms as civilization's most spectacular birthday, but, as it approaches, the occasion also sends out nagging threats of comeuppance.

The millennial date is an arbitrary mark on the calendar, decreed around the year 525 by the calculations of an obscure monk. The celebrated year 2000, a triple tumbling of naughts, gets some of its status from humanity's fascination with zeros—the so-called tyranny of tens that makes a neat, right-angle architecture of accumulating years, time sawed into stackable solidities, like children's blocks. And it is true, of course, that the moment may signify little to non-Christians.

Nonetheless, the millennium is freighted with immense historical symbolism and psychological power. It does not depend on objective calculation, but entirely on what people bring to it—hopes, anxieties, the metaphysical focus of their attention. The millennium is essentially an event of the imagination.

Thousand-year blocks of time enforce a chastening standard of weight and scale. The millennium has a gravitational pull that draws in the largest meanings, if only because its frame of reference is so enormous. The millennial drama represents nothing less than the ritual death and rebirth of history, one thousand-year epoch yielding to another. Such imponderable masses of time overwhelm and humble the individual life span, reducing human tragedies and accomplishments to windblown powder.

The year 2000 has long been a fixed point in the distance, a horizon line. In recent years the young have begun to calculate how old they will be at the turn of the millennium. Older people have wondered if they would live to see it. The millennium has also served as a projected launch platform for humankind's most ambitious, far-reaching projects. The year 2000 would be the Year One of a better age, the decisive border at which the Future would start. Now that the destination of 2000 is approaching with a kind of dopplered urgency, people are bound to wonder what the future will look like after that. What will be the new frontier beyond 2000?

The passage into a new millennium will occur this time in the global electronic village. It will be the first (obviously, given the state of technology in the year 1000) to be observed simultaneously worldwide, with one rotation of the planet. Almost every human intelligence will be focused for an instant in a solidarity of collective wonder and vulnerability—Mystery in the Age of Information.

The millennium is almost by definition a moment of extreme possibilities, arousing fantasies that veer wildly between earthly paradise and annihilation.

Dark meanings still reverberate like distant thunder from the last millennial passage. There was no widespread panic at the approach of the year 1000, as some writers have claimed, but an inescapable note of Armageddon was in the air. Men pondered over the text of the last days in the book of Revelation: "And I saw a new heaven and a new earth: for the first heaven and the first earth were passed away; and there was no more sea" (Revelation 21:1).

In the year 1000, the Four Horsemen of the Apocalypse—War, Plague, Famine and Death—were riding unimpeded. To be sure, the apocalyptic four have a sort of chronic credibility: They have been prominent in every century. The world would be paradise indeed if they visited only at each turning of a thousand years. But in the centuries since the first millennium, zealous, punitive preachers have endlessly invoked the four, backing up their threats of doom with Revelation.

Millennial expectations at the beginning of this century brightened, however, and for a while shone with optimism and self-confidence. The 1939 World's Fair (just before Hitler marched into Poland) was organized around the sleek theme "Building the World of Tomorrow." In 1965 (just before the Vietnam War began in earnest), the American Academy of Arts and Sciences brought together its Commission on the Year 2000. The chairman, sociologist Daniel Bell, declared, "The problem of the future consists in defining one's priorities and making the necessary commitments."

But in the past quarter-century, millennial visions have grown darker, lurid as a Brueghel. The best-selling nonfiction book of the 1970s in America was Christian author Hal Lindsey's *The Late Great Planet Earth*. Among many other things, Lindsey predicted that the Soviet Union would invade Israel and that, after millions of the righteous were gathered up in the eschatological event known as the "rapture," Jesus would descend from the heavens to preside over the real New World Order. In his 1974 book *Armageddon, Oil and the Middle East Crisis,* John F. Walvoord projected his vision: "Destruction on a formerly incomprehensible scale is clearly predicted for the end time in the book of Revelation and may be the result of nuclear war." Evangelist Pat Robertson has said that in the millennial age the saved will be empowered to control geologic faults spiritually and thereby prevent earthquakes.

Where science and technology once seemed to offer a redemptive promise, they have grown more problematic. As the second millen-

nium approaches, they often appear to be agents of either nuclear destruction or materialistic overconsumption and earth poisoning. The
naively shining Cities of Tomorrow have deteriorated into a vision of
Blade Runner, wherein a sinister polyglot brainlessness reigns, a sort of
neofeudal brutality in the air. An Italian engineer, Roberto Vacca,
warned in *The Coming Dark Age,* "Our great technological systems of
human organization and association are continuously outgrowing ordered control [and] are now reaching critical dimensions of instability."
The Club of Rome described The Limits of Growth in neo-Malthusian
terms, reaching the dismal conclusion that the earth's resources probably could not support the rates of economic and population growth
much beyond the year 2100. (Later researchers questioned the computer models on which the project was based.)

Yet the report had an effect upon global morale. Like oil spills and
acid rain, the Club of Rome report seemed to be part of the evidence
of a planetary trend. In this uncertain atmosphere, the traditional an-
tagonists, religion and science, edged toward the idea of a truce based
on a concern and reverence for the endangered life of the planet.
Nature ceased to be either a savage force to be conquered (science) or
a lower temporal form, inferior to heaven (religion). Instead the earth
came to seem an innocent and fragile victim of human excess.

The pressures of such anxieties have encouraged in some quarters
an ethic of millenarian asceticism, a New Age impulse to withdraw
from the older promises of the consumer society and its plenitude.
Barkun predicts that the approaching millennium will bring an increasingly skeptical attitude toward gratuitous technology and a
renewed attraction to life in small, self-sufficient rural communities.
People will tend to cultivate spiritual and aesthetic values in opposition
to material gratification. And the emotional view of the future will
swing sharply back and forth, from exultant hope to bitter despair. The
millennium will be the best of times. Or else it will be the worst of
times. An age of unprecedented wonders will begin. Or else all the
planetary debts will come simultaneously and cataclysmically due.

The year 1991 brought the disintegration of the Soviet Union and
with it the effective end—for the moment—of the world's nuclear

nightmares. But still it seemed that the slower-working apocalypses of vanishing ozone and overpopulation and world hunger and AIDS were menacingly clustered around the end of the millennium. Perhaps the world's imagination needs an agenda of dooms, if only to make it focus upon its New Millennium resolutions. So all Four Horsemen seem to be up and riding again, joined possibly by the environmental Fifth.

We say that time will tell. But time is elastic and mysterious and, in its wild, undifferentiated state, uninhabitable by humans. Life needs its days and nights, its waking and sleeping, its seasons, its routines, its appointment books. People organize their lives by drawing lines, segmenting time, measuring their progress—clocking themselves. Time is the organizing principle of conscious human effort. Time may be difficult to understand sometimes, but it is what we have, all we have, the medium in which we swim.

In that lies the meaning of the millennium. Delineated time is history's narrative framework—the way to make sense out of beginnings, middles and ends. Everyone is born, and dies, in the middle of history's larger story. The millennium is a chance (the rarest) to see, or to imagine that we see, the greater human story, filed in the file drawer with a click of completeness. Envisioning the end of one era and the beginning of another somehow infuses life with narrative meaning. And surviving the millennial passage, for those who do, may even have about it a wistful savor of the afterlife.

The Hereweareagain Gaieties

October 24, 1988

> GLENDOWER: I can call spirits from the vasty deep.
> HOTSPUR: Why so can I, or so can any man;
> But will they come when you do call them?
> —SHAKESPEARE, *HENRY IV*, PART I

THAT EXCHANGE WAS ONE OF JOHN KENNEDY'S FAVORITES.
His instruments were sensitive to the bogus. He might find it very
funny that the politicians of 1988 keep trying to summon spirits, no-
tably his own, from the vasty deep of 1960.

Rhetoric comparing 1988 with 1960 has a wistful, if cynical, political
purpose. It attempts to make a live political connection through the increasingly important American sacrament of memory. It wishes to
mobilize nostalgia in order to give glamour and energy to a dismal,
weightless campaign. It is politics as séance.

The real connections between the races of 1960 and 1988 are wispy
to the point of mere coincidence. A youngish Democratic candidate
from Massachusetts (Dukakis, at fifty-four in 1988, is eleven years
older than Kennedy was in 1960) with an older running mate, a senator from Texas, campaigns against a sitting vice president who for eight
years served an aging, popular Republican father figure.

They are surface similarities and no more. But they have an interest
as wishful symbols, and are an index of the changes that have occurred
in America and the world in the past twenty-eight years. The real
meaning of a comparison between the elections of 1960 and 1988 is the
difference that separates them.

The elections of 1960 and 1988 are brackets enclosing a period of
transformation—change that has placed the two campaigns in different eras. In 1960 the candidates for the first time debated on television,

and politics began an almost metaphysical transformation: The external world was miraculously reconvened as images upon America's internal screen. Electrons fetched out of the air poured the circus directly into the living room, into the bloodstream—just as they would inject Vietnam into the center of American consciousness.

The year 1988 represents something close to a dismantling of the American presidential campaign. The candidates perform simulations of encounters with the real world, but the exercise is principally a series of television visuals, of staged events created for TV cameras. The issues have become as weightless as clouds of electrons, and the candidates mere actors in commercials.

Some of the imitations and reincarnations of JFK have had traces of farce. In 1984 Gary Hart, during the primaries, slipped into a bizarre physical impersonation that had him descending the stairs of airplanes with just the gingerly JFK inclination of bad back and his right hand tucked into his jacket pocket, the thumb protruding in the way that Kennedy's always did. The American voter began to think of Madame Tussaud's, or of Elvis impersonators.

Dan Quayle, in his debate with Lloyd Bentsen, was heedless enough to bring up Kennedy's name. Bentsen, who has good reflexes, saw the opening: "Senator, you're no Jack Kennedy." Michael Dukakis has been more dignified, but more relentless, about comparing himself with Kennedy, or at any rate comparing 1960 with 1988. Again and again, from the Democratic Convention on, he has told audiences, "Twenty-eight years ago, another son of Massachusetts and another son of Texas were our nominees." Dukakis wants to borrow a small radiance of analogy. Ted Sorensen, the author of so many of Kennedy's speeches, including the inaugural, is recycling the rhetoric for Dukakis. The Kennedy themes recur in Sorensen's Dukakis: "It's time to get the country moving again." It does not work.

In strange ways, 1960 is sacred in grainy national memory. Americans feel a wistfulness about that election, if only because it was a moment when they and the world were younger. Was the race a classic encounter between two smart and well-matched athletes working the game in its last good moment? Maybe. The drama lingers in images of black and white as a moment of moral sunshine for Americans, or of remembered innocence. The candidates, youngish veterans, connected the American people to the days of their last good war. The election of 1960 was the end of America's postwar political order and the beginning (starting 1,110 days later) of a long, tumbling historical free fall (assassinations, riots, Vietnam, Watergate, oil embargoes, hostages in Iran, the economic rise of the Pacific Rim nations, on and on—glasnost, China) that has created a new world and left America searching for its place therein.

America used to be the New World. Now the world is the New World.

What has happened in the world as a whole between 1960 and 1988, and especially during the 1980s, is analogous to what occurred in the United States in the years after the Civil War, between, say, 1875 and 1900. The railroads spreading west, the telephone, mass manufacture, elevators, a thousand other new items of technology— all transformed America, opened its markets and shortened its distances. The world today is becoming a global society, and a much smaller planet, because of satellites, computers, jet travel, the interpenetrations of world markets, and the fact that Communism has grown cold in its extremities.

The nation is no longer moated—economically, militarily—by the Atlantic and Pacific. As Vietnam instructed, what America touches does not necessarily become sacred—an end of the Wilsonian illusion. America, which once cherished the conviction that God had endowed its national idea, began feeling lost in what might be called the Brownian motions of history—Brownian movement being the term for molecules that fly about with no discernible pattern or reason. The American preeminence in manufacturing is gone.

Many Americans have been retreating to the shrine of national memory. Never have so many anniversaries been observed, so many nostalgias set glowing, as if retrospection were now the only safe and reliable line of sight. You are, among other things, what you remember, or believe you remember. The past has become a persistent presence in the American mind.

Ronald Reagan, a genius at this kind of thing, managed to recrystal-ize the national morale through his evocations of a simple and virtuous small-town America. He performed an optical illusion that was the equivalent of having Mickey Rooney, as Andy Hardy, standing tall in the saddle. That has been one trouble with Reaganistic good feeling: a suspicion that it was based upon camera angle.

The evocations of the election of 1960 are a somewhat more youth-ful play upon the illusion, and more self-serving. Those candidates who have evoked the 1960 election were calling back not a time or place so much as a glamorous man—John Kennedy.

James Joyce had a lovely phrase in *Finnegans Wake:* "The hereweareagain gaieties." A Kennedy campaign always had the hereweareagain gaieties, that Irish quality of politics as frolic, overlaid with a unique elegance and a ruthlessness that advanced upon you with the brightest of teeth. No wonder that in the presidential cam-paign of 1988, Americans feel a nostalgia for the festive in their politics. American politics used to be fun. Once upon a time, lively, funny peo-ple practiced the art. In a priceless line about the 1988 race, Robert Strauss, former Democratic Party chairman and an accomplished hu-morist, said Dukakis reminded him of Cary Grant. Depressingly, Strauss was not, in this case, trying to be funny.

In gloomy moments, one believes that some alchemy of television packaging and American decline in the world has ruined presidential politics and turned it into a dreary and cynical transaction. After eight years of a former actor in the White House, perhaps it is just as well that neither candidate this time behaves remotely like an entertainer. Who ever said that the president of the United States had to be charming?

The example of John Kennedy said so, and the message is implanted in the collective memory.

Chet Atkins, on a stage in the bright sunshine of Jackson, Tennessee, is warming up the crowd. He stands with Pat Boone in front of the Old Country Store in Casey Jones Village, named for the famous train engineer who lived there at the turn of the century. Atkins, the genius of American country guitar, is singing now: "Would Jesus wear a Rolex?"

George Herbert Walker Bush and Dan Quayle materialize on the stage in brilliant early-fall sunshine. Great cheers, but little warmth for Quayle, who walks on like a mistake in the illusion.

"Read my lips!" cries Bush. "No . . . new . . . taxes!" Read my lips. George Bush is ever at odds with language, as if he does not regard it as a reliable vehicle of thought. At his worst moments on the stump, Bush is a sort of amateur terrorist of language, like an eleven-year-old Shi'ite picking up a Kalashnikov assault rifle for the first time and firing off words in wild bursts, blowing out the lamps, sending the relatives diving through the windows. Bush is mostly oblivious to the nuances of language, as if some moral or cultural dyslexia were knotting up the thought (which may explain why he keeps using oafishly wrong expressions like "read my lips" and "kick a little ass"). He seems to regard words as dangerous, potentially treacherous. Odd: It is a tenet of conservative intellectuals that "ideas have consequences." Bush sometimes sounds as if he regards ideas, and words, as an inconvenience and an irritation—perverse, buzzing little demons that need to be brushed away periodically like flies.

Sometimes Bush's speech has a chameleon quality. One day during a tour through central Illinois farmland, Bush and his wife, Barbara, rode in a bus with the country singers Loretta Lynn, Crystal Gayle and Peggy Sue, all sisters. At a stop in the town of Wenona, Bush told the crowd that the three sisters had been giving a country concert in the bus, and "I thought I'd died and gone to heaven." George Bush, out of Kennebunkport and Houston, out of Andover and Yale, had a little mountain twang in his voice when he said it, standing in twill trousers and a cowboy shirt. Loretta Lynn, the coal-miner's daughter out of Butcher's Hollow, Kentucky, told the crowd she loved George Bush "'cuz he's country!"

No, he is not. George Bush is a man who seems to be searching for the country. He sometimes seems to have misplaced America, and to be intently seeking it, trying out different accents, different styles of thought, as if seeking his own authenticity. Or perhaps fleeing it. Bush used to be a moderate Republican. Now, inheriting the Reagan legacy, he is constrained to run as a right-winger. He trumpets right-wing "values"—

and panders unapologetically to the Know-Nothing instincts in the crowd, but one listens to him always with a smudge of doubt: Does he really believe that?

Bush went from patrician Connecticut to the Texas oil fields as a young man; he has gone from moderate Republican to right-wing Republican, from one identity to another, from one appointive office to another, and these transitions seem at last to add up to a sense of permanent motion and quest, of search for something that is finally his own. It is possible, of course, that after so many years, he is closing in upon that something right now, and will discover both America and himself in the most spectacular way.

Bush is a puzzling man. Dukakis, in an equally troubling way, seems an unpuzzling man. Study the way that the two men walk. If the candidates would not disclose themselves in other ways, they would surely express a little of themselves thus.

Dukakis trudges. He is a compact and gravid man, like a wrestler, with feet apart and stance wary, as if afraid of being knocked down. He is a man careful beyond the ordinary standards of prudence. He holds the railing tightly as he descends the stairs from an airplane.

Dukakis's vectors point downward, as if gravity were pressing on him especially hard. Even the words that leave his lips seem to have weights on them. When he says, as he often does in a speech, "My friends," the expression carries a curious gravamen of reproof or irony—but no warmth. His speeches, however, have much of his body's compactness and concision and a certain driving force about them.

One fresh morning on a farm in Idalou, in the flatlands of West Texas, with an ashy-silver half-plate moon in the blue sky, the rally crowd was being warmed up by Texas agriculture commissioner Jim Hightower, a charismatic populist with a talent for comic fulmination. Dan Quayle, said Hightower, is so dumb he "thinks Cheerios are doughnut seeds." And: "If ignorance ever goes to forty dollars a barrel, I want the drilling rights on George Bush's head."

Dukakis, with his weighty, even slightly oppressive air of self-possession and the small eyes that give his large head a somehow sealed look, like a tank turret even without his famous tank, applauded in an odd slow motion and dipped his left shoulder and gave a slow-motion thumbs-up sign, as if to say, "Way to go, Big Guy!" Then he came forward and started to tell the crowd about John Kennedy and Lyndon Johnson, and about how "we can do better" and how 1960 had rolled round again. History, said Dukakis, repeats itself. And at least some of the crowd wanted to bring Hightower back for an encore.

George Bush's vectors fly upward, as if he were about to launch himself. His rangy walk would be a John Wayne saunter, except that he goes on his toes with a springy stride, with profile high and prowing the wind. It is his father's walk, the dark-suited, dignified swagger that one saw in the early 1950s when Prescott Bush of Connecticut crossed the Senate floor. On a dazzling day, the blue sky washed cloudless, George Bush performed such a swagger at the Columbus airport.

An American scene: The candidate came down the front steps of his plane and walked across an agoraphobia of tarmac to a crowd of red-white-and-blue flag-waving, sign-pumping Republicans gathered behind the rope to cheer. In the Kodachrome sunshine, one saw the sharpshooters on the airport roof and the shiny black Secret Service van with black tinted windows, an agent standing on the tailgate with his hand inside a black nylon bag that concealed his automatic weapon. The sunshine itself became sinister and a chill of premonition crossed the mind—the dank American underdream—and in a small spasm of panic, one frisked the faces in the crowd. The sudden foreboding had a specific primal antecedent in time and place and noon sunshine: The nerves were reaching back exactly to the imprint made upon the American mind on November 22, 1963, in Dallas. And as one boards the Dukakis plane in San Francisco, a frisky German shepherd pokes around the luggage, sniffing for high explosives.

The sociologist of religion Emile Durkheim once said that the contrast between the sacred and the profane is the widest and deepest of all contrasts that the human mind can make. In retrospect, in the churchier precincts of the memory, the election of 1960 has, for some, a numinous glow. The election was the prologue to everything that happened after. It was the American politics before the fall. Its protagonists went on to their high, dramatic fates. Perhaps part of the magic of that race is that we know the tale to its dramatic completion.

One man who helped transform that election campaign into instantaneous myth was Theodore H. White. *The Making of the President 1960* was the first of a series. White's description of the 1960 race, as one reads it now, seems an endearing period piece. One cannot conceive of writing such prose now, about the 1988 campaign. White invented the form. He absorbed politics and hymned it in an act of reportage and imagination that was a variation on Walt Whitman. White's descriptions of the 1960 race are bardic, Homeric. Political bosses are "chieftains." The "clashes" between Kennedy and Nixon sound like something that occurred between Achilles and Hector outside the walls of Troy. The premise that gives his narrative its dramatic drive is a broad foundation of certitude about the rightness and preeminence of American power and, therefore, the absolute centrality of the presidential race in the drama of the world. It was then a Ptolemaic universe, revolving around the White House. What higher story to tell? Americans did not then lose wars. Presidents did not get assassinated, or lie, or have to barricade themselves in the White House.

Heraclitus said a man cannot stand in the same river twice, the flow of things being what it is; not only are 1960 and 1988 different rivers, but they run in different courses altogether. It is startling to remember now that Kennedy's Catholicism was the single greatest issue of the campaign and almost unhorsed him in a race he won by less than 120,000 votes. It is a trivia question to ask which two islands off the coast of mainland China received inordinate attention during the second and third television debates between Kennedy and Nixon (Quemoy and Matsu). Both candidates were dedicated to strong national defense. The Soviet Union and the Cold War and the nuclear threat dominated everyone's horizon, with anxieties rising over the U-2 spy plane that the Soviets shot down on May 1, 1960, and the Soviets' launching of Sputnik 1 three years earlier. The rocket that took the satellite aloft punched a hole through American self-confidence and made education a central issue.

In the television debates, the camera was endlessly kind to Kennedy, whose charm passed through the lens and directly into the American consciousness. Nixon fared badly on the camera. It exaggerated the depth of his eye sockets, picked up the sweat on his upper lip and the shadow of his heavy whiskers. Kennedy had the video sense to address the camera and the American people, while Nixon addressed himself to Kennedy, as a prevideo debater would. Some had thought the forty-three-year-old Democrat a depthless rich-boy dreamboat who missed too many votes in the Senate. His only previous executive experience ended with his getting his PT boat sawed in half by a Japanese destroyer. But the first debate established him in the public mind as at least the equal of the two-term vice president.

The professionalism of the media handlers in 1988 invigorates the political process infinitely less than did the emotional intimacy of the 1960 campaign. For all its spooky powers, television rarely achieves any ignitions of the personal in a campaign. Never in the 1988 campaign does one see anything like the public passion that was displayed, for both candidates, during 1960. Kennedy had his "jumpers"—females who forested the parade routes, who swooned and leaped and shrieked. "It was flat-out every day and most of the night, ten or fifteen days at a time without a day off," remembers Ted Sorensen. "Today it feels more like a missile exchange instead of war in the trenches. Kennedy would saturate a state. He'd do ten or fifteen events a day. Now they do two, usually timed carefully to make the evening network news. There aren't many large crowds now. Kennedy would go after the largest possible crowds."

Herb Klein, Nixon's press secretary then, says, "We'd come into a city concentrating on a downtown noon rally. Pierre Salinger [Kennedy's press secretary] and I would compete to get the biggest crowd estimate out of the local police chief. The biggest difference between the two campaigns is that the candidates now are not exposed to the public the way they used to be."

As Arthur Schlesinger Jr. remarks, "Television has replaced the political party." It controls agenda and voter turnout at the polls, two key traditional functions of the party. In the election of 1880, the political parties were so good at motivating voters that 80 percent of them voted, despite two weak candidates—Garfield and Hancock—and no strong issues.

Michael Dukakis's campaign caravan, like a sleek, sinuous dragon, all flashing lights, police outriders, limo, station wagons, Secret Service, staff, two buses for the press, sweeps through Sacramento at eight in the morning, all traffic halted at intersections by leapfrogging police cars with astonishing precision. Not an instant's impedance in the arteries of democracy. The campaign dazzles by to its event and comes to rest at a glistening green public park in the most splendid of California mornings. A soccer field, roped off. Twenty or thirty small boys in their soccer uniforms, their parents and friends on the sidelines. The candidate appears, wearing khakis, red crew-neck sweater and jogging shoes. He saunters in his freighted way across the grass toward the boys, and then, without transition, starts idly toeing a soccer ball toward them, again in that curious slow-motion way he has, his body doing not the act itself but the slo-mo replay. The photographers click away. Dukakis, one thinks, may have made a mistake—in his outfit, with his large head, he looks like Charlie Brown, and something in his almost rueful body English suggests that Lucy is about to snatch the ball away again just as he kicks. Unfair: A reporter remarks, "This is part of Dukakis's relentless search for a constituency shorter than himself." In a few moments it is over. The kids yell in little voices: "Two, four, six, eight, who do we appreciate? Dukakis, Dukakis, yea!" Absolutely nothing has happened. The caravan sweeps away. Next morning, the newspapers carry a picture, sure enough, of Michael Dukakis toeing a soccer ball toward a child.

Or George Bush's long procession of buses pulling off Route 51 in central Illinois one afternoon at 3:30 and sweeping up to the Del Monte canning factory. The press corps (numbering some 120 now) dutifully takes its place not far from enormous piles of corn that are being dumped onto the vast concrete acreage, then pushed by special dozers toward the trench that will catch the corn on conveyer belts and carry it with a kind of clanking *Modern Times* idiot ingenuity up a ramp to be mechanically husked and then borne inside the maw of the factory to its fate. So much corn has an unexpected rich barnyard kind of smell, a cloying excess of smell. Bush appears with his two oldest grandchildren, walks toward a monster mound of corn, and as photographers record the event, he acts like a man waiting for a train on a platform. Loretta Lynn and Crystal Gayle and Peggy Sue appear, dressed in tall spike heels, skintight pedal pushers and Bush T-shirts. On the other side of the factory, for the thousandth time that day, the sisters introduce Bush by singing "Coal Miner's Daughter," "Amazing Grace," "The Man from Galilee," and "I Saw the Light." The crowds all day, surprised to find someone really famous among them, give the singers squeals of delight and that sudden sharp liveliness of the eyes, the predatory gladness, that announces recognition of a celebrity. Loretta Lynn!

The novelist John Gardner once wrote a version of Beowulf that was told from Grendel's point of view. There is a scene in which a wandering bard arrives among the drunken cretins and begins to sing beautiful songs to them about what they have accomplished that day in battle. Atrocity becomes glory, bloodletting becomes heroic. It is a shrewd point about mythmaking, and perhaps about the making of the myth of Camelot.

But there is, more and more, a countervailing mood of antimyth that may also be one of the insoluble dilemmas of American politics. What able man or woman is willing to submit to the inquisitions of the press into private lives, into any previous lives they might have led? Would John Kennedy have survived in the politics of 1960 if his extracurricular adventures had been investigated?

White's book about 1960 is in some ways a hymn and a poem not only to American democracy but to the American landscape and American people, to their varieties and resonances. White's writing then strikes a heroic note that sounds odd to the American ear now. But perhaps a sense of eloquence and size has passed out of history's favor.

A presidential campaign is still a fascinating trajectory, over time and vast landscape. In the very American way, it is a moral itinerary, an idea proceeding across both biographies and territories.

Now the candidate's chartered plane fires back across the continent against the direction of old westering tracks thirty thousand feet below. Inside the plane, the clerisy of "spin," that is, the priesthood of partisans sent around to see reporters after major campaign events and impart the right spin, have done their work up and down the aisles, like Polonius and Hamlet discussing the shapes of clouds. The candidate is dozing up front. The jackals of the press have settled into their routines of mild carousal.

The jackals haven't the barnacled, bad-liver look of some who covered the 1960 campaign. They don't, like Teddy White, smoke unfiltered cigarettes, or filtered either. They play poker sometimes, or blackjack, and one throwback even asks for a Jack Daniels. A group clusters around the seats behind and plays a game of Jeopardy on a laptop computer—in answer to which the candidate's press staff, quite justly, chants in rallentando: "Boring, boring, BORING!" The journalists all have toys White never imagined—cellular telephones, laptops, tiny portable television sets, all the magic paraphernalia connecting them to the New World that America has entered.

Still, it is the old America, too. The plane drops into cold drizzle at Green Bay, and there awaits a crowd that would have been no different from the people Kennedy or Nixon might have descended to visit. The band, a little forlorn in the night, is drums, electronic keyboard piano and electric guitar, and it sounds like a Milwaukee roadhouse on a Saturday night. It plays "Happy Days Are Here Again." The scene is fervent and lonely.

Then the plane vacuums up the particles again, and again sails east. American landscapes are so resonant—the sere wrinklings of Nevada mountains that hold the topaz lake, the Badlands, the great agricultural geometries of the Midwest, the stretch of Georgia that Sherman blackened. We fly now steady east, against the time zones, into darkness. At last Boston, below, slides toward us like Christmas, strings of light on velvet. How festive American cities look from the air at night.

Chicago, 1968

August 26, 1996

Outside the Hilton, at the corner of Michigan Avenue and Balbo Drive, I stood talking to Winston Spencer Churchill. Churchill was kicking around the world as a correspondent. I noticed he liked to watch the reaction when he stuck out his hand and said, "Hullo, I'm Winston Churchill." For he resembled his grandfather's pictures taken when that young Winston covered the Boer War at the turn of the century—boyish and freckled, greedy for trouble. Now, behind the police lines, Churchill and I chatted with a guilty, voyeur's air, as if awaiting some illegal sporting event—a cockfight or a sloppily organized human sacrifice.

It was early evening on Wednesday, just after seven. Even on the lakefront, the air stank. The tear gas dispensed by one side and the stink bombs set off by the other lingered in mouth and throat. Across the scene (phalanxes of blue-helmeted cops, battle jeeps with barbed wire like mustaches across their grilles, the guerrilla-idealist young in tantrum, their faces contorted with rage) there swept not only rhythmic waves of sound ("Hey, Hey, LBJ, how many kids did you kill today?") but an amazing satanic smell, a yippie genius's brew that simulated vomit, decomposing flesh, death, cloaca and kindred flavors. It was what evil would smell like if it were available in an aerosol can— bad enough to make the South Side stockyards, next door to the convention, smell almost wholesome. This exotic moral stink had drifted halfway around the world, after all, from Vietnam.

In front of the Hilton, on Michigan Avenue, two sides of America ground against each other like tectonic plates. Each side cartooned and ridiculed the other so brutally that by now the two seemed to belong almost to different species. The 1960s had a genius for excess and caricature. On one side, the love-it-or-leave-it, proud, Middle

American, Okie-from-Muskogee, traditionalist nation of squares who supported the Cold War assumptions that took Lyndon Johnson ever deeper into Vietnam. On the other side, the "countercultural" young, either flower children or revolutionaries, and their fellow-traveling adult allies in the antiwar movement, the Eugene McCarthy uprising against LBJ, people whose hatred of the war in Vietnam led them into ever greater alienation from American society and its figures of authority.

Mayor Richard Daley's frontline forces in Chicago must have been chosen for immovable heft, men built like trucks. Now they silently palm-smacked their clubs, their eyes as narrow as the slits in an armored car. Most of the convention delegates and dignitaries quartered in the fortress Hilton were at the moment three miles away at the convention hall, preparing to bestow upon poor Hubert Humphrey the nomination he thought would redeem the years of humiliation and corrupting self-abasement he had endured as Johnson's vice president.

The police needed to protect the Hilton nonetheless. It housed not only delegates and candidates but also the country's besieged political process, its apparently crumbling legitimacy. Recollect the famous sequence at the front end of 1968, that bizarre and violent year:

1. The war that America was fighting for inaccessible reasons in an obscure little Southeast Asian country seemed to blow up in America's face with the communists' Tet offensive in late January.
2. Minnesota's Democratic senator, Eugene McCarthy, challenged his president, Lyndon Johnson, in the New Hampshire primary and won 42.4 percent of the Democratic vote. Seeing that, Robert Kennedy hurried into the race.
3. LBJ withdrew as a candidate for reelection.
4. Martin Luther King Jr. was assassinated, a murder that precipitated days of riots in cities across the country.
5. Robert Kennedy was killed in Los Angeles in early June.

And so on. It is a part of the folklore, each act more amazing than the one before, a dark jack-in-the-box of history. On Tuesday night of the Democratic Convention week, the Soviets invaded Czechoslovakia and eradicated the Prague Spring.

Now there was silence on the cops' side of the barricades—an ominous, hurricane stillness. On the other side: the dirty, skinny, red-eyed, hyper, unslept, screaming, antiwar young, their youthful energy converted to electrical fury. Rage shot out of them like sparks, like flaming snakes. No flowers in their hair now. The foresighted wore football helmets.

Then the cops charged. They moved with surprising speed and a nimble fury like that of a rhinoceros attacking. A flying wedge of blue drove down Balbo into the noisy, ragged flesh on Michigan. The cops bent to their work, avengers at harvest time, chop-swinging clubs with methodical ferocity, a burst-boil rage. And in the midst of it, I began to detect a certain professional satisfaction of the kind a hitter feels sometimes. The cops had found a ghastly sweet spot. The sound that a club makes when it strikes a human skull—in earnest—awakens in the hearer a sickened, fearful amazement. No kidding now: a thunk! resonant through the skull and its wet package of thought and immortal soul.

It dawned on me that I was now an animal as much in season as the protesters, for the blue rhino was wheeling back, flailing through the bloodied crowd. I skittered into the Hilton lobby. A cop lumbered after me with club upraised and aimed at my skull just above the left ear. I held up my press credentials like a ridiculous little magic shield, like a clove of garlic or the sign of the cross, and the cop went into freeze-frame and thought about the matter long and hard before at last he lowered his club, a flicker of disappointment in his eye, and moved on to hunt for other game deeper in the lobby.

The cops outside went on banging heads almost indiscriminately. Middle-aged bystanders were as likely to be bloodied as young radicals. People were dragged feetfirst, heads bouncing on pavement, to paddy wagons and hurled in.

The demonstrators knew their McLuhan and chanted, "The whole world is watching." After a delay caused by strikes that prevented live transmission, the television networks finally broadcast the footage of what a national commission would later call a police riot. Uncle Walter

Cronkite was visibly furious. Tom Wicker would write in the *New York Times,* "Those were our children in the streets, and the Chicago police beat them up."

The bashing on Michigan Avenue was only one of a series that week. In the last, just before dawn on Friday after the convention adjourned, the police permitted themselves to go berserk in the halls of the Hilton, rousting sleeping McCarthy workers from their rooms and beating on their skulls. Police claimed the workers had been throwing things (beer cans, ashtrays, bags of excrement) down on cops from the windows above.

The 1968 Democratic Convention was part of the ur-mess of the 1960s and in a sense the big bang of the American culture wars. And here we are now: More or less the same two tectonic plates are still grinding against each other in America. Their surfaces may be a little smoother now.

Before Johnson fell for the tar baby of Vietnam, Americans believed their presidents almost always told them the truth. The level of trust and therefore respect for authority was probably foolishly high. All of that changed in the fatal asininity of Vietnam. The baby boomers' rites of passage turned into a huge Oedipal overtoppling of authority, an assault on Dad that was disorientingly successful.

It takes years for all the myth and trauma to work through the system. Maybe they have done so only this summer of 1996, after twenty-eight years have passed and the Democrats feel free, as adults now, leaders of the party, to return to the old slaughterhouse. This year the Democrats have conducted a lottery for groups that want to hold protests at their convention.

After the police charged on Michigan Avenue, I lost track of Churchill and did not see him again at the convention. Chicago that week was crawling with famous names, including an unusual number of literary celebrities, all bent on getting high on a snort of antiestablishment danger and writing about it—Norman Mailer, Jean Genet, William Burroughs, Allen Ginsburg, the last of whom went about dispensing his Buddhist "oms" through the tear gas. Next week the Chicago convention may run more to Hollywood celebrities. None will be teargassed.

ELEPHANT LAKE

August 23, 2001

JUST AT SUNSET, A BRIGHT THREE-QUARTER MOON COMES UP IN the south, pillowed in golden clouds. The wind blows from the north now, cool and steady across central Ontario after days of unnaturally warm and humid air transplanted from the Gulf of Mexico and days of hot haze and Turneresque fog that would go electrical late every afternoon in brilliant, theatrical thunderstorms.

The new wind is clean, and whips the lake to a brisk chop, the water lively, with a metallic sheen. Canadian order has been restored.

The loons are numerous this year, and in fine voice. The silence as we fish, casting over a weed bed, is broken now and then by the quavering and slightly hysterical cries that make up loon conversation; they remind me, in this key, of Mrs. Mead, the doctor's dithering wife in *Gone with the Wind*. The loons' other mode of talk is their famous lonely alto wail, which has something of the wolf on the tundra in it. A Jack London note.

But the loons seem remarkably sociable this August, gathering in groups of up to seven in midlake, so relaxed that they tolerate a boat's approach to within five yards or so, at which distance they do their magic trick of vanishing beneath the surface and popping up long seconds later in some other quarter of the lake. Sleight-of-loon.

We give up casting and troll. As the sun disappears over the ridge, the judge abruptly stands up in the boat and wrestles a strong, invisible something that churns up the water just astern, stripping line from the reel whose drag the judge has set generously loose. The muskie, having had enough of this indignity and thinking to settle the matter, jumps spectacularly, his whole body three feet out of the water, writhing in a three-and-a-half gainer, hitting the water again bent nearly head to tail in a fiercely muscular C-shape—a lovely jump.

Minutes pass. I have reeled in my line and stand by with the net. The judge, a muskie fisherman of many years' experience, has played the fish smoothly to the side of the boat. We see the muskie prowling caged-tiger circles in the water two feet down. I dip the big net to the water. The fish is about thirty-eight inches long, and plump as a banker—no monster but a respectable keeper, if we cared to keep him (which we don't).

But now, quite casually, as if he has decided the game has gone far enough, the muskie gives his head an expert shake and tosses the hook and flashes away into the green, weedy dusk of Elephant Lake.

Ah, well. He has saved us the trouble of leaning like fish dentists into his big prehistoric mouth to extract the hook, which is my least favorite part of fishing. (Sometimes the hook is halfway down the gullet and you have to use pliers, wrenching and pulling inside the mouth of a thrashing, gasping fish as the seconds tick away and you worry you are going to kill the creature though it was not your intention. Then, the hook finally out, you set the dying fish back in the water and move him back and forth to get the gills going again and wait until, as usually happens, he recovers his senses, like a prizefighter after a knockout, and makes off blearily through the water, promising himself to be more careful in the future about impulsive gobbling.)

This is the private news from Elephant Lake, where the judge, my father-in-law, has been coming to fish for muskie every summer for forty-three years and where I have joined him for the last nine summers or so.

I got a great northern pike last night—well, not great but respectable. When you are fishing for muskie, a northern seems an anticlimax, though better than nothing. Trouble is that a northern is a defeatist and gives up after a few seconds of brave combat. I also got a muskie on the line, but like the judge's fish, he threw the hook just before I boated him.

Under the dock here at Elephant Lake Lodge, there dwells a kind of house muskie that has opted for the soft life. Kids fishing for sunfish off the dock are shocked out of their wits from time to time: Just as they are landing a sunfish, the muskie flashes up—like *Jaws*—and snatches it off their hook. The kids either think this is neat, or else they go pale and vow never to go near the water again.

The house muskie has been caught several times; he figures, I suppose, that this is the cost of doing business.

E. B. White wrote a famous essay called "Once More to the Lake," about a father taking his young boy in the summer to go fishing in the same changeless lake where the father had gone when he was a boy. The essay has a sweet sense of stopped time. I thought of it last night when we met a lawyer from Toronto who sat in the dining room of the lodge with his son, a boy of nine or ten; the lawyer had gone to camp at a place nearby on Baptiste Lake thirty years ago and was bringing his son to see the camp and to do some fishing hereabouts. We told the boy about the house muskie, and today the boy spent hours on the dock trying to conjure him up. He wanted to see the muskie come up from the depths like Jaws. But the fish, perversely shy for the moment, did not materialize.

PART TWO

---ᘯᘯᘯ---

People

Chuck Jones,
Physicist and Philosopher

March 6, 2000

THE GAUDY FUSS EVERYONE MADE OVER THE MILLENNIUM MAY have obscured the real significance of the year 2000: It marked the fiftieth anniversary of the debut of the Coyote and Roadrunner. As such, 2000 represented a milestone in the career of the greatest living American, Chuck Jones.

Progenitor of Wile E. Coyote, the Roadrunner, Bugs Bunny, Daffy Duck, Elmer Fudd and the rest, the great animator has turned eighty-seven and remains (or so he claims) devastatingly attractive to women.

That the Nobel Prize committee has overlooked Chuck Jones tells us what we need to know about the stolidity of the Scandinavian mind. There is no Nobel Prize for comedy. (If there were, Chuck would have won it four or five times.) That being so, I propose Chuck Jones for the Nobel Prize in physics, on the basis of his pioneering formulation of the Coyote-Roadrunner Dynamic, illustrated, for example, when Coyote sets in motion giant boulder A, which whistlingly descends into a canyon to strike seesaw lever B, catapulting giant boulder C into orbit . . . and so on. "Pure mass moving, for perhaps the first time, in pure space," according to another animator, Don Graham. Chuck Jones's work is a bridge that carries Isaac Newton across into chaos theory. Or how about Chuck's discovery of "Illudium Phosdex, the shaving cream atom"? How about his miraculous reduction of Wagner's fourteen-hour *Ring of the Nibelung* to the six-minute "What's Opera, Doc?" during which Elmer Fudd, as Siegfried, sings to Bugs-in-blond-pigtail-drag: "Oh, Bwoonhilduh, you're so wovewy!"? How about "One Froggy Evening," in which Michigan J. Frog leaps out of a building's cornerstone singing "The Michigan Rag"? If that is not Nobel material, none exists.

The first time I met Chuck Jones, at a reception in the early 1990s, I saw a slender, dandyish man standing with his head cocked and his weight reared back on his right heel, in a quizzical posture that reminded me, unmistakably, of . . . Bugs! Replace Chuck's glass with a carrot, and behold—"Eh, what's up, Doc?" Chuck had about him an air of the raffishly boyish and the richly amused. If he's in the mood, he can ratchet things up to trickster-as-philosopher. But you have to buy him lunch for that.

Some friends and I formed Chester A. Arthur Post Number One of the Chuck Jones Fan Club of America, meeting sporadically at a round table in a New York restaurant under the gavel of Post Commander Stefan Kanfer, author of, among other books, a fine biography of Groucho Marx.

Visiting from California, Chuck condescends to appear from time to time at these luncheons, usually with his wife, Marian, who, as I told Chuck once, is much too good for him. At the last lunch, a film crew recorded the occasion for a Columbia Artists Management documentary about Chuck, featuring Robin Williams and Whoopi Goldberg.

Chuck reminisced and clowned a little and doodled his famous creations on cloth napkins that the rest of us snapped up and preserved like religious relics. Chuck is an anthology of quotes from his hero Mark Twain. His mind is stocked with oddments, like the line from the artist Grant Wood: "All the good ideas I ever had came to me while I was milking a cow."

Chuck has codified what he has learned. His rules, in shortened form:

- Love what you caricature.
- Respect the impulsive thought and try to implement it.
- Character is all that matters.
- Timing is the essence.

Chuck says that "the most important and stunning discovery I made at art school was the ability to live by the single line . . . no shading, no multiple lines, no cross-hatching, no subterfuge. Just that line."

His one-liners have hilarious clarity. He first thought of the Coyote as "a sort of dissolute collie." Or: "It is easier and more believable to humanize animals than it is to humanize humans."

Chuck is an authentic American genius, and the line of his life, I think, has been beautifully drawn.

Don't Spit in the Fire

February 21, 2000

When George Washington was a boy, he copied out 110 "Rules of Civility and Decent Behavior" from a sixteenth-century training manual prepared by French Jesuits for young noblemen. The rules still make sense.

Rule 9, for example, instructs: "Spit not in the fire." Rule 13 counsels us: "Kill no vermin [such] as fleas, lice, ticks, etc., in the sight of others. If you see filth or thick spittle, put your foot dexterously upon it. If it be upon the clothes of your companion, put it off privately. . . . "

Other rules, less colorful, offer good social and political advice.

Rule 1: "Every action done in company ought to be with some sign of respect to those that are present."

Rule 17: "Be no flatterer."

Washington's program covered negative political campaigning as well. Rule 49: "Use no reproachful language against anyone; neither curse nor revile."

Washington constructed his formidable character upon these rules, which he observed for all his life. This year's campaign is said to be about character, not issues. Of course, Washington could afford to be high-minded about negative campaigning. He did not want the presidency. He got it by unanimous vote of the electoral college. Hamilton and Jefferson, founders of the two-party system, were the first two great negative campaigners.

Jefferson presents himself as "the quiet, modest retiring philosopher," Hamilton said sarcastically as he warmed up in 1792. It's time Jefferson were exposed as "the intriguing incendiary" that he really is. Sixty-eight years later, Abraham Lincoln's opponents had him down as a backwoods baboon.

Negative campaigning enjoyed periods of folkloric charm. In an election campaign a couple generations ago, North Carolina's Senator Robert Rice Reynolds denounced his opponent for his alleged habit of eating caviar.

"You know what caviar is?" Reynolds would ask, with a squinty and meaningful eye. In a paroxysm of disgust and incredulity, he would answer his own question: "Why, it's fish eggs! Fish eggs from Red Russia!"

Reynolds told the backcountry crowds that his opponent had once sunk so low as go up to Harvard (pronounced HAW-vud). What did the man do there? Why, he "matriculated"! And, worse, he became "a thespian"! Imagine.

Naturally, Reynolds won the race.

In an age of unrelenting saturation television, however, an all-negative campaign hisses like an infestation of snakes, tongues flicking from the television set, voices coiling and insinuating the darkest evils.

Unfortunately, our remedy for negative campaigning has landed us in a state of did-so-did-not prissiness that is tiresome and occasionally hilarious. Politics as nyaaah-nyaah-nya-nyaaah-nyaaah. Thus does virtuousness make us nostalgic for sin.

All the negatives this time are about whether the other candidate went negative. In his "concession" speech in South Carolina on Saturday night, John McCain fired off a few rounds at George W. Bush, and the Sunday morning commentariat went tsk-tsk-tsk about the negativity.

It has become part of the script to treat negative campaigning as a political offense equivalent to murdering your father and marrying your mother. But the crimes cited—marginally misstating the other candidate's record on Social Security or health care, or comparing him to the current president (what savagery, what outrage!)—are so bathetic that the grand, ignoble tradition of mudslinging is trivialized. The political pendulum swings between viciousness and childishness—between tattling and spitting in the fire.

KATHARINE GRAHAM

July 19, 2001

THE PUBLIC KATHARINE GRAHAM WAS BORN, AT THE AGE OF forty-six, out of a catastrophe—the suicide in 1963 of her brilliant and unstable husband Philip, a manic depressive who was publisher of the *Washington Post.*

That sudden, involuntary propulsion into public life and, in a modest way, into history gave to Kay Graham's story a mythological quality. She was a privileged nonentity—a mother and housewife, with all the meanings, and demeanings, that that ruffly serfdom suggested in 1963. She rose to the occasion. She became an exemplary woman in power in a way that was all the more persuasive because she was without feminist ideology. Her life was the story itself, the action, not the commentary.

Harry Truman came blinking onstage in somewhat the same way in April 1945, when Franklin Roosevelt died in Warm Springs, Georgia. The obscure vice president from Missouri was called to the White House from his bourbon-and-water in Sam Rayburn's hideaway in the Capitol, just as Kay Graham was called from her children and domestic routine. Truman said he felt as if the sun, the moon and all the planets had fallen on him. Kay Graham did not exactly enjoy the moment, either.

Truman became the common man as unexpected force, a marvel of feisty and principled adequacies, and much tougher than the smug suits thought. Substitute "woman" for "common man," and you have Kay Graham. Low expectations at the start lead on to a handsome kind of vindication.

I don't mean to compare Truman and Graham otherwise. Of course the personalities were different (Truman crisply combative, Graham rather shy, for example). And Kay Graham did not become president of the United States. She just took over a newspaper, and, at that time, not a great one, either. She (with Ben Bradlee and others) made it great. She presided, at crucial moments, over a radical transformation of American journalism and its relationship to government and power. The publication of the Pentagon papers in 1971 and the Woodward-Bernstein investigation of Watergate starting a year later were acts of gambler's courage and historic significance.

Katharine Graham represented the virtues of the best Washington, a certain homeliness—sophisticated, but likeably homely all the same, as Washington once was: an atmosphere that implied power allied to decency and intelligence and real guts. She was part of the best of the permanent government, the part that stays in town as administrations come and go.

The worst part of that permanent Washington is mere slick K Street venality—unelected money catering a hog's buffet. The best of the tenured Washingtonians, represented by Kay Graham at the top of her game, joined good human instincts with intelligent principle, and a certain thoughtful unfoolability about people (Richard Nixon, for example . . .).

What I liked about Kay Graham was the continuity she carried with her, and the honest human touch evident in her autobiography. She was born the same year as my father, who was for many years a Washington reporter and editor, and I always felt in Kay Graham a re-assuring connection to his generation, to an older Washington, to people who had some of the seasoning of big history (depression, World War II). Of course the old Washington could be vividly brainless and fraudulent and god-awful, too. Kay Graham seemed to me a very good judge of men in power. She brought a large sense of occasion to problems like the Pentagon papers and Watergate, which were her most dangerous and finest moments.

THE DEATH OF DANIEL PEARL

March 4, 2002

Ask a roomful of fledgling journalists if they would be "willing to die for the truth," and not a hand will be raised; they do not mean no, exactly. They simply give the hypothesis a pocket veto. They think, for one thing, that the question is too darkly phrased, and even implies an obscure promise of martyrdom—and martyrdom is not normally the journalist's line of work.

Ask the young roomful, instead, whether they would be "willing to risk your lives to cover extreme situations in faraway places and report the truth," and the best in the room will get a gleam in their eyes—an ignition of curiosity and romance and professional aspiration, even a trench coat wanderlust, as if their minds were flickering in black and white for a moment, a few frames of 1930s movies.

Daniel Pearl, I gather, had the gleam. A sheer avidity to know things is the most endearing trait of any journalist. Long ago, the novelist John Hersey wrote in a sketch of Henry Luce: "He was amazed and delighted to learn whatever he had not known before." Curiosity is the noblest form of intellectual energy; in any case, your mind goes nowhere without it—except maybe to fanaticism.

For the polar opposite of Daniel Pearl's intellectual curiosity was the sort of dogmatism that took his life. An ideologue with a closed mind killed a splendid young man with an open mind. Not the first time that the desire to know has been murdered by the need not to know. Half the world belongs to candle-snuffers—to people who have no curiosity to find out, so to speak, how to take off or land.

Journalists are not often idealized or romanticized these days. Rather the reverse. Journalists' poll numbers are low. They have a corrupted image of lowest-common-denominator tabloid sensationalism, of superficiality and bias. Commentators, left and right, howl dogmatisms. Some of them take fat fees from companies like Enron in exchange for a few hogsheads of bloviation.

But there should still be enormous respect and affection for the curiosity that you find in the eyes of real journalists, people like Daniel Pearl—not the mere entertainers and careerists, but the intelligent ones who ask questions and respect facts.

Journalists are a varied assortment, of course—some of them as shabby, venal or self-important as the cast of Evelyn Waugh's *Scoop*, the 1930s novel that is still, I suppose, the most hilarious depiction of foreign correspondents and their publishers in the grip of a vigorous incomprehension of just about everything. (John Boot, who writes a nature column, "Lush Places," for a British newspaper called *The Beast*—composing sentences like, "Feather-footed through the plashy fen passes the questing vole"—is recruited by mistake to join a collection of journalistic mountebanks and hacks in covering coup and countercoup in the fictional African land of Ishmailia.) Much has changed in journalism since Waugh wrote, but no one who knows the current corps of foreign correspondents would fail to recognize a few types from *Scoop*.

Still, I think I would rather have dinner—in Belgrade or Islamabad or Jerusalem—with people like Daniel Pearl than with either the faculty of Harvard University or the first one hundred names in the Boston telephone book. Why? It's their true journalists' knowledgeable, companionable talk, the stories that their curiosity has unearthed and accumulated—their confidence that the world is a fascinating place, and that journalism, though it may sometimes be wrongheaded or squalid, is also critically important, and, quite often, a huge amount of fun. Correspondents like Pearl are the true students of the world's diversity (as opposed to narrow-gauge group-identity ideologues at home, each crowd sitting at its own table in the cafeteria and glaring at the others through a haze of grievance).

It's fun, but also dangerous work. Journalists are sometimes naive about their own safety—prone to an illusion that they are either bulletproof or invisible. In the mid-1960s, I walked blithely through the mobs during a riot in Harlem, with Molotov cocktails sailing off the roofs of apartment houses; I imagined that as a journalist, I was merely an invisible witness, as harmless as a recording secretary, as if I had letters of transit allowing me to pass between cops and rioters completely without consequence. The rioters left me alone, but only because, with my blue eyes and flopping forelock of light-brown hair, they thought, in the half-light, that I was Bobby Kennedy. . . . Otherwise, why would a white man be dumb enough to wander around like that in the middle of a riot in Harlem? So, like a jerk, I walked as a god among them for a little while.

Daniel Pearl, it is said, did not take stupid chances. But the world, as we see, sometimes has horrible surprises.

Hedley Donovan Ascends to the Forty-Sixth Floor

March 5, 2004

In the earliest days of trains, someone advanced the theory that traveling at such a high rate of speed (15 or 20 mph) would cause the passengers to go insane.

I subscribe to a similar theory about the velocity of information in the early twenty-first century—that the breakneck speed of data, news, ideas, causes each individual item to become a mere blur as it fires by, unassimilated, unexamined, a fast-forward gibberish, the Doppler effect of maddening media. The speed and quantity of fragmented information overloads the intellectual and emotional faculties of absorption. We adapt, of course, as we adapted to trains and later to planes, but I have a lingering suspicion that the original theory about insanity and trains may have been right, and that we have been getting crazier ever since we laid the first tracks, though it may be part of our dementia not to recognize it.

The human brain, it may be, was made to grope its way—or anyway to amble along at a seemly pace, carrying a walking stick, taking in the sights and digesting them before moving on.

This line of thought leads me around—by certain weedy back roads of memory—to the singular intellectual metabolism of Hedley Donovan.

Hedley was the editor in chief of Time Inc. for some years after Henry R. Luce stepped down in 1965. Hedley had Gravitas. Hedley had Probity. The words were invented for him. Hedley had a large, impressive head, like a boulder with brains, and intelligent eyes the color of clear, gray ice, like remnants of the glaciers that once covered his native Minnesota. He seemed to have a glacial metabolism. His most attractive quality was an imperturbable stillness.

Hedley was famous for his silences. He could abruptly go as silent as the tundra. To call them pregnant silences would be wrong; they were evolutionary silences. While he thought something over, it was protocol among his underlings not to speak, but rather, to sit in mute expectation around the long luncheon table in a private dining room on the forty-sixth floor of the Time-Life Building in New York, where he would be seated on a Friday with managing editors and writers from all the Time Inc. magazines (*Time, Life, Fortune, Sports Illustrated, People, Money,* and so on). Hedley's brain, marinated in the large tub of vodka martini set before him (of which he would drink three and possibly four during the lunch, to no apparent drunkening effect), probed the matter at hand, at a sort of . . . *Darwinian* pace, his thought, so to speak, emerging from the sea, from the primordial slime, and making its way slowly and awkwardly up the mental beach until it arrived at the tree line . . . and pausing there for an eon . . . betimes would begin another painful ascent, up the trunk toward the higher branches, where, having attained such altitude, Hedley's thought would painfully grow feathers and at last flap its wings in the form of words. Hedley would speak.

Heavy words upon the heavy air . . . sonorous words . . . judicious words . . . widely spaced for dramatic emphasis, and rumbling forth from Hedley with deep resonance, as from an echoing chamber at the center of the earth, or as if (to relocate to a different perspective) God were Br'er Bear sitting at the top of Rockefeller Center, pronouncing *de haut en bas.*

I was sometimes one of the writers sitting around the table, and I intend this satire in a friendly way. Hedley, who died in 1990, was usually right about things. I liked him immensely. He had a large and decent mind, well informed by experience, and was, I thought, the best kind of American—fair, compassionate, careful, and generous. He could be fooled, but he did not stay fooled. He possessed some of Henry Luce's best qualities—an immense curiosity organized by a strong moral faculty. Hedley had an admirable, likable, honorable sense of responsibility—his own and his country's, and his magazines'.

Hedley's ponderous, judicious intelligence presided over the large and important print media empire that Luce founded. I wonder about the lightning-quick electronic information metabolism of the early twenty-first century—the rapid-response atmosphere in which bloggers, for example, operate. I am trying to decide which atmosphere I prefer, and which metabolism best serves the long-term interests of sanity.

There is something to be said for Hedley's way.

His ponderous thought processes could make him sound like a horse's ass sometimes. A lot of people thought the entire hierarchical, patriarchal Luce empire was a horse's ass. But consider the alternative, as the late *Life* magazine used to say in its advertisements. A *Time* correspondent once described to me a cocktail party in London at which Hedley, with his formidable stillness, was surrounded by a dozen fast-talking and furiously articulate Oxbridge types, yipping and yapping and fluting ever so wittily, one-upping one another. As they capered and parried and thrust, they would steal disconcerted glances at the American Br'er Bear, who was magnificently, inscrutably unimpressed. My kind of guy.

It is possibly a generational preference. Hedley spoke with the earned authority of a decent white American male of his time who had passed through the Depression and World War II. To call it "the Greatest Generation" is to overstate things, but it deserved respect and its mind was, in my view, often more interesting, humane, and seasoned than the sort of Americans we got later. On the other hand, "Tail Gunner Joe" McCarthy was also part of the Greatest Generation.

Sanity is relative, as speed is relative. Now I take the Acela when I want to slow down.

Isaac Newton

December 31, 1999

Standing in an unstable universe where distances contract and clocks slow down, and time and space are plastic, Albert Einstein cast a wistful backward glance at Isaac Newton. "Fortunate Newton, happy childhood of science!" Einstein wrote. "Nature to him was an open book, whose letters he could read without effort."

A child's first tasks are to walk and talk and understand his little universe. Newton, the seventeenth century's formidable prodigy, simply enlarged the project. The first of his family of Lincolnshire yeomen to be able to write his name, Newton grew into a touchy, passionately focused introvert who could go without sleep for days and live on bread and wine, and, at an astonishingly precocious age, absorbed everything important that was known to science up to that time—the works of Aristotle and, after that, the new men who superseded him: Copernicus, Kepler, Descartes and Galileo (Galileo died in 1642, the year Newton was born). Riding on the shoulders of giants—and correcting the giants where they went wrong—Newton began assembling and perfecting the Newtonian universe, a miraculously predictable and rational clockwork creation held together by his universal gravitation and regulated by his elegant laws of motion.

Amazingly, the bulk of Newton's formative thought was accomplished at twenty-three and twenty-four, while he was rusticated to Lincolnshire by the Great Plague, which shut down Cambridge University several months at a time from 1665 to 1667. Newton lived to be eighty-four. Before he was done, his comprehensive intelligence—with which he seemed to have thought and tinkered his way into the very mind of God—had set off not one but four scientific revolutions—in mathematics (he invented calculus, as did Leibniz in Germany, independent of Newton), in optics (he invented the reflecting telescope, and his experiments with spectra established the nature of color and the heterogeneous components of sunlight), in mechanics (his three laws of motion changed the world) and with his understanding of gravity. The last explained the phenomena of heaven and earth in a single mathematical system—or did until Einstein arrived.

Newton imagined and proved a rational universe; he in effect re-designed the human mind. Newton gave it not only intellectual tools undreamed of before, but with them, unprecedented self-confidence and ambition. If Shakespeare incomparably enlarged humanity's conception of itself, Newton—working later, in the turmoil of the English civil war and Restoration—set in place those cooler universals that were the premise of the eighteenth century's Age of Reason and the dynamic of the nineteenth century's age of revolutions—industrial, political and social.

In a sense, all the change that shaped the world until the onset of modernity had its origins in Newton's mind. For what he showed was this: The universe is knowable and governed by universal laws—therefore predictable, therefore perfectible by human reason and will. Go beyond science to politics and society: If all bodies, great and small, are subject to the same universal laws, the idea leads on to democracy (equality of all humans, great and small) and the principle of universal justice. Newton's laws ousted older preferments of feudal hierarchy and magic (though Newton himself devoted frustrated years to the study of alchemy) and installed the authority of the inquiring human mind.

In a way, Newton's was the greatest magic of all: the thought (owing something to alchemy) that for all phenomena of nature and society, there must be not only a discoverable secret but a generalization with the force of law—a solution to every problem, scientific, social or moral.

We live in the consequences of that immense ambition; we have seen its results, both splendid and ghastly (space exploration, Marxist utopias). If religion taught faith and the mystery of the Causeless Cause (the ultimate secret, God), Newtonianism located human intelligence in a cosmos of magnificently impassive reciprocities, celestial mechanics working by God's infinitely reliable and predictable cause and effect. Perhaps Newton merely codified what we intuitively knew (equal and opposite reactions, for example). As Einstein said, "The conceptions which he used to reduce the material of experience to order seemed to flow spontaneously from experience itself, from the beautiful experiments which he ranged in order like playthings."

The Newtonian heritage to us, in any case, is pervasive. W. H. Auden wrote in 1939:

> *I and the world know*
> *what every schoolboy learns.*
> *Those to whom evil is done*
> *do evil in return.*

What is that but Newton's third law of motion? Einstein's image of Newton as a child occurred, oddly enough, to Newton himself. Maybe that's where Einstein got it. Just before he died, Newton remarked, "I do not know what I may appear to the world; but to myself, I seem to have been only like a boy, playing on the seashore, and diverting myself in now and then finding a smoother pebble or prettier shell than ordinary, while the great ocean of truth lay all undiscovered before me."

MONICA LEWINSKY MEETS RWANDA

October 12, 1998

I HAVE SPENT A FEW DAYS FLIPPING BACK AND FORTH MENTALLY between the Clinton-Lewinsky business, still dragging on, and a new book by the *New Yorker's* Philip Gourevitch. The book is entitled *We Wish to Inform You That Tomorrow We Will Be Killed with Our Families: Stories from Rwanda.*

The disproportion between the two subjects is of course grotesque. To crowd Lewinsky and Rwanda into the same viewfinder is not just to discuss apples and oranges but to compare, forgive me, apples and severed heads. Each of the dramas discloses a different nation in moral crisis, but as Bill Clinton might point out, it depends what you mean by "moral." What a difference in the nations—and in the crises.

An unexpected juxtaposition—an interesting surprise, like a rattlesnake in the mailbox—may disturb and clarify the mind. When you put the Clinton scandal and the Rwandan genocide side by side, each becomes a slightly different thing.

First, perspective: The moral weight of a national crisis is in inverse proportion to a nation's wealth and power. America in its opulence gets presidential *docu-porn*—what the Washington lawyer Lloyd Cutler calls "Full Monty impeachment," the risky, tiresome romp of a resourceful president who, caught in violations of the school's honor code, violates it further in protesting his innocence.

By contrast, Rwanda (average monthly income: less than twenty-five dollars) gets rivers clogged with corpses. America's wealth entitles its citizens to work themselves into a moral froth over office fellatio. America's vast first-world privilege also means that its scandals are infinitely less dangerous to the man and woman in the street. America's samurai of opinion scream at one another on talk shows; political argument in

Rwanda is done with machetes, and leaves a million people hacked to pieces.

I thought of the reporting devoted to the two subjects: Gourevitch's book ranks among the best examples of the journalism of moral witness. It speaks with an austerity enforced by the mystery and horror of the genocide.

True evil versus pathetic misbehavior: The Lewinsky coverage unfolds in a drearily gamy continuum; prime cuts and messy chitterlings from the meat-packing firm of Starr, Tripp & Drudge get mass-packaged in cling-wrap and cardboard for the gaudy supermarkets of the information age.

But you do notice one damning convergence. In 1994, the United States, having been burned in Somalia, was desperate to stay out of Rwanda. How to manage that? By pettifogging. By arguing about semantics: the Clinton way. His administration, pressed to honor the 1948 Genocide Convention (not to mention human decency) by intervening, quibbled at a furious rate about the meaning of the word *genocide*. Madeleine Albright, who was Clinton's ambassador to the United Nations in 1994, temporized as the death toll in Rwanda climbed into the hundreds of thousands. It was, as Gourevitch writes, "the absolute low point of her career as a stateswoman." What works first for tragedy will serve later for farce. The casuistry pressed into service to dodge an inconvenient genocide made a later, lighter appearance in Clinton's Jesuitical parsing, under oath, of "is" and "sexual relations." As this convergence suggests, character matters.

During his African tour last March, Clinton stopped in Rwanda and eloquently apologized to the survivors gathered at Kigali airport. He used the phrase "never again"—two words of grave historical weight. He said, "And never again must we be shy in the face of the evidence." Shy? In any case, did he mean it?

It is worth asking these things in the face of the approaching winter in Kosovo: The genocidal impulses that led the Hutu to slaughter one million Tutsi (give or take) in 1994 are (allowing for a few regional differences, such as machetes and skin color) identical to the tribal bloodlusts at work in the Balkans. Eerily the same: the neighbors who suddenly turn a killing fury upon neighbors, the roving bands fueled round the clock on alcohol, the strange, dull light in the murderers' eyes, the sudden civic duty to exterminate the Other.

There is little for the American people to like in the public performances they see. The polls professing satisfaction may mask an alienation, just below the surface, and a generalized disgust at everyone: screaming media, nitwit Congress, ignoble president. Nero gave the people circuses. Clinton is the circus.

The dangerous part now is not the president's distraction by scandal and the prospect of impeachment. The risk lies, rather, in something that the Lewinsky-Rwanda convergence shows: Clinton's willingness to use words as if he did not understand that they have real meanings and consequences, as if his intense, fleeting sincerity—his shoeshine and his smile, or his wagging finger, or sidelong laser glance, or his bitten lip: his sheer performance—were sufficient. We are headed into historical country where they are not. And they never were.

STALIN'S SANCHO PANZA

April 7, 2003

WHEN THE SOVIET SHIP *BALTIKA* THROBBED INTO NEW YORK Harbor one morning in September 1960, demonstrators on a chartered sightseeing boat waved placards: ROSES ARE RED, VIOLETS ARE BLUE; STALIN DROPPED DEAD. HOW ABOUT YOU? Nikita Khrushchev laughed and pointed. A few weeks later at the United Nations, a Philippine delegate gave a speech complaining about the Soviet occupation of Eastern Europe. Khrushchev astonished the General Assembly by taking off his brown loafer and banging it on the table as if it were a spoon on an infant's high chair, except that in this case the banging had an apocalyptic implication.

That is the iconic memory of Khrushchev—squat, pinkish, piggy, with glittering eyes, a survivor's cunning and an impishly brutal sense of theater. At the Vienna summit, he gave John Kennedy a famous mugging. JFK came away muttering, "I never met a man like this. I talked about how a nuclear exchange would kill 70 million people in 10 minutes, and he just looked at me as if to say 'So what?'"

What did Kennedy expect? Khrushchev understood that style of statecraft. He had learned from the monster himself, sitting at Joseph Stalin's right hand—or in his savage vicinity—for decades as cheerleader, yes-man and ideological dogsbody: a "nice guy," as his Kremlin cronies called him, who cheerfully survived Stalin's almost recreational paranoia even when so many of the evil crew (including Yezhov and Beria) were led offstage and shot.

Yet Khrushchev, unlike his mentor, ultimately lined up more on the side of life than on the side of death. The fascination of William Taubman's splendid new biography, *Khrushchev, the Man and His Era* (Norton; 876 pages), lies in tracking the abundantly human struggle in the man between his native humanity and the temptations of power and glamour. Early on, Stalin took a shine to young Khrushchev (some thought because Khrushchev was even shorter than Stalin). Between 1929 and 1938—the most lethal years of Stalinism, starting with the enforced collectivization that left some 10 million kulaks dead, and running through the Great Terror and the show trials of the late 1930s—Khrushchev's career skyrocketed. The darkest period of Russian history was his golden age.

"At the height of the terror," writes Taubman, a professor of political science at Amherst College, "Khrushchev gave violent, bloodcurdling speeches rousing 'the masses' to join in the witch-hunt. As Moscow party boss he personally approved the arrests of many of his own colleagues and their dispatch into what he later called the meat grinder." He had other sins on his head, many from a later time; he brutally crushed the 1956 Hungarian uprising, for example.

After such knowledge, what forgiveness? Taubman's exploration of Khrushchev's complicity in Stalinist horror is probing, subtle. "Like many others," Taubman writes, "Khrushchev thought he was building a new socialist society, a glorious end that justified even the harshest means." So he "practiced deception and self-deception. He never fully owned up to his complicity." Touching a chillingly familiar chord, Taubman explains, "His complicity in great crimes . . . was tied to nothing less than his own sense of self-worth, to his growing feeling of dignity, to the invigorating, intoxicating conviction that Stalin, a man he came almost to worship, admired him in return."

Khrushchev came of peasant stock; he possessed a peasant's shrewdness and wit—a garrulous, storytelling gift the newspapers called earthy; what they meant was that he referred to excrement a lot. With only two years of schooling, he had a fierce, uncouth animation that was shadowed by feelings of intellectual inferiority.

Yet Stalin's pudgy Sancho Panza was the man who, in February 1956, delivered the famous four-hour "secret speech" to the party congress in which he set forth Stalin's crimes and began the complex, much delayed process of de-Stalinization. Out of guilt or common decency, he began to rinse the terror out of Soviet life. Writes Taubman: "His daring but bumbling attempt to reform communism began the long, erratic process of putting a human face (initially his own) on an inhu-mane system."

When Khrushchev was at last deposed in 1964, in part because his shoe-banging performance at the United Nations had embarrassed the Soviet Union, he profited from his own reforms. Instead of shooting him, the party heavies sent him off to a retirement dacha at Petrovo-Dalneye, where he tended his garden like Don Corleone.

Jackie Kennedy

May 30, 1994

Vaclav Havel was talking about the heavies who ran Czechoslovakia during the communist years.

One of the worst things about them, Havel said, was their awful taste. Havel gestured around a sitting room in his presidential residence in Prague. The room was handsomely simple and bathed in morning sunlight. "This was hideous when they were here," he said. "The furniture, the curtains . . . " Bad taste, he suggested, corrupts government.

I thought of Havel's idea when Jacqueline Bouvier Kennedy Onassis died, and wondered what it is that good taste does.

In Havel's mind, brutality, stupidity and kitsch all belonged to the same local gang: dead-drunk communists and evil smells, ghastly heavy velvet drapes and torture. Havel's formula was a variation on Stendhal's rule: "Bad taste leads to crimes."

It depends: Bad taste in what? There were Nazis who came home from work at Auschwitz and listened to Mozart. An elegant emperor may also be a sadist or an idiot or a weakling. If good taste were the qualification for leadership, the greatest presidents might be interior decorators.

I am not sure about the bad-taste rule as it applies to styles of government, except in the way that it points to a sometimes desirable elegance of leaderly thought, or might remind Americans of a president long ago who designed his own house at Monticello.

But Jacqueline Kennedy Onassis proved something about the rules of good and bad taste as they apply to the strange and sometimes rotten religion of the late twentieth century—celebrity. It is a religion that, as she knew as well as anyone, demands human sacrifice.

Somehow, she managed to escape. And the escape was the most stylish part of her life.

Young Mrs. Kennedy, in her early thirties, in the pillbox hat, or the bloody pink suit, or the black veil, became one of the ur-divinities of the paleotelevision age. By the time she died, she was still arguably the most famous woman on earth. Who else—Madonna? Princess Di? (The falloff in quality is steep.)

It may seem an odd way of appreciating Jacqueline Kennedy, but think for a moment what she might have been had she possessed a different character. And, for that matter, what her children might have become, given their fame, their money, their trauma—their excuse. Instead, she was what she was, and they are, admirably, one gathers, what they are, thanks to their mother. Important things are unfakeable.

She had excellent taste in art and music, of course; the "classy" (to use John Kennedy's word) side of Camelot—the stylish redecorations, Pablo Casals at the White House and so on—was her doing, mostly. But it seemed to me that over the years her truly superb taste expressed itself in what might be called the stylishness of her privacy.

Part of John Kennedy's charm derived from his reticence, from a sense one had of something withheld. That was his personality. In a more difficult way, in an earned way, Jacqueline Kennedy's achievement was what she was able to withhold. Celebrity Zen, perhaps: the mystique of reticence.

She belonged to a time—a tragedy—when large literary lines did not seem off, or ridiculous, as they might now. Hamlet and Lear, "if worthy their prominent part in the play," wrote Yeats, "do not break up their lines to weep." She, magnificently, did not break up her lines to weep. There was another thought that was associated especially with her husband: Courage is "grace under pressure." But that line applied to her in some truer way than it applied to him. She earned it in a harder fashion.

Jacqueline's father-in-law Joseph Kennedy went off to Hollywood decades ago and figured out the fundamental rule of the Age of Celebrity: "It doesn't matter what you are, it only matters what people think you are." The principle works for the short run, which is usually the only run that celebrity needs. Jacqueline Kennedy endured in the long run. Even in the earliest days after the inauguration in 1961, she located the saner and contrary principle in a memo she wrote to her press secretary: "I feel strongly that publicity in this era has gotten completely out of hand—and you must really protect the privacy of me and my children."

She was a civilized woman (John Kennedy was about half-civilized). Her civilized quality derived in large part from her insistence that her life belonged to her and her children. It is hard enough for a celebrity to be sane; fame is a distorting, corrupting and even psychotic environment. People in a healthy community gossip about people they know. It must disturb something in human nature to gossip so addictedly about people one doesn't know—all of those brightly painted, artificial familiars.

Jacqueline Onassis was clearly a sane woman. She kept a seemly silence. And for all the fragility she may have suggested in the big, round sunglasses and the head scarf, she wore some inner armoring; she possessed an eerie talent (a strategy of self-protection well known to those who handle dangerous animals) to make herself disappear, to dematerialize. If you saw her on the street, she would seem to abstract herself out of public attention, a kind of elegant vanishing. She would be, as she finally is now . . . elsewhere.

RATS LIVE ON NO EVIL STAR

September 23, 1991

ANNE SEXTON WAS A POPULAR, PULITZER PRIZE—WINNING poet who was capable occasionally of a dark brilliance. She had a favorite palindrome: RATS LIVE ON NO EVIL STAR. The trick of her work has first of all its bright little surprise of words, and then, on second look, a deeper, perverse magic—a double negative of meaning that ends in a metaphysical buzz. RATS LIVE ON EVIL STARS would work in a sane world, or else RATS LIVE ON NO GOOD STAR. But as it is . . .

Like her contemporary Sylvia Plath, Sexton had a gift of the self-dramatizing and self-destructive kind. She was the mad housewife of Weston, Massachusetts, beautiful if you caught her in the right light, "a possessed witch," as she thought of herself sometimes, "haunting the black air, braver at night." Both Plath and Sexton wound up as cautionary tales. In 1963 Plath stuck her head in an oven in London. Sexton told her psychiatrist, "Sylvia Plath's death disturbs me. Makes me want it too. She took something that was mine, that death was mine!" Eleven years later, in 1974, at the age of forty-five, Sexton poured herself a tall glass of vodka, went into her garage and closed the door, started up the old red Cougar, turned on the car radio and waited for the exhaust fumes to kill her.

It was not an impulsive act. Sexton tried to kill herself many times in the course of her adult life. Or anyway, she had a long flirtation with death by overdose. She carried a virtual pharmacy around in her pocketbook. She drenched herself with alcohol. As she wrote in an early poem, "the odor of death hung in the air / like rotting potatoes." She checked in and out of sanitariums. Doctors tried to minister to her hysteria, depression, anorexia, insomnia, wildly alternating moods, lacerating rages, trances, fugue states, terrible confusions, bouts of self-disgust.

Anne Sexton was Ophelia, all grown up and turned into suburban mother and basket case. She was an obsessive who used up all the oxygen in the room. Now, posthumously, the poet, the generator of her own myth, is achieving a certain celebrity at the expense of the family that put up with her for years. Her version of the story, elaborately unpretty, is the one being told, the tale that survives. Her family gets dragged into the nightmares of its most disturbed and most articulate member. Literature 1, Life 0.

Sexton was both a victim and a manipulator, as these things often go. She was shrewd, self-centered, half cracked. She abused her children. In episodes of rage she would seize her daughter Linda and choke or slap her, and one day she threw the little girl across the room. Linda says that when she was older, in her teens, her mother sexually abused her. The poet had many love affairs during her twenty-four-year marriage, including a long sexual involvement with her psychiatrist. Sexton actually paid for these appointments. (A second psychiatrist, Dr. Martin Orne, raised a different question of ethics by turning over to biographer Diane Wood Middlebrook some three hundred hours of audiotapes he had recorded during sessions with Sexton, but Middlebrook seems to have used them with discretion.)

All of the untidy history is told in Middlebrook's *Anne Sexton: A Biography*. Middlebrook, a professor of English at Stanford University, is judicious and canny. She appreciates both Sexton's gifts as a poet and her attractive side as a human being (humor, intensity), but looks at her destructive weaknesses with a steady eye. Linda Sexton, who is now thirty-eight and executor of her mother's estate, cooperated with the biographer and on the whole admires the end result.

Some members of the family are outraged. They think the biography opens windows on a universe of Sexton's own disturbed imaginings—which, being a good biography, it does. Two of the poet's nieces, Lisa Taylor Tompson and Mary Gray Ford, sent a letter to the *New York Times Book Review*, in which they try to rescue the family from Anne's messy version. They assert the rights of the sane and normal. "We take pride in her art and her accomplishment," the nieces write. "But we strenuously object to the portrayal of people we knew as libidinous, perverted beasts whose foul treatment of this deeply troubled soul drove her to the anguish she felt."

The worst parts of the published story, the nieces say, involve suggestions that Anne's father sexually abused her and that her sainted great-aunt, Nana, administered erotically disturbing back rubs to Anne as a girl. Middlebrook's book makes it clear that these suggestions almost surely originated in Sexton's mind and had no basis in fact.

But sanity screams at the innuendo, like a gull blackened in an oil spill. It wants to cleanse itself. The poet's version has the power of her black magic, her words on paper. "Where others saw roses," the nieces write, "Anne saw clots of blood." The sick, brilliant woman has the inestimable advantage of being dead and therefore beyond examination on questions of who abused whom and how.

Does the poet's work redeem the poet's mess? Sexton was working in a rich literary tradition. Her immediate American predecessors were not a wholesome precedent: John Berryman (alcoholic, suicide), Robert Lowell (episodically psychotic), Delmore Schwartz (alcoholic), Theodore Roethke (manic-depressive), Elizabeth Bishop (alcoholic). Sexton had shrewd instincts. "With used furniture he makes a tree," she wrote. "A writer is essentially a crook." Maybe.

Anne Sexton was a pain, in the real, physical sense. Every large family has a pain or two: an iridescent liar, a middle-aged infant, a little Iago. But somehow, in Sexton's case, it turned out that the pain was also entangled with a miracle: the miracle of her forty-five-year-long survival, for one thing, when such a terrible undertow was pulling her, and the miracle of her poems, or some of them at least—the dark, intelligent objects that she floated toward shore before she went under.

The Death of John Kennedy Jr.

July 8, 2000

THE AIR IS CLEAR, BLUE-GOLDEN—SUCH A SWEET, FRICTION-less light that from a hilltop I see the Catskills across the Hudson, miles to the west. In a wetland by the road, a great blue heron prospects for frogs, standing poised in the early evening clarity, utterly still . . . then strikes with a lightning-flash of beak. At my approach, the heron rouses itself in a cumbersome fluster, and rises in the air and flaps off in prehistoric, slow-motion grace, topping the red pines.

Coming home, I settle down at the computer screen and read the news on the Web. Something catches my eye—old business. The National Transportation Safety Board has decided that John Kennedy Jr. probably became disoriented in the night sky almost a year ago off Martha's Vineyard. The novice pilot's "spatial disorientation" caused the crash. We knew that, didn't we?

Time is elastic. That weekend seems either two days, or possibly ten years, ago. On that evening, by chance, we were having dinner with a friend at her house on Martha's Vineyard. The sun had gone down. We ate dinner in the afterlight, looking out over Vineyard Sound. We peered toward the mainland and one of us said, "There's going to be a storm." A dark, ominous haze had gathered—disorienting indeed. The water of the sound had become indistinguishable from the air—all was an inky continuum, a squid's cloud. Only when we looked higher, into the upper air, did we see vestiges of light.

We lit a fire and talked awhile, and night descended. The storm never came. We went to sleep.

The next morning as we had breakfast, Coast Guard helicopters clattered back and forth across the sound, flying low, searching in patient grid patterns. I logged on to check my e-mail, and saw a news headline: "JFK Jr.'s Plane Missing."

I knew John, but only slightly—liked him, admired him. The things they said, after the crash, about what a nice guy he was—all that was true. He had patience, and, I thought, a suave acumen. I'm fairly certain that he had political plans—that he might have methodically beefed himself up for a Senate run sometime after he had matured into his forties. And after that, after he had left the mere gorgeous hunk image far behind, then. . . . Instead, he died at thirty-eight.

John's father said, "Life is unfair." There's an essay question: Has life been unfair to the Kennedys? Discuss. (Give due attention to both sides of the question.) Was life unfair to John?

There is a scene in the movie *The English Patient* in which the party is riding across the dunes of the Egyptian desert. All is laughter and good humor until, in the fraction of an instant, a flicker of inattention, the car's wheels turn wrong, the vehicle flips over, and the characters' universe is suddenly, irreversibly changed—all in that laughter-to-disaster instant.

We recognize the moment; we have all, at one time or another, felt the shock and disbelief of the decisive stroke that alters everything. It strikes the famous and the obscure impartially. I knew an aged cowboy in West Texas, with the unlikely name of Cecil, who was driving down a highway one morning and took his eyes off the road for a second in order to reach for his tobacco pouch, and veered fatally into the path of an eighteen-wheeler.

What's the lesson, if any, of something like John Kennedy Jr.'s death? I feel, still, an anger and a disgust that just about overwhelm the sense of sadness: What a dumb, inexcusable thing! And the two women died with him.

The Kennedys have been testing the limits of their dispensation for three generations now. In the last generation (Joe Jr. and John and Bobby), death had historical context and therefore the dark prestige of tragedy. But when planes go down in incompetent or reckless moments, or when a guy skis into a tree while playing high-speed downhill touch football in the Rockies, there's not enough tragedy involved to make a hero.

And there's not much more to tell your children except: For God's sake, be careful! Stop showing off! Don't be an idiot! Don't act like a Kennedy!

GEORGE WALLACE

October 11, 1982

GIVEN THE HISTORY, WHAT ASTONISHES ONE IS THIS TENDER-
ness. An odd, sweet quiet comes upon the field and grove in the
September afternoon. The people, after their rally, rest almost dreamily on the threadbare grass. George Wallace has spoken. He sits in his
wheelchair on the small flatbed metal stage in the park at Noccalula
Falls near Gadsden, Alabama. The people come to him. They fall into
a long, orderly line to file past and take his hand and have him sign
their Wallace posters.

Their gazes mix awe and deep familiarity and shyness. They are
blue-collar people, or else small farmers who work these hills. Mostly
they have rough, country faces and washed, flat, distantly Celtic eyes.
People in wheelchairs are pushed up to his wheelchair, and George
Wallace reaches out the gentlest communing hands to them, and
spends long moments with each, consoling and almost, one thinks,
healing. He has the nimbus of saint and martyr—or at any rate, of a
celebrity who has passed through the fire and the greater world; he has
come back to them from history, come back with powder burns.

Northerners should watch Wallace with his people. The process is
tribal, a rite of communion. Only by watching it can one begin to ana-
lyze the disconcerting news that a fairly large number of Alabama
blacks have, in 1982, joined the Wallace tribe.

One of George Wallace's heroes, Stonewall Jackson, had a military
premise: "Mystery. Mystery is the secret of success." Jackson meant a
mystery of action, a talent for moving armies unpredictably. George
Wallace's gubernatorial campaign this year is exploring a few deeper
mysteries of the human character or, at any rate, of the human memory: questions that involve the capacity of the politician's heart to

change, the mind to forget and the Alabama black to forgive. In the South, even the shallows may be mysterious, profound.

Last week Wallace won the Democratic nomination to become governor for what would be an unprecedented fourth term (or fifth, if one counts the partial term served by Wallace's wife, the late Governor Lurleen). Wallace, at sixty-three, beat a well-heeled moderate Birmingham suburbanite, George McMillan. Alabama liberals wince at the choice available in November: either George Wallace or the Republicans' pistol-packing law-and-order Reaganite mayor of Montgomery, Emory Folmar. In the weird way that these things happen, Folmar, fifty-two, is playing the part of the old George Wallace in this race, running against the new George Wallace, the aging and re-upholstered seg.

The chief mystery of the campaign, at least to those with memories that run back to the 1960s, is that many black Alabamians are voting for Wallace, and even working in his cause. The Deep South is supposed to be the one American region where the past means something.

The Alabama Democratic Conference, the state's black political machine, strongly supported McMillan in the primary. They brought in Jesse Jackson and Coretta Scott King to speak against Wallace, to remind blacks of what Wallace had been. The majority of blacks (an estimated 65 percent) went against Wallace. Still, it was the combination of rural blacks and rural whites and blue-collar workers that won for Wallace. That any blacks at all enlisted with Wallace is reason to reflect.

The poison and paranoia have mostly gone out of the issue of race in Alabama. (Look for them more in South Boston, say, there in a cradle of abolitionism.) The countryside is peaceful now along the route from Selma to Montgomery, through Dallas County and "bloody Lowndes," the old Black Belt over which so many gusts of racial violence have passed. But still one looks across the cotton fields at the tall, deep Alabama forests that are primordially rich and inviting and sinister.

Something of the quality of those woods occasionally comes out in George Wallace's voice: a slurred dankness and a warning. But mostly his message is one of populist conciliation. Wallace is a born-again Christian. He appeared before the assembled blacks of the Southern Christian Leadership Conference in Birmingham last summer and apologized for his old segregationist politics. Have you changed in your attitude toward blacks? Wallace is asked today. "No," he replies. "I have respected and loved them always."

It is spiritually disorienting to see a black driving a car with Alabama plates and a Wallace bumper sticker. It is surreal to walk into Wallace's state campaign headquarters, a neobellum low-rise former furniture store on the edge of Montgomery. There, amid the deep shag carpeting and the clickity-click of computer printers churning out voter lists, sits Mrs. Ollie Carter, a black Wallace worker. All day she phones around the state with a gentle, churchgoing courtesy, asking blacks for their support, reminding them to vote.

Mrs. Carter claims that 98 percent of the blacks she calls say they are supporting Wallace. She taught elementary school for nineteen years in rural Shelby County, and remembers that none of her pupils had their own textbooks until George Wallace became governor. Wallace people almost always mention his record in improving Alabama education (though the state still ranks among the lowest in literacy), especially those free textbooks for the children, and the system of twenty-six junior colleges he started around the state. And the fact is that, leaving aside the low growls of race, Wallace was generally quite a good governor. As for all of that racial viciousness, Mrs. Carter squares her frank and open countenance, earnest and astonishing: "He has made some mistakes. But haven't we all? You have to understand. The races are more bold and honest with each other in the South." That is true. So is the opposite; the exchange between the races in the South has also been a drama of long silences, of the unstated.

One theory has it that Alabama blacks have always been cynically knowing about George Wallace, that they have figured all along that his segregationist behavior and rhetoric were matters of political expediency. There is some truth in the theory. Alabama today has the second highest (after Michigan) unemployment in the nation: 14.5 percent. Everywhere in Alabama the message is the same: "Folks are hurtin'." Wallace has argued, so far successfully, that as an internationally known figure and the most experienced governor in Alabama history, he can bring new industries and new jobs to the state. So many Alabamians, black and white, have accepted the logic that the chances are good Wallace will move back into the governor's office.

What holds the mind in the Wallace race, however, is the symbolism rattling around in the play. Wallace in the past has been accused of a mean and opportunistic depthlessness. Yet his career now opens upon unexpected dimensions of passion and forgiveness and redemptive possibilities. If Wallace is an opportunist, as every politician is, he has also displayed resources of courage and endurance and temperament and even of grace.

One recent night, George Wallace Jr. was riding up to Scottsboro—that resonant Alabama place name, home of the Scottsboro Boys—to give a talk to some Wallace workers at the courthouse. As the Cadillac sedan fired up the interstate from Montgomery in the dusk and into a soft Alabama night, George Jr. talked about his father. They are close. A few nights before his father was shot in Maryland, George Jr. had a dream in which just such a shooting occurred, except that in the dream, George Sr. died. George Jr., a poised, intelligent, decent young man with his mother's eyes and his father's eyebrows, who works as director of student finance at Troy State University, is thirty now. He has been giving political speeches since he was seven and his daddy stood him up on chairs so he could reach the microphone at political rallies.

Once in Michigan, George Jr. remembered, "I watched while my father just set a crowd on fire. Set them on fire!" Was that frightening? he was asked. A pause. "Yes." But then: "I thought to myself: I wonder why it takes a man from south Alabama to set these people on fire. Why isn't there a man from Michigan who can set these people on fire?"

George Wallace, the senior George, promises his people that he will never go out trying to set the rest of the country on fire again. "I already been shot outta the presidential race once," he jokes sardonically. Besides, he says, "everything I was saying in the '60s and '70s is now the conventional wisdom." It was never race at all, it was Big

Government interference that was the issue, it was states' rights. That always sounded like a self-serving and morally evasive line. But maybe in the deeper levels of Confederate psychology, down in the almost pagan sources of Southern Scotch-Irish defiance, there is some truth in it. It is the truth of a profound sense of community, touchy and estranged and quick to take offense and to punish. It is essentially a tribal ethic. The tragedy of the South was that the honor of the white tribe came to depend upon the subservience of blacks.

But in a sense, the tragedy of race was secondary in the drama of George Wallace. He used it, when convenient. But when he ventured into the presidential primaries, it was the honor of the tribe of outraged Middle Americans that he was riding forth to rescue and avenge. It was Pickett's Charge across a vast suburban parking lot, and it ended in a bloody mess. But in a way it succeeded. The Reagan victory of 1980 was a vindication of Wallace's social conservatism, if not of his populist economics.

Driving back down from Scottsboro well past midnight, George Jr. turned in his seat with a small, inspired smile and said: "You remember *The Last Hurrah*? Well, in that one, at the end, Skeffington lost the election. Down here, we're going to have *The Last Hurrah*, with a twist. We're gonna win!"

Then he rode in silence all the way to Montgomery.

Scribble, Scribble, Eh, Mr. Toad

February 24, 1986

NATIONAL HANDWRITING DAY HAS PASSED WITHOUT PARADES. But the occasion may deserve to be celebrated, belatedly, with an updating of a part of *The Wind in the Willows*, a new chapter in the life of Toad of Toad Hall:

Toad gave up pen and pencil years ago, when he discovered the Smith-Corona manual portable typewriter. Toad loved his Smith-Corona. He played upon it like a flamboyant pianist. Now he massaged the keyboard tenderly through a quiet phrase, now he banged it operatically, thundering along to the chinging bell at the end of the line, where his left arm would abruptly fire into midair with a flourish and fling home the carriage return.

If Toad ever put pen to paper, it was reluctantly, to scribble in the margin of a college textbook ("Hmmmmm" or "Sez who?" or "Ha!"), or to write a check. Over the years, Toad's handwriting atrophied, until it was almost illegible. Who cared? Sonatas of language, symphonies, flowed from the Smith-Corona.

At length, Toad moved on to an electric model, an IBM Selectric, and grew more rapturous still. Toad said the machine was like a small private printing press: The thoughts shot from his brain through his fingers and directly into flawless print.

Then one winter afternoon, Toad came upon the marvel that changed his life forever. Toad found the word processor. It was to his Selectric as a Ferrari to a gypsy's cart. Toad now thought that his old writing machines were clattering relics of the industrial revolution.

Toad processed words like a demon. His fingers flew across the keys, and the words arrayed themselves on a magic screen before him. Here was a miracle that imitated the very motions of his brain, that teleported paragraphs here and there—no, there!—as quickly as a mind flicking through alternatives. Prose with the speed of light, and lighter than air! Toad could lift ten pounds of verbiage, at a whim, from his first page and transport it to the last, and then (hmmm) back again.

A happy life, until one day, Toad, when riding his bicycle in the park, took a disastrous spill. Left thumb broken, arm turned to fossil in a cast, out of which his fingers twiddled uselessly, Toad faced the future. He tried one-handing his word processor, his hand jerking over the keyboard like a chicken in a barnyard.

It was no use. There is no going back in pleasure. "Bother!" said Toad. He picked up a No. 1 Eberhard Faber pencil. He eyed it with the despair of a suddenly toothless gourmand confronting a life of strained carrots and peas. He found a schoolboy's lined notebook and started to write.

The words came haltingly, in misshapen clusters. Toad's fingers lunged and jabbed and oversteered. When he paused to reread a sentence, he found that he could not decipher it. The language came out Etruscan.

Yet Toad perforce persisted. It had been years since he had formally and respectfully addressed blank paper with only pen or pencil in hand. He felt unarmed, vulnerable. He thought of final exams long years ago—the fields of rustling blue-book pages, the universal low, frantic scratching of pens, the smell of sour collegiate anguish.

Toad drove his pencil onward. Grudgingly, he thought, This is rather interesting. His handwriting, spasmodic at first, began to settle after a time into rhythmic, regular strokes, growing stronger, like an oarsman on a long haul.

Words come differently this way, thought Toad. To write a word is to make a thought an object. A thought flying around like electrons in the atmosphere of the brain suddenly coalesces into an object on the page (or computer screen). But when written in longhand, the word is a differently and more personally styled object than when it is arrayed in linear file, each R like every other R. It is not an art form, God knows, in Toad script, not Japanese calligraphy. Printed (typed) words march in uniform, standardized, cloned shapes done by assembly line. But now, thought Toad, as I write this down in pencil, the words look like ragtag militia, irregulars shambling across the page, out of step, slovenly but distinctive.

Toad reflected. What he saw on the penciled page was himself, all right, not just the content of the words but the physical shape and flow of thought. Some writers do not like to see so much of themselves on the page and prefer to objectify the words through a writing machine. Toad for a moment accused himself of sentimentalizing handwriting, as if it were home-baked bread or hand-cranked ice cream. He accused himself of erecting a cathedral of enthusiasm around his handicap.

At length Toad could see his own changes of mood in the handwriting. He could read haste when he had hurried. He thought that handwriting would make a fine lie-detector test, or a foolproof drunkometer. Handwriting is civilization's casual encephalogram.

Writing in longhand does change one's style, Toad came to believe, a subtle change, of pace, of rhythm. Sentences in longhand seemed to take on some of the sinuosities of script. As he read his pages, Toad considered: The whole toad is captured here. *L'écriture, c'est l'homme* (Handwriting is the man). Or: *L'écriture, c'est le crapaud* (Handwriting is the toad). What collectors pay for is the great writer's manuscript, the relic of his actual touch, like a saint's bone or lock of hair. What will we pay in future years for a great writer's computer printouts? All the evidence of his emendations, his confusions and moods, will have vanished into hyperspace, shot there by the Delete key.

Toad found himself seduced, in love, scribbling away in the transports of a new passion. Toad was always a fanatic, of course, an absolutist. He bought the fanciest fountain pen. His word processor went first into a corner, then into a closet with the old IBM.

Toad thought of Henry James. For decades, James wandered Europe and the United States, staying in hotels or in friends' houses. He was completely mobile. He needed only pen and paper to write his usual six hours a day. Then in middle age, he got writer's cramp. He bought a typewriter, and, of course, needed a servant to operate the thing. So now James was more and more confined to his home in Sussex, pacing the room, dictating to the typist and the clacking machine. James became a prisoner of progress.

Toad, liberated, bounded off in the other direction. Light of heart, he took to the open road, encumbered by nothing heavier than a notebook and a pen. Pausing on a hilltop now and then, he wrote long letters to Ratty and Mole, and folded them into the shape of paper airplanes, and sent them sailing off on the breeze.

PART THREE

Images

TABLOID SHAKESPEARE

April 7, 2000

WE HAVE PERFECTED A FORM OF NEWS THAT MIGHT BE CALLED Shakespearean tabloid. We live in a golden age of the genre.

The classic of Shakespearean tabloid in our time was the O. J. Simpson case, which had everything (grisly murder, fame, sex, race and more, all played out before an audience of billions from Judge Lance Ito's courtroom).

Since the first days of the Senate Judiciary Committee hearings on Clarence Thomas (another courtroom-type setting, with power, sex, race and gender conflict acted out before a hilarious cast of U.S. senators), American news audiences have witnessed an extraordinary procession of such dramas. The death of Princess Diana (death, youth, beauty, sex, royalty, etc., with the media themselves playing a villainous role in the form of the paparazzi) offered Shakespearean tabloid that seemed unsurpassable until . . . John Kennedy Jr. fell from the sky with his wife and sister-in-law, a tragedy (death, youth, beauty, royalty of the American kind) compounded by its heartbreaking blood tie to the ur-tabloid story of the century—the assassination of John's father in Dallas in 1963.

The Elian Gonzalez story—a heartbreaking business in a different way, a Solomonic dilemma with high cultural flavoring and an added dimension of exiles versus the old Stalinist dictator—turns out to have legs. Whether it will be one of the classics of our time remains to be seen.

This is an unpleasantly cynical way to write about ordeals that, for the people involved, are painful and real. But the very authenticity of the original tragedy is, by definition, bankable, and attracts to itself the gaudy luminescence of media spectacle. The three-ring circus comes to town. Bardic electronics record it all, and twenty-four hours a day, the footage plays, and commentators dramatize, colorize and moralize the pain.

Shakespeare might have felt himself inadequate to do justice to some of this. The Monica Lewinsky–Bill Clinton story (great power brought almost to ruin by sleazy sex, with a blue dress playing its decisive part, like Desdemona's handkerchief) unfolded in the manner of great Shakespearean tabloid—constantly topping itself.

Columbine High School was the nightmare classic of what, in the 1990s, became an American subgenre, the school shooting. Columbine did not have sex or fame or power, but instead offered the familiar dynamic of impotence with a satanic overlay: a disturbed desire to achieve fame and power by committing powerful outrage. The bombing of the federal building in Oklahoma City had some of that aspect.

Events of history have come to participate in the Shakespearean tabloid form. What was more indelible than the night the Gulf War started, live on television from Baghdad? That war, a peculiarly compact production as wars go, had Christiane Amanpour and Arthur Kent, "the Scud Stud," to dress up professional journalism in a lightly sexual glamour.

Where did it start? In the Pleistocene of the media, there was the Lindbergh kidnapping, a tragedy with relentless media legs that drove Charles and Anne Morrow Lindbergh out of America and, ever since, has provided sound argument for anyone who wishes to prove that journalists are subhuman.

The modern era of history as tabloid began in the 1960s; almost the entire decade was Shakespearean tabloid—especially the year 1968, which started with the Tet offensive, moved on through Lyndon Johnson's abdication, Martin Luther King's assassination, nationwide racial uprisings, Bobby Kennedy's assassination, and the photogenic Walpurgisnacht of the Chicago Democratic Convention.

You can identify classic Shakespearean tabloid by the way that it becomes an obsession of both audience and media and uses up the available oxygen. In this golden age, the god of news seems to have become providential and has, for some time now, been providing big sagas with a disturbing regularity.

FRANK CAPRA'S AMERICA

January 14, 2002

On a cold night just after New Year's, I watched one of Frank Capra's movies—not a bad way to keep warm, if you choose the right Capra. I wanted to tune in on an old American wavelength. A Capra resonance, an atmosphere, seemed to have returned off and on during the fall. It suggested some earlier American self-image, a kind of innocence arising from vulnerability and loss: post-traumatic sweetness. (The trauma in Capra's case, of course, was the stock-market crash and the Great Depression.) Had we renewed our citizenship, for a little while, in Frank Capra's America?

Capra's movies are the garden from which Americans were expelled, years ago, by their success and power and diversity—and by their bitter internal wars over, among others, Joe McCarthy, Martin Luther King Jr. and Ho Chi Minh. The films archive the country's grainy common-man myth of itself, more generous and neighborly and decent, and a lot whiter (in a Norman Rockwell way) than America has proved to be, decades later, having made all that money and opened its doors to the world.

That night I did not want to see one of Capra's political films (*Mr. Smith Goes to Washington* or *Meet John Doe*, for example), all chicken fat and diatribe, in which endearing little people go up against incipient corporate fascism. I wanted the pure, innocent allegory of *It Happened One Night*, which won five Oscars in 1934.

Movies don't change. Ellie Andrews (Claudette Colbert) is still a rich, spoiled heiress with a daddy problem who thinks she wants to marry a phony named King Westley, an "aviator" who arrives for their wedding by landing on Daddy's sumptuous lawn in an autogyro. Peter Warne (Clark Gable), an unemployed newspaperman and wisecracking paragon, rescues Ellie from the phonies at the last moment and bears her away to the true America, for a honeymoon in a roadside motor camp in Michigan.

All of that occurs in the last few minutes of the movie. Most of the story takes place aboard a bus making its slow way up from Miami toward New York City, with Gable acting as Colbert's chaste protector—honorable knight disguised as roadwise cynic—as she tries to elude her father's detectives. The bus is the real Frank Capra America, a gallant little vessel pushing through sparsely settled American countryside, the passengers, ensemble, singing "The Daring Young Man on the Flying Trapeze," checking into roadside motor cabins when a bridge washes out and waiting in line next morning for the outdoor showers.

It Happened One Night dances charmingly along the fence between lark and allegory. It is, among other things, a dissertation on what it means to be an American phony. King Westley—"the pill of the century," as Gable says, a café-society parasite with the face of a small reptile—wants to marry Ellie for her money and in the end accepts a bribe of $100,000 to go away. King's narcissistic autogyro is a sort of 1930s version of the Osprey, or of those personal motor-scooters-of-the-air that the writer James Fallows envisioned, pre-9/11, as universal transport in a coming yuppie paradise. In Capra the real Americans take their chances with one another traveling overland. (Contemplating the current plan to use $15 billion of taxpayers' money to bail out the aviation industry, one thinks that Capra, long ago, had his heart in the right place.)

As often in Hollywood's version of the 1930s, the rich are sleek, fat, boozy, faintly ridiculous. The media (newspapers and their editors, in this case) make idiots of themselves in a montage of pinwheeling banner headlines: LOVE TRIUMPHANT! screams the *New York Mail* over the phony "yarn" of Westley and Ellie being madly in love.

When authentic love triumphs (after the long journey in which Gable's newspaperman has almost prudishly refused to take advantage of Ellie's ardor and has declined her father's reward of $10,000), it is the victory of an ordinary American's honor over the opulent phoniness of too much money and of gaudily dishonest media.

Capra had an eye for basic American themes that keep reformulating themselves from one generation to another. You watch *It Happened One Night* with a sense that it's a contemporary story. Play a game: Set down the Peter Warne character and the King Westley character as American archetypes and relocate them in the present. Which of them, would you judge, emerges triumphant in 2002?

Until September 11, I would have said the sleek fraud King Westley (with his autogyro and chiseled money and bogus media) would get the girl and take over America. Now I am not sure. We'll see. The movie's not over.

Welcome to the Global Village

May 29, 1989

The effect has been contradictory: a sense of sunlight and elegy at the same time, of glasnost and claustrophobia.

Whenever the world's molecules reorganize themselves, of course, someone announces a new reality—"All changed, changed utterly: A terrible beauty is born," in W. B. Yeats' smitten lines about the Irish rebellion of Easter 1916. Seventy-three years later, the Irish troubles proceed, dreary, never beautiful—an eczema of violence in the margins.

But the world in the past few years has, in fact, profoundly changed. In Tiananmen Square last week, many of the demonstrators' signs were written in English. The students knew they were enacting a planetary drama, that their words and images in that one place would powder into electrons and then recombine on millions of little screens in other places, other minds, around the world.

The planet has become an intricate convergence—of acid rains and rain forests burning, of ideas and Reeboks and stock markets that ripple through time zones, of satellite signals and worldwide television, of advance-purchase airfares, fax machines, the miniaturization of the universe by computer, of T-shirts and mutual destinies.

The planetary circuits are wired: an integrated system, a microchip floating in space. Wired for evils—for AIDS, for example, for nuclear war, for terrorism. But also for entertainment, knowledge and even (we live in hope) for higher possibilities like art, excellence, intelligence and freedom. Justice has not gone planetary and never will. But the village has indeed become global—Marshall McLuhan was right. No island is an island anymore: The earth itself is decisively the island now.

Travel and travel writing are enjoying a sort of brilliant late afternoon, what photographers call the magic hour before sunset. But the romantic sense of remoteness shrivels. Even the trash announces that the planet is all interconnection, interpenetration, black spillage, a maze of mutual implication, trajectories like the wrapped yarn of a baseball.

A scene: blue plastic bags, bags by the thousands, struggle out of the Red Sea onto the shores of Egypt.

The wind dries them, and then they inflate like lungs and rise on the desert air. They come out of the sea like Portuguese men-of-war and then, amphibious, as if in some Darwinian drama, sail off to litter another of the earth's last emptinesses. Reverse Darwin, really: devolution, a flight of death forms.

Those who actually read Salman Rushdie's notorious best seller *The Satanic Verses* may have absorbed Rushdie's perception of what the planet has become: old cultures in sudden high-velocity crisscross, a bewilderment of ethnic explosion and implosion simultaneously. The Ayatollah Khomeini's response to Rushdie is (whatever else it is) an exquisite vindication of Rushdie's point. Khomeini's Iranian revolution was exactly a violent repudiation of the new world that the shah had sponsored. The struggle throughout the Middle East now is, among other things, a collision between Islam and the temptations and intrusions of the West. In the new world, everything disintegrates: family, community, tradition, coherence itself. The old community perishes in deference to a new community not yet born.

So the world is exactly Salman Rushdie's Indian characters passively seat-belted in their flight from Bombay to London, then blown apart by a random, idiot bomb and soon seen pinwheeling down to a soft landing off the English coast—the England where Kipling comes home to roost and the empire will implode and intermingle.

A media tale: American television correspondent covering a unit of government troops moving against a guerrilla post in El Salvador keeps eyeing his watch and asking the commander when he will order the attack. Distracted commander says, "Not yet, not yet." Correspondent finally explodes, "Goddammit, I've a bird [satellite feed to the network] at six o'clock!" The leader, understanding perfectly, orders his attack immediately.

The definition of conquest changed. Japan proved that territory, sheer acreage, means nothing. The Soviet Union's geographical vastness avails little in productivity.

The deepest change may be an intuition that military war is pointless. Except in atavistic places like the Middle East and Ireland, conquering territory is a fruitless and counterproductive exercise. Why conquer land? The Soviets have more trouble than they can manage with their nationalities. The new world's battlegrounds are markets and ideas. The Japanese and Germans, having learned their military lessons the hard way, re-entered the war by other means.

Cities like Cairo, Lagos, Nairobi, Mexico City are slouching toward the new world in the darkest way. Life and death struggle with one another: great birth rates, great death rates. This is the new world's suffocation, of population, poverty, pollution. The country people crowd into the cities. Their continuities are broken, their communities, their village frameworks wrecked, with nothing to replace them.

In the new world, America has lost some of its radiant pride of place. Japan has risen. Europe is organizing itself into a new collective power. The Soviet Union is struggling to escape the dustbin of history. Gorbachev, a magician of much élan, tried to rescind the hoax of communism without denouncing its idea. It was fascinating to watch a smart man trying to defend a premise that is beneath his intelligence. And Gorbachev, an allegedly world-historical man, presently vanishes.

What is the meaning of the new world? Like the older one, it goes dark and then goes light. It flies through the air. It is perhaps too intimate to be heroic anymore. It is, on balance, better than the one before, because it is more conscious. So we hope.

TIME IN A RECTANGLE

October 25, 1989

Balzac had a "vague dread" of being photographed. Like some primitive peoples, he thought the camera steals something of the soul—that, as he told a friend "every body in its natural state is made up of a series of ghostly images superimposed in layers to infinity, wrapped in infinitesimal films." Each time a photograph was made, he believed, another thin layer of the subject's being would be stripped off to become not life as before but a membrane of memory in a sort of translucent antiworld.

If that is what photography is up to, then the onion of the world is being peeled away, layer by layer—lenses like black holes gobbling up life's emanations. Mere images proliferate, while history pares down to a phosphorescence of itself.

The idea catches something of the superstition (sometimes justified, if you think about it) and the spooky metaphysics that go ghosting around photography. Taking pictures is a transaction that snatches instants away from time and imprisons them in rectangles. These rectangles become a collective public memory and an image-world that is located usually on the verge of tears, often on the edge of a moral mess.

It is possible to be entranced by photography and at the same time disquieted by its powerful capacity to bypass thought. Photography, as the critic Susan Sontag has pointed out, is an elegiac, nostalgic phenomenon. No one photographs the future. The instants that the photographer freezes are ever the past, ever receding. They have about them the brilliance or instancy of their moment but also the cello sound of loss that life makes when going irrecoverably away and lodging at last in the dream works.

The pictures made by photojournalists have the legitimacy of being news, fresh information. They slice along the hard edge of the present. Photojournalism is not self-conscious, since it first enters the room (the brain) as a battle report from the far-flung Now. It is only later that the artifacts of photojournalism sink into the textures of the civilization and tincture its memory: Jack Ruby shooting Lee Harvey Oswald, an image so raw and shocking, subsides at last into the ecology of memory, where we also find thousands of other oddments from the time—John John saluting at the funeral, Jack and Jackie on Cape Cod, who knows?—bright shards that stimulate old feelings (ghost pangs, ghost tendernesses, wistfulness) but not thought really. The shocks turn into dreams. The memory of such pictures, flipped through like a disordered Rolodex, makes at last a cultural tapestry, an inventory of the kind that brothers and sisters and distant cousins may rummage through at family reunions, except that the greatest photojournalism has given certain memories the emotional prestige of icons.

If journalism—the kind done with words—is the first draft of history, what is photojournalism? Is it the first impression of history, the first graphic flash? Yes, but it is also (and this is the disturbing thing) history's lasting visual impression. The service that the pictures perform is splendid, and so powerful as to seem preternatural. But sometimes the power they possess is more than they deserve.

Call up Eddie Adams's 1968 photo of General Nguyen Ngoc Loan, the police chief of Saigon, firing his snub-nosed revolver into the temple of a Vietcong officer. Bright sunlight, Saigon: the scrawny police chief's arm, outstretched, goes by extension through the trigger finger into the V.C.'s brain. That photograph, and another in 1972 showing a naked young Vietnamese girl running in arms-outstretched terror up a road away from American napalm, outmanned the force of three U.S. presidents and the most powerful army in the world. The photographs were considered, quite ridiculously, to be a portrait of America's moral disgrace. Freudians spend years trying to call up the primal image-memories, turned to trauma, that distort a neurotic patient's psyche. Photographs sometimes have a way of installing the image and legitimizing the trauma: the very vividness of the image, the greatness of the photograph as journalism or even as art, forestalls examination.

Adams felt uncomfortable about his picture of Loan executing the Vietcong officer. What the picture does not show is that a few moments earlier the Vietcong had slaughtered the family of Loan's best friend in a house just up the road. All this occurred during the Tet offensive, a state of general mayhem in South Vietnam. The Communists had no qualms about summary execution.

But Loan shot the man; Adams took the picture. The image fired around the world and lodged in the conscience. Photography is the very dream of the Heisenberg uncertainty principle—the act of observing a physical event inevitably changes it. War is merciless and bloody, and by definition it occurs outside the orbit of due process. Loan's Vietcong did not have a trial. He did have a photographer. The photographer's picture took on a life of its own and changed history.

All great photographs have lives of their own, but they can be as false as dreams. Somehow the mind knows that and sorts out the matter, and permits itself to enjoy the pictures without getting sunk in the really mysterious business that they involve.

Still, a puritan conscience recoils a little from the sheer power of photographs. They have lingering about them the ghost of the golden calf—the bright object too much admired, without God's abstract difficulties. Great photographs bring the mind alive. Photographs are magic things that traffic in mystery. They float on the surface, and they have a strange life in the depths of the mind.

THE BLOOD SPORT OF
MORAL DILEMMAS

May 4, 1992

WELCOME TO AMERICAN MORAL BLOOD SPORTS—LIVE AND in color. On the program: from Buffalo, the Pro-Choicers meet the Pro-Lifers for another in-your-face metaphysical infuriator. And from San Quentin, California, after a fourteen-year legal preliminary, a night of ghastly last-minute appeals and strap-him-in-take-him-out action as double-murderer Robert Alton Harris flirts with cyanide and exhales death-row doggerel. (Close-up. Harris, macho-sardonic: "You can be a king or a street sweeper, / But everybody dances with the Grim Reaper.") Back after this . . .

Television has all but swallowed American politics and sport. Now it is closing in on the nation's moral dilemmas. Debates of the toughest questions (abortion, the death penalty, for example) look like wrestling or professional football. When Robert Harris was executed in California last week, the event had a strange gaudy quality, somehow commercial and electronic. Perhaps one day prisoners will go to the gas chamber with product-endorsement logos on their prison pajamas.

Americana: Harris's last meal was two large pizzas, a bucket of Kentucky Fried Chicken, a six-pack of Pepsi, a bag of jelly beans, a pack of Camel cigarettes. Junk food was a motif in the case. In 1978 Harris murdered two teenage boys in order to steal their car for a bank robbery, and having killed them, he finished the burgers they had been eating. (My theory is that Harris would be alive today if he had not eaten the burgers. That detail must have struck the jurors as the cool, novelistic touch of Satan.)

The state of California might as well have executed Harris on the fifty-yard-line at halftime of the Super Bowl—the two moral constituencies, pro–death penalty and con, cheering or shrieking from either side of the stadium, the federal judiciary hovering overhead like a black blimp. When Harris was finally dead, America saw the postgame show: witnesses to the execution describing how the prisoner may or may not have mouthed the words "I'm sorry" to the father of one of the victims; breathed the fumes; convulsed and drooled; then died.

Socrates did not say the untelevised life is not worth living. He said the unexamined life. The unexamined death is a waste too. Socrates spent the hours before his execution by hemlock in 399 B.C. discussing the immortality of the soul. Reflection is not television's strong suit. The medium is a fairly crude moral filter, a kind of brilliant, overstimulated cretin. Its brain waves are discontinuous.

Leave aside the question of whether capital punishment is right or wrong. If the people choose to execute a criminal, how should it be done? Before what audience? In full video, retribution as spectacle?

The Eighth Amendment forbids "cruel and unusual punishments." Some of the witnesses to Harris's execution thought the cyanide, which took some minutes to kill Harris, was barbaric. That is an insult to centuries of creative barbarians, who have administered capital punishment by boiling in oil, burning at the stake, flaying to death, crushing, impaling, drowning, crucifying, drawing and quartering, disemboweling, gibbeting, garroting, throwing to lions and much, much worse. Cyanide, by comparison, is a sweet pink poof of cessation. Would last week's witnesses have been happier if California had used a neat bullet to the base of the brain (the method the Chinese authorities favor now)? Or if the state had injected Harris with a lethal shot of cocaine so that he would depart in a blinding rush of pleasure? What was truly cruel and unusual—virtually sadistic—was the way that the quarreling judicial stage managers jerked Harris in and out of the gas chamber, the man not knowing whether he was to die or be spared. In that long night, he died several deaths.

Executions in past centuries were public events—part ritual of citizenship, part savage entertainment. Every self-respecting English town had its gallows. As prisoners were carted from jail to noose, their friends along the route passed them strong drink and might turn the last mile into a macabre, hilarious, rolling party. Later, the decorous nineteenth century thought it more humane and seemly to execute people out of sight, behind the prison walls.

Maybe that was a mistake. In a poem, Robert Lowell wrote, "My eyes have seen what my hand did." Does the public have a right, even a duty, to watch its executions, to see exactly what its hand has done? What would be the effect?

If TV cameras had been present during the American Civil War to record the slaughters of Cold Harbor, say, or the Wilderness, the public might have been so sickened that it would have abandoned the struggle. The country might have split into the United States and the Confederate States; slavery might have survived a long time. Some think seeing executions on television would so repel the public that it would abolish capital punishment. Some believe showing such vivid evidence of the punishment would deter people from committing the crimes. Perhaps. Or would televised executions become something like what they were once—grisly popular entertainments?

The answer is all of the above. Emphasis on the entertainment. People pay millions to watch terminators and terminations. They have a taste for it. The distinction between actual death and special effects gets blurry in this culture. It thins to vanishing. Reality and unreality become ugly, interchangeable kicks. Perhaps if Harris had been spared, he might have been hired to play himself in the docudrama.

When Artists Distort History

December 23, 1991

King Richard III was a monster. He poisoned his wife, stole the throne from his two young nephews and ordered them to be smothered in the Tower of London. Richard was a sort of Antichrist the King—"that bottled spider, that pois'nous bunch-back'd toad."

Anyway, that was Shakespeare's version. Shakespeare did what the playwright does: He turned history into a vivid, articulate, organized dream—repeatable nightly. He put the crouchback onstage, and sold tickets.

And who would say that the real Richard known to family and friends was not identical to Shakespeare's memorably loathsome creation? The actual Richard went dimming into the past and vanished. When all the eyewitnesses are gone, the artist's imagination begins to conjure.

Variations on the King Richard effect are at work in Oliver Stone's *JFK*. Richard III was art, but it was propaganda too. Shakespeare took the details of his plot from Tudor historians who wanted to blacken Richard's name. Several centuries passed before other historians began to write about Richard's virtues and suggest that he may have been a victim of Tudor malice and what is the cleverest conspiracy of all: art.

JFK is a long and powerful harangue about the death of the man Stone keeps calling "the slain young king." What are the rules of Stone's game? Is Stone functioning as commercial entertainer? Propagandist? Documentary filmmaker? Historian? Journalist? Fantasist? Sensationalist? Paranoid conspiracy-monger? Lone hero crusading for the truth against a venal establishment? Answer: some of the above.

The first superficial effect of *JFK* is to raise angry little scruples like welts in the conscience. Wouldn't it be absurd if a generation of younger Americans, with no memory of 1963, were to form their ideas about John Kennedy's assassination from Oliver Stone's report of it? But worse things have happened—including, perhaps, the Warren Commission report.

Stone's movie and the Warren report are interestingly symmetrical: The Warren Commission was stolidly, one might say pathologically, unsuspicious, while in every scene of the Stone film, conspiracy theories writhe underfoot like snakes. In a strange way, the two reports balance one another out. It may be ridiculous to accord Stone's movie a status coequal with the Warren report. On the other hand, the Warren report has endured through the years as a monolith of obscure suppression, a smooth tomb of denial. Stone's movie, for all its wild gesticulations, at least refreshes the memory and gets a long-cold curiosity and contempt glowing again.

The fecklessness of the Warren report somehow makes one less indignant about Stone's methods and the five hundred kitchen sinks that he has heaved into his story. His technique is admirable as storytelling and now and then preposterous as historical inquiry. But why should the American people expect a moviemaker to assume responsibility for producing the last word on the Kennedy assassination when the government, historians and news media have all pursued the subject so imperfectly?

Stone uses a suspect, mongrel art form, and *JFK* raises the familiar ethical and historical problems of docudrama. But so what? Artists have always used public events as raw material, have taken history into their imaginations and transformed it. The fall of Troy vanished into *The Iliad*. The Battle of Borodino found its most memorable permanence in Tolstoy's imagining of it in *War and Peace*.

Especially in a world of insatiable electronic storytelling, real history procreates, endlessly conjuring new versions of itself. Public life has become a metaphysical breeder of fictions. Watergate became an almost continuous television miniseries—although it is interesting that the movie version of Woodward and Bernstein's *All the President's Men* stayed close to the known facts and, unlike *JFK,* did not validate dark conjecture.

Some public figures have a story magic, and some do not. Richard Nixon possesses an indefinable, discomfited dark gleam that somehow fascinates. And John Kennedy, despite everything, still has the bright glamor that works best of all. Works, that is, except when the subject is his assassination. That may be a matter still too sacred, too raw and unassimilated. The long American passivity about the death in Dallas may be a sort of hypnosis—or a grief that hardened into a will not to know. Do not let daylight in upon magic.

Why is Stone's movie different from any other imaginative treatment of history? Is it because the assassination of John Kennedy was so traumatic, the baby boomers' end of childhood? Or that Americans have enshrined his death as official tragedy, a title that confers immunity from profane revisionists who would reopen the grave? Are artists and moviemakers by such logic enjoined from stories about the Holocaust? The Holocaust, of course, is known from the outset to be a satanic plot. For some reason—a native individualism, maybe—many Americans resist dark theories about JFK's death, and think those retailing them are peddling foreign, anarchist goods. Real Americans hate conspiracies as something unclean.

Perhaps the memory of the assassination is simply too fresh. An outraged movie like Stone's intrudes upon a semipermanent mourning. Maybe the subject should be embargoed for some period, withheld from artists and entertainers, in the same way the Catholic Church once declined to consider sainthood until the person in question had been dead for fifty years.

No: better to opt for information and conjecture and the exhumation of all theories. Let a hundred flowers bloom, even if some of them are poisonous and paranoid. A culture is what it remembers, and what it knows.

GRAVITAS

March 14, 1988

THE PRESIDENTIAL CAMPAIGN PROCEEDS IN A DREAMY WEIGHT-lessness. Multiple images of multiple candidates float through the night air—the bright auditorium, the shiny "hopefuls." The audience almost unconsciously makes a ritual calculation. They do not judge the men on the issues, really, so much as on the unarticulated question of gravitas. Which of the candidates has the weight, the size, the some-thing, to be president?

Gravitas is a mystery, just as the presidency itself is something of a mystery. Gravitas is a secret of character and grasp and experience, a force in the eye, the voice, the bearing. Sometimes—as with, say, Winston Churchill—it announces itself as eloquence, and sometimes it proclaims itself as a silence, a suspension full of either menace or Zen. The Japanese believe a man's gravitas emanates from densities of the unspoken.

Sicilians speak of a "man of respect," a phrase suggesting, at its darkest reach, a gravitas that can not only hurt but even kill in order to enforce that respect. Gravitas is a phenomenon of power, but the forms and styles of power are various. Dictators are forever strutting the tinhorn's impersonation of gravitas. Brute power is only one of the cruder types, and it is sometimes subdued by other forms: a moral gravitas, for example. Martin Luther King Jr. brought his gravitas to bear against men of power who were morally vacant. Gravitas may be aggression, but it may express itself otherwise, as something withheld, as a dignity and forbearance.

A peculiarly powerful form of gravitas may arise out of suffering. It draws its authority not only from the redemptive example of Christ but also from Greek tragedy: the terrible moral power of woe. Mother Teresa has that gravitas of the redemptive. Whole cultures may be judged weighty or weightless by the calibration of suffering. Russian history sometimes seems an entire universe of gravitas: Always there is the heavy Slavic woe, the encroaching dark and metaphysical winter.

And yet Mikhail Gorbachev, a figure of gravitas among world leaders, achieved his effect precisely by reversing the Slavic inevitabilities: opening the windows, airing out the old system. The earlier generations of Soviets (Leonid Brezhnev, for example) sat upon the world's stage like dark boulders. Weight is not enough. Gravitas is weight with complexities of life and intelligence in it.

Pope John Paul II has gravitas. Jimmy Carter does not. Nor did Gerald Ford. Richard Nixon displayed a bizarre and complex gravitas that destroyed itself in sinister trivialities. Did Ronald Reagan have gravitas? In some ways, Reagan seemed a perfect expression of the anti-gravitas of his America, a place that seemed weightless and evanescent, as forgetful as a television screen. Gravitas, a deep moral seriousness, is not necessarily the virtue for an electronic age. And yet Reagan possessed a gravitas of authenticity. In any case, lame ducks always suffer from diminished gravitas. People don't take them as seriously as before, when the days of power lay ahead.

Margaret Thatcher undoubtedly had gravitas. One thought of Barbara Jordan as a figure of gravitas (the voice, the steady, strong intelligence).

In the long preliminary stages, the campaign seemed depressing, a drama in wan search of heroes and meanings. Such diminutive choices must mean that the nation itself has grown diminished. The Old Testament, that thunderous text inhabited by nothing less than the gravitas of God, recorded, "There were giants in the earth in those days." Americans now alive remember Franklin Roosevelt, Harry Truman, Dwight Eisenhower, John Kennedy—not all giants in any consensus but men of weight and consequence. But history is full of optical illusions.

In 1861 President-elect Abraham Lincoln made his way east from Illinois. Much of the world regarded him as a coarse and faintly ridiculous country lawyer. Lincoln proved to be a complex historical surprise.

Something of the same error of premature judgment occurred with Franklin Roosevelt. As he took office in 1933, FDR hardly seemed a savior to anyone. Edmund Wilson wrote at the time that Roosevelt was a decent man, but "was there anything durable?"

When Roosevelt died, the nation watched in horror as a depthless little haberdasher from Missouri, a seeming nullity out of the old Pendergast machine in Kansas City, moved into the White House. Over the years, however, Harry Truman acquired historical size and force.

George Washington invented the form of American presidential gravitas. His political successors lived with a perception of decline, of a falling off from the golden age. When Warren G. Harding (a falling off indeed) expressed doubt that he had the size to be president, an Ohio political boss named Harry Daugherty told him, "Don't make me laugh. . . . The days of the giants in the presidential chair [are] passed. . . . Greatness in the presidential chair is largely an illusion of the people."

Americans every four years have to talk themselves into something. They need to see a kind of plausibility in a candidate. The Nobel Prize committees go through the same exercise: The candidates have to be elevated to the general vicinity of the mythic in order to be worthy. But it may be a law of the drama that the presidential choices almost always seem inadequate. People feel an underlying anxiety, not necessarily because the candidates are no good, but because at a moment of such change, an entire society is suspended, awaiting the next act.

In a campaign with no incumbent running, a candidate's presidential gravitas is hypothetical. Only the enactment of a presidency can make a president. Now, all is faith, or hope, or dispirited guessing.

Gay Marriage

February 8, 2003

IF I PURSUE A CHAIN OF HUMANE SYLLOGISM, I CANNOT ARRIVE at any conclusion except that gay marriage is a good thing and should be legal.

Those against it say that marriage is only between a man and a woman. That thought seems to have the atmosphere of common sense and of long human experience.

But if you turn the matter slightly in your mind and allow a different light to play upon it, it seems to me that what you saw as common sense may morph into something less admirable, into dogmatism; and you may begin to see that long human experience is not rigidly changeless, but instead is an evolution. It may be time for an evolutionary change regarding marriage—one that, in any case, seems to me not only *not* harmful but potentially beneficial to society as a whole. The legalization of gay marriage will, I think, strengthen, not weaken, the institution of marriage.

Marriage is not necessarily—not significantly, not essentially—between a man and a woman. It is between two people.

The essence of marriage—the physical and metaphysical logic of it, the purpose, the point—is not, necessarily, to have children.

The essence of marriage is love and the commitment of two people to one another. Children may or may not be part of it. That depends on God's, or Nature's, or the couple's will.

If the essence of marriage were the production of children, then before permitting a man and a woman to be legally married, the law would have to require fertility tests to make sure the union would result in children.

If the essence of marriage were having children, then a man and a woman aged sixty, say, would not be permitted to marry: No kids, no marriage.

In any case, what does it mean to "have" children? A gay couple can adopt. Or, as often happens today in a relationship of two women, one of them may be impregnated by donor sperm. Nothing in our experiences teaches us that gay couples are less good parents than straight couples; on the contrary, the effort and advertence involved in gay parenthood probably mean that gays will be good parents. They have chosen the role; they focus upon it at least as thoughtfully as straights do.

We know enough about evil in an evil world to know that its enemy and antidote is love. Whatever fosters love (generosity, charity, forbearance, decency, human connection, understanding) is good.

If marriage adds to the overall sum of love—and therefore, of good—in the world, then legalizing gay marriages adds to the sum and improves the world. If marriage does not add to the overall sum of love and constructive good, then the institution of marriage is not worth protecting, anyway.

I favor the full legalization of gay marriages on libertarian grounds. Marriage is not easy; it is a complicated life-graft with unforeseeable difficulties, emotional and financial. It's an intimate and dangerous gamble. If two people want to be married, it's their commitment, their love, their risk, and their responsibility. It is not my business to interfere one way or another, and certainly not my job to check their genitals.

This Land Is Whose Land?

July 8, 2002

W<small>OODY</small> G<small>UTHRIE</small> <small>SANG ABOUT THE</small> L<small>EWIS AND</small> C<small>LARK COUNTRY</small>. Instead of his usual hobo's plainsong, Guthrie broke into an anthem that might have been written by the National Association of Manufacturers:

> Roll on, Columbia, roll on
> Roll on, Columbia, roll on
> Your power is turning our darkness to dawn,
> so roll on, Columbia, roll on.

Guthrie ardently wired up the dawn of manifest destiny to hydro-electric power:

> Tom Jefferson's vision would not let him rest
> An empire he saw in the Pacific Northwest
> Sent Lewis and Clark and they did the rest
> So roll on, Columbia, roll on.

The beautiful, wild river made Guthrie see factories and dams and mines that would put people to work to feed and clothe hungry children in *Grapes of Wrath* time. He heard the music of jackhammers.

Times and priorities change. It's disconcerting to the environmentalist to hear the author of "This Land Is Your Land, This Land is My Land" sounding like a booster from Midland, Texas, with a pump-jack for a metronome. But the 1930s were then, and had a cold reality staring them in the face. This is now. Political correctness is addicted to committing the sin of anachronism—imposing the current sense of racial and environmental decorum upon earlier times. Consider

Thomas Jefferson's descent from Enlightenment philosopher and naturalist to slave-master and debaucher of Sally Hemings—a fair enough revisionist correction (if kept in disciplined perspective) that has metamorphosed into tabloid history.

Of course, one age's evil is another's accepted routine. By the banks of the Columbia River in 1805, Meriwether Lewis, as specimen-collecting naturalist, blasted away at a condor—a barbarous breach of ecological etiquette today. (He missed.) Audubon slaughtered a thousand birds for every one he painted. Teddy Roosevelt, the greatest conservationist president and the father of the national parks, was a hunter who wiped out more wildlife than all other presidents combined. National Public Radio would reprehend all of this behavior in the twenty-first century.

In the 1930s, Woody Guthrie's Columbia River song turned into the *Marseillaise* of the "public power Democrats." After Franklin Roosevelt's reelection in 1936, the massive Bonneville Dam became the first neo-pharoanic project on the Columbia. This land is your land, and it's my land, but for what, exactly? The Bonneville Power Administration (BPA) enticed power-needy businesses to settle in the Pacific Northwest—pulp mills on the coast, iron foundries on the river, vineyards in the high deserts, nuclear plants on the sagebrush prairie. Guthrie got his wish.

Now the BPA, and the dams and the varied industries—all are at the center of the great battles of the Pacific Northwest. Whose land, indeed. In the state of Washington, two geographic consciousnesses have emerged—development versus environment. West of the Cascades, a largely urban population evaluates industry by its environmental impact. East of the Cascades, a mostly rural population judges environmental initiatives by their impact on business. Guthrie's public power Democrats—liberals of long ago—created a status quo of irrigation and hydropower that today's conservative east-of-the-Cascades is desperately trying to maintain. Deference to salmon or spotted owl, says the east, takes food away from the grandchildren of the hungry kids Guthrie worried about.

But demographics have shifted the balance of power. The deciding votes are now in the west—in Tacoma, Seattle and Bellevue—while the overwhelming majority of public lands affected by the west's environmental enthusiasms lie to the east of the mountains, which are the Northwest's cultural wall, its Mason-Dixon line. To apple farmers in Okanogan County, six hours east of Seattle, it was the "damned environmentalists" of the Clinton administration who brought down upon their heads something that felt to the locals like an economic Waco. Apple orchards had prospered there because of irrigation made possible by diversion dams in the Columbia watershed. After the salmon was placed on the Endangered Species List, the irrigation canals dried up; farmers burned their crops and cursed Washington, D.C.

Urgencies vary. In wartime, for example, security trumps civil liberties—but not absolutely. In Lewis and Clark country, if there is any visionary thought of Jeffersonian scope going on, it is directed to reconciling economic development with environmental protection. Ward Parkinson, the cofounder of Micron, Idaho's largest employer, thinks long-term about educated work forces and quality of life, and says that when the state's politicians "decide to protect the salmon on the Snake River, that's when we will know they are serious about developing industry." There may be a convergence of environment and industry coming, but it is still somewhere downstream.

THE PLEDGE OF ALLEGIANCE

July 8, 2002

I LEARNED THE PLEDGE OF ALLEGIANCE BEFORE THE WORDS "under God" were inserted into it. We did not know anything was missing.

Even without God, it was a Norman Rockwell scene: little white boys and girls with their hands over their hearts, facing a flag in the corner of a classroom in northwest Washington, D.C., struggling with the tough five syllables of "indivisible," while children across the racial divide in all-black schools in northeast and southwest Washington ghettos recited the same patriotic words to begin the school day. The colored children grasped the details of the affirmation as little as we white children did, I'd guess. At the same hour on Capitol Hill, Alger Hiss and Whittaker Chambers raised their right hands to be sworn in before the House Un-American Activities Committee. And so the Cold War's First Battle of Bull Run began, eventually producing divisions in America almost as dramatic as the racial ones.

That word "indivisible" is a handsome thought, which we rally to in wartime and generally preserve as an ultimate ideal, but the term has rarely described American history as it is enacted on the ground. America is more interesting than the pietisms it lavishes upon itself.

In 1954, around the time of the Supreme Court's decision outlawing school segregation, and around the time that Vice President Richard Nixon discussed the use of nuclear weapons to relieve the French garrison at Dienbienphu in Indochina, Congress and President Eisenhower promulgated a bill to add the words "under God" to the Pledge of Allegiance. Oppose Godless Communism with Godful Americanism. By then I had converted to Catholicism and left public school for a Jesuit school where we began class not with the pledge but with a Hail Mary—a mood-setter that, like the pledge, lost its force through unthinking repetition.

After 1954, whenever I heard the pledge recited (in the ritual stream-of-consciousness way that one says, "thirtydayshathSeptember-AprilJuneandNovemberalltheresthavethirty-one"), it sounded somehow tampered with, and wrong. The original version had been grooved into my brain. I mistrusted the addition of "under God" first of all on unconscious aesthetic grounds. The new phrase, set off by tendentious commas, was a hiccup in the flow of the drone, the mumbled civic music, the schoolkids' *ommmmmmmm*. Even at that age, I sensed that someone had intruded an alien and politicized bromide into the pledge. Again, the adjacent word "indivisible" banged up against a new divisive irrelevance, a phrase that seemed to demand, somewhere below the surface, "what God—if any—do *you* worship? Is He the God of America? He damn well better be!"

The pledge became one of those gestures of an innocent and anodyne "ceremonial deism"—like "In God We Trust." Here's where we stand: The pledge is no big deal—not an organized religious agenda or otherwise a threat to the Constitution, but rather a vague reassurance of collective goodwill. If you challenge the pledge, however, it becomes a big deal indeed, sacred, indispensable, and not to be messed with.

The Ninth Circuit Court of Appeals in San Francisco—ruling last week that schoolchildren should not recite the pledge, because that phrase "under God" violates the establishment clause of the First Amendment—certainly chose a ridiculously inappropriate moment to mess with it. The decision—at a time when America's post-9/11 flags are still truculently out and its nerves frayed by a now-you-see-it-now-you-don't war against terrorists, by a doubtful economy, and by a longer-term anxiety that a deluge of immigration is swamping the American identity—seemed stupid: fetishistic about the First Amendment, and almost wanton in its cluelessness about the American mood.

Howls arose. The Senate and House—fearlessly doing the difficult, unpopular thing—came out four-square in favor of the Pledge of

Allegiance; so did President Bush. Profiles in courage. The Ninth Circuit, obviously abashed, said it would reconsider.

The Pledge of Allegiance has the comfort of custom about it, and should certainly be preserved. It's too bad the highly dispensable "under God" language cannot be quietly dropped. Fat chance, of course. But why not render unto Caesar an affirmation of flag and country, but keep God in our hearts, where God belongs, and out of politics? Christ himself was scathing about pharisaical display. Don't try to nationalize the deity. It's a little cheap. The Almighty likes to work on a case-by-case basis anyway.

I'm all for patriotism and all for religion. But they need to be watched. Sometimes patriotism becomes the next-to-last refuge of a scoundrel. And sometimes—as Osama Bin Laden and certain pederast priests should have proven to us by now—religion becomes the last resort.

A Thousand Stockings

May 21, 2001

Last night, I sang for duh Sultan of Pasha. He offered me his harem of
500 wives. But I toined him down. Know why? 'Cuz when I get up in
duh mornin', who wants to find a thousand stockings hangin' in duh
bathroom!

—Jimmy Durante

I KNEW A MAN — SHORT, BALD, OF UNDETECTABLE CHARM —
who was a virtual bigamist. He had a wife and family in the suburbs
and something of the same arrangement, though without benefit of
clergy, in town. He lived a complex double life—a secret agent in his
own existence, half of him a stranger to the other half. Which was perhaps his way of keeping himself amused. He often had to eat two
dinners: once, in early evening after work, with his in-town woman,
and a few hours later—after "working late at the office"—with his wife.
No wonder he was fat. Lie management is intricate work, as every philanderer knows. But my friend domesticated the danger, so to speak.
He possessed an eerie serenity, and the twinkle of a man with a secret.
He saw the same movies twice. He had to remember which movies he
had seen with which woman. I wonder if he wrote it down—double-
entry bookkeeping. I would have been a nervous wreck.

I have followed the case of Tom Green with some wonder. Green, a
self-proclaimed Mormon living in the Utah desert, has five wives and
thirty children (the Mormon Church excommunicated Green in 1980
for his belief in polygamy). He has just been convicted of bigamy in
Provo, and could get twenty-five years—five years for each wife—for
doing what all self-respecting male waterbuck, eland, and gnu do as a
matter of course.

Of course the domestic redundancies of my bigamous friend and of polygamous Green are different in spirit, or at least in arrangement. Green—a stern, bearded and Biblical sort of character—has lived, without duplicity, the life of a robust gnu. This begetting is hard work. The sultan of Pasha without the silks, he collected all his wives there in the desert, and they share a common life. My friend, by contrast, conducted a symmetrical, binary life covertly—keeping the right hand ignorant of the left hand's adventures. I think, paradoxically, that in his deepest heart, my friend did it because he needed confirmation of his intuition of the essential loneliness of the world. Or else, less gloomily, he operated on the principle that since the grass is always greener on the other side of the fence, maybe he ought to own territory on both sides.

It also needs to be said, while we are being metaphysical, that two-timing is an effort to thwart the fatal fact that you only go around once. It doesn't work, but it keeps you busy.

Simplify, said Thoreau, who married no one. Monogamy is complexity enough. One of my favorite cases involved François Mitterrand, the former president of France, who had a wife but also many mistresses. He possessed, evidently, an orderly mind. Five days of the week, as I heard the story, he took a different mistress out to dinner, always dining on the same night with the same woman at the same restaurant. Thursday meant Babette and Le Cochon d'Or, or some such. Tuesday meant Françoise and Le Bistro de l'Ennuie. This was cosmopolitan but drearily bureaucratic polygamy, and I cannot help wondering if the women did not get terribly bored, not just with the Great Man, but with the schedule. Might they not have called one another up and tried to swap nights and restaurants, just to get a change of menu?

Tom Green could not possibly have found five good restaurants out there in the Utah desert. On the other hand, I imagine he eats well at home.

No Census for Moses

March 20, 2000

WHEN I WAS ON ASSIGNMENT TO WRITE A MAGAZINE ARTICLE, years ago, about the animals of Africa, I lived for a time with a group of Masai in the remote Loita Hills of Kenya. Their leader was an elder named Moses.

At the time I knew him, Moses owned a herd of upwards of one hundred cows, by my count. He took great joy and satisfaction in them; cattle are the only wealth that means anything to the Masai. Moses knew each of his cows by name, by appearance, even by the place in the line of march she would assume when the herd traveled to water at the river. But when I asked Moses how many cows he had, he became mysterious and evasive. The Masai, like many other people around the world, hate to enumerate. They believe that if the number of cows, for example, is known, it might be easier for someone to place a curse upon them. The evil eye likes to work with numbers, much as a social scientist does.

The U.S. Census Bureau would never get anything out of Moses.

The world is divided between (1) those who, like Moses, resist all quantifications as vaguely menacing, even evil, or at least as being what we, in advanced societies, call invasions of privacy; and (2) those with the social engineer's ambitious turn of mind. I side with Moses.

My short form of the U.S. Census 2000 arrived in the mail the other day, in an envelope that warned: "Your Response Is Required By Law."

The form started by asking "1. How many people were living or staying in this house, apartment, or mobile home on April 1, 2000?" All right. It's not April 1 yet, but never mind. The Constitution says the government should count the citizens from time to time.

But then the bureaucratic oyster-shuckers begin to work the blade between the shells and into the private life: name, phone number, sex, date of birth. Okay, the IRS has all this anyway. And so much more.

As we came to questions eight and nine, however, my adrenaline began to flow. The shuckers wanted to know: Is "Person 1" Spanish/Hispanic/Latino? Mexican, Mexican-American, Chicano? Puerto Rican? Cuban? White? Black? American Indian or Alaska Native? Asian Indian? Chinese? Filipino? Japanese? Korean? Vietnamese? Native Hawaiian? Guamanian or Chamorro? Samoan? Other Pacific Islander?

Why not also ask: Turkish? Bulgarian? French? Basque? Nepalese? Maori? Egyptian? Sicilian? Finnish?

The correct answer is "American." Refuse to cooperate with a racial inquiry that in its implications is bizarrely reminiscent of Nazi practice or of the blood rules of South African apartheid. The Census Bureau, in trying to count Americans, seems to have misplaced the entire meaning of America. The long form of Census 2000, sent to one in every six households, is considerably more intrusive, filled with questions about personal finances and even household plumbing.

The intentions of the census are allegedly benevolent. But racial sifting and enumeration and categorization are inherently wrong. If the purpose is to provide a citizen count in order to determine congressional districts—fine. But, insidiously, we are told it is necessary to have all the detail, racial and otherwise, in order to apportion some $182 billion in federal government funds. In other words, we are being bribed, with $182 billion of our own money, to accept intrusions that should trouble not only antigovernment crackpots but anyone concerned about the way that social engineers, basing their work in the widely accepted but bogus assumptions of the social sciences, endanger freedom.

The social scientist's false assumption is this: That human beings and human behavior can be measured, quantified, predicted and manipulated in the same way, with the same rigor, that prevails in the natural sciences. It is not true. No end of evil and stupidity have proceeded from the premise, an essentially utopian conceit responsible for various totalitarian idiocies (Stalin, Mao, Pol Pot, for example) and lesser homegrown follies of social engineering like St. Louis's Pruitt-Igo, the nightmare high-rise ghetto that had to be blasted to rubble in 1972, only a few years after its erection by the visionary social engineers of the U.S. Department of Urban Development, who had all the numbers and social theories on their side.

My friend Moses was right. Beware the evil eye.

The Right to Wear T-Shirts

March 17, 2003

President George W. Bush took an oath—as he said at his press conference last week—to "protect and defend the Constitution" of the United States. It's good that the Constitution is in the forefront of his mind. It should stay there. It should be engraved on his shaving mirror. It should be embroidered on Attorney General John Ashcroft's bath towels.

Sometimes wars are necessary for the preservation of peace and the enforcement of international law. I think that is what is going on now, although I respect the credible fear that the effect of American action will be the reverse of peace and order. We don't yet know.

Meantime, the least we can do is reread the Constitution and refresh our gratitude and submission to it. Keeping the Constitution will be as vital to the American future as fending off terrorists. More so. If Americans win a war (not just against Saddam Hussein but the longer-term struggle) and lose the Constitution, they will have lost everything.

The terrible freedom of war—with its rush of animal adrenaline, its wild all-is-permitted, its violent necessities—inverts the moral order. Killing, normally forbidden, is suddenly sanctioned, even deemed heroic. Stakes are high. So is fear. Paranoia drifts on the wind like mustard gas. Disagreement may look like treason. Due process may appear to be an unaffordable luxury. The First Amendment may seem optional. The peacetime fail-safe checks and balances (Congress and courts keeping the presidency honest) may strip themselves down to a military principle—deference to the chain of command, and to the commander in chief.

All this is especially true at the start of the twenty-first century, when the urgencies of nuclear weapons, anthrax and other horrors getting hatched in any tinhorn's basement make it even more difficult to keep a watchful and reverent eye on an eighteenth-century document that, for all its service to the republic, can seem a tiresome inconvenience when the blood is up.

With the approach of war, a familiar recklessness boils up from the American id; you catch it, for example, in the talk-show braying about various ingeniously horrible ways that the United States ought to be torturing Khalid Shaikh Mohammed. (I have been trying to decide how much anti-Arab bigotry goes into this: Would the braying be as graphic and gleeful if the terrorist were a Whiffenpoof? Maybe.)

There was a stupid incident last week at the Crossgates Mall in Guilderland, New York, where a sixty-one-year-old lawyer and his son put on T-shirts that read "Peace on Earth" and "Give Peace a Chance," and were ordered by mall security guards to remove the shirts or leave. The lawyer refused, and was charged with trespassing. At high schools across the country, some students were threatened with suspension if they cut classes in order to participate in antiwar demonstrations. The incidents caused a stir, but were insignificant compared with the damage that the Ashcroft Justice Department has inflicted on American freedom since 9/11—a zealot's agenda of illegal detentions, denials of due process and invasions of privacy. If the war on terrorism is open-ended, that means "emergency" measures to combat terrorism can go on indefinitely. That way lies the police state.

Americans should also be careful about Bush's ram-it-and-jam-it, get-real style of preemptive global law enforcement—Wyatt Earp on a mission of Napoleonic Wilsonianism. On the other hand, humility and self-doubt can get you killed in a dangerous world.

In the obscurities of a bad moment, we need the clarity of the Constitution. Just as the Constitution is clear about freedom of speech, it is explicit about the power to make war. Article 1, section 8, gives Congress the authority to declare war. Article 2, section 2, makes the president the commander in chief of the armed forces. Is it constitutionally necessary for Congress to declare war in order for a president to make war? No: The United States has declared war only four times (1812, Spanish-American, World War I, and World War II). Bush has congressional resolutions authorizing force. But you do not want to go into a (to say the least) controversial war, opposed by much of the world, when protected merely by the fine print. I wish Bush had the full constitutional writ behind him. He is a gambler, of course. He's going to be awfully lonely if this goes wrong. Will he be a hero if it goes well?

A hard rain, in any case, is going to fall. Keep the Constitution dry and legible. The danger to America is that in trying to protect what it has, it will lose the very thing that is worth having.

Gramsci Versus Tocqueville

February 1, 2001

Are you a Gramscian or a Tocquevillian?

At the time of the 2000 presidential campaign, George W. Bush was an emphatic Tocquevillian. His plan enlisting faith-based organizations to solve social problems was a Tocquevillian project.

Al Gore, by contrast, ran a somewhat Gramscian campaign, noodling themes of class warfare and identity politics, speaking on the veiled premise that society is divided between oppressors and oppressed, between bloated white Republican clubmen and a rainbow coalition of everyone else. Oddly enough, Gore's running mate, Joe Lieberman, had been on record as a devout Tocquevillian, on the side of religion, morality, patriotism and the American exceptionalism—the United Colors of Bill Bennett. Or at least he was Tocquevillian until Gore telephoned. Lieberman sold a few of his principles down the river to run with the Gramscians.

In the February 2001 issue of *Policy Review,* the bimonthly published by the conservative Heritage Foundation, John Fonte, a senior fellow of the Hudson Institute, makes the case that for all the famous convergence at the center of American politics (supposedly a legacy of Clintonism—not too liberal, not too conservative, but a little of both), America remains in the grip of a profound culture war.

Fonte identifies the opposing armies in the war as Gramscians and Tocquevillians. The Gramscians take their name from the twentieth-century Marxist intellectual and politician Antonio Gramsci (1891–1937). As Fonte remarks: "Despite [Gramsci's] enormous influence on today's politics, he remains far less well-known to most Americans than does Tocqueville," the prescient young French visitor who figured out America so brilliantly a hundred years before Gramsci's death.

Left brain, right brain: Gramsci and Tocqueville represent radically different ways of thinking about America. "Like Marx," Fonte writes, "[Gramsci] argued that all societies in human history have been divided into two basic groups: the privileged and the marginalized, the oppressor and the oppressed, the dominant and the subordinate." Europe is that way—and America is no exception. Gramsci went beyond Marx to include "also women, racial minorities, and many 'criminals.'" Therefore: The personal—in fact, all life—is political. There are no absolute moral standards: Morality is socially constructed. And so on.

Gramsci's American descendants, as Fonte notes, include feminists like Catharine MacKinnon ("a rape is not an isolated event or moral transgression or individual interchange gone wrong but an act of terrorism and torture within a systemic context of group subjection, like lynching") and others (in interest groups, government, universities and major corporations) who speak the neo-Marxian rhetoric of categories and conspiracies—who speak, in effect, of oppressed moral proletarians (gays, women, the disabled, people of color) and "enemies of the people," usually meaning (by process of elimination) heterosexual white males.

The Tocquevillians, on the other hand, say America is an exception. They "take Alexis de Tocqueville's essentially empirical description of American exceptionalism and celebrate the traits of this exceptionalism as normative values to be embraced." In the contemporary Tocquevillians' view, says Fonte, "Americans today, just as in Tocqueville's time, are much more individualistic, religious, and patriotic than the people of any other comparably advanced nation."

Is this Gramscian-Tocquevillian split the same as the red-blue fifty-fifty division we saw on the electoral map in November 2000? Yes, but not exactly. In millions of individual citizens' minds, elements of the two views blend. For example, I am essentially Tocquevillian, but the Tocquevillian American should nurture an enormous tolerance that is enabled by the assumptions (1) that American life ought, above all, to be fair, and (2) that there's enough here for everyone. But tolerance to a Tocquevillian is condescension to a Gramscian. Gramscianism lives on an invidious and Europeanized zero-sum kind of thinking about power.

Gramscian ideas are far advanced in America. You see them in "hate crimes" laws, in gender equity legislation, in forced corporate "sensitivity" training, in the menace of coerced "right thinking" in the universities. You feel the nuances of it in casual conversation. It's an attitude at a cocktail party. To speak Tocquevillian (the deepest American cultural tradition) is as bad as lighting up a cigarette at a dinner party on the Upper West Side.

The Tocquevillian is the Gramscian's right-wing fascist. But the Gramscian, you see, is a vicious Kluxer in her own right. As Bugs Bunny says, "This means war."

BEFORE THE FALL

January 11, 2001

IN A BOOK ABOUT HIS BOYHOOD, *AN HOUR BEFORE DAYLIGHT*, Jimmy Carter describes the close friendships that he had with black children when growing up in south Georgia in the 1930s.

I listened to Carter on National Public Radio the other day as he discussed that time. His familiar soft drawl—a sweet voice, with that undercurrent of regret and wonder that signals a Southerner's nostalgia drifting back over a considerable distance—called back in my own mind a summer in southern Maryland many years ago, when I was a nine-year-old white boy and my best friend was Charles, the son of a black tenant farmer.

It's a familiar memory to people who remember the South in the days before *Brown v. Board of Education*—the days of Jim Crow racism (I have thousands of memories of that) accompanied by the bittersweet, paradoxical business of real, exuberant friendships between black children and white children: innocent intimacies, prelapsarian. Those friendships have the quality of Mark Twain boyhoods—not entirely a matter of Tom Sawyer's rapscallion innocence, but something of boyhood bitterly shadowed, as *Huckleberry Finn* was, by violence, alcoholism, hatred, vicious stupidity and the precocious knowledge of evil. Harper Lee had the atmosphere in *To Kill a Mockingbird*.

My ten-year-old brother, Hugh, and I had been, in effect, exiled for the summer, in the care of our teenage Aunt Sally, to a small vacation cottage (no electricity, no running water) on a backcountry farm absentee-owned by a friend of my father's. You went a mile down a dirt road crusted with crushed oyster shells until you came to the cottage. The yard was overgrown with tall grass, and if you weren't careful you might fall into the small, empty cracked-concrete swimming pool. A path led down to Charles Creek, a tributary of Chesapeake Bay.

There was a ramshackle dock with many planks missing, and a skiff, from which we caught crabs by trailing knotted twine behind us in the weedy, brackish-green water. We were impressed by the stupidity of the crabs, which clung stubbornly to the twine as we hauled them up to die in the skiff.

Hughie and I preferred to live with the tenant farmer's family in their unpainted, weathered house half a mile down the road. My brother, Charles and I stayed up poring over the Montgomery Ward's catalog by the coal oil lamp, fantasizing about the cowboy boots that were available for $5.95 (an impossible sum of money), and falling asleep in sleeping bags on the living room floor. (The news the other day that Montgomery Ward's had gone out of business bumped in my mind against Jimmy Carter's voice and memories—all items from a lost world.)

Charles aspired to be a jockey, and he would gallop from place to place, slapping the back of his thighs with his hands to make the sound of a horse's hoofs. His father had a plow-horse named Bill, a long-suffering white mare. The three of us boys would climb aboard the broad acreage of Bill's back and ride her down the oyster-shell road to the blacktop and then on to Chink's roadhouse, where we would go in by the "Colored" entrance, and there, in a barroom twilight amid the stale beer and dead cigarette smells, Charles would with utmost deference approach the owner Chink and place our morning's bets on the numbers. We never bet more than ten cents, all in pennies, money collected from Aunt Sally and Charles's mother, Leola, and from our own stash. We never won, never hit the number, though we tried elaborate systems (jumbled birthdays and the like). But the trip to Chink's remained all summer a hopeful ritual, an adventure.

I have not revisited this memory in years. It represents, I think, a sort of private racial Eden, previous to the knowledge of color differences and all the ugliness in America that has always proceeded from those.

Heraclitus

March 19, 2001

Heraclitus—"the obscure philosopher," the pre-Socratic thinker who was 2,500 years ago a contemporary of Confucius, Lao Tzu and the Buddha—is best known as the man who said that you cannot put your foot into the same river twice.

Here is how the poet Brooks Haxton, in his fine new translation of Heraclitus, puts the thought:

> *The river*
> *where you set*
> *your foot just now*
> *is gone—*
> *those waters*
> *giving way to this,*
> *now this.*

The Fragments are all that are left of Heraclitus's book, *On Nature*, which was lost many centuries ago. The Fragments have a scattered, enigmatic quality—epigrams and bits of poetry saved from the ruins. But they have a wit, and, for an "obscure" philosopher, a prismatic clarity that travels well across centuries. The thoughts remain fresh and profound. Haxton's translation shines them up handsomely.

> *To a god the wisdom*
> *of the wisest man*
> *sounds apish. Beauty*
> *in a human face*
> *looks apish too.*
> *In everything*

we have attained
the excellence of apes.

Heraclitus was of royal blood but renounced his heritage. He looked on his fellow Ephesians with a certain aristocratic disdain. He hated the mediocrity of those who "eat their way/ toward sleep like nameless oxen." The Ephesians, he wrote,

say, No man should be
worthier than average. Thus,
my fellow citizens declare
whoever would seek
excellence can find it
elsewhere among others.

It's bracing to come upon an intelligent elitist long, long dead, especially when we live in an Ephesus of our own, filled, as his was, with mediocrities and idiot intoxications. Haxton writes in his introduction: "To a sober mind, the drunkenness of cultic worshipers must have been particularly unappealing in a cosmopolitan city like Ephesus, with gods of wine on every side, drunken Greeks initiated into the Thracian ecstacies of Dionysius running amok with drunken Phrygians worshipping Sabazius, Lydians possessed by Bassareus, and Cretans in the frenzy of Zagreus, all claiming in their cups to have transcended understanding."

Heraclitus said:

Stupidity is better
kept a secret
than displayed.

And:

Seekers of wisdom first
need sound intelligence.

He was sardonically hard-headed:

> *Hungry livestock,*
> *though in sight of pasture,*
> *need the prod.*

And disdainful of mystic transports:

> *Pythagoras may well have been*
> *the deepest in his learning of all men,*
> *and still he claimed to recollect*
> *details of former lives,*
> *being in one a cucumber*
> *and one time a sardine.*

The Fragments speak in an eerily contemporary voice. Heraclitus anticipated Einstein in the realization that energy is the essence of matter:

> *All things change to fire,*
> *and fire exhausted*
> *falls back into things.*

The metaphor of Heraclitean fire posited an absolutely unstable world, in constant flux, consuming and creating, the alternation and reconciliation of day and night, waking and sleeping, life and death, wet and dry, good and evil.

> *What was cold soon warms,*
> *and warmth soon cools.*
> *So moisture dries,*
> *and dry things drown.*

And:

The earth is melted
into the sea
by that same reckoning
whereby the sea
sinks into the earth.

Here is the ultimate economy:

As all things change to fire,
and fire exhausted
falls back into things,
the crops are sold
for money spent on food.

But at least these words have, for 2,500 years, survived the fire.

THE PLAGUE MENTALITY

September 23, 1985

An epidemic of yellow fever struck Philadelphia in August 1793. Eyes glazed, flesh yellowed, minds went delirious. People died, not individually, here and there, but in clusters, in alarming patterns. A plague mentality set in. Friends recoiled from one another. If they met by chance, they did not shake hands but nodded distantly and hurried on. The very air felt diseased. People dodged to the windward of those they passed. They sealed themselves in their houses. The deaths went on, great ugly scythings. Some adopted a policy of savage self-preservation, all sentiment heaved overboard like ballast. Husbands deserted stricken wives, parents abandoned children. The corpses of even the wealthy were carted off unattended, to be shoveled under without ceremony or prayer. One-tenth of the city's population died before cold weather came in the fall and killed the mosquitoes.

The plague mentality is something like the siege mentality, only more paranoid. In a siege, the enemy waits outside the walls. In a plague or an epidemic, he lives intimately within. Death drifts through human blood or saliva. It commutes by bug bite or kiss or who knows what. It travels in mysterious ways, and everything, everyone, becomes suspect: a toilet seat, a child's cut, an act of love. Life slips into science fiction. People begin acting like characters in the first reel of *The Invasion of the Body-Snatchers*. They peer intently at one another as if to detect the telltale change, the secret lesion, the sign that someone has crossed over, is not himself anymore, but one of *them*, alien and lethal.

In the plague mentality, one belongs either to the kingdom of life or to the kingdom of death. So the state of mind glints with a certain fanaticism. It is said that when children saw the telltale sign during the Black Death in the fourteenth century, they sang, "Ring around a rosie!" That meant they saw a ring on the skin around a red spot that marked the onset of the Black Death. "A pocket full of posies" meant the flowers one carried to mask the ambient stench. The ditty ended in apocalypse: "All fall down." The Black Death eventually took off half the population of Europe.

During the American Civil War, more soldiers died of typhoid than died in battle. The epidemic of Spanish influenza in 1918–1919 killed more than 500,000 Americans. Before the Salk vaccine, nearly 600,000 Americans were infected by poliomyelitis, and 10 percent of them died. The polio epidemic caused memorable summers of trauma, during which swimming pools and shopping centers across the United States were closed.

Between 1981 and 1985, some 6,000 people have died of AIDS in the United States. From a statistical point of view, AIDS is not a major plague during this time frame. Still, one detects a plague mentality regarding the disease and those who carry it. Paradoxically, homosexuals are both victims of the plague mentality and themselves perpetrators of it. Because 73 percent of those who have AIDS in the early 1980s are homosexuals, the general populace tends to look with suspicion on all homosexuals. Because the virus is often transmitted by homosexual intercourse, homosexuals themselves bring to their intimate lives a desperate wariness and paranoia.

A plague mentality results from ignorance and fear, but not in the way that is usually meant. When medicine is ignorant about a lethal disease, then the only intelligent approach, by mothers or anyone else, is to be fearful and intensely cautious. But, like a plague itself, a plague mentality seems an anachronism in elaborately doctored postindustrial America. The discussion in recent years has gone in the other direction: Has medicine got so good that it is keeping people alive past their natural time? At a moment when rock fans of the First World undertake to cure a biblical scourge like the Ethiopian famine with twenty-four hours of music bounced off a satellite, AIDS, implacable and thus far incurable, comes as a shock. It arrives like a cannibal at the picnic and eats the children.

Cancer used to be the most dreaded word. But cancer no longer means a virtual sentence of death. AIDS does. AIDS sounds with a peculiar and absolute resonance in our minds. It catches echoes of the voice of God and of nuclear doom. AIDS carries significances that go beyond the numbers of those afflicted.

In some minds, AIDS is a validation of Judeo-Christian morality—a terrible swift sword in the hand of God, a punishment for transgressions against his order. Thus the disease partakes, so to speak, of the prestige of the infinite. AIDS becomes a dramatically targeted refinement of the doctrine that all disease is a form of God's retribution upon fallen and sinful man. "Sickness is in fact the whip of God for the sins of many," said Cotton Mather. AIDS renews in many minds, sometimes in an almost unconscious way, questions of the problem of sin: Is there sin? Against whom? Against what? Is sex sometimes a sin? Why? And what kind of sex? And so on.

The psychological reaction to AIDS, apart from the real fears it engenders, represents a collision between the ordered world of religious faith—God presiding, commandments in force—and a universe that appears indifferent to the Decalogue or the strictures of St. Paul, one in which a disease like AIDS, a "syndrome," is as morally indifferent as a hurricane: an event of nature. Beyond that argument, which itself now seems ancient, it is probable that in most minds a vague dread of the disease is accompanied by a sympathy for those afflicted. Sympathy, alas, is usually directly proportional to one's distance from the problem, and the sentiment will recede if the virus spreads and the sympathetic become the threatened.

AIDS suits the style of the late twentieth century. It becomes a death-dealing absolute loose in the world. Westerners for some years have consolidated their dreads, reposing them (if that is the word) in the Bomb, in the one overriding horror of nuclear holocaust. A fat and prosperous West lounges next door to its great kaboom. It is both smug and edgy at the same time. Now comes another agent of doomsday, this one actually killing people and doubling the number of its victims every ten months as if to reverse the logic of Thomas Malthus. The prospect of nuclear holocaust may be terrible, but the mind takes certain perverse psychological comforts from it. It has not happened, for one thing. And if it does happen, it will be over in a flash. AIDS is slower and smaller, and may not add up ultimately to a world-historical monster. But the bug has ambitions, and is already proceeding with its arithmetic. Meantime, science, which dreamed up the totalitarian nuke, now labors desperately to eradicate its sinister young friend.

TRAGEDY AS CHILD'S PLAY

April 6, 1998

WE PLAYED *LORD OF THE FLIES* IN THE REMOTER WOODS OF Rock Creek Park in Washington, D.C. We collected stones in bushel baskets and hid them among the dogwood blossoms. And then, nasty little sociopaths, ten or twelve years old, we lay in ambush and at the signal hurled rocks full force at our enemies, who were led by the boy with yellow teeth.

One day an older boy, who was almost ready to shave, brought a pellet pistol to the war, not a feckless Daisy that would merely sting but a penetrating gas-fired model, almost as wicked as a .22.

That same day, in the midst of battle, I flanked the boy with yellow teeth and sidearmed a perfect strike at his head. I knew I'd nailed him the instant the rock left my fingers. The missile hit him in the temple, and he clutched his head and fell to his knees, blood gushing through his fingers. I fled in horror, and the war was over. But I secretly cherished a certain involuntary glow of pleasure at the perfect bull's-eye I'd thrown.

What if we'd had automatic rifles? Would we have used them? Our violent imaginations were in business for themselves, loose in the wildwood. We had not signed the Geneva convention. We did not desire blood, but we had not thought the play through to consequence; our fun lay in a kind of self-obliterating game of action and in the glee of power.

I do not mean to say, God knows, that boys will be boys. But it is part of childhood to enter into parallel universes of "play" that may be sinister and that may become the more captivating the more it simulates reality. Usually the play, a form of testing and learning, is not fatal. But boys back to the dawn of human experience have had it in their bones to play violent games. Even the priggish Henry Adams, as a boy in the middle of the nineteenth century, joined the Latin School's army in a bloody rock-in-the-snowball battle on Boston Common against a mob of "blackguards from the slums."

It seems grotesque to think of the Jonesboro, Arkansas, slaughter in terms of play. But that is a way to approach the otherwise mystifying spectacle of children gunning down children. First of all, play is not necessarily innocent. Nor is childhood. The innocence of children (which was the unspoken premise of much horrified commentary last week about the Arkansas school shootings) is an adult myth. The reality is children's extreme vulnerability; their storms of anger and irrationality and their dramatically imaginative lives, which conjure monsters and heroes and set them in motion—whole Iliads. Those imaginations sometimes indulge crazy fantasies of revenge and annihilating vindication. The vulnerability, anger and extreme fantasies of children have been a constant over the centuries, I think. The late twentieth century has not reinvented human nature, even though American perfectionism, in league with what is perhaps the amnesia of the dollar people on the subject of human tragedy, may encourage that illusion.

The little Arkansas shooters were not entirely different from the dysfunctional brat in the park in Washington (me) who nearly killed the boy with yellow teeth. But some things were different in Jonesboro.

We ex-children have created an elaborate culture of fantasy. The more brilliantly our moviemakers and television makers succeed in their work of the technological and artistic imagination, the more their audiences are transported back into the realm of the child-id that is most hospitable to fantasy—a zone of suspended disbelief wherein all things become possible, including deeds of graphic violence. It is sometimes said that too many television shows and movies are cynically targeted at twelve-year-olds. That's not exactly the point: The makers of those shows in effect appropriate the imaginative world of the child because the youthful brain is the environment most frictionlessly sympathetic to fantasy, no questions asked. The tiresome, responsible brain of the adult breaks into the action and says, Now wait a minute.

We pay a moral price. Our profitable fantasy culture has set up a resonance by which, in the minds of children, a murderous dream of revenge, say, slips easily through the looking glass into actuality. The greater our creativity, in some sense the more we disturb the ecology, the balance of nature, between the universes of fantasy and actuality. Naturally, this disturbance is most dramatically manifested in children, who lack the reality-testing resources of experience and self-possession to make the necessary distinctions, and to subdue the animals that sometimes get loose in their brains.

So when you link a fantasy culture to the wondrous American inventory of guns, you may now and then spawn a little terrorist. Guns fire vicious daydreams into the actual. Squint and point, and one magic trigger-finger's twitch, the merest spasm of impulse, may send the world into mayhem. That is a power so seductive that it might even have a little Satan in it.

An Elegy for Integration

October 30, 1995

W HEN THE OLD SOUTHERN RACISTS FILIBUSTERED A CIVIL rights bill, they would serve up fatback inanities to an almost empty Senate chamber—homily grits to obstruct the hours.

Minister Farrakhan's performance at the Million Man March, playing to a packed house, rose through Washington's sweet October air and bounced off satellites. Louis Farrakhan banged on the American mind with a silk umbrella and the handle of a broom: Mumbo jumbo will hoodoo you. He went on about obelisks and the intricate, unintelligible meanings of mystical, pseudo-pharoanic numerologies. He sounded by turns menacing and Rotarian: a salesman in a sharp bow tie, the hallucination of Mussolini channeling Booker T. Washington. Behind him postured his son from the Fruit of Islam, in sunglasses and paramilitary Graustark.

Farrakhan had his moment in history. But he talked too long, and the moment went away. He was strange while it lasted.

And the white marble city was washed in a tide of black men's anger, yearning, hope, self-affirmation and, during Farrakhan's weirder passages, restless bewilderment.

There was more to the manifestation in Washington than Farrakhan. But what did the numbers and energy mean? Was the Million Man March a Woodstock of black American manhood—a vivid but perishable spectacle? A protest without a program, the dictum has it, is mere sentimentality. Or was the march a turning point, a moment of moral liftoff, a Great Awakening? And would there be, down the road when nothing changes, another Great Disillusioning?

I came away with the thought—melancholy, unhopeful—that it is getting to be time for Americans to clarify their minds about integration. Time for blacks and whites to stop indulging themselves—as

Farrakhan does—in separatist fantasies and to return to the text of that infinitely superior speech that Martin Luther King Jr. delivered at the march on Washington in 1963. Time to return to the ideal of an individualist, integrated, color-blind society—and to understand that that ideal will require yet more time and hard work. But perhaps I also am guilty of a sentimentality without a program. I don't know anyone of any race in multicultural and coreless America who acts as if he or she thinks integration is a good idea.

The country, almost without knowing where it was going, has wandered down unpaved roads that vanish into swampland. The Farrakhan march—warmhearted, festive, lovely in its way—was a sort of culminating symptom. On respectable op-ed pages, writers have been suggesting that we might as well consider breaking off part of the United States to form a separate Republic of African America. The arrangement would confirm a secession that has already occurred in millions of minds all over the country. The attitude is that it was a horrible marriage from the start and has long since dissolved in chronic dysfunction, occasional riot and permanent mutual contempt. Why keep the ugly, abusive charade going? (Was it some such domestic metaphor playing in the unconscious mind that made the Simpson case so fascinating?)

With the O. J. Simpson verdict and with the country about to turn the autumn corner into the 1996 presidential election, I keep returning to the sentiment that Americans could find, if they were looking, in the old hymn "Lord, Plant My Feet on Higher Ground." King was right: The content of one's character, not the color of one's skin, is what matters. Stop defining people by color, by groups (blacks, whites, Asians, gays). Stop practicing the politics of tribal identity. But you would have to rescind a universe of political correctness and poisonous identity politics in order to restore the old moral order.

Still, I think wistfully, America has made a career of transcending itself, of leaving its worse selves behind. If it had not, the United States would have devolved into a sort of continental Beirut long ago. The worse self that should now be left behind may be the oldest residual American self—the racial-tribal. The continuation of the American idea depends upon the nation's transcending that. All Americans will arrive at civilization together, or they will not arrive at all.

It is too bad that the main speaker at the Million Man March was not Glenn Loury, the Boston University economist and author (*One by One from the Inside Out: Essays and Reviews on Race and Responsibility in America*) who brings more clarity and decency to the subject of race in America than almost anyone else. Is integration mere sentimentality? Is justice not the deeper need, the more attainable? Can there be justice without integration? What kind of justice, and for whom?

Unlike Louis Farrakhan, writes Loury, "Dr. King was a leader of both black and white Americans." Part of his accomplishment, Loury points out, lay in "assuring the 'good people' on each side of the racial divide that their counterparts on the other side do in fact exist. He sought to create a dynamic within which growing numbers of Americans could embrace a strategy of reconciliation among decent people of both races." Today it is the bad people on either side who know for certain that their counterparts exist.

POSTSCRIPT, YEARS LATER: Glenn Loury eventually changed his mind. He reversed his opinion about affirmative action and condemned those who, like me, used Martin Luther King's words to argue against racial preferences. I still believe that Loury was essentially right the first time.

THE MUSEUM OF SLAVERY

August 14, 1995

I SAY, "BLACKS SHOULD FOCUS ON WHATEVER INCREASES BLACK self-respect and pride. That is the answer." He—old friend, old comrade—leans across the table, voice angry, eyes flame throwing. I should not have said "should."

"Listen," he starts, meaning, Listen, Whitey. "After everything that has happened, no white man has the right to tell blacks what they should be doing—about anything!"

I have a temper too. I stifle an impulse to reply with what W. C. Fields called an evasive answer. I pause and let the adrenaline subside; I roll my eyes to the ceiling and raise my open palms, priestlike: Peace.

But I am right—presumptuous and prim but on the money: self-respect. The answer is in the black mind. Forget about the white mind. The Muslims have been saying it for years.

But when a white man says such things, the truth, arriving from the wrong direction, becomes an enemy truth to blacks—less welcome than a lie. (Enslave them, and then lecture them about self-respect—cutely done, Mr. Charles.) Still, my inner ranter is awake and would push even further. He wants to say, "Forget about racism, about racists. They are always there, and irrelevant. What matters is the content of the black mind, not the white. Building the black mind, its morale." I do not say it. I have no right. My friend ascribes the ills of the universe to racism.

My friend is handsome, brainy, son of a distinguished family, successfully married, light-skinned in a city (Washington) where—a source of ideological discomfort—light skin proclaims the black elite. He was educated in the Ivy League, has climbed high in his profession. But precisely the reasons for which he should feel self-respect, airtight reasons for a white man, raise confusing interior questions about his identity as a black man. Or so I surmise. Hence the anger. Ellis Cose wrote a book called *The Rage of a Privileged Class* about black executives and law partners who earn half a million dollars or more a year and feel sorry for themselves. My friend is a flashing electrical display of privileged rage.

And thus upon our lunchtime dialogue at Washington's Jefferson Hotel (named for that numinous slave-owning paradox) there descends the ancestral "twoness," something of the familiar racial veil W. E. B. DuBois wrote about in 1903.

But my friend and I retreat from the battlefield. We part as friends. For days I continue our conversation in my mind.

I look up DuBois's great book *The Souls of Black Folk* and admire again its rolling thunder:

> After the Egyptian and Indian, the Greek and Roman, the Teuton and Mongolian, the Negro is a sort of seventh son, born with a veil, and gifted with second-sight in this American world—a world which yields him no true self-consciousness, but only lets him see himself through the revelation of the other world . . . One ever feels his twoness,—an American, a Negro; two souls, two thoughts, two unreconciled strivings.

Will DuBois's famous refrain—"the problem of the Twentieth Century is the problem of the color line"—be just as valid in the twenty-first? I like to doubt it.

What will cure the twoness? So many of the problems remain the same. But everything is changed too, mainly because of the emergence of a black middle class. I take up Glenn Loury's *One by One from the Inside Out*. Loury, a professor of economics at Boston University, is black and writes, among many other things, "No people can be genuinely free so long as they look to others for their deliverance."

In my imaginary conversation, I echo Loury: Affirmative action confuses the racial issue, placing all blacks in the same category and obscuring the differences between the black middle class and the black poor. The need is not affirmative action for the black middle class (for whom it may turn into a moral scam and irrelevance). The imperative is massive intelligent help for the poor, whose condition is an American apocalypse—a disgrace to the nation and, although many may not accept it, a disgrace to the black middle class. That middle class preaches conservative values to its children but excuses the destructive world of the poor as a somehow "authentic" snoop-doggie gangsta-rap culture whose misery results from white racism. That continuing misery is also a form of moral capital for the black middle class.

Yet at our lunch it occurred to me that the essential problem also revolves, at a deeper level, around myths. We have the founders' story (Washington et al.), the frontier story (endless folklore there) and the Ellis Island story (sepia-tinted immigrant myth). What is the great void in the national tale?

"What would you think," I ask my friend, "about a museum and memorial on the Mall in Washington, something called the American Museum of Slavery and Freedom—a national acknowledgment of the history? There is still this terrible suppression of what happened—or half-suppression. There's denial and ignorance—or else a lot of fatuous political correctness. And yet American culture has been more powerfully formed by black energies than almost anyone knows. Wouldn't it accomplish something to lift the history into full sunshine? The Vietnam Memorial, after all, worked in a healing way."

"Oh, it's a good idea," my friend says. "It wouldn't solve anything, though."

I think: It might be a modest start.

Hiroshima

September 19, 1994

ONE MORNING IN HIROSHIMA, I WATCHED AS HUNDREDS OF Japanese schoolchildren—a newly minted generation in their navy-and-white uniforms—poured out of the Peace Memorial Museum. The Japanese authorities take children there every day, busload after busload, to see the evidence: the photographs taken on August 6, 1945, and the days afterward; the drawings that the child survivors made to show what they had seen; the blinding thousand-sun light; the river choked with bodies; the melted clocks; the nuclear soot that fell upon the city—"black rain." These sights are implanted in the minds of today's Japanese children as . . . what? Warning? Against what exactly? Accusation? Against whom precisely?

Now it is common for Japanese children to practice their English on the *gaijin,* and seeing me outside the museum, a little boy danced up, peered into my face and said brightly, "Murderer! Hello!"

I thought of the Japanese schoolboy in recent months at Washington's Smithsonian Institution as I shuffled through one script after another, trying to figure out how to deal with Hiroshima in a fiftieth-anniversary exhibition about the end of the war and the dawn of the nuclear era. Around the Smithsonian, the task brought on profound moral discomfort.

The first script for the exhibition, which will display a part of the re-assembled Enola Gay, was way left of the mark. It interpreted Hiroshima and Nagasaki in a way that managed to transport a righteous 1960s moral stance on Vietnam ("Baby killers!") back in time to portray the Japanese as more or less innocent victims of American beastliness and lust for revenge. As if the Japanese had been conquering Asia by Marquess of Queensbury rules. The curators said to the American public, "Murderer! Hello!"

The spirit of the text struck some Americans who had the advantage of having been there at the time as a revisionist travesty. The curators seemed to be confused about who started the war and who pursued it (in China, the Philippines and elsewhere) with relentless inhumanity. To turn the Japanese into the victims of World War II, and the Americans into the villains, seemed an act of something worse than ignorance; it had the ring of a perverse generational upsidedownspeak and Oedipal lèse-majesté.

The anger of World War II veterans and others who knew what they were talking about descended upon the Smithsonian. The curators produced a revised script earlier in the summer and last week a third try, which finally puts Hiroshima and Nagasaki into the historical context of Japanese aggression and its many victims and of a long and vastly destructive war.

Of course, the metaphysics is confusing. Hiroshima, introducing the nuclear age, lifted war out of its traditional (and more or less manageable) place in human affairs and into a realm of the absolute, of doomsday.

When the Italian author Primo Levi was in Auschwitz, a guard told him, *"Hier ist kein warum."* (Here is no why.) He was right. That was the terror, the mystery and the evil.

But you have to make distinctions, even—or especially—when using the vocabularies of seeming absolutes. At Hiroshima there was, precisely, a *warum,* an excellent why.

To understand the reason, it may be necessary to return to the moment. Events occur in contexts. At the time, it seemed that nothing less than such a devastation would serve to eradicate a Japanese militarist regime that had killed many more innocent civilians than died on those two nuclear mornings. The scales of death were pretty heavy, well before the Bomb. Four months earlier, Americans suffered 48,000 casualties taking Okinawa. And in March 1945, the incendiary-bomb raids had burned down much of Tokyo and killed at least 100,000, a toll approaching the combined carnage at Hiroshima and Nagasaki. To have possessed a weapon that would end such a war almost instantly and not to have used it would have been inexplicable and, to those who would have died in the longer war, inexcusable.

It is possible in hindsight to entertain hypothetical doubt about whether an invasion of the Japanese home islands would have been absolutely necessary at that stage of the war. Perhaps the Japanese would have submitted, although nothing in experience predicted that. One may argue whether the nuclear bombs really saved a million or two or more lives, Japanese and American, that might have been lost in a protracted endgame. But sometimes hindsight is decadent and a little fatuous.

Last week, a couple of days after the Smithsonian released its third Hiroshima script, Elie Wiesel was speaking in Washington, D.C., at the new U.S. Holocaust Memorial Museum. He was addressing 120 teenagers from five Middle Eastern countries who had spent a summer session at a Maine camp in the Seeds of Peace program. A Palestinian boy in the program minimized the Jews' Holocaust under the Nazis and said bitterly, thinking of his own people, "There are many holocausts!"

Elie Wiesel embraced the boy and told him, "Don't compare! Don't compare! All suffering is intolerable."

A Holocaust of Words

March 2, 1988

The library in Leningrad burned for a night and a day. By the time the fire was out at the National Academy of Sciences, 400,000 books had been incinerated. An additional 3.6 million had been damaged by water. In the weeks since the fire, workers have been shoveling blackened remains of books into trash bins and hanging the sodden survivors on lines to dry in front of enormous electric fans.

A holocaust of words. No one died in the fire. And yet whenever books burn, one has a sense of mourning. Books are not inanimate objects, not really, and the death of books, especially by fire, especially in such numbers, has the power of a kind of tragedy. Books are life-forms, children of the mind. Words (in the beginning was the Word) have about them some of the mystery of creation.

Russians have always loved their books profoundly. Literature has sometimes sustained the Russians when almost everything else was gone. During the siege of Leningrad, the city's population, frozen and starving down to the verge of cannibalism, drew strength by listening to a team of poets as they read on the radio from the works of Pushkin and other writers. "Never before nor ever in the future," said a survivor, "will people listen to poetry as did Leningrad in that winter—hungry, swollen and hardly living." Today Russians will fill a stadium to hear a poetry reading.

There is some irony in the Russian passion for books. Knowing the power of written words, Russian authority has for centuries accorded books the brutal compliment of suppression. It has slain books by other means than fire. Book publishing first flourished in Russia under Catherine the Great, and yet it was she who used local police, corrupt and ignorant, to enforce the country's first censorship regulations. Czar Nicholas I conducted a sort of terrorism against certain books and writers. He functioned as personal censor for Pushkin and banished Dostoyevsky to Siberia. Revolution only encouraged the Russian candle-snuffers. Lenin said, "Ideas are much more fatal things than guns," the founder telling his successor, in effect, *nihil obstat,* and setting in motion the years of poet destruction (Osip Mandelstam, Marina Tsvetaeva) and book murder under Stalin.

For generations of Russians, books have been surrounded by exaltation and tragedy. In a prison camp in the Gulag during the 1960s, the poet and essayist Andrei Sinyavsky hid hand-copied pages of the Book of Revelations in the calf of his boot. He wrote, "What is the most precious, the most exciting smell waiting for you in the house when you return to it after half a dozen years or so? The smell of roses, you think? No, mouldering books."

Vladimir Nabokov carried his love of Russian into exile:

> *Beyond the seas where I have lost a sceptre,*
> *I hear the neighing of my dappled nouns,*
> *Soft participles coming down the steps,*
> *Treading on leaves, trailing their rustling gowns . . .*

Americans don't take books that seriously anymore. Russians don't either: Their popular culture has begun to succumb to television. In America one rarely encounters the mystical book worship. Everything in the West today seems infinitely replicable, by computer, microfilm, somehow, so that if a book chances to burn up, there must be thousands more where that came from. If anything, there seem to be entirely too many words and numbers in circulation, too many sinister records of everything crammed into the microchips of FBI, IRS, police departments. Too many books altogether, perhaps—too much information, anyway. The glut of books subverts a reverence for them. Bookstore tables groan under the piles of remaindered volumes. In the United States more than fifty thousand new titles are published every year.

It was the Dominican zealot Girolamo Savonarola who presided over the Bonfire of the Vanities during Carnival in Florence in 1497.

Thousands of the Florentine children who were Savonarola's followers went through the city collecting what they deemed lewd books, as well as pictures, lutes, playing cards, mirrors and other vanities, and piled them in the great Piazza della Signoria of Florence. The pyramid of offending objects rose sixty feet high, and went up in flames. One year later Savonarola had a political quarrel with Pope Alexander VI, was excommunicated, tried and hanged. His body was burned at the stake. Savonarola went up in smoke.

The Leningrad library fire was a natural disaster. Deliberate book burning seems not only criminal but evil. Why? Is it worse to destroy a book than to kill its author? Is it worse to destroy a book by burning it than to throw it into the trash compactor? Or to shred it? Not in effect. But somehow the irrevocable reduction of words to smoke and poof! into nonentity haunts the imagination. In Hitler's bonfires in 1933, the works of Kafka, Freud, Einstein, Zola and Proust were incinerated— their smoke a prefiguration of the terrible clouds that came from the Nazi chimneys later.

Anyone who loves books knows how hard it is to throw even one of them away, even one that is silly or stupid or vicious and full of lies. How much more criminal, how much more a sin against consciousness, to burn a book. A question then: What if one were to gather from the corners of the earth all the existing copies of *Mein Kampf* and make a bonfire of them? Would that be an act of virtue? Or of evil?

Sometimes it seems that the right books never get burned. But the world has its quota of idiotic and vicious people just as it has its supplies of books that are vicious, trashy and witless. Books are eventually as mortal as people—the acids in the paper eat them, the bindings decay and at last the books crumble in one's hands. But their ambition anyway is to outlast the flesh. Books have a kind of enshrining counterlife. One can live with the thought of one's own death. It is the thought of the death of words and books that is terrifying. For that is the deeper extinction.

The Holocaust Museum

April 26, 1993

A STORY TOLD BY AN ISRAELI ARMY COLONEL WHILE DRIVING through blinding sunlight from the Dead Sea to the Jordan River:

The colonel's parents lost seven children in the Nazi death camps. But the parents survived. After the war, they made their way to Israel, where they conceived a son (the colonel), whom they called their miracle child. Though they doted on him and loved him dearly (as may be imagined), they sent him off at an early age to be raised on a kibbutz—away from his parents. For the Holocaust, the mother and father felt, had left such a terrible darkness of grief in them, such a residue of adhesive evil, that they feared the communicated memory of it would haunt the child and blight his life. Better he should be a sabra and kibbutznik, raised in the sunshine of Eretz Yisrael.

The politics of memory is complicated. Never remember? Or never forget? Or simply, Never again? Now the parents' generation, the survivors of the Hitler years, are in their seventies and eighties and are dying off. The generation's memory—along with whatever objects and images and cautionary knowledge may be salvaged—needs to find permanent residence. Or else it will be lost. This week, a powerful—and controversial—fortress against forgetting is being dedicated in Washington, D.C.

The United States Holocaust Memorial Museum, more than a dozen years in planning and construction, has been built at the edge of the Mall, L'Enfant's expanse that is a kind of spacious American myth-yard. There the eye sweeps across the Capitol and Washington Monument, Lincoln Memorial and Jefferson Memorial, the white marbles softened at this time of year by dogwood and cherry blossoms. The Mall bespeaks eighteenth-century Enlightenment come to America, a certain lucidity and ideal. The Holocaust museum is like the twentieth-century "Endarkenment," a dense, evil mystery set down in the new world, an ocean away from where it happened.

That is what most of the argument is about. At Washington dinner parties, you hear the questions: Why put it in Washington? Why not in Berlin, say? Or else: Why should the Germans suffer this kind of permanently installed American rebuke, as if the years of Hitler were all of German history? And why would Americans build a memorial and museum to the European Holocaust before installing a remembrance, say, of slavery and the black American struggle, or of the devastation of American Indian life? The premise is that America's sacred statuary memory belongs to things that happened on native grounds. An odor of anti-Semitism sometimes gusts around these dinner tables, the half-stated thought being: It's Jews imposing, trying to push into the American club of myth with their alien memories. Further: Do we have to go through all this again, the hand-wringing, the Holocaust?

Does the Holocaust museum belong? Well, it does. Those who object to it are just as wrong as the other people who (for different reasons) campaigned against the Vietnam Veterans Memorial, calling it a depressive exercise, an insult to the American military and a "black gash of shame." The Vietnam wall transcended the criticisms and became an American shrine.

The Holocaust museum stands beside the U.S. Bureau of Engraving and Printing. Architect James Freed, of Pei Cobb Freed & Partners, gave one side of the exterior a sort of bland grandness of facade, a little like the Department of Agriculture as it might have been done by Albert Speer. But the facade, like Speer's overblown neoclassical productions, masks an emptiness, and behind that, a horror. Within, Freed's design encloses all the menacing, grim functionalism, the history and the instruments, of bureaucratically enacted genocide: Hannah Arendt's "banality of evil" done up in the Bauhaus of hell.

Freed, who grew up in Nazi Germany but escaped to America in 1939, has twisted the death factory to a surreal dimension. The roof is a procession of camp watchtowers. The enormous Hall of Witness is a sort of evil atrium with steel-braced brick walls reminiscent of crematoria. A staircase narrows unnaturally toward the top, crowding the visitors together, like a trick of perspective, like receding railroad tracks made abruptly real—the Final Solution machine. Angles are skewed, expectations thwarted and sight lines intolerably torqued. No exit.

These touches (sometimes just barely) transcend mere surreal trickiness because of the truth they express. The real power of the museum is in its concrete narrative details, which gather themselves into an intense course in humanity and inhumanity. The place assumes no prior knowledge of the Holocaust and all that surrounded it, but through films, photographs, heartbreaking human artifacts and placard narratives, it tells the story—not only of Europe's Jews but also of the Gypsies, homosexuals and others the Nazis set about trying to annihilate.

Here is a tower gallery of Jewish life before the deluge in the Lithuanian town of Ejszyszki, presently to be extinguished—picnics, children, a beautiful young woman, faces like quizzical flowers. Here is a railroad boxcar of the kind that carried people to Auschwitz. With one or two exceptions (such as a casting of the notorious iron *Arbeit Macht Frei* sign over the entrance to Auschwitz), nothing is simulated, every object is authentic, the real thing. Some of the film footage is grisly to the point of being unwatchable. Those images too disturbing for children are screened off to a height of five feet or so.

The best argument for the museum is this: It is a civilizing place that deepens the ideas of justice and humanity on which the United States depends. America needs its comprehensive moral ambition, the universal idea of itself as the last best hope. The country succeeds by renewing its idea of justice and by striving toward it. The Holocaust was a catastrophe of the civilized heart and of justice, and no one, including Americans, can be whole without trying to understand it.

Americans refused to take in the "Ship of Fools" in 1939, the liner *St. Louis,* even though it sailed as close as Havana with its 1,128 refugees fleeing Hitler. The American military in 1944 declined to bomb the death camps or the rail lines leading to them. These decisions (documented in the museum) have a contemporary resonance: bureaucratic cowardice and fecklessness, indifference, appeasement, denial, tribal intolerance and fanaticism, racial hatred. This is the way these things happen. The Holocaust is a densely compacted drama of warning that needs to be remembered repeatedly. In the world at the end of the twentieth century, geography matters less; borders are porous, ideas go at the speed of light. A European apocalypse is not alien to America. The lessons are here—played out to an extreme that has become the world standard of evil, a sort of baseline.

The enslavement of blacks in America, an immense historical tragedy, was, however, different from the European Holocaust. Slavery did not threaten the extinction of black Africans; in biblical terms, it was more like the Egyptian captivity, not the apocalypse. But it is ridiculous to engage in a competition of comparative tragedies. A Museum of Black America in Washington is just as necessary, and would be just as civilizing, as the Holocaust museum.

The claim that the Holocaust never occurred has been spreading in America. The statement gets laundered, like dirty money, as it is passed along, especially to the young. A Midwestern mother, Jewish, hired a fifteen-year-old gentile girl to help with the children one summer. The mother had a number of books on her shelves about the Holocaust. The bright fifteen-year-old said one day, in a nice way, as if stating simple fact: "Why do you have so many books on that? It never happened, you know."

In the future such a girl's high school class might make a spring trip to Washington and visit the museum, and come away with a moral and political immunization that may be as useful, in the real world, as the Salk vaccine.

COLLATERAL DAMAGE

May 7, 2001

THAT NIGHT IN THE MEKONG DELTA, THE WOMEN AND CHIL-dren who died were, in the heartless phrase, *collateral damage*. They were victims of the fog of battle, or of the atrocity of Oops! You can't make an omelet without breaking a few eggs.

Vietnam was some omelet. But it was a war, after all—a tragic, confusing, mishandled business in which the enemy merged with the civilian population, and the girl who did the laundry might blow you up with a grenade hidden beneath the folded underwear. Brave, decent men like Bob Kerrey got hurt or killed and sometimes made mistakes that killed the innocent.

Timothy McVeigh appropriated the term *collateral damage* to describe the nineteen children whom he murdered in Oklahoma City. But what exactly was McVeigh's war? A freelance fanaticism that is idiot cousin to the real thing, I suppose. McVeigh's victims, his collateral damage, were just as dead. They perished without the small prestige of having died in a conflict that meant something—anything.

The military historian John Keegan ended his classic study *The Face of Battle* (published a year after the last helicopters lifted ignominiously off the American embassy roof in Saigon) by saying that, what with Vietnam and nuclear weapons, "the suspicion grows that battle has already abolished itself." It is pretty to think so. What we have left, in any case, is chronic but localized messes—and terrorism of the McVeigh or bin Laden variety.

If big war is for the moment obsolete, collateral damage remains, as if to keep up tradition. We no longer have the higher moral purposes (such as eliminating Hitler or saving human freedom), but keep the ghastliness of war. We have drifted far out of sight of the Geneva conventions, or of any rules at all. "Women and children first," once the formula of lifeboat gallantry, takes on an evil meaning.

Serbian snipers at work in the hills above Sarajevo a few years ago kept themselves dosed with slivovitz around the clock (as extra insurance against inhibitions of conscience) and potted away at women and children darting through the city under their cross hairs. Collateral damage is supposed to mean a mistake, but this killing was deliberate, focused and recreational. War is a great and terrible permission. A spirit of satanic play shoots a jolt of lethal impulse through the trigger finger. This is absolute power, on a person-to-person basis. It tends to corrupt absolutely. Degenerate violence takes on a life of its own. It feeds especially on women and children, the victims of convenience. It seeks them out. In the drug wars, a shadow struggle, an American woman and her adopted daughter were carelessly shot down the other day over Peru.

The devils snipe. The giants brawl; they trample the flowers. They break things. *Sunt lacrimae rerum*—the world's sad mortality. But collateral damage is a wily concept, and you have to make distinctions. There are varieties. Sometimes, as at My Lai, it occurs as atrocious revenge. (One detail made My Lai indelible in my mind: the American slaughterers took a lunch break.) Sometimes, as at Kent State, or Amritsar in 1919, the damage may be the consequence of bad crowd control. Stupidity and atrocity are closely related.

True awfulness sets in when collateral damage is no longer collateral but becomes the intended point. Innocents are terrorized as a matter of policy. Stalin's Ukrainian famine, the rape of Nanking, the London Blitz, Dresden, the Tokyo fire bombings—all these accomplished a purposeful slaughter of bystanders in order to break an enemy's will. Sometimes the collateral damage has a moral justification—kill more than 100,000 civilians at Hiroshima, for example, in order to end the war and spare millions of lives, American and Japanese, that might have been lost in an invasion of the home islands. That argument persists, of course.

Now and then, collateral damage has even aspired to achieve an extermination. The Holocaust represented the ultimate infliction of the form. Tribes less well organized than the Germans (Serbs and Croats, Hutu and Tutsi) conduct raggedy versions of a similar ethnic malevolence.

The term *collateral damage* implies something secondary and unimportant. But it's the collateral damage that most haunts us later on. It's because of My Lai, or incidents like Bob Kerrey's night in the Mekong Delta, that that war keeps coming back and back and back to the surface of the American conscience, all these years later—unquiet ghosts that you may still see flickering, from time to time, in Kerrey's troubled eye.

MUNICH AND VIETNAM

October 11, 2003

THE LESSONS AND MODELS FROM THE TIME STILL RESONATE, like muffled voices from another part of the house: Munich, for example, the paradigm that advised hitting aggressors early and hard. In the 1960s and early 1970s, Munich crashed head-on into the contradicting Vietnam quagmire narrative that in the guise of attacking "Amerikan" imperialism counseled something of the same isolationism that prevailed in America up to Pearl Harbor and had a contemptible manifestation in the views of Ambassador Joseph P. Kennedy.

Last night I was reading a letter that Captain Basil Liddell Hart, the defense correspondent of the London *Times* and a much respected military expert, wrote to the ambassador's son, young John F. Kennedy, in 1940 (a time when the price for Munich was being paid in the skies over London).

Liddell Hart's innovative theories in the 1920s about tank warfare had been studied and digested for future use by Hitler's Panzer generals. Now Liddell Hart wrote an unexpected eight-page letter to congratulate Kennedy on his book called *Why England Slept,* which was based on Kennedy's undergraduate honors thesis at Harvard, much doctored and fluffed up by his old man's media flunky, Arthur Krock of the *New York Times.*

Liddell Hart noted that the trouble with his own brilliant ideas about mass surprise armored assault was that they were designed for use by aggressor nations and not by the democracies, which would not attack without provocation. So Liddell Hart ruefully turned his mind to devising defensive means to protect democracies against mass surprise assault.

He told Kennedy that the situation in 1940 was akin to that of Britain during the Napoleonic wars:

Our fundamental purpose must be vitally different from that of our opponents. While their natural object was expansion, through conquest, our proper object was not merely to defeat that purpose, but to take care that civilization was not destroyed in the process of fighting to defend it. Since our [democratic] conditions deprived us of the possibility of gaining a quick victory by surprise, any conflict was bound to be a lengthy one.

Does this have any application to Iraq and the Middle East? If so, what? Does this quotation support the George W. Bush conception of the war, or that of his critics? Depends, I suppose, on whom you consider the expansionist aggressors. And where you think the values of "civilization" lie. How does the Bush doctrine of preemption align itself with Liddell Hart's concept of civilized defensiveness?

As I have said before, Iraq equals Munich versus Vietnam and is, among other things, a generational conflict being waged in the American mind between the Greatest Generation and the . . . Not So Greatest Generation.

Which one is right? The Reagan obits remind some of us, for a little while, that it is possible for a president of the United States to be vilified by the *bien pensant* as a simplistic dunce, an imbecile (the liberal intellectuals' sneering contempt for Reagan was not unlike the sneering contempt in the 1950s for Eisenhower, or, to fetch back a ways, the sneering contempt to be heard in Henry Adams's parlor on Lafayette Square in the 1870s about the moron in the White House, Ulysses Grant, who was actually not a bad president, all in all)—to be vilified and still, in the fullness of time, to come out looking pretty good.

A Convert's Confession

October 3, 1994

I was converted to the Roman Catholic Church in my adolescence. But I never had a convert's zeal. I never acquired that instinctive deep structure, that internal universe, that is installed in the cradle Catholic from the start—the spiritual DNA. Half in the church, half out, a kid who read too much Graham Greene and Thomas Merton, I embraced, it may be, the surface things: the brocaded rituals, the Latin Mass of those days, the rich atmospheres.

Nor did I acquire the true deep structure of the church's doctrinal rationales, its ideals and distastes. The strictures involving family and divorce were fine print that I was too young to care about. The view of sex, which I cared about a lot, seemed punitive and refracted: At the margin of every sunny adolescent day there hung a black Jesuit thundercloud of reproach.

Growing older, I have realized that the fine print is more important, more powerful than ritual or atmospherics. Still half in, half out of the church, wistfully faithful, I find myself puzzling over those contractual details. The church's ideals of family, for example, strike me as, by turns, heroic, profound or quaint.

Or as self-destructive. Despite my respect for the church and my contempt for some of the overstimulated moral idiocy of the secular world, I think that in two areas—(1) contraception and (2) ordination and the role of women—the church has gone needlessly, dangerously astray. John Paul II, one of the greatest popes, has settled for a stolid "Here I stand."

Any institution in business for two thousand years is bound to be condescending about passing fads. Rome's attitude alternates between suggesting that concern about these issues (birth control, women's rights) is an ephemeral ideological trend and implying that such concern represents the vanguard of forces infinitely darker. Both reactions are wrong, I think.

American Catholics—and millions elsewhere—understand that the church is simply out to lunch on the subject of birth control. If abortion is clearly wrong—and it is—the way to begin preventing abortions is to encourage contraception. Contraception sinlessly heads off the unwelcome pregnancy that might occasion the sin of abortion, that is, the destruction of rudimentary life. Only abstracted celibates and moral neurotics (I think) insist that a pill or condom contravenes the divine design for sex. On the contrary, contraception is an act of moral responsibility perfectly consistent with marital virtue and family cohesion.

One can embrace the principle of contraceptive discretion without entering into the Cairo debate—Thomas Malthus versus the More the Merrier School. Many conservatives, and such resolutely un-alarmed observers of the world environment as the economist Julian Simon, see more people as the planet's greatest asset, economic and otherwise, and argue that in a free-market economy, sperm, ovaries and Adam Smith conspire to produce the best of all possible worlds. Let a billion flowers bloom. I consider this also to be a form of argu-mentative neurosis.

I have puzzled for years over the church's dark, astigmatic view of sex. But sex is merely the narrow focus. The broader perspective—and failure—involves the church's view of women and their role in the world. It seems clear to me that a full, welcoming embrace of women as ordained equals in the priesthood, the hierarchy and the work of the church would refresh the institution, infuse it with new life, energy, hope and purpose.

Strange that the church's leaders, with their intellectual tools and twenty centuries' experience, would fall into what might be called the fallacy of incidentals. Women are not ordained priests, because Christ, in human form, was a man and chose male apostles. But surely male-ness was incidental to the essence of Christ's teaching and importance. Those who build cathedrals of principle, unassailable tra-ditions, around an unimportant or incidental distinction—one that is rooted in custom of distant time and, interminably preserved, becomes essentially inhuman—are doomed.

The continuing damage done to the Catholic Church by the exclusion of women from the priesthood is hard to estimate. What is lost by keeping women out of the full priestly life amounts to a tragedy for the church. In that policy, a world of opportunity has been closed; life that might have flourished, women's souls sharing in the heart of the church, has been shut down.

I hate the doctrinaire reductionism that coarsens all relationships between men and women into trench warfare. As the late Allan Bloom wrote, "The worst distortion of all is to turn love, a relation that is founded in natural sweetness, mutual caring, and the contemplation of eternity in shared children, into a power struggle." Some similar distortion of religion's natural sweetness and profound reciprocity has been too long accepted as part of the Catholic Church's design (male authority, female submission). I suspect that John Paul II feels that if the design is altered now, the whole structure will collapse.

It is not so. The danger lies in the continuing distortion, the airless stasis of a bad tradition. All of this is one reason that I do not go to Mass much anymore.

THREE TAKES ON AMERICA

April 10, 2000

How Americans look to themselves and to others, in three takes:

1) Some weeks ago, I was on the air with a radio talk show host in Texas, discussing the Confederate battle flag flying over the state capitol in South Carolina. The radio man was affable, polite, so I said—affably, politely—that I thought it was discourteous to fly a flag that offended so many of South Carolina's citizens. It caused them pain. Remove it. Besides, polls say the majority of South Carolinians, white and black, want it to come down.

But, said the man, for many the flag has nothing to do with race; it is a matter of Southern heritage.

Not so politely, I replied: "The swastika does not fly over the Reichstag now. The Nazis, after all, lost the war."

I felt the flare of rage through the phone line, a palpable heat:

"DO YOU MEAN TO COMPARE . . . ???!!!!!"

To compare what went on in Nazi Germany to what went on in the American South was, in the man's mind, an obscenity, an outrage.

2) On the other hand, if you were to visit the New York Historical Society's current exhibition, entitled, "Without Sanctuary: Lynching Photography in America," you might find yourself staring into something like the same moral abyss that presents itself if you visit Auschwitz. Before the question "How could this be?" the mind goes into a state of moral shock.

Elie Wiesel, my teacher in these matters, warns: "Don't compare." But evil has its universality, and in the lynching photographs—a ghastly race-based "American Death Trip" of snapshots assembled mostly from the first several decades of the twentieth century—we are in the presence of unmistakable evil, unmistakably American.

This is not the "banality of evil," as Hannah Arendt described Eichmann's bureaucratic Final Solution. The photographs present, rather, a sort of festivity of evil. Well-dressed white people—the men in jaunty straw boaters, the women in pretty Sunday dresses, the children (children!) neat as a pin—are posed as they inspect mutilated and naked black corpses. People have brought picnic baskets. The pictures were sent as postcards through the mail.

America idealizes itself, and indeed has achieved much of its stunning success in the world, by believing the best of itself (against sometimes powerful evidence to the contrary), by hewing to its most optimistic myth (consider Ronald Reagan) and holding itself almost metaphysically blameless among the nations. This is American exceptionalism.

Is it not provocative and unproductive and maybe even a little voyeuristic to conjure up such old evils as the "lynching bees"? I have talked to Israelis who do not want to hear another word about the Holocaust. Some American blacks are, in the same way, impatient with those who dwell on the past. They understand that tragic memory, while sometimes instructive, can also be destructive and transfixing. Surely Americans—a lucky and headlong and creatively forgetful people in many ways—live in a happier village than do, for example, memory-obsessed Bosnians, Serbs, Croats and Kosovars.

3) Whether or not Americans are oblivious about the past, it's troubling that they seem relatively heedless about the way that others may see them in the present. The *New York Times* has done an interesting roundup piece about "a growing backlash of anti-Americanism in Europe, especially in France, where a member of parliament named Noël Mamère has written a book called 'No Thanks, Uncle Sam,' a catalogue of American gaucheries and moral derelictions ranging from too much crime and too many guns to capital punishment to inadequate health care for the poor." For all of my life, Europeans have been

intermittently anti-American in one way or another, especially the French, who have a genius for ingratitude and superciliousness.

What's most troubling in all this, though, is not the French mind-set, but the American—the insularity of Americans in their role as the smug, sole superpower, and even worse (because it is potentially dangerous), their apparent lack of curiosity about what goes on in the rest of the world. The stupid side of the American exceptionalism has always been the American narcissism. It's a paradox that globalization seems to make the narcissism worse.

NAMES

March 8, 1993

A NAME IS SOMETIMES A RIDICULOUS FATE. FOR EXAMPLE, a man afflicted with the name of Kill Sin Pimple lived in Sussex, in 1609. In the spring of that year, the record shows, Kill Sin served on a jury with his other Puritan neighbors, including Fly Debate Roberts, More Fruit Fowler, God Reward Smart, Be Faithful Joiner and Fight the Good Fight of Faith White. Poor men. At birth, their parents had turned them into religious bumper stickers.

Names may carry strange freights—perverse jokes, weird energies of inflicted embarrassment. Another seventeenth-century Puritan child was condemned to bear the name of Flie Fornication Andrewes. Of course, it is also possible that Andrewes sailed along, calling himself by a jaunty, executive "F. F. Andrewes." Even the most humiliating name can sometimes be painted over or escaped altogether. Initials are invaluable: H. R. (Bob) Haldeman, of the Nixon White House, deftly suppressed Harry Robbins: "Harry Haldeman" might not have worked for him.

Names have an intricate life of their own. Where married women and power are concerned, the issue becomes poignant. The official elongation of the name of Hillary Rodham Clinton suggests some of the effects achieved when customs of naming drift into the atmospheres of politics and feminism.

The history of "Hillary Rodham Clinton" goes back in time, like a novel: At birth, Bill Clinton was William Jefferson Blythe, his father being a young salesman named William Jefferson Blythe III, who died in a car accident before Bill was born. In a story now familiar, the fifteen-year-old future president legally changed his name to Bill Clinton to affirm family solidarity with his mother and stepfather, Roger Clinton. In 1975, when Bill Clinton got married, his new wife chose to keep the name Hillary Rodham. But five years later, Clinton was defeated in a run for reelection as Arkansas governor, at which point, to assert a more conventional family image, Hillary Rodham started calling herself Hillary Clinton. But she was not exactly taking Bill's name either, since "Clinton" had not originally been Bill's. Bill was once removed from his own birth name, so now Hillary was, historically speaking, twice removed.

A name may announce something—or conceal something. In some societies, such as the Arab or Chinese, a beautiful child might be called by a deprecating name—Dog, Stupid, Ugly, say—in order to ward off the evil eye. Hillary Rodham knew that in some parts of the political wilds, she attracted the evil eye to the 1992 Democratic ticket. So during her demure, cookie-baker phase, she was emphatically Hillary Clinton, mute, nodding adorer and helpmate of Bill. She half-concealed herself in "Hillary Clinton" until the coast was clear. With the inauguration, the formal, formidable triple name lumbered into place like a convoy of armored cars: Hillary Rodham Clinton.

The name problem for married women is a clumsy mess. Married women have four or more choices. (1) Keep the last name they were given at birth. (2) Take the husband's last name. (3) Use three names, as in Hillary Rodham Clinton, or, as women did in the 1970s, join the wife's birth name and the husband's birth name with a hyphen—a practice that in the third generation down the road would produce geometrically expanded multiple-hyphenated nightmares. (4) Use the unmarried name in most matters professional, and use the husband's name in at least some matters personal and domestic. Most men, if they were to wake up one morning and find themselves transformed into married women, would (rather huffily) choose option number one.

Variations: One woman who has been married three times and divorced three times uses all four available last names, changing them as if she were changing outfits, according to mood or season. More commonly it happens that a woman has made her professional reputation, in her twenties and thirties, while using the name of her first husband, then gets divorced and possibly remarried, but remains stuck with the first husband's name in the middle of her three-name procession.

Names possess a peculiar indelible power—subversive, evocative, satirical, by turns. The name is an aura, a costume. Dickens knew how names proclaim character—although anyone named Lance is bound to hope that this is not always true. Democrats used to have fun with "George Herbert Walker Bush." The full inventory of the pedigree, formally decanted, produced a piled-on, Connecticut preppie–Little Lord Fauntleroy effect that went nicely with the populist crack that Bush "was born on third base and thought he had hit a triple."

How many names does a person need? For ordinary getting around, two, as a bird requires two wings. More than two, as a rule, is overweight. Only God should use fewer than two.

The words with which people and things are named have a changeful magic. Some cultures invent different names for people in different stages of life. In Chinese tradition a boy of school age would be given a *book name,* to be used in arranging marriages and other official matters. A boy's book name might be "Worthy Prince" or "Spring Dragon" or "Celestial Emolument." (Does a father say, "Hello, have you met my boy, Celestial Emolument?")

Hillary Rodham Clinton may find her name changing still further as her career evolves. Perhaps by next year, she will be known as H. R. Clinton. Maybe the year after that, she will be H. R. (Bob) Clinton.

DIANA'S FAME

September 15, 1997

THE TALE CAME TO A CLOSE IN ONE OF THOSE RITUALS OF shared planetary theater: a joining of tragedy and gossip in universal soap opera. But whatever emotional residue lingered as the world dried its eyes, two slightly hard-edged questions presented themselves in another part of the brain. The questions were not necessarily unkind. They were churned up by the undercurrent of sadness and disgust and fatalism that ran through one's thoughts on hearing the news from Paris that night, and in the days that followed.

The first question was this: Why on earth would anyone want to be famous, especially now? (What a nightmare! What a disaster!)

And the second question (the obverse of the first): Why do masses of men and women feel such intense emotion about the life and death of people who are strangers to them—strangers, that is, except to the extent that masses of people have been deceived by the tabloids into an illusion of intimacy with the famous?

If the intimacy was an illusion, is the grief an illusion as well? Or how exactly do we assess the emotional truth of these outpourings? A moment of poignant communion in the Family of Man? A cheap exploitation of sympathies one centimeter deep? Or is there a third possibility? Something to do with mortals and gods and goddesses?

To be famous is among the basic human ambitions, of course, an all-but-universal fantasy. Who—except for nuns and monks, say, who are content with God's radiant attention—sets out in life to remain obscure? Fame is fun—and vindication. One need never be lonely, anywhere, ever. Fame has style, glamour, money, attention; it ignites the sudden light of recognition in strangers' eyes, commands the comic deference of headwaiters as they sweep you past the serfs and hoi polloi to the best table.

Some who have come to be famous see in retrospect that the daydream may have been touchingly adolescent, self-inflating in the style of Mr. Toad. In some personalities, the need for attention is darker and more retrograde: neurotic, infantile, a sort of baby's unappeasable love craving, a raw, screaming hunger.

In any case, one should beware of answered prayers. Those with hard experience at being famous know that while celebrity can occasionally be delightful, it may become a burden, an arduous and menacing bore. Just how menacing it can be we saw in the middle of that recent night in Paris.

It was always a primitive terror to be cast out of the tribe and made to wander as a stranger. Today a famous person—Arnold Schwarzenegger, say, or Sylvester Stallone, those universal action figures whose films require the fewest subtitles and therefore address masses most eloquently in remote cultures—might go anywhere on earth and never be a stranger. Is that desirable? Or a horror? Such planetary recognition may be as dangerous, in a different way, as being an unknown alien once was.

The famed one is paradoxically as naked as an exile dispossessed. The celebrity enters into a powerful and potentially dangerous force field, a relationship with masses of people gone slightly insane; sometimes celebrity encounters that side of human nature that forms lynch mobs: the beast. A surreal dynamic goes to work. The famous may find their fortunes held hostage by the moods and attention spans of people they do not know. The unstable affections of fandom have a life of their own and acquire an unpredictable but nearly absolute power over one's personal and professional fate. Fame becomes a form of primitive, dangerous religion, like snake handling.

The most extreme danger comes in the form of the sort of lethal nonentity who gunned down John Lennon. Other stalkers are less murderous but more numerous. In fandom, boundaries of individuality break down and enthusiasts come to think they own the celebrity in some way. They behave with a bizarre, intrusive, proprietary aggression, as if the icon had entered their own head (as indeed the icon has) and thereby relinquished all rights of privacy and courtesy and become a plaything of fans' fantasy. Madonna has said that one of the worst things about being famous is that you cannot put your trash out on the sidewalk in front of your house: Someone will plunder it. Autograph hunters are the most benign of stalkers. The press, to a divorced princess, an actress or the U.S. president, represents a complex evil and professional necessity. The predations that celebrities fear most from the press, especially photographers, are intrusions into the lives of their children.

Sane, well-balanced celebrities accept their fame as part of their working life, but also an irrelevance and an intrusion and a pain in the neck. It is true that people live more comfortably with fame when they are confident that it is something they have earned by their own merit and hard work over a period of time.

The trouble is that fame at the end of the twentieth century—a global, multicultural and multimedia saturation—gets distributed by a sort of cultural chaos theory, detached not only from merit in many cases but also from any comprehensible framework of value and virtue. And so beneath the surface floats a fierce sense of injustice—a sense of ethical dislocation, as if the laws of cause and effect had been rescinded. In such a culture, to be obscure is by definition to be a failure. The obscure man asks bitterly, "Why is he famous, and not I? What's he got that I haven't got?" Manifestly, nothing. It is not the Salieri-Mozart configuration, mediocrity envying genius; today, let some unsung brilliant political thinker wonder why Dick Morris is famous for sucking a call girl's toes.

A guilty sense of the injustice of fame assaults the famed one as well: "Why am I famous? Why do all these people seem to love me? I don't deserve it. I am a fraud." The anguished, neurotic internal monologue gets dramatized in self-destructive ways (drug overdoses, alcohol, rampages, broken marriages, suicides or, if the celebrities are lucky, a trudge through the rehab that ends with confession and absolution in prime time: "I feel more centered now, Barbara"); all this mess forms up as part of the great sobbing dysfunctional pageant on display at the supermarket checkout counters.

Fame is the delicious toxin that addicts the troubled famous—including Diana, for example, and, in different ways, Elvis, Marilyn Monroe, Marlon Brando and Brigitte Bardot—the waifs and shipwrecks. The troubled famous develop a virtually sadomasochistic, I-hate-it/I-need-it dependency on fame. They are married to it as unhappily as Strindberg couples are married to each other. They are imprisoned and isolated by their fame. In a curious fashion, the metaphysical loneliness of their fame may expose and energize their worst latent flaws and turn them into monstrous distortions of themselves: Fame tends to draw their spirits away from them in the way that some tribal people fear that being photographed will steal their souls. Fame distributes their souls to the masses as in Communion. The famous get ingested by the world in some primitive manner.

That is the pathological side—the part of fame that appeals to the tabloid groundlings. Many famous people, of course, are worthy and righteous, and have even been much improved by their fame; all the public attention actually encourages them to rise to the occasion. One thinks of veterans in show business like Sophia Loren, with her sexy, humorous sense of self and her feet on the ground; or the late Audrey Hepburn; or Gregory Peck, who in 1997 is still to be seen around Beverly Hills with majestic white mane and bushy black thundercloud eyebrows and his air of formidably screwy gravitas. But in general the sane-and-sober famous, in show business or elsewhere, pose the same problem to their chroniclers and their public that God presented to John Milton when the poet was writing *Paradise Lost*: Satan was a more interesting character to describe, and to read about, than God.

Fame is a nasty Faustian bargain, the famous find, but with an inversion of the classic deal. Instead of selling one's soul to the devil in order to know all things, as Faust did, one sells one's soul in order to be known. A devolution from the active to the passive. The outcome is not happy in either case.

The ancient Greeks savored stories from Olympus that in our culture fill the *People* columns. Celebrities are what we have instead of gods and goddesses. We mortals may get more out of the famous than the famous get out of us. We get gaudy entertainment; life's possibili-

ties and absurdities all heightened and tarted up with sex and sermon-
ettes; vicarious excursions outside the confines of oneself; a kind of
narrative structure to contemplate in our otherwise formless lives; fa-
bles with suspense and denouement—as in Diana's story, which has a
fairy-tale beginning, a troubled middle and a climax of pageant at the
sad end.

It is a strange transaction. People projected all sorts of fantasies
upon Princess Diana in somewhat the way girls project little play scenarios upon Barbie dolls. Diana was a sort of Barbie-Ophelia—except
that Barbie is an inanimate doll and Ophelia a part played by an actress who, after her performance, takes off her makeup and goes out
for a late supper. Who would want such sacrificial fame for keeps?
Diana, a real person, died, and stays dead.

Literature has better consolations than either life or tabloids. After
Diana's funeral, one wistfully looks up the quote at the end of George
Eliot's *Middlemarch* and reads: "For the growing good of the world is
partly dependent on unhistoric acts; and that things are not so ill with
you and me as they might have been, is half owing to the number who
lived faithfully a hidden life, and rest in unvisited tombs."

THE DEATH OF J. PETERMAN

February 8, 1999

WHEN I HEARD LAST WEEK THAT J. PETERMAN HAD FILED FOR bankruptcy, I searched for a predictable joke in the Peterman style.

I said that, with Peterman gone, I felt the way I had when Gerald and Sarah Murphy closed down the Villa America at Cap d'Antibes—Scott was sober and unavailable to make scenes, anyway, and Zelda was crazy and the magic was gone.

Or—trying again—I said I felt as I had that night at the Muthaiga Club when Karen Blixen told us the coffee plantation was finished; hadn't been the same since Denis died.

But it is not so easy to compose a parody of the Peterman catalog. Its style, a bubbly kitsch of knowingness, creates surprising little fantasies that are part Harlequin Romance, part Cole Porter lyric, now and then a touch of the bodice-ripper, or when flying high, of Evelyn Waugh—a soigné escapism that is a parody of sophistication, so bad that it is great fun. All that literary ingenuity gone to sell clothes in the mail . . . and to end up bankrupt, besides. *Sunt lacrimae rerum,* as an unforgettable 'Cliffie whispered to me that night in the Mt. Auburn Club, just before Joanie Baez came on . . .

Here is an item from Peterman's "Owner's Manual" Number 72, fall of 1998: "Sir Rupert met him just beyond the gate of Penworth House. At first he thought he recognized the man. An old mate from Rugby? Trinity College? No, that would have been foolish. MI5 wouldn't have chanced it. Not like this anyway. Still, the man had the right look about him. The windowpane blazer. Nicely non-bureaucratic." Windowpane Blazer. 100% wool. $225. Too much Bond, I think—a little over the top. So is this, from the same catalog: "Fabiana whistled for the stable boy. He came. She whipped her crop against her boot. 'Saddle my horses.'" Tie-back chiffon blouse. $135. Then there is the turtleneck sweater from a "Bohemian aunt . . . says Dylan Thomas gave it to her at 3 A.M. outside the White Horse Tavern."

The trick of the catalog, as art form and selling tool, is to create an idealized world. On the planet of J. Crew, for example, it is always the weekend of the Princeton game; translucent blonde girls, clones of Mia Farrow long ago, smile at guys who don't tuck their shirts in, and touch the guys (on the calf, for example) in a lightly intimate way that is somehow proprietary. For the summer catalog, the setting switches to some Martha's Vineyard of the mind that, similarly, will know neither death nor gingivitis.

The universe of L.L. Bean resembles Maine, with a suppressed memory of hard winters in the woods long ago. Bean's world, robustly cozy, is subliminally less privileged and more autonomously practical than Crew: The young people are off-beautiful and went to state schools; no undercurrent eroticism here, no touching except for mom's hugs at Christmas and Thanksgiving. Clothes are called "good-looking" or "comfortable," and at the most extravagant, as an inside joke: "wicked good." A rosy-cheeked geezer and crone trudge around in Thinsulate snow sneakers—this last is a touch of AARP, Mia Farrow in real time, that would never make its way into J. Crew.

J. Peterman's world, on the other hand, has never been one particular place. Rather, Peterman retails an evoked time, a diffuse, multifaceted past located somewhere between the two world wars, sometimes drifting back into the Edwardian. A thought along these lines appears in the text presenting an Indian Elephant Caftan (No. AAF7744. Silk crepe de Chine. $180. Bangalore, India): "Comeliness and the passions of the past happen to mean a lot to me, perhaps you."

Seinfeld parodied Peterman—the tribute, perhaps, of one insubstantial 1990s style to another. Illusion is everything, self-deception is indispensable, and Peterman works behind a scrim of pastness, sometimes hilarious but curiously sweet nonetheless. Peterman sells interesting and fairly good-quality stuff. The danger, of course, is that you may get the thing in the mail and try it on (a Sherlock Holmes hat or cape, say, or one of those flouncy, too-much-by-half fin de siècle velvet gowns: "We drank Veuve Clicquot") and find you look absolutely ridiculous in it. I always thought it would be risky to go out in the classic horseman's duster that was one of Peterman's hottest items when he started the business. Even if you look like Clint Eastwood, the duster is not advisable. Though we all like to dress up—and the baby boomers especially, for they sprang from the costume party of the 1960s—you must beware lest some kid in the crowd is laughing and pointing, not at the emperor's nakedness, but at your Peterman outfit.

I am speaking of Peterman only at his extreme, though I confess I think the Peterman contribution has been more to the culture of fantasy than to clothing. I search for Peterman moments in real life. For example: A foreign correspondent, old Asia hand, Brit I've known for years, has us up to his tiny, steamy Manhattan apartment for dinner. He makes Peking duck, and when he notices an awkward pause in the conversation, pops his head out of the kitchen and begins an anecdote in that fluting voice of his: "You know, once when I was playing fan-tan in Macao . . . "

PART FOUR

Outrages

The World Trade Center

September 11, 2001

[Author's Note: Contrary to this volume's title, the following essay was very much a first draft, written a couple of hours after the second tower went down and published in a special edition of TIME *that closed the evening of 9/11.]*

FOR ONCE, LET'S HAVE NO "GRIEF COUNSELORS" STANDING BY with banal consolations, as if the purpose, in the midst of all this, were merely to make everyone feel better. We shouldn't feel better.

Let's have no fatuous rhetoric about "healing." Healing is inappropriate now, and dangerous. There will be time later for the tears of sorrow.

A day cannot live in infamy without the nourishment of rage. Let's have rage.

What's needed is a unified, unifying, Pearl Harbor sort of purple American fury—a ruthless indignation that doesn't leak away in a week or two, wandering off into Prozac-induced forgetfulness or into the next media sensation (O.J. . . . . Elian . . . Chandra . . .) or into a corruptly thoughtful relativism (as has happened in the recent past, when, for example, you might hear someone say, "Terrible what he did, of course, but, you know, the Unabomber does have a point, doesn't he, about modern technology?").

Let America explore the rich reciprocal possibilities of the fatwa. A policy of focused brutality does not come easily to a self-conscious, self-indulgent, contradictory, diverse, humane nation with a short attention span. America needs to relearn a lost discipline, self-confident relentlessness—and to relearn why human nature has equipped us all with a weapon (abhorred in decent peacetime societies) called hatred.

As the bodies are counted, into the thousands, hatred will not, I think, be a difficult emotion to summon. Is the medicine too strong? Call it, rather, a wholesome and intelligent enmity—the sort that impels even such a prosperous, messily tolerant organism as America to act. Anyone who does not loathe the people who did these things, and the people who cheer them on, is too philosophical for decent company.

It's a practical matter, anyway. In war, enemies are enemies. You find them and put them out of business, on the sound principle that that's what they are trying to do to you. If what happened on Tuesday does not give Americans the political will needed to exterminate men like Osama bin Laden and those who conspire with them in evil mischief, then nothing ever will and we are in for a procession of black Tuesdays.

This was terrorism brought to near perfection as a dramatic form. Never has the evil business had such production values. Normally, the audience sees only the smoking aftermath—the blown-up embassy, the ruined barracks, the ship with a blackened hole at the waterline. This time the first plane striking the first tower acted as a shill. It alerted the media, brought cameras to the scene so that they might be set up to record the vivid surreal bloom of the second strike ("Am I seeing this?") and then—could they be such engineering geniuses, so deft at demolition?—the catastrophic collapse of the two towers, one after the other, and a sequence of panic in the streets that might have been shot for a remake of The *War of the Worlds* or for *Independence Day*. Evil possesses an instinct for theater, which is why, in an era of gaudy and gifted media, evil may vastly magnify its damage by the power of horrific images.

It is important not to be transfixed. The police screamed to the people running from the towers, "Don't look back!"—a biblical warning against the power of the image. Terrorism is sometimes described (in a frustrated, oh-the-burdens-of-great-power tone of voice) as "asymmetrical warfare." So what? Most of history is a pageant of asymmetries. It is mostly the asymmetries that cause history to happen—an obscure Schickelgruber nearly destroys Europe; a mere atom, artfully diddled, incinerates a city. Elegant perplexity puts too much emphasis on the "asymmetrical" side of the phrase and not enough on the fact that it is, indeed, real warfare. Asymmetry is a concept. War is, as we see, blood and death.

It is not a bad idea to repeat a line from the 19th century French anarchist thinker Pierre-Joseph Proudhon: "The fecundity of the unexpected far exceeds the prudence of statesmen." America, in the spasms of a few hours, became a changed country. It turned the corner, at last, out of the 1990s. The menu of American priorities was rearranged. The presidency of George W. Bush begins now. What seemed important a few days ago (in the media, at least) became instantly trivial. If Gary Condit is mentioned once in the next six months on cable television, I will be astonished.

During World War II, John Kennedy wrote home to his parents from the Pacific. He remarked that Americans are at their best during very good times or very bad times; the in-between periods, he thought, cause them trouble. I'm not sure that is true. Good times sometimes have a tendency to make Americans squalid.

The worst times, as we see, separate the civilized of the world from the uncivilized. This is the moment of clarity. Let the civilized toughen up, and let the uncivilized take their chances in the game they started.

The French Have the Right
Not to Have Existed

July 16, 2001

There was once a sardonically funny and useless device, the self-canceling black box.

You pushed a button on the outside of it, it made a whirring sound, a lid opened, a small plastic hand reached out of the box, and pushed the button again . . . The hand withdrew, the box lid closed, and all was silence again. A battery-operated metaphysical joke.

France's highest court of appeal, the Cour de Cassation, has reproduced the self-canceling black box as law. It has ruled that disabled children are entitled to be compensated if their mothers were not given a chance to abort the defective fetus: that is, the complainant himself! The court has decided in favor of the families of three children—one with a malformed spine, two born with only one arm—whose lawyers argued that if doctors had detected the fetuses' disabilities, the physicians would have had the pregnancies terminated.

The metaphysics is spectacularly French. A child stands in court, and demands the legal right never to have existed. The judges on the bench nod gravely. Except that it is not the "deformed" child that stands in court. It is parents and lawyers, collaborating in the odious work of attempting to annul an inconvenient life.

The filmmaker Jean Cocteau remarked, "Stupidity is always astounding, no matter how often one encounters it." Stupidity's first cousins are evil and venality, which carry briefcases and are ingenious. God knows this decision is an ingenious, not to say hilarious, piece of work. I sometimes think that the absurdities of the French, philosophical and otherwise, result from the beauty and seductive elegance of their language, with which they can talk themselves into anything.

The Cour de Cassation persuaded itself to uphold last year's Perruche decision, in which a mentally retarded boy received damages because he had not been aborted.

The abandonment of common sense is not an exclusively French problem. But it is disturbing to find the French courts affirming Nazi principles of eugenics. The decision savors of Vichy. The court's logic—a true deformity—would encourage wholesale prenatal slaughter. It stigmatizes the handicapped and states, as a principle of law, that they never should have been born. Such children are an error that would, in the utopia toward which the idealism of the law (and perhaps of the French language) aspires, be eliminated, pre-emptively.

Under the menace of this decision, French doctors, whenever the slightest shadow turns up on the sonogram, will advise: Abort. Perfect children are mandated by law. Parents will be considered irresponsible if they bring forth a specimen less than perfect. Think of the charming effect this decision would have if it were applied in those many countries around the world where a fetus that turns up with a vagina rather than a penis is considered to be defective.

We proceed, one generation to the next, through genes and memes. The Oxford evolutionary biologist Richard Dawkins proposed some years ago that, just as genetics has genes, culture must have its own units of transmission, which he called "memes"—ideas of all kinds, images, tunes, games, concepts, movies, books, gestures, all the propagating thoughts that leap from mind to mind and, in our interactive information culture, have become a chaotically boiling universal soup.

The idea of perfectibility by abortion is an evil meme that should have vanished with Dr. Mengele. But instead, it has survived and prospered. Instead of being tried as a war criminal, the idea ends up being validated by a French court. The French beguilement with paradox mates with the principle of genocide. It ends up as a chief option of what might be called the hubristic scientific override, the mechanism whereby human expertise may correct the blunders of the genes.

Some miraculous medical preemptions are possible. But the promise of them has tended to override the wholesome memes of humility and common sense. That way lies tragedy, farce and paradox: You try for the perfect human . . . you arrive at the ultimately inhuman.

FLAG BURNING

March 29, 2000

I REMEMBER RIDING ON GEORGE HERBERT WALKER BUSH'S
campaign bus through the countryside of downstate Illinois in the
early fall of 1988. The candidate was in his pork-rinds mode: A display
of exuberant populist condescension designed to neutralize Bush's
Waspiness around election time and provide camouflage on missions
of good-natured political slumming. Loretta Lynn was on the bus.
Bush sang along to country music. In every public square, he hammered away at big, cheap themes: (1) Willie Horton, the Black
Monster on Furlough; (2) Read My Lips, No New Taxes; and (3)
Uncouth Radicals Want to Burn Your Flag.

Bush, a fine man in all sorts of ways, ran a disgusting campaign that
year. Issue number one was racist, issue number three was bogus, and
Bush's mantra on issue two was notoriously insincere. (He betrayed
that promise by raising taxes once elected.) But working the big bogus
vein has a way of paying off in American politics. If 1988 was a gridiron,
the Democrat, poor Michael Dukakis of Massachusetts, was playing
high school football. Bush was doing it the way they do it in the
NFL—rough stuff and the killer instinct.

One generation passeth away, and a new generation arriveth to
make the same mistakes, as if they had never been made before. I
guess I had gone to sleep on the subject of flag burning. I was astonished to wake up, all these years later, to find that the Senate has been
seriously considering an amendment to the Constitution to prohibit
flag burning. I thought we had evolved beyond that one. (On the other
hand, why would I have thought that?)

Then, and now, and for the future, a flag-burning amendment is a
terrible idea. Why does it keep coming back?

Flag burning (even though it occurs rarely) originated as one of the vivid, button-pushing ur-outrages committed during the great 1960s deconstruction of American authority (which some boomers consider the beginning of the world). It was engraved on the national memory by photographs of the time—images that merge with black-and-white shots of an Abbie Hoffman type giving the finger to "Amerika," or of the student radical Mark Rudd smirking and smoking a cigar with his feet up on the desk of the president of Columbia University. Burning the flag has a force of Oedipal transgression.

It outrages veterans. It outrages lots of Americans. It is intended to. It is not difficult to sympathize with the anger. Vietnam outraged people, too—just as World War I outraged the poet e. e. cummings, who wrote, in "The Song of Olaf":

> *There is some s—— I will not eat*
> *I will not kiss your f—— flag.*

The Constitution—onto which patriots or opportunists are eager to nail wanton amendments from time to time—was not designed for the purpose of making people feel good by silencing opinions that make some people feel bad.

These truisms need to be repeated from time to time: The First Amendment functions as an indispensable shock absorber. It protects all speech, not merely popular or majority speech. If you enjoy the freedom of America, you must put up with the disgusting freedom of your fellow citizens. Other people's freedom is sometimes offensive. If America's freedom were designed only for you and people who think as you do, then it is by definition not freedom.

The idea of a flag-burning amendment is advanced mostly by conservatives who seem not to understand that its logic partakes of the worst of coercive and morally negligent thinking from the other side of the ideological aisle. How does the rationale for prohibiting flag-burning differ from the politically correct fascism on university campuses that, for example, denies a hearing to Ward Connerly, the Californian behind the legal drive against affirmative action?

Such suppressions, from either side, are more dangerous to America than burning a flag could ever be.

Death in Texas

March 8, 1999

After the sentencing, a black bystander outside the courthouse in Jasper, Texas, told a reporter, "I am not in favor of the death penalty. But in this case, I will make an exception."

There are any number of Americans who would make an exception for John William King, the white man who chained a black man, James Byrd Jr., to a pickup truck last year and dragged him along a rough country road that skinned him alive and dismembered him. To object to putting King to death for the deed requires a saintliness I do not possess. In one sense, King's case is almost a moral free ride. My conscience would remain untroubled by some other death sentences, but John William King's execution will seem especially just and fitting— and, though it is ghastly to say so, a rather handsome American moment.

What happened in Jasper stands slightly to one side of the usual argument about capital punishment. It mobilizes different issues of justice. Here, racial payback overrides the familiar philosophical dilemma presented by executions.

The jurors, in any event, did their best to avoid large issues. They imposed the death penalty, it seems, on practical grounds, as if King's execution were an urgency of public health, like disposing of an incurable case of rabies. If sentenced to life, King would probably kill someone else in jail, the prosecution reasoned—another black, or a Jew perhaps, so lively and irrepressible boils his hate. He displays no shadow of remorse, and even in the Jasper jail, awaiting trial, he managed to get hold of an eight-inch knife. The jury did not find it hard to conclude that, among other reasons to execute him, he is simply too dangerous to go on living.

Besides, no one doubted King's guilt; no danger here of running up against the strongest argument opposing the death penalty: You might execute the wrong man. He's the right one, all right. Few will weep when the injection stops King's heart.

But after the melodrama, after the white devil disappears offstage, snarling like Cagney, a scruple (call it ACLU logic, a schoolmarm in the mind) begins to wave its hand in the back of the hall. Easy cases make bad law, or bad principle. The powerful emotional sway of this one is unsettling.

I confess that I have puzzled for years over the death penalty. At times I have defended it, at times argued against it. I am thus only half civilized—and to make things worse, am not even sure on which side civilization lies. If I were a state's governor, I would have to choose one side or the other on certain midnights of the year, when executioners awaited my go-ahead. As it is, I have the luxury to persist in ambivalence, going case by case, preserving the option of the noose.

A way of understanding Jasper may lie in these questions: Can capital punishment possibly be civilizing? Might it be sometimes indispensable? Human nature, without a social contract, leads people to pursue and punish murderers in their own way. The social contract restrains the human impulse toward rough justice. The contract states: Our authorities, acting under law for the community, will find the killers, try them and punish them. Implicit is the promise that the punishment will be sufficient to satisfy the need not only for moral satisfaction and justice but also for some measure of emotional satisfaction, a catharsis by—to admit it—legally ritualized revenge. A public hanging used to be a celebration of justice. The catharsis may have barbaric roots, yet by paradox is an essential civilizing instrument.

But race skews any discussion of capital punishment in America. Arguments against the death penalty focus on the disproportionate number of blacks on death row. What does Jasper give us? Something astonishing: the spectacle of a vicious white sent to death row—for killing a black man. Hence the high-fives among blacks outside the courthouse. The natural jubilation is philosophically inconsistent, of course. It is difficult to argue that whites should be executed but blacks should not. What celebrating blacks really mean is something simpler: It's about time.

The promising novelty of Jasper is that for a moment, it aligns the black social contract with the white social contract. That is all that racial justice is ultimately about: the equality of the contracts. In the past they have been two different documents, with very different protections under the law.

The State of Texas under the old social contract would not have executed the white man King for murdering the black man Byrd. (To have done so, in fact, would have violated the white community's contract with itself.) Whatever misgivings arise from the fact of execution itself, the jury's decision declared a happy change in the social organism. One white juror made the argument that King required the death sentence because the community had to show that the murder was "something we cannot accept." If there was encouragement to be taken from Jasper, it lay in the juror's use of the word *we*.

PART FIVE

Dilemmas

I Came, I Saw,
I Spoiled Everything

July 10, 1995

At three in the morning, a serpent of lights begins to coil up Mount Sinai—up the path Moses took, a sparkling procession of tourists' flashlights. As dawn arrives, you see less lovely effects—the litter of candy wrappers, soda cans and Kodachrome boxes people have discarded on the ascent.

In the highlands of Papua New Guinea, in a village near Goroka, the warriors, all but naked, smear their bodies with a pale mud and don surreal mud masks. Taking up clubs and spears and bows, they crouch and advance, ghostly, out of the Stone Age (which they inhabited until the day before yesterday) and into a clicking horde of tourists from a cruise ship that docked on the coast this morning. The "mud men" mime ferocity for a little while; then they mingle shyly in the crowd of rich white aliens and try to make sense of the paper money the strangers offer for weapons and boar's-tusk necklaces. It may not be too many months before the mud men start accepting the American Express card.

By the Doge's Palace in Venice, down the little canal from the Bridge of Sighs, the Ponte de Paglia groans under the weight of Japanese, Germans, Americans, Frenchmen, Scots, English, Indians, Spaniards, Scandinavians—the whole world milling about in T-shirts, polyglotting. It takes five minutes for a pedestrian to push across the bridge, a distance of thirty yards. Venice vanished centuries ago into its tourist-shop-museum self, forfeit to the ever flattening demographics of mass tourism.

Against expectations, the summer of 1995 will be a booming one for tourism and travel. At a moment when the dollar is faring badly against other currencies and when hotel and airline prices are climbing, the 1995 season's tourism is likely to break records. The great, global middle class is in motion.

Is this a wonderful thing? Familiar pieties collide, good news and bad news: (1) Peaceful mobility on a planetary scale proclaims victories for freedom, democratic pluralism, frequent-flyer programs and unfettered competitive markets; (2) a radioactive cloud of banalizing sameness threatens the earth; the sacred and beautiful places, all the uniquenesses, have been invaded, desacralized, franchised for the masses, dissolved into the United Colors of Benetton.

Both versions are true; the second follows from the first. The travel industry cherishes Piety 1. The traveler drifts through the world trying to fend off the truth of Piety 2, which declares itself in spasms of denied disappointment. At worst, a nostalgic heartache goes to work, the travel snob's regret, grandchild of an Evelyn Waugh–Somerset Maugham steamship elitism. Lucretius wrote: "Whenever a thing changes and alters its nature, at that moment comes the death of what it was before." A new metaphysic of distances and destinations has taken over the world.

Werner Heisenberg's famous uncertainty principle stated that some physical events can never be accurately observed because the scientist's intrusively observing eye changes the event itself. The summer may be remembered as the moment when Heisenberg Tourism achieved a sort of global critical mass. A few weeks ago, a monk at St. Catherine's Monastery on Mount Sinai looked gloomily at the tourists and stated the new Heisenberg principle: "They come, and everything changes."

The idea that tourism inevitably strips off some holiness of place, some magic, may be descended from the primitive conceit that a camera steals the soul of the person photographed. The sacred place (Mount Sinai, Mount Fuji, the Grand Canyon) is an onion, and each new wave of Visigoths with video cameras peels away a layer of mystique, until the magic that drew the stranger in the first place is gone, and instead the tourist finds—other tourists. And with them, the hotels and fast foods and souvenirs and globally identical amenities. A real traveler hates all that.

Why travel, after all? In order to have a paper sash over the toilet seat? To enjoy a comfortable, momentary change of perspective—a vacation as the equivalent of rolling over in one's sleep? Or to lose oneself? To pass through distance into some new place where the eyes become capable, for a moment, of a fresh transparency. Slide into the Pleistocene: Under a thorn tree in Masai Mara, say, a cheetah tears at the Thomson's gazelle it has nailed for lunch. All around in a semicircle, the minibuses sprout glaring bwanas from their sunroofs. The onion peels.

Is it inevitable that tourists corrupt the places they visit? Probably. But wait: Maybe we could turn it around. Make tourism a moral force, a technique for civilizing war zones, for example. In Papua New Guinea, tribes firing arrows at one another across an unpaved track through the forest have been known to break off hostilities to allow a tourist bus to pass.

Would not Bosnia—I hear it's lovely this time of year—profit if tens of thousands of tourists were to descend with dollars and cameras? Would the Heisenberg gaze of strangers shame the ethnic purifiers and spoil the snipers' aim? Would commercialism defeat tribalism? Or maybe Disney could take over the war and give the fighters blanks and dummy mortar shells to fire: They would enact their hatreds daily as a permanent tourist attraction.

And Rwanda would be developed as a jungle theme park.

THE SIXTIES WILL NEVER END

May 6, 1996

First, Prince Yusupov and the others fed poisoned cakes and wine to Rasputin. The czarina's dissolute monk seemed to thrive on them. He called for more wine and went on with the party.

Next, the conspirators shot the *starets* a few times, and that slowed him down. He was still alive, but less chipper. Assassination as low comedy: Now they doggedly carried Rasputin out to the frozen Neva and shoved him through a hole in the ice. He kept bobbing to the surface.

Finally, at the end of the assassins' long night of work, the old charlatan got worn out and sank, reluctantly, for the last time.

I like to think that Rasputin stayed dead for a half-century and then, irrepressible, achieved reincarnation, not as one person this time, but as an entire decade—the 1960s. This expansive metaphysics would have allowed him to show off all his facets: as holy man and party boy, as faith healer, sexual omnivore, purveyor of mystic salvations and bogus profundities, enemy of soap, hairy narcissist . . .

And survivor. The 1960s have proved to be just as difficult to eliminate as Rasputin was. Or, to be bipartisan, as hard to dispose of as Richard Nixon, who went down into the frozen river a hundred times during his career and always bobbed back. Nixon and the 1960s, though they hated each other, were each driven by a fierce relentlessness. Nixon finally died. The 1960s go on and on.

Three events in recent days, however, have breathed hope into a nation that has lived long under the baby boom's army of occupation. If you look, you know that the 1960s had a core of nobility and tragedy. It breaks the heart still to think of Medgar Evers or Martin Luther King Jr., or the night Bobby Kennedy was shot. But so much of the time turned to meretricious junk, an idealism gone clueless and narcissistic.

We saw traces of the pattern again in the case of the Unabomber, for example—Rasputin with a chemistry set.

And then April 1996 brought Sotheby's yard sale of Jacqueline Kennedy's bric-a-brac. Jackie belonged to the founding myth of the 1960s. Now the saint's relics of Camelot have turned to kitsch. The gavel-banging crassness of the sell-off may help bring Americans to that objectivity and even disillusionment necessary for what grief specialists refer to as closure.

Any decade seems ridiculous in retrospect, its absurdities left exposed after the smoke has cleared. In memory, the 1970s seem wincingly stupid—that idiot disco music, those haircuts, those shirts and ties. Why pick on the 1960s?

For this reason: Most decades have the good grace to die of their own accord, a natural and seemly death. The old decade goes into the dustbin precisely because in looking back, we see its follies and feel a healthy eagerness to get on with something better.

The 1920s went off the cliff and pinwheeled onto the rocks below, a world economic crash that seemed a retribution for too much heedlessness and gin. By the end of the 1930s, W. H. Auden's "low, dishonest decade," the Nazis were spreading out all over Western civilization. And so on. The 1940s—the first half of them given over to world war, the second half hardening into cold war and nuclear anxiety—did not make anyone want to linger.

Intellectuals finished off the lamentable 1950s even before Eisenhower left office. Each decade gets reduced to a formula. The 1950s were conformity, McCarthyism, the Silent Generation, Ike in senility, cold war, suburban ticky-tacky. By 1960 America's thinkers had taken the 1950s to the ice floe and abandoned them there; we saw young John Kennedy on the horizon.

But with the 1960s, something different happened. We've been over this material before, but the baby boomers, born of the pent-up desires and deferred domesticity enforced by World War II, were so numerous that they transformed their coming of age into the genesis of an entire new culture, or so they thought. It was not merely a new version of the old motifs but instead a new consciousness, wired to television, a new sexuality, a new music, a new spiritual way. It was a new universe altogether, all the ghastly nonsense of Woodstock, the simultaneous arrogance and ignorance: overprivileged, pretentious, self-righteous, self-important, artificially proliferated by its own electronic imaging, and, as the years have passed, sadly resistant to the usual generational cleansing. They came to cultural power unnaturally early, when still adolescents, really, and now they hold the institutional power for real, from the White House on down.

Once demographers liked to use the disgusting pig-in-the-python image to describe the boomers moving through the stages of their lives. It would be more accurate to say that the pig (that huge generation) tried to swallow the snake of history—a messy and unappetizing spectacle.

What a fate: The American story turned into a continuous sequel to *The Big Chill*. Will this movie ever end?

A Boy Dies

October 20, 1997

In Cambridge, Massachusetts, two men lured a ten-year-old boy named Jeffrey Curley with promises of fifty dollars and a new bicycle. The police said that when the boy refused to have sex with the men, one of them, Charles Jaynes, who weighs 250 pounds, sat on Jeffrey and smothered him with a gasoline-soaked rag. Then, according to the police, the men had sex with the corpse and, after that, bought a fifty-gallon Rubbermaid container, sealed the body in it with duct tape and dumped the container into a river on the Maine–New Hampshire border.

The police located the child's body in the river in October 1997 and arrested the two men, who had literature in their trunk from the North American Man-Boy Love Association.

The night the body was found, five hundred people from the boy's community packed into an auditorium in Cambridge. It is a measure of our progress as a civilization that the five hundred did not get a rope and march on the police station. Instead, they listened to a local child psychiatrist, who told them, "It's beyond our comprehension." The boy's father, a firefighter, said he hoped the men would be executed. My own mental sentence upon them (before I calmed down) included execution, but was more vivid and, so to speak, Islamic. Massachusetts has outlawed the death penalty, however, and surely would not countenance what I had in mind.

This kind of news is hard to cope with. First comes shock and a flash of retaliatory rage. Then the mind begins to subdue itself to a state of sullen depression—reflecting that these things happen, and always have. There was a double horror not long ago involving, first, an older man from Long Island and a New Jersey fifteen-year-old whom the man had met through the Internet and sexually abused. Second, that same abused fifteen-year-old then raped and murdered an eleven-year-old.

But why should our outrage be dampened, rather than inflamed, by knowing that these atrocities are common? Well, you cannot focus your rage against an evil that is universal. You deepen your sadness with stories—think back to the Leopold-Loeb case in 1924, for example. Everyone in America wanted to hang those two in Chicago for murdering fourteen-year-old Bobby Franks as a sort of Nietzschean thrill; Clarence Darrow, with a magnificent speech against the death penalty, got the idiots off with life imprisonment. Nathan Leopold was released in 1958 and lived to the age of sixty-six, strolling upon a beach in Puerto Rico.

We oscillate between two moral poles. The left brain says, "Nothing human is foreign to me," a dictum that floats in like elegant driftwood from the second century B.C., when the Roman playwright Terence said it. The line describes the ideal state of today's movie and television audience: a morally promiscuous and passive receptivity, a tolerant consumer's connoisseurship of vice and weirdness.

The right brain, meantime, goes to the other extreme and lays down, "Nothing foreign is human to me"—a thought that is not merely a nice motto for xenophobes, but also points, if you think about it, toward one of the deepest dynamics of human nature. A healthy character, in its raw state, is a nasty little fascist, equipped with an intolerant immune system; it rejects such deeds as the Cambridge murder and necrophilia in the way that a healthy body rejects an invasion of microbes. This vigorous state of mind has no sympathy for what it identifies as alien life-forms and thinks such sympathy would be dangerous weakness, a breakdown of a society's natural defenses. In some ways, of course, it is right.

But "Nothing foreign is human to me" is the cry of the lynch mob. The mob does not wish to listen to the psychiatrist—or to the theologian, or to the lawyer. A civilized mind, on the other hand, has all four voices (mob, theology, psychiatry, law) speaking to it at once. That interior argument is confusing.

The theologian in us speaks of evil and has the floor when outrages against children are committed. For evil is a concept that blossoms out of the causeless, and crimes against children seem the least explicable of human brutalities.

The psychiatric appeaser goes to work on causes: If an act can be explained and is therefore part of behavioral cause and effect (well, Hitler had an unhappy childhood, therefore . . .), then it does not deserve the name of evil. Which, the theologian replies, is nonsense: The person who did the deed may be a victim himself or may have merely been having a bad-hair day, as someone remarked in trying to figure out Susan Smith's murder of her children in a South Carolina lake. But the deed is, indelibly, evil.

The voice of the law will have to sort the other voices out. And after all the screaming in our mental auditorium, we acquiesce at last to that. But the screaming itself is exhausting. What have we learned from it? Anything new? Perhaps. But even the knowledge is contaminating.

The Seductiveness of Guns

March 3, 2000

WHAT DO WE SAY ABOUT A SIX-YEAR-OLD GIRL WHO DIES OF A gunshot wound?

What do we say when the gunshot was fired by a six-year-old boy? At school.

Do we say, "Guns don't kill people, six-year-old boys kill people?"

That's one way to look at it.

Thus does outrage cool down to the merely sardonic. It's interesting how quickly we cover the range from shock to acceptance.

Each new episode is merely another chapter of what has become the turn-of-the-century American Gun Drama—a cultural Kabuki in which teenagers or tykes go to school one morning and blast away. The site of the explosion may be anywhere (Colorado, Arkansas, Pennsylvania, Michigan)—fate showing up on the doorstep like Ed McMahon with a surprise. Tabloid theater: the same scurry of panic, same expressions on the kids' faces, same emergency swooping-in, too late, of adult authority (ambulances, cop cars, local TV trucks), same aftermath of "grief counselors" and fatuous talk of "closure."

And meantime, the house divides—pro-gun, anti-gun. The same stylized arguments gallop out of the fax machines, two armies with different emotional techniques. The gun-control tribe has the momentary advantage of shock. The National Rifle Association has developed a sort of rope-a-dope genius for slipping the punch: All you have to do is enforce the laws already on the books, say the gun conservatives, and anyway, that kid in Michigan was living in a crack house with guns everywhere, and criminals aren't deterred by gun-control laws, so what's the point of them? Let the outrage drain off a little (it takes only a day or so, a news cycle), and then focus, in a certain manly way (subtly denigrating emotionalism) upon specific details of the case.

I suspect it will go on and on, like Israel-Palestine, or Northern Ireland, or the Balkans, until there comes some changing of the cultural tide, a force that will overwhelm mere arguments over policy. That is what happened in the case of cigarettes. When I was a child, nothing was more glamorous than smoking. In fact, there was something vaguely wrong with you if you did not smoke.

Guns possess a similar seductive glamour, especially to children. I have always loved guns—their machined steel, significantly weighty, their dark dynamic, the spiraled rifling when I sighted down the inside of the barrel to the tab of blue sky at the muzzle.

Guns were the things that heroes carried, transformative instruments that giants used to save the world from Hitler and lesser bad guys. And when I walked as a ten-year-old through Adirondack woods, slipping through birches and hemlocks, carrying a .22, I possessed secrecy and manhood and power.

Guns are seductive. Listen to the word *seductive*—the language of cunning love. Guns seduce children, and men as well. The American male's love of guns has a kinship to his love of cars: Both have to do with beautiful machinery, with individual power and control and aggression-on-demand. Of course, guns and cars have different purposes. Both may be instruments of rage; the gun is more single-minded in accomplishing its aim.

Pending the cultural sea change, I have a suggestion. New entertainment industry standards should require that in all movie and television productions in which guns are used, only live ammunition may be employed, so that an actor who is portrayed as being shot must, in actuality, be shot. Every character who is portrayed as dying by gunshot must, in fact, die. All blood from gun wounds must be the actors' actual blood.

This rule would restore a wholesome cause-and-effect verisimilitude to our entertainment, and, overnight, would reduce gun violence in media to zero. It's a thought.

Rape in War

February 22, 1993

Rape and killing are chief among the vicious pleasures, a man's recreations on the dark side. Medieval kings reserved for themselves alone the right to do such things, in peacetime anyway. In war, the privileges were distributed to the lowliest foot soldier: every man a king.

Killing is what soldiers are trained to do. The disciplined destruction of the enemy is their military duty. Soldiers may be court-martialed for not killing.

Rape is a disreputable half-brother to that. No glory attends it. The story of rape in war is murky. Rape after battle has usually been regarded as an ugly side effect. The spoils of war, Homeric booty: Kill the men, and take the women as prizes. Does after-battle rape merely serve to illustrate the human tendency to take things too far once taboos have been breached, especially in the midst of much danger and adrenaline and anarchy? Everyone knows that atrocity has a life of its own, a quality of evil ecstasy.

No one can hear accounts from the war in Bosnia-Herzegovina without sensing that the conflict there has taken the matter of rape in war down into deeper, more sinister dimensions. It is not known how many rapes have been committed since the fighting began in the breakup of Yugoslavia. A European Community (EC) team of investigators calculates that twenty thousand Muslim women and girls have been raped by Serbs. Other estimates run much higher. The Bosnian government claims that as many as fifty thousand Muslim women have been raped. Serbs are undoubtedly committing most of the rapes at the moment; they have also seized the most land. But as Amnesty International reported last month, others in the conflict, Muslims and Croats, have also been guilty of widespread rape. The hideous moral ecology of the region has left no one innocent.

The fighting has opened a door upon horrors—the wanton siege of Sarajevo, the death camps and other atrocities of "ethnic cleansing"— suggesting that atavistic nationalisms, or tribalisms, may lie just beneath the civil veneers. The abuses of Bosnian women open a perspective upon wartime rape that is equally terrible. In Bosnia, rape, far from being a side effect of war, has become one of the indispensable instruments of war. The battleground is not only villages and countryside but also women's bodies.

Amnesty International's report *Bosnia-Herzegovina: Rape and Sexual Abuse by Armed Forces*, describes the nature of rape in this war: "The available evidence indicates that in some cases the rape of women has been carried out in an organized or systematic way, with the deliberate detention of women for the purpose of rape and sexual abuse." Rather than being the random indiscipline of soldiers, many of the rapes in Bosnia have almost certainly been committed as a matter of deliberate policy.

And as a weapon of war, rape works—sometimes even better than killing does. Killing may make martyrs, and thus inspirit and strengthen the morale and solidarity of the victims. Rape, on the other hand, not only defiles and shatters the individual woman but, especially in traditional societies, also administers a grave, long-lasting wound to morale and identity. Rape penetrates the pride and cohesion of a people and corrodes its future. When a woman is raped in war, she and her family and ultimately her community internalize the assault upon their identity. Rape in war is only sometimes an act of simple lust or sadism.

The Serbs not only vehemently deny encouraging mass rape but also deny that such rapes have even occurred. Croats and Muslims have also denied such practices. The Balkans reverberate to this counterpoint of denial, a victim symphony of outraged innocence. Radovan Karadzic, who is a poet and a psychiatrist as well as the ruthless commander in chief of the Bosnian Serbs, tries a reverse approach. He says soldiers on all sides are committing rape. He sounds the note of bogus fatalism that is also a kind of blessing of rape: "It is tragic. But these dreadful things happen in all wars."

The first indications began to emerge in the summer of 1992, when Muslim and Croat victims described mass rapes by Serbs to the International Red Cross and the U.N. High Commissioner for Refugees. The women—some escaped to Croatia, some still living in Bosnia, some in concentration camps—all told of being forcibly taken by Serb troops, often to temporary "camps" in inns, hotels, schools, town halls and even restaurants. There they would be raped by a procession of Serb soldiers, then either released or sent to one of the larger concentration camps in Bosnia. Other women have been repeatedly raped in their own homes by Serbs, and some were reportedly killed afterward. A number of pregnant victims ended up in Croatian hospitals as refugees, awaiting the birth of unwanted children. Some of the victims were said to be held by Serb soldiers until they gave birth.

In the past few months, there have been reports of Muslim and Croat soldiers committing mass rape, but the cases have been less well documented. Says a senior EC official: "The Red Cross, the U.N. and we know that some mass rapes have been committed by non-Serbs. The information has come from similar sources: the victims."

In December the EC, at its summit meeting in Edinburgh, expressed its outrage at "these acts of unspeakable brutality." So did the U.N. Security Council. The EC summit appointed a twelve-member team, which found mass rape had been committed "in the context of expansionist strategy"—that is, ethnic cleansing. The investigators reported that "daughters are often raped in front of parents, mothers in front of children, and wives in front of husbands." David Andrews, a member of the commission, who was at the time Ireland's foreign minister, said it was clear that rape had "become an instrument, not a by-product, of war."

How does rape work as a weapon of war?

In the Balkans ethnic purity is a primitively overriding value. Bosnian Muslims believe that the mass rapes are intended to break down their national, religious and cultural identity. In part, they assume, the Serb objective is to use rape and enforced pregnancy as a form of revenge and humiliation. Says Mark Wheeler, a lecturer on modern Balkan affairs at the University of London's School of Slavonic and East European Studies: "The idea of nationality in the former Yugoslavia is based on descent, and the greatest debasement is to pollute a person's descent."

Neatly done: Mass rape achieves ethnic cleansing through ethnic pollution. Serbs do not care about the fate of the children of rape: The offspring are not Serbs but of mixed blood, therefore debased. Mass rape contaminates the gene pool.

The Balkans have become a sort of Bermuda Triangle into which human decencies vanish without a trace. In the post–cold war era, it is unsettling to think that conscienceless tribal ferocity may catch on around the world. Rape, of course, has been an apparently inevitable part of war since men first threw rocks at each other—or anyway since Rome was founded upon the rape of the Sabines. Joseph Stalin expressed a prevailing (male victor's) view of rape in war. When Yugoslav Milovan Djilas complained about the rapes that Russians had committed in Yugoslavia, Stalin replied, "Can't you understand it if a soldier who has crossed thousands of kilometers through blood and fire and death has fun with a woman or takes some trifle?" In 1945, Soviet soldiers raped two million German women as a massive payback for everything the Nazis had done to Russia. Alexander Solzhenitsyn, who was a Soviet army captain in East Prussia in 1945, reported: "All of us knew very well that if the girls were German, they could be raped and then shot. That was almost a combat distinction."

Revenge, soaked in hatred and hormones, may explain some of the Soviet troops' behavior. But it is not a good all-purpose explanation. Revenge—which in the Nazi-Soviet context perversely takes on the color of almost a kind of brutal justice—does not explain Nanjing in 1937. The Chinese had not committed atrocities against the Japanese people when the Japanese marched into Nanjing and raped—and often murdered—tens of thousands of Chinese women. Nor can revenge entirely explain the behavior of Pakistani troops who in 1971 raped more than 250,000 Bengali women and girls in Bangladesh.

Achilles sulked in his tent because Agamemnon denied him his just plunder in war, the beauty Briseis. "Rape has always been endemic with armies," says John A. Lynn, military-history professor at the

University of Illinois. "There have been armies in which rape was treated as a disciplinary problem, and armies in which it was institutionalized. In most European armies in the first half of the 17th century, rapes by unpaid soldiers occurred in large numbers in front of officers and were not stopped because they were part of the quid pro quo of what you got for being a soldier."

Once there were even elaborate rules about permissible rape in war. Lynn mentions an early European convention: If a besieged town surrendered in timely fashion, its women would be spared rape. If the town resisted, wholesale rape was justified. Says Lynn: "That kind of legitimized rape had a political reason—to intimidate other towns to surrender without resistance."

Armies in all civilized countries receive intensive indoctrination on decent behavior and on what offenses, including rape, will result in court-martial. It is the job of officers to control their men. Elite units are the least likely to commit rape and other atrocities, although SS men in World War II proved the exception. Says the military historian John Keegan: "Elite units have a rather high opinion of themselves and consider atrocity to be beneath them." A soldier who murders or rapes disgraces his comrades and damages esprit de corps.

But Bosnia shows how that logic can be turned upside down. There, "elite" units of Serbian irregulars such as the White Eagles have evidently made rape a gesture of group solidarity. A man who refuses to join the others in rape is regarded as a traitor to the unit, and to his Serbian blood. Sometimes, that impulse to bond with the male group becomes a kind of perverse inflaming energy inciting to rape. Lust is only a subsidiary drive.

And sometimes, young men in war may commit rape to please their elders, their officers, and win a sort of father-to-son approval. The rape is proof of commitment to the unit's fierceness. A young man willing to do hideous things has subordinated his individual conscience in order to fuse with the uncompromising purposes of the group. A man seals his allegiance in atrocity.

It should be possible to draw a graph predicting the level of rape that would occur in a battle context according to the officers' degrees of tolerance or disapproval. The greatest number of rapes would happen if (1) the soldiers were under direct orders to commit rape. Slightly fewer would take place if (2) there were fully articulated official approval of rape, as with the Soviets entering Germany in 1945. The levels would descend with (3) tacit official approval of rape, (4) official neutrality on the subject, (5) tacit official disapproval, (6) spoken official disapproval, (7) direct orders not to rape or (8) a written code of conduct prohibiting rape and mandating punishment for such behavior.

Even armies operating under conditions 7 and 8 may commit numerous rapes. Rapes increase geometrically if the soldiers feel that civilian women are implicated in the war against them. American soldiers in Vietnam committed an unknowable number of rapes, including those at My Lai, in part when the units were incompetently or viciously led, but also in part because it was hard for the Americans to distinguish officially friendly Vietnamese civilians from the Vietcong.

Richard Mollica is the director of the refugee-trauma program of the Harvard School of Public Health and director of the Indochinese Psychiatry Clinic at St. Elizabeth's Hospital in Brighton, Massachusetts. He and his colleagues have worked with some 3,500 refugees, half of them Cambodians. The subjective meaning of rape in war, Mollica suggests, is created by the historical and cultural traditions that surround the deed: "Every society and subculture has a different way of dealing with rape." In some societies the taint of rape is indelible and toxic. In Indochina, as in many areas with traditional societies, rape means the loss of a woman's sexual purity, the highest gift she can give her husband. The Cambodians have a folk saying: "A woman is cotton, a man is a diamond. If you throw cotton in the mud, it's always soiled. But if you throw a diamond in the mud, it can be cleaned."

On the other hand, some women from Nicaragua and other parts of Latin America were proud of being raped in war because their political beliefs told them that they had given their bodies to the revolution. Rape as sacrifice: The crime creates a living martyr.

In Bosnia the cotton-and-diamonds tradition, alas, applies, and the rapists know it. Part of the enduring disaster of rape is this: The husband often enough blames the woman who was raped as much as he blames the man who raped her. All the dynamics of rape are ingeniously destructive. It tears the social fabric apart. It profoundly degrades the women and disgraces—absolutely—the men who were unable to protect the women.

Rape is inherently unforgivable: No woman has ever forgiven the man who raped her. No man has ever forgiven the man who raped his wife or daughter or mother. There is little hope of reconciliation. Rape is also inherently unforgettable. No one who has been raped ever forgets, as long as she lives. No raped woman can look at men without fearing it will happen again. Rape lives on and on in the anger and grief and depression and adhesive shame that it creates in one evil burst of violence.

Rape in the Bosnian war is clearly a policy of scorched emotional earth with intent to achieve ethnic cleansing. The only possible benefit one can see emerging from the rapes might be a grace of widened perception, a clearer moral focus on the idea that rape is really a form of warfare, like, say, germ warfare, and that sometime in the future, it will become unthinkable. It is pretty to think so.

Busybodies, Crybabies

August 12, 1991

THE MOST CONSPICUOUS CHILDREN ON THE AMERICAN PLAY-
ground are the busybody and the crybaby.

The busybody, gauleiter of correctness, a bully with the ayatollah
shine in his eyes, barges around telling the other kids that they cannot
smoke, be fat, drink booze, wear furs, eat meat or otherwise noncon-
form to the new tribal rules.

The crybaby, on the other hand, is the abject, manipulative little
devil with the lawyer and, so to speak, the actionable diaper rash. He
is a mayor of Washington, arrested (and captured on videotape) as he
smokes crack in a hotel room with a woman not his wife. He pro-
nounces himself a victim—of the woman, of white injustice, of the
universe.

Both these types, the one overactive and the other overpassive, are
fashioning odd new malformations of American character. The busybodies infect American society with a nasty intolerance—a zeal to
police the private lives of others and hammer them into standard
forms. In Freudian terms, the busybodies might be the superego of the
American personality, the overbearing wardens. The crybabies are the
messy id, all blubbering need and a virtually infantile irresponsibility.
Hard pressed in between is the ego that is supposed to be healthy, tolerant and intelligent. It all adds up to what the *Economist* calls "a
decadent puritanism within America: an odd combination of ducking
responsibility and telling everyone else what to do."

Zealotry of either kind—the puritan's need to regiment others or the
victim's passion for blaming everyone except himself—tends to produce a depressing civic stupidity. Each trait has about it the immobility
of addiction. Victims become addicted to being victims: They derive
identity, innocence and a kind of devious power from sheer, defaulting

helplessness. On the other side, the candlesnuffers of behavioral and political correctness enact their paradox, accomplishing intolerance in the name of tolerance, regimentation in the name of betterment.

The spectacle of the two moral defectives of the schoolyard jumping up and down on the social contract is evidence that America is not entirely a society of grown-ups. A drama in Encino, California: A lawyer named Kenneth Shild built a basketball court in his yard, sixty feet from the bedroom window of a neighbor, Michael Rubin, also a lawyer. The bouncing of the basketball produced a "percussion noise that was highly annoying," according to Rubin, who asked Shild and his son to stop playing. Shild refused, and Rubin, knowing that his rights allowed him to take action to stop a nuisance, sprayed water from his garden hose onto the neighbor's basketball court. Suit and countersuit. Rubin's restraining order limiting the hours of the day during which the Shilds could play was overturned by an appeals-court judge. Each side seeks more than $100,000 in punitive damages. Shild argues mental stress. Rubin claims that his property has been devalued.

Fish gotta swim. Locusts devour the countryside. Lawyers sue. For all the American plague of overlitigation, lawyers also act as a kind of priesthood in the rituals of American faith. Most religions preach a philosophical endurance of the imperfections of the world. Suffering must be borne. Americans did not come to the New World to live like that. They operate on a pushy, querulous assumption of perfectibility on earth ("the pursuit of happiness"—their own personal happiness). That expectation, which can make Americans charming and unreasonable and shallow, is part of their formula for success. But it has led Americans into absurdities and discontents that others who know life better might never think of. A frontier self-sufficiency and stoicism in the face of pain belong now in a museum of lost American self-images.

Each approach, that of busybody or crybaby, is selfish, and each poisons the sense of common cause. The sheer stupidity of each seeps into public discourse and politics. *Idiot,* in the original Greek, meant someone who cared nothing for issues of public life. The pollster Peter Hart asked some young people in a focus group to name qualities that make America special. Silence. Then one young man said, "Cable TV."

Asked how to encourage more young people to vote, a young woman replied, "Pay them."

In her book *Rights Talk,* Mary Ann Glendon of Harvard Law School argues that the nation's legal language on rights is highly developed, but the language of responsibility is meager: "A tendency to frame nearly every social controversy in terms of a clash of rights (a woman's right to her own body vs. a fetus's right to life) impedes compromise, mutual understanding, and the discovery of common ground."

But of course deciding about abortion is not easy. Compromise and common ground are difficult to find on many issues. The American social contract is fluid, rapidly changing, postmodernist, just as the American gene and culture pool is turbulently new every day. Life improvises rich dilemmas, but they fly by like commercial breaks, hallucinatory, riveting, half-noticed. What is the moral authority behind a social contract so vivid and illegible? Only the zealously asserted styles of the new tribes (do this, don't do this, look a certain way, think a certain way, and that will make you all right).

When old coherences break down, civilities and tolerances fall away as well. So does an ideal of self-reliance and inner autonomy and responsibility. The new tribes, strident and anxious and dogmatic, push forward to impose a new order. Yet they seem curiously faddish, unserious: Youth culture unites with hypochondria and a childish sense of entitlement. Long ago, Carry Nation actually thought the United States would be better off if everyone stopped drinking. The busybodies today worry not about their society but about themselves—they imagine that they would be beautiful and virtuous and live forever, if only you would put out that cigar.

FIFTEEN CHEERS FOR ABSTINENCE

October 2, 1995

DURING THE 1950S, WHEN THERE WAS NO SEX, THE JESUIT retreat master would tell us, "Boys, sometimes you are going to find yourselves having what we call Impure Thoughts. And when that happens, boys, I want you to play basketball."

Thus in the concrete courtyard outside the cafeteria at St. Aloysius Gonzaga—before classes, between classes, in any weather, in the demon energy of our hormones—we played basketball. A boy would launch a set shot from the outside that rose steeply and dropped like a mortar shell. Swish! Another teenage pregnancy averted.

Basketball as birth control: the sublimating trajectory of ball to hoop cartooned the urgent, intimate quest of sperm to ovum—and, so to speak, contracepted it. Basketball converted raw adolescent pagan fuel to a useful chastity—that is, to play. For years when I saw teenagers on the court shooting baskets, I would say to myself, "I know what's on your minds, you dirty boys!"

What will keep today's young safe from the downward spiral—which is not only the familiar descent of children bearing children and disintegrated families and AIDS, but also the more general American sexual devolution, the swamp of the id? Basketball has lost its sublimating magic.

I offer fifteen cheers for abstinence.

I do not suggest saying, "Ricky, instead of sex tonight, why don't you work on your stamp collection?" Heroic individual self-denial is not viable long-term adolescent policy. What might work, however, would be an entire context of abstinence, a culture of abstinence: what philosophy would call "enlightened abstinence, rightly understood."

The chief health official of the state of Virginia, Kay Coles James, attracted the usual supercilious ridicule by urging abstinence as a policy to reduce teenage pregnancy. It will not do, of course. Teenagers will no more abstain from sex than will the frisking neighborhood dogs, and it is fatuous, punitive, Neanderthal to expect them to; the best that adult authority can do is to distribute condoms to the beasts and hope they will pause long enough to slip one on before their urgencies of crotch propel them into the hedge. If they do not take the precaution, well, then, the fallback: a morning's visit to the abortionist. Melancholy, perhaps, but—um—c'est la vie. The condom-slinger's mentality takes a ruthlessly un-ennobled view of human nature. The young tend to fulfill expectations. Government-sponsored condom distribution announces that the society officially expects to get copulating dogs.

Long ago, Jesuit father and finger-wagging mother understood truths that return to us now with what Emerson called "an alienated majesty." The cultural big bang of the 1960s destroyed the authority of common sense. The homeliest folklore comes back now as a ghost of lost knowledge or else shows up in the polyesters of what liberals dismiss as the religious right.

Isn't adolescence madhouse enough—with sufficient confusion, shame and manic, grandiose-despairing energy of its own? The years from puberty to the first full-time job are a rough passage through which the child, if tough and lucky, evolves into a creditable, honorable, responsible grown-up. You cannot light a candle in a high wind. What's needed for the development to occur is shelter, safety. A context of abstinence is the beginning of such shelter.

The mentality of abstinence demands a certain elementary moral metaphysics. Teach this: The more you indulge in anything, good or bad, but especially bad—in drugs, casual sex, violence, idiot music, stupidity, driving 90 mph, bad manners, rage—the more you lose. The more you abstain, the more you gain. This is not cheap rhyming paradox but a good truth that in the past generation or two has been swept away by raw sewage. For an adolescent, abstinence means security and, therefore, the freedom that comes with self-possession. Abstinence becomes a medium of clarity, the window through which it is easier to recognize, among many things, one's work and one's mate.

America has become a society that makes too much of its living by marketing its own Impure Thoughts: a corrupt dynamic. Secular realists reply to the idea of abstinence with some snorting variant on what Hemingway's Jake Barnes told Brett Ashley at the end of *The Sun Also Rises*: "Isn't it pretty to think so?" (Jake's problem was not sexual indulgence, of course, but the reverse—grim chastity enforced by a war wound.) Get real.

But I remember that the Jesuits at Gonzaga High School maintained a chokingly blue-hazed "senior lounge" wherein we privileged men in our fourth year could light up cigarettes between classes. By graduation I was up to a pack of unfiltered Camels a day. The culture and its sustaining icons (Humphrey Bogart, for example) loved smoking. Today smoking cigarettes is disreputable, to me and practically everyone else. Change the myth, and the values follow.

PART SIX

Metaphysics

Stem Cells and Sin and

J. Robert Oppenheimer

August 15, 2004

MOST PEOPLE APPROACH THE MORAL DIMENSION OF EMBRYONIC stem cell research by using a metaphor of weighing and balancing. What could be more civilized, more moderate, than balance? President George W. Bush said he wanted his policy on government funding of such work to reflect the "need to balance value and respect for life with the promise of science, and the hope of saving life." Even Bush's critics would not object to that formulation.

A more militant approach waves the uncompromising banners of rights—whether that means, on one side, the right of free scientific inquiry, unimpeded by government or by ideological zealotry or, on the other side, the rights of nascent life, as represented by embryos in laboratory freezers. Rights are nonnegotiable; this line of argument hardens almost immediately into a stalemate of absolutes—which is where another debate in America, the abortion rights dispute, has ended up.

Neither the moderate weigh-and-balance strategy nor the categorical rights approach is morally satisfactory when applied to stem-cell research. They are Potemkin villages. Both the approaches collapse, or become irrelevant, in the face of the essential question: Should the embryo be considered human life? Potential human life? What are the rights, if any, of a human who is merely "potential"?

Either/Or:

If the embryo is human life, then no amount of weighing and balancing will make it all right to destroy that human life in hope of scientific gain; otherwise our science has turned into the workshop of

Dr. Mengele. If the embryo is *not* human life, then you need not balance anything: Go after the Alzheimer's, and sleep easy.

As for the rights front: If the embryo is human life, then it has rights. Stop the work now. If the embryo is not human life, then it is mere stuff, and does not have rights.

But if, as we say, it is to be regarded as potential human life, then we enter into that feckless, undignified dialogue of legalistic scholasticism that prevails now, a branch of metaphysics in which we hold up mirrors to the mouth and nose of the poor minuscule hypothetical tyke—how many embryos can fit on the head of a pin? We fashion an opinion about embryonic stem cell research that is not so much reasoned (since the matter of when we become human, of when we achieve "ensoulment," is mysterious) as it is retrofitted to our existing prejudices.

I suspect that wisdom on this subject may lie elsewhere.

A few months ago at Caltech I talked to a physicist, now in his nineties, who, as a young man, worked with J. Robert Oppenheimer at Los Alamos. The physicist told me that one day in the spring of 1945, Oppenheimer asked, in effect, How are we going to set off this thing? And the young physicist got out his pad and pencil and designed the trigger mechanism for the Nagasaki bomb. (Someone else handled Hiroshima.)

I asked this distinguished, noble-looking, deeply intelligent man about both the scientific and the moral dimensions of his work on the Manhattan Project, and about how he felt about what the team was doing, and how it turned out. I asked, of course, about the death toll, and he astonished me.

He said: "Well, we were focusing on knocking down the buildings." He meant that it had not quite occurred to him and his colleagues that such horrible carnage would result. It was the buildings that they were concentrating on, and they did not quite see, um, the people.

Though I am a layman, I allow myself to generalize that even the most brilliant scientists do not always grasp the implications of their work.

Fairly or unfairly, my mind keeps aligning these two subjects beside one another, to see if the juxtaposition has anything to say. Hiroshima was an ultimate act of war, intended to destroy, to obliterate. Embryonic stem cell research is meant to cure diseases and save lives. Harry Truman and those who defended the use of the atom bomb argued—and they had no other argument—that it was dropped in order to stop the war immediately and to save lives (Japanese as well as American). Which it did. Embryonic stem cell research has about it (to my imagination, anyway) a touch of the disquieting metaphysics of the hidden and tiny and immensely potential world of the atom and the sperm and the egg (death from diddlings of the atom, life from unions of sperm and egg—the cosmic potency of the potential), a troubling hallucinatory glimpse of "half-lives" in the stem-cell refrigerators, all those millions of frozen embryos, those microscopic hypotheses of discarded human beings.

After the bombs were dropped on Japan, Oppenheimer, a difficult, mystic and possibly unknowable man, had the humility to describe this ultimate flowering of the Enlightenment in atavistic theological terms. He said that the scientists "have known sin."

I find similarly atavistic thoughts creeping into my reflections on embryonic stem cell research. Extraordinary promises are made for this kind of research—the medical equivalent of a healer's tent meeting, proffering cures for Parkinson's, Alzheimer's, diabetes, spinal cord injuries, and much more. (As far as I know, there is no reason yet to believe that these cures will actually materialize.) The drama of the widow Nancy Reagan testifying—witnessing—for such research brings to the tent the spectacle of a conservative convert whose mind presumably has passed from medieval dark to Enlightenment. *Newsweek*'s Jonathan Alter writes, with the condescension of the *bien pensant*, that "these days, a liberal on health issues is a conservative who's been mugged by an illness in the family."

Well, in May 1947, *Collier's* magazine promised that a new "golden age of atomic medicine" would cure cancer and practically everything else. Robert Hutchins at the University of Chicago rhapsodized that in the new atomic age, "the atomic city will have a central diagnostic center, but only a small hospital, if any at all, for most human ailments will be cured as rapidly as they are diagnosed." *Coronet* magazine in 1948 promised that atomic energy would abolish diabetes, heart disease and cancer. The Nobel Prize in medicine that year, 1948, went to the man who invented DDT.

So I repeat that I am not dead certain that scientists always understand, as they should, the implications of their work; sometimes, they see even less than non-scientists do, because, like the people at Los Alamos, scientists may be narrowly if passionately focused on their work, and by definition they have a partisan's perspective. In any case, they can get as carried away as the rest of us.

It seems to me that embryonic stem cell research should be viewed in a longer-range and wider perspective than it is now. The discussion should not in any case degenerate into pettifogging about how much medical progress would justify how much of an ugly moral trade-off, or about whether there occurs an instant of human ignition when paternally and maternally contributed haploid pronuclei combine to form a unique diploid nucleus of a developing zygote.

The problem concerns the dangers of introducing a principle of research that, while seemingly tolerable or acceptable or even admirable in its present application (saving lives, finding the cure for diabetes or Parkinson's) may become the gateway to irreversible evils farther down the line. I think from time to time of the example of Franz Stangl, an apparently decent Catholic family man and Viennese policeman who was recruited by the Nazis in the late 1930s to take over as head of security at an Austrian mental hospital. In due course, the hospital proposed gassing a few of its most hopeless cases—virtual vegetables who had no lives at all, immobile, imbecilic; it would be a mercy to put them gently to sleep. Stangl reluctantly agreed to preside over the procedure . . . and in the fullness of time, one procedure leading to another, the decent family man became the *kommandant* of Treblinka, the Nazi extermination camp.

It is not far-fetched, I think, to worry that some biotech manipulations will have very bad consequences. We should be careful and patient, and cultivate the most neglected virtue, humility, the one that came to Oppenheimer when he talked of sin. Human beings are not garbage, no matter how relentlessly they treat one another as such, and any process, such as industrial in-vitro fertilization, that inevitably generates hundreds of thousands of unused embryos that will be frozen and eventually discarded is, I fear, leading the human race down the corridor toward the last room in Bluebeard's Castle.

Aha! the argument flies back: You have just argued in favor of embryonic stem cell research. Those hundreds of thousands of unused embryos, which otherwise would go out with the garbage, should be salvaged and used in embryonic stem cell research: Medical good might thus come out of what might be otherwise—let us admit it—an unfortunate business.

No, sorry, that is a transient and morally dubious side question.

The real issue, the larger one, concerns the decency and self-respect of the human race over the long range. It really is not all right to treat human life as garbage, no matter how ambitious your scientific and medical reasons for doing so. If using adult stem cells for research proves unsatisfactory, then scientists in their ingenuity must find other ways. It is good to relieve suffering, but it is not paramount. The human race will continue to suffer in any case. It was sad that Ronald Reagan spent his last decade with Alzheimer's, and it was an ordeal for his wife; but the man had eighty-three good and rich and prosperous years. Let us not be greedy.

The Fire Hose of History

April 17, 2000

I WENT TO HIROSHIMA. I WAS SURPRISED BY THE VIGOROUS, flashing, neon normality of the city. Nuclear apocalypse had come and gone. How could it have left so little trace?

I remembered this the other day when I was talking with a college student about Vietnam. I mentioned the Tet offensive. I was astonished (though I should not have been) to realize she had never heard of Tet. I remember every minute of Tet, in early 1968, when the entire South Vietnamese countryside erupted with the Communist offensive and when, back in the States, you could see the war turning 180 degrees and becoming, suddenly, a disaster in the minds of the men who had made and supported American policy. The light at the end of the tunnel went out.

And now in 2000, it is twenty-five years—a quarter of a century—since April 1975, and the surreal days (long after the Americans had cravenly Vietnamized the struggle and said good-bye) when Hanoi's regular army came down from the north like the blade of a guillotine. I am trying to find the right image: The fall of South Vietnam at the end of April 1975 was like the demolition of Pruitt-Igo three years earlier, when that vast imbecility of social engineering (a huge high-rise housing project for the poor in St. Louis) was at last rigged up with dynamite and reduced to rubble, the ritual suicide of the highest, most expensive hopes. Vietnam was the Pruitt-Igo of American wars. Both had been designed by the same mentality.

April 1975, the end of the American role in Vietnam, was ignominious and indelible—the last choppers lifting off the American embassy roof, Marines hammering the fingers of desperate Vietnamese trying to cling to the skids, and then the millions of dollars' worth of helicopters being pushed off the flight decks of carriers into the South China Sea to make way for more incoming helicopters. "Numbah Ten," as they said in Vietnam, the rout of the Dollar People.

The memory recedes at generational warp speed. Those who remember, remember. But a senior in college now was born three or four years after Saigon fell and changed its name to Ho Chi Minh City. I see the black POW-MIA flag still flying (though frayed) above a post office or police barracks in Massachusetts. No one raised an outcry of political correctness when John McCain referred some weeks ago to his North Vietnamese jailers as "gooks"—the feeling being, I guess, that his years at the Hanoi Hilton earned him a pass.

Memory is made of a weird elastic. World War II may be fresher now in the public mind than Vietnam. *Saving Private Ryan* brought it back, along with Tom Brokaw's book *The Greatest Generation.* But in the next week, because of the anniversary, Vietnam will zoom close again in its vividness for those of us who remember it. To the young, it might as well be the Punic Wars.

Robert Frost wrote a poem called "Out, Out—" in which a boy using a buzz saw to cut stove wood is momentarily careless and cuts his own hand off, and then dies of shock. The others in the farmyard are stunned. But Frost ends the poem with an interesting chill:

> *And they, since they*
> *Were not the one dead, turned to their affairs.*

We, because we are not the ones dead (the ones on the heartbreaking Vietnam memorial wall), have long since turned to our affairs, which since then have been moving at a blinding velocity. I sometimes wonder what the furious acceleration in the rate of change in our lives does to the faculty of memory and to the moral meanings we are capable of absorbing from our experience. It is now a year since Colombine (so long ago), which shares the marker with Oklahoma City, ten thousand news cycles gone.

A Pope Apologizes

March 13, 2000

It was a Day of Pardon Mass in St. Peter's Basilica in Rome. John Paul II wore purple vestments, the color of repentance. The pope is frail now. His hands shook with Parkinson's. Attended by five cardinals and two bishops, he leaned on a silver staff, an old man in a new millennium, sighting back across two thousand years.

Normally when a Catholic confesses his sins, he must be specific—about how often he committed an offense, for example, and with what premeditation. He must declare his remorse and a determination not to commit the sin again. Only then may forgiveness and absolution come.

The pope was not explicit about the historical sins of Catholics. And he insisted on a critical distinction: John Paul did not speak of the sins of the church per se, but of the erring men and women who make up the church. The holiness and infallibility of the church as the Mystical Body of Christ remain intact: Whatever evils were done by Catholics, the Catholic Church itself remains unsullied. The sins were a deviation, a falsification of the church.

What then were the sins? It was clear that John Paul meant primarily the Crusades, the Inquisition and a terrible inaction and silence in the face of the Holocaust. Later this month, the pope will go to Israel, where he will visit the Holocaust museum at Yad Vashem. A couple of years ago, the Vatican issued a "call to penitence" expressing "deep regret for the errors and failures" of Catholics who kept silent. At Yad Vashem, he will surely have more to say on the subject.

John Paul cannot be accused of political correctness. His apology has no taint of that cheap grace that attends smug breast-beating—what might be called feel-good remorse.

Still, does the pope's apology matter? What's done is done—the ashes of heretics burned centuries ago are cold indeed. The silence surrounding Auschwitz has a terrible integrity that need not be intruded upon by moral pettifogging about why an earlier pope, Pius XII, did not speak out. John Paul said his mass of pardon was an attempt to "purify memory." Whose memory exactly is to be purified? The victims' memories? By what easy magic would that occur? The victims of the Crusades and Inquisition are long, long dead. Did he mean the memories of the descendants of victims? Surely he did not mean merely to purify the memories of the guilty, or the descendants of the guilty? That would be cheap grace indeed. Apology takes a fascinating variety of forms; it may have many intentions—at worst, to excuse oneself merely, or to prepare the way for a new cycle of abuse, in the way of certain contentedly inveterate sinners.

What was the point of the pope's apology?

It was to set in motion the dynamic of apology and forgiveness and transcendence, a powerful and liberating force. (Consider the power of the opposite: hatred, grievance, revenge, *lex talionis* and the bloody shirt, the Balkan way of perpetuating rage.) Only apology and forgiveness—acts of moral clarification and, incidentally, of leadership—can lift the weight of the past.

THE RAZOR BLADES' GRAVEYARD

April 26, 2001

IN THE BACK OF OLD MEDICINE CABINETS, YOU MAY STILL SEE the little mail slot—blackened with rust at the edges—through which a man of another time would push a used razor blade, dropping it into a mysterious, never-seen depository, the graveyard of unkeen but still raggedly dangerous blades: a black hole.

When I was a child the blade slot fascinated me. Children have a highly developed sense of metaphysics. The slot seemed a tear in time, as if the blade that had just shaved my father, nicking his jawline, had for punishment been exiled to another dimension. That bourn from which no traveler returns. The wafer-thin blue blade was condemned to slide out of this world and to turn slowly in the black space that began on the far side of the inside of the mirror.

I saw such a slot yesterday, unused for years, I suppose. I am not nostalgic for the deadly old blades, which you screwed down into what was called a safety razor—an instrument that might leave the face dappled with bloodied toilet paper wads. The blades now rusting in the depository drew more blood in their time than the guillotine. For years, since the perfection of miraculous little whisker-reapers that come in cartridges, I have shaved blind, with impunity, without a mirror. I haven't cut myself since the Carter administration.

But the sight of the blade slot made me think—excuse these featherweight reflections—about the old rituals. Long ago, when men wore hats, shaving was a more serious and ceremonial business than it is now. I keep to some of the old forms. I use a shaving brush, for example.

But shaving once had the gravitas and danger of a masculine order now vanished. You went about it with the focus of a surgeon. If you hacked away at your face when you had a hangover, you emerged from the bathroom looking as if you'd been in a knife fight. A perversely in-fallible rule of adolescence held that when shaving just before a date, you would open two or three unstoppable bleeding wounds.

In the presence of acne, shaving devolved to massacre. At the tough Jesuit high school I attended, a prefect of discipline, Father Donahue, confronted a Polish kid who, for three days running, refused the pre-fect's order to shave the dirty shadow of down from his cheeks. Finally, Father Donahue led the kid into his office by the ear and dry-shaved him with a "safety razor." Maybe Father Donahue learned about the operation from reading about the Mohawks and Iroquois, who sent Jesuit martyrs to heaven centuries ago.

My father shaved with focused nonchalance, pausing now and then to study his work and take a drag from the unfiltered Camel parked on the edge of the sink. Now and then he brought his left hand into play, to hold his nose aside (face abruptly grotesque) while he worked the bristles on the high upper lip.

A ceremony of the patriarchy, if you like. Gillette Blue Blades spon-sored other ceremonies: prizefights on black-and-white television, the boxing-ring bell orchestrated into the jingle . . . "To LOOK sharp DING / ev'ry time you shave!" I cherish a hazy recollection, the haze being snow on the television set, perhaps, and the bluish cigarette smoke lay-ered above the ring—of Sugar Ray Robinson throwing the most beautiful punch ever thrown, a straight jab, pure lightning that sent his man into another dimension, as if used boxers and used blades alike would spin in black space forever.

Books for Emergencies

April 29, 1991

I KNOW A WOMAN WHOSE SON DIED BY DROWNING ON THE NIGHT of his high school graduation. She told me she got through the weeks and months afterward by reading and rereading the works of Willa Cather. The calm and clarity of Cather's prose stabilized the woman and helped her through the time.

We have rafts that we cling to in bad weather—consolations, little solidarities, numbers we dial, people we wake up in the middle of the night.

It is not much fun to wake up the television set. The medium is a microwave: It makes reality taste wrong. Television transforms the world into a bright dust of electrons, noisy and occasionally toxic. Turn on the set, and lingering dreams float out to mingle with CNN. Dreams are not an electronic medium.

During a crisis, during a war, television, the escapist magician, makes urgent reality inescapable. TV becomes spookier than usual in its metaphysical way: the instant global connection that is informative and hypnotic and jumpy all at once—immediate and unreal. The sacramental anchors dispense their unctions and alarms.

I find shelter in books in the middle of the night. They are cozier. The global electronic collective, the knife of the news, can wait until the sun comes up. The mind prefers to be private in its sleepless stretches.

I am not talking exactly about reading to escape. Nor about reading to edify and impress oneself. *Paradise Lost* is not much help at three in the morning, except of course as a heavy sleeping potion. I mean the kind of reading one does to keep sane, to touch other intelligences, to absorb a little grace. In Vietnam the soldiers said, "He is a man you can walk down the road with." They meant, a man you can trust when the road is very dangerous. Every reader knows there are certain books you can go down the road with.

The books you keep for the middle of the night serve a personal purpose, one of companionship. Your connection with them is a mystery of affinities. I like certain books about fly fishing, for example, especially Norman Maclean's *A River Runs Through It*, which, like fishing itself, sometimes makes sudden, taut connections to divinity.

One man rereads the adventures of Sherlock Holmes. He likes their world, the fogs and bobbies, the rational wrapped in an ambient madness, the inexplicable each time yielding its secret in a concluding sunburst, a sharp clarity.

Television news, when it flies in raw and ragged, can be lacerating. The medium destroys sequence. Reading restores to the mind a stabilization of linear prose, a bit of the architecture of thought. First one sentence, then another, building paragraphs, whole pages, chapters, books, until eventually something like an attention span returns and perhaps a steadier regard for cause and effect. War (and television) shatters. Reading, thought reconstruct. The mind in reading is active, not passive-depressive.

There is no point in being too reverent about books. *Mein Kampf* was—is—a book. Still, some books have the virtue of being processed through an intelligence. Writers make universes. To enter that creation gives the reader some intellectual dignity and a higher sense of possibilities. The dignity encourages relief and acceptance. The universe may be the splendid, twittish neverland of P. G. Wodehouse (escape maybe, but a steadying one) or Anthony Trollope's order, or Tolkien's. I know a married couple who got through a tragic time by reading Dickens to each other every night. Years ago, recovering from a heart operation, I read Shelby Foote's three-volume history of the American Civil War—a universe indeed, the fullest, most instructive tragedy of American history, all of the New World's Homer and Shakespeare enacted in four years. People find the books they need.

I like writers who have struggled with a dark side and persevered: Samuel Johnson, for example; his distinction and his majestic sanity both achieved the hard way. He emerged very human and funny and with astonishing resources of kindness. I have been reading Henry James's letters in the middle of the night. If James's novels are sometimes tiresome, his letters, which he produced in amazing quantity, are endlessly intelligent and alive. To a friend named Grace Norton, who was much afflicted, he wrote, "Remember that every life is a special problem which is not yours but another's and content yourself with the terrible algebra of your own. . . . We all live together, and those of us who love and know, live so most." He told her, "Even if we don't reach the sun, we shall at least have been up in a balloon."

Odd that nineteenth-century writers should write a prose that seems so stabilizing in the late twentieth. Ralph Waldo Emerson is good to have beside the bed between three and six in the morning. So is the book of Job. Poetry: Wallace Stevens for his strange visual clarities, Robert Frost for his sly moral clarities, Walt Whitman for his spaciousness and energy. Some early Hemingway. I read the memoirs of Nadezhda Mandelstam (*Hope Against Hope; Hope Abandoned*), the widow of Osip Mandelstam, a Soviet poet destroyed by Stalin. I look at *The Wind in the Willows* to admire Mr. Toad.

The contemplation of anything intelligent—it need not be writing—helps the mind through the black hours. Mozart, for example; music like bright ice water, or, say, the thought of the serene Palladian lines of Jefferson's Monticello. These things realign the mind and teach it not to be petty. All honest thought is a form of prayer. I read Samuel Johnson ("Despair is criminal") and go back to sleep.

Mars As Divine Cartoon

August 19, 1996

The great American metaphysician Chuck Jones discerned some years ago that the universe operates in sequences of violent Newtonian reciprocities. Jones dramatized his ideas in the famous Wile E. Coyote–Road Runner Dynamic: Coyote sets in motion giant boulder A, which whistlingly descends into a canyon to strike seesaw lever B, catapulting giant boulder C into orbit . . . and so on. Jones's work is a bridge that carries Isaac Newton across into chaos theory.

And now Jones is vindicated: We see that some sixteen million years ago, the slapstick asteroid A slammed into planet B (Mars, the fourth rock from the sun), dislodging spud-size meteorite C, which spitballed through space and whammed into planet D (Earth). Betimes, the alien microspud wakes up in the Antarctic and assumes the shape of an outlandishly hot idea, E (LIFE ON MARS!!!!), which pinballs hectically through earthling media, knocking vases off the mantelpiece, toppling assumptions, causing tabloid amazement and theological consternation.

More vindication: Jones anticipated last week's news by suggesting long ago that life on Mars takes the form of a supercilious ass who wants to disintegrate Earth with his "Iludium pew—36 Explosive Space Modulator" because Earth obstructs his view of Venus. Earthkind's hero, Bugs Bunny, snuffs out Marvin the Martian's modulator fuse and saves the world, a feat that, theologians agree, must rank slightly ahead of Daffy Duck's space exploration in quest of "Aludium Phosdex, the shaving-cream atom."

The mind resists reducing cosmogony to cartoons. On the other hand, what could be more in the spirit of Coyote and Road Runner than the big bang? Science instructs us that the universe is made of beer suds, or of string. Time bends like a pretzel and vanishes into a black hole. What if the universe is the hysterically funny work of a trickster-comic?

When humans confront the unknown, they may, at one extreme, resort to humor, or, at the other extreme, to theology. Both impulses (one disciplined, the other not) are forms of speculation, and both may be, in different ways, profound. Anarchic humor tends to inherit the universe when theology falls apart. The humor is either a refreshing relief or a prelude to despair.

The wandering piece of Mars reminds everyone of cartoons and fantasies that the Red Planet has always stimulated; among other things, it has brought radio talk shows alive with the voices of vindicated UFO spotters, the Mars rock being their Rosetta stone, the key that unlocks the mystery. But does the rock threaten the centuries-long assumptions and designs of theology?

Most of the world's faiths are content to enlarge the franchise and embrace the possibility: If life exists on Mars, or anywhere else in the universe, God put it there. "In my Father's house are many mansions." Humankind has been living in one small room.

Interesting questions do arise among Christians. For example: If life exists on other worlds, is it intelligent life? Mars's fugitive microbial traces are a long, long way from the ensoulment that distinguishes humankind. If creatures on other planets have souls, are they fallen in the Christian sense? Or are they an unfallen, sinless race? If fallen, does the earthly incarnation and sacrifice of Christ redeem all extraterrestrials as well? Or will—must—Christ redeem each planet's souls separately by taking an incarnation in their form? C. S. Lewis worried about these questions years ago, and quoted poet Alice Meynell's "Christ in the Universe":

> . . . in the eternities
> Doubtless we shall compare together, hear
> A million alien Gospels, in what guise
> He trod the Pleiades, the Lyre, the Bear.

The possibility that life exists elsewhere is of course a blow to the incorrigible human sense of self-importance. People accustomed to thinking of themselves as significant—masters of the universe to whom God made all else in creation subsidiary—might be demoted to distant cousins tenant-farming on their speck of dust.

Sentimentalists have clung to the thought that life gives meaning to a barren, indifferent universe. What if life—surprise!—turns out to be a miracle almost infinitely replicated across the universe? Is its meaning thereby infinitely augmented, or is it instead reduced to a commonplace, as the miracle of human flight became ordinary? The moment, of course, is far off.

As early as the eighteenth century, British scholar Richard Bentley pursued the argument that God's omnipotence and glory might require many planets, many arenas, for their display. Comedy might reconcile with theology along the same line of thought, by suggesting that perhaps God is a performer who created intelligent life because he needs an audience.

"Good evening, ladies and germs," begins the Voice across the deep. "I know you're out there. I can hear you breathing."

The Moon and the Clones

August 3, 1998

> Why should a dog, a horse, a rat, have life, and thou no breath at all?
> —King Lear

The news of the death of astronaut Alan Shepard, the first American in space, arrived at the same time last week as a report that scientists in Hawaii have cloned fifty mice.

With Shepard's death, time seemed less elastic than we thought it was. The old outleaping moment of the race to the moon, science and technology's heroic counterpoint to the 1960s rage and mess, was now, as embodied in the first young all-American leaper, dead of leukemia at the age of seventy-four. You may rescind the laws of gravity but not of mortality.

John Glenn will head into space again this year on a shuttle at the age of seventy-seven—an admirable feat for a geezer but no longer the irreplaceable original. In those days, rockets named for the god Apollo went up from Cape Kennedy like chariots of fire and carried a cargo of such elemental significance and mystery that even Norman Mailer was awed and knocked off his ego for an hour or two. Mailer wrote that Cape Kennedy was "the antechamber of the new creation."

Today the new creation involved in cloning is no doubt visionary (Frankenstein goes partners with Henry Ford in the mass production of life) and also plunges forth into mystery, though of a different sort from that approached by astronauts. Think of the fifty Hawaiian mice and then extrapolate, taking your metaphysics as far as your imagination will carry you. What, exactly, are the implications of unsouled reduplication?

As gods, we are cautious. We send the animals before us. The Soviets launched a dog called Laika on a Sputnik 2 space vehicle in 1957; in 1961 the Americans fired up a chimpanzee named Ham in a

Mercury capsule. Presumably Ham, with his evolutionary advantage, had a richer experience in space than the astronaut dog. When America at last committed a human life to the venture, Shepard advanced the space program by an evolutionary quantum leap. He lived to become more famous still by playing golf on the moon during his Apollo 14 expedition in 1971.

The cloners also send the animals before us. First, in 1997, came the single sheep Dolly. Now the fifty mice. First the individual, then the horde. Charles Lindbergh crossed dangerous virgin atmosphere to get over the Atlantic to Paris in 1927; that same air is now dense with flying auditoriums of people.

The space agenda remains splendid though underfunded. If the leading edge of popular curiosity trends for the moment away from space and toward cloning, we may sense that in the transition the future has grown a little retrograde, at least from a moral and theological point of view. As the American space program began in the 1950s, rockets routinely exploded on the launch pad and collapsed into their own ruins like defunct Las Vegas casinos. The nation's leading rocketmeister was the boy wonder of Peenemünde, Wernher von Braun, inventor of Hitler's Vengeance Rocket, the V-2. (*I Aim at the Stars* was the title of von Braun's memoir; comedian Mort Sahl's suggested subtitle was *But Sometimes I Hit London.*)

But after Shepard's flight and Glenn's earth orbit the following year, and on through the expensive brilliance of the Apollo moon sequence, the space program became for a time numinous. One night in the late fall of 1972, I sat beside Kurt Vonnegut Jr. in a chigger-ridden field at Cape Kennedy and waited for the firing of Apollo 17, the only night launch of the Apollo program. All of us (VIPs, press and, on the roads beyond, the entire Winnebago nation) had assembled essentially and inarticulately to worship. Civilization going back thousands of years (the Greeks, Pythagoras, Galileo, Newton, Einstein and on to the NASA geeks with slide rules) was poised to ride up out of the sandy, swampish Florida ooze. The great rocket, with its conical nubbin of human life up top, glowed in a radiance of light beams—mysterious, still and white.

Action: clouds of billowing fire. The earth quivered. The mighty thing that we had extracted from the earth with our tools and shrewd opposable thumbs rose from the earth and shot up, stately, to the moon. It seems a long time ago.

At the moment of an Apollo launch a few years earlier, Norman Mailer found himself saying aloud, "Oh my God, oh my God, oh my God, oh my God!" He was pointing, like the rocket, toward another dimension.

It's hard to know exactly where the cloning points. Maybe it would not be a bad idea to put a payload of fifty mice aboard the next space shuttle. Perhaps in the farther future, our clones should do the space colonizing for us while we originals stay back at our messy headquarters on earth. Would that parse theologically?

A Mystic of Houses

June 30, 1997

I CLAIM, HALF-SERIOUSLY, TO BE A MYSTIC OF HOUSES. WHEN I
walk into a house, I think I know—that is, I feel—the emotional history of the place. Everyone knows that a house has an aura, as a person
does—an atmosphere, a vibration that is characteristic and unmistakable. I am abnormally sensitive to houses, as a dog is a genius about
smells, or as a soldier who took a bullet a long time ago might be sensitive to changes in weather. I mention all this because a ghost has
turned up.

My wife and I went house hunting in a rural county. The exercise
sharpened my house-mystic's faculty. We inspected dozens of houses,
led up and down dirt roads and blacktops by a real-estate agent. He
would recite the history of each house and, most discreetly, tell something about the owners ("The kids are grown; they're moving back to
the city," or, once the agent knew us better, "They're getting a divorce—she's taken up with the contractor"). As I skimmed up gossip,
my eyes would frisk the house in an abstracted way, taking in mood,
angles of light and shadow and, after that, piecing together what I
thought was the house's story.

Once we inspected a yellow brick farmhouse nestled in a fairy-tale
little valley, its cow pastures enclosed by wooded ridges of old-growth
maple, birch and hemlock. I wanted the house. Then I walked inside
and knew I didn't want it anymore. I picked up . . . a kind of rage, a
claustrophobia, a violence. The atmosphere of the house was red and
gave off a low, unwholesome electricity, a Satan's hum. The ceilings
pressed down. The walls seemed to be stained by anguish. I burst out
of the house as if from a room full of poison gas.

A house's joy may announce itself as vividly as its misery, or an inherent contentment as readily as a permeating sorrow. The personality

embedded there may be stolid, smug, hospitable, plainspoken, snob-
bish. I cannot explain the physics, but I imagine that the passions and
attitudes and conversations, the laughs and screams of past occupants
come, over a period of years, to saturate the walls and wallpapers and
paints and floors and beams, as the sweats and oils of a man's head get
into the band and felt of his hat. Something in our core detects house
moods in the way a forming infant picks up the moods of its domicile,
the womb. A house transmits different influences in the way a pregnant mother does, depending on whether she gets drunk at night or
listens to Mozart.

It is easy to detect an alcoholic house—it smells of its sorrows,
smudged rages and dead brain cells. A house may be possessed more
easily by a demon than a person may; a person has consciousness and
mobility and a measure of will, all of which he may use to flee. A house
is immobile, a cruder and more passive organism, though possessing a
soul nonetheless, and is articulate in its own language. A house may be
in a state of grace or in a state of mortal sin. If it harbors hatred or in-
cest or violence or some other misery, the house will absorb the facts
and become an archive of the unhappiness. The reverse is true. Love
gives a house a radiance. All of us know these things.

The resonances of a new house may be premonitions rather than
memories. One day at dusk in late November, I visited the freshly
minted suburban house of a young woman, recently married. Her husband was at work. The woman did not work. She sat alone at home and
waited for his return—a bride marooned in desolate, treeless suburbia.
I visited the woman in the early 1970s. I pieced together, from that
half-hour, what proved to be an accurate scenario of the course that
American feminism would follow. The house predicted everything.

My wife and I finally bought a 150-year-old white farmhouse on a
dirt road. Everyone who visits speaks with wonder about the house's
emanations. A family lived here happily for many years. The old man's
wife died in her seventies; he lived on in the house and died at an advanced age. The house radiates an astonishing sweetness.

Several times in the past two weeks, my wife has wakened at four in
the morning and heard footsteps in the house—a man's footsteps, she

thinks, not stealthy, but matter-of-fact, like those of a man going about early-morning chores. I have listened, heard the sounds and gone to look, and concluded that the furnace has been making footstep noises.

I don't quite believe it. An amputee may harbor in his nerves the ghost of the missing leg—his former completeness. Perhaps out of habit, our house believes, down in its planks and nails, that the old man still gets up at four and busies himself at coffee and oatmeal. A puttergeist. I am happy to share the house with the ghost (though I sleep later than four in the morning and wish that at that hour he would keep it down). I trust my wife and I will eventually replace the old man's ghost in the house's affections.

Evil Twins

January 25, 2001

Americans have always been each other's evil twins — tribes of opposites, Hatfields and McCoys at one another's throats. They have been Hamiltonians and Jeffersonians, nativists and immigrants, slave owners and abolitionists, rebs and federals, wets and dries, isolationists and internationalists, believers and secularists, hippies and the silent majority.

And, so equally matched that it took a 5–4 Supreme Court to judge the election, we had Al Gore's blue-liberal America, trailing its agenda (pro–big government, pro-choice on abortion, anti-gun, pro-labor, environmentalist, anti–capital punishment, etc., etc.) and its conviction that it was robbed of the 2000 election, pitted against Bush's red-conservative (pro-life, anti–central government, pro-business, pro-development, pro-voucher, pro-prayer, pro-flag, etc. etc.) America.

I imagine two possibilities in the wake of the 2000 election:

1. Divisive anger will dissipate as the months go by and the new red-conservative administration creates a program and a record—facts on the ground—and as the realities of power organize their own dynamic. Americans in the past have been pretty good at outgrowing their hatreds; they have had the Constitution, material abundance and vast physical space to help them do so.

2. The rage, grievance and bitterness will harden, with what ugly result down the road? America will become a superpower Northern Ireland of the mouth, and the election of 2000 will seem like the Battle of the Boyne, and the Troubles will go on and on. Within limits, of course, that is just political normality, only nastier.

Arguing for the first scenario is the fact that Americans are not only a fairly tolerant people but usually have short attention spans. Twenty-four/seven cable television may unnaturally inflame and prolong a story (Elian Gonzalez, let us say). But once it is over, it is over. New dramas and sensations supersede the old one, and in time people will not quite remember what a chad was. Further, it would be against the interests of blue America—self-destructive, in fact—for the Democratic leadership to overdo its righteousness and its demonization of the Bush administration. The columnist Michael Kelly [who was to die covering the early phases of the American invasion of Iraq] has pointed out that a Democratic ideological jihad might have the same result as the Republicans' disastrous overinterpretation of their mandate in 1994.

But there are reasons to expect the second scenario. For one thing, the two chief channels of our discourse as a people, television and the Internet, encourage emotionalism and abhor compromise. Machines get more brilliant; people get more volatile, superficial, unreasonable.

The Japanese have a word, *haragei,* which refers to the *hara,* the belly (as in *hara-kiri*) which is, in Japanese culture, what the heart is in the Western tradition: the core and home of will, authentic emotion, sincerity. *Haragei* (a sumo wrestling match of contesting authenticities; the art and politics of the gut, basically) is not articulate or rational, but merely asserts its mystic will. Some Japanese have worried that their country's politicians rely too much on *haragei,* and have suggested that Japanese should westernize themselves toward more rational, systematic debate.

I fear that Americans, inflamed by television, are moving in the opposite direction—toward *haragei* and away from intelligent argument about anything. Television detests an open mind. An open mind is bad theater. What television wants is passion, vivid characters defined only by the positions that they hold, the ideas that they enact: heroes and villains, politics as extreme fighting. Television's idea of good civics is people screaming at each other from opposite sides of an issue for the entertainment of a nation of groundlings. And television's bottom-feeding, bottom-lining imperatives (a noisy swordplay of issues for the simple-minded masses, translated to high ratings and profits) have conspired with the instantaneous capabilities of the Web. Rage fires and cross-fires through the ether at the twitch of a billion mouse-fingers to create toxic political weather systems, an atmosphere of unthinking scorn, slur and shallow but blinding indignation.

It's raining indignation, contempt and vicious stupidity across much of America.

The Greatest Invention
in the World

January 29, 1990

When Mel Brooks's Two-Thousand-Year-Old Man was asked to name the greatest invention in the history of the world, he answered without hesitation: "Saran Wrap." A nice try, but wrong. The greatest invention in the history of the world was—is—the telephone.

The telephone is a commonplace item on a much-wired planet. The idea of being able to throw your voice around the world and in a few seconds hit precisely the ear you wanted among all the globe's ten billion ears has lost its capacity to surprise. But the telephone has strange powers. The sudden little ice age of deregulation that descended upon AT&T last week may have given some Americans a subliminal dose of the spooks.

One hundred fourteen years ago, Bell's instrument began the electronization of the earth. The telephone system has amounted to the first step toward global mental telepathy. The telephone and its elaborations (computer modems, fax machines and so on) have endowed the planet with another dimension altogether: a dissolution of distance, a warping of time, a fusion of the micro (individual mind) and macro (the world). Charles de Gaulle declined to have a telephone, undoubtedly because he had already fused micro and macro—*Le monde, c'est moi.*

With the telephone, reality began to dematerialize and go magic, disintegrating here to recombine over there. Information began riding around the world on electricity. The abrupt disconnection of such a familiar yet mysterious faculty, the telephone, must be unsettling—like a glimpse of a dead world, a premonition of absolute cold.

The telephone is one of those miracles one can discuss in terms either sacred or profane. (The same is true of babies.) The phone is of course a mere home appliance and business tool, and by the standards of the twenty-first century, a primitive one. To bring electronic mysticism to the telephone may seem something like illustrating the wonders of flight by discussing pigeons.

If you think of the telephone purely as a secular voice thrower, it arrives in the mind at its most irritating. For example, no one has yet devised a pleasant way for a telephone to come to life. The ring is a sudden intrusion, a drill in the ear. Pavlov's dog hears and picks the damned thing up. The satanic bleats from some phones are the equivalent of sound lasers. Don't hurt me again, says the dog. I'll talk. The phone that looks like a duck decoy and quacks instead of ringing may breed phones that bark or baa or moo or, maybe, sound like distant summer thunder.

But the ring cannot be subtle. Its mission is disruption. The phone is the instrument we were issued for a march into the age of discontinuity. The telephone call is a breaking-and-entering that we invite by having telephones in the first place. Someone unbidden barges in and for an instant or an hour usurps the ears and upsets the mind's prior arrangements. Life proceeds in particles, not waves. The author Cyril Connolly wrote lugubriously about the sheer intimacy of intrusion that a telephone can manage. "Complete physical union between two people is the rarest sensation which life can provide—and yet not quite real, for it stops when the telephone rings."

Something about telephones is comic, related to some manic vaudeville. In your fist you clutch to the ear an object that looks ignominiously like the shining plastic cousin of a shoe. Designers have produced more streamlined models, but an essential ungainliness is inescapable. It results partly from the pressing of technology against anatomy. The technosmooth circuitry is pushed bizarrely against the old Darwinian skull. The talker's being comes unfocused from the visual immediate room and refocuses—through the ear!—elsewhere. The Here communes with There through sudden activations of breath, vocal cords, jawbone, tongue, lips, eyes, emotions. Through the thing held to the ear, we hear voices from another world. We would be amazed by this spectacle if we were not so used to it.

In 1886 a poet named Benjamin Franklin Taylor caught both the metaphysics and, unintentionally, the comedy when he wrote this rhapsody to the phone:

> *The far is near. Our feeblest whispers fly*
> *Where cannon falter, thunders faint and die.*
> *Your little song the telephone can float*
> *As free of fetters as a bluebird's note.*

Alexander Graham Bell thought the telephone should properly be answered by saying, "Hoy! Hoy!"—an odd term from the Middle English that became the sailor's "Ahoy!" and reflected Bell's sense that those speaking on early telephones were meeting like ships on a lonely and vast electronic sea. The world has now grown electronically dense, densest of all perhaps among the Japanese, who answer the phone with a crowded, tender, almost cuddling, quick-whispered *mushi-mushi*. The Russians say *slushaiyu* (I'm listening). The hipper Russians say *allo*. Italians say *pronto* (ready). The Chinese say *wei, wei* (with a pause between the words, unlike the Japanese *mushi-mushi*). *Wei, wei* is meaningless, except as a formula to answer the phone.

Why is the telephone the greatest invention in the history of the world? Forget its existential oppressions (the disruptions, the discontinuities of mind or, if you want to look for trouble, the thought of the sheer obliterating noise that would be made if all the telephone conversations of the earth at a given moment were audible at once). All of that is nattering. The telephone, with the fluidities of information that it has enabled, has proved to be a promiscuously, irrepressibly democratic force, a kinetic object with the mysterious purity to change the world. The telephone, like the authority to kill, might have been legally restricted to kings and dictators. But it is in a way the ideal instrument of freedom—inclusive, unjudging, versatile, electronic but old-fashioned (here so long no one really fears it). The telephone, like democracy, is infinitely tolerant of stupidity; it is a virtual medium of stupidity, a four-lane highway of the greedy and false and brainless. But it is (unless tampered with) a faithful channel of words from mouth to distant ear, mind to mind, and that is, absolutely and exactly, the meaning of freedom.

The Future of War

November 29, 1993

Genghis Khan sat with his Mongol comrades-in-arms debating the question What is life's sweetest pleasure? One man ventured that it surely was falconry. Genghis Khan—who was not Genghis Khan for nothing—answered, "You are mistaken. Man's greatest good fortune is to chase and defeat his enemy, seize his total possessions, leave his married women weeping and wailing, ride his gelding, and use the bodies of his women as a nightshirt."

The Khan's agenda—war and atrocity—is still pursued, although with less candor about the pleasure involved: Some tribal or nationalist rationale ("Greater Serbia!") is proclaimed. Even after the cold war has ended and big-battle war seems to have become extinct—the Gulf War perhaps a last set piece of tank warfare—parvenu nations tinker in their basements with homemade nuclear weapons. Even more ominous is the global inundation of conventional weapons, a planetary democratization of firepower trickling down to Third World villages and the hip-pockets of American schoolchildren.

Margaret Mead argued that "war is only an invention." She refused to regard it as an inevitable part of human baggage, the curse of the reptilian brain. John Keegan is agnostic in the nature-nurture argument. "All we need to accept," he writes in *A History of Warfare*, "is that, over the course of 4,000 years of experiment and repetition, war-making has become a habit." Whether it is a filthy habit or, as sometimes happens, a dirty necessity, war obviously has transcendent excitements, temptations and mysteries. And it is the oldest drama: the epic of the limbic system.

Homer gave to each death in battle a vivid, ghastly intimacy, a perfect uniqueness that would flash-freeze the instant: no two deaths the same. Keegan has a similar eye for the memorable in war. The eye is connected to the mind of one of the century's most distinguished military historians.

Keegan shares the usual civilized revulsion at war: a richly knowledgeable antipathy, in his case. His gaze is clear, steady and morally complicated. He has been drawn all his life to military culture and the subject of war. Complications from a teenage case of tuberculosis left him lame, unfit for military duty. But he went on to teach military history at Sandhurst, the Royal Military Academy, for many years—a soldier's life by association, at an intellectual remove.

Keegan is instinctively sympathetic to warriors and ruthlessly unromantic about the specifics of their work:

> [I remember] the look of disgust that passed over the face of a highly distinguished curator of one of the greatest collections of arms and armor in the world when I casually remarked to him that a common type of debris removed from the flesh of wounded men by surgeons in the gunpowder age was broken bone and teeth from neighbors in the ranks. He had simply never considered what was the effect of the weapons about which he knew so much, as artifacts, on the bodies of the soldiers who used them.

A History of Warfare represents a synthesis of what Keegan has absorbed in more than three decades of studying war, teaching military men and listening to them. Like his 1976 work The Face of Battle, his new book is alive with sudden, unexpected details and delights of knowledge—a treatise, for example, on how to make a composite bow, that revolutionary asset of the horse warrior; a detour into the institutionalized vengeance of Maori war-making; or a splendid interlude on the effects of geography on war, including a disquisition on why Adrianople (Edirne in modern Turkey) has been the most fought-over place in the world (it stands at the land bridge between Europe and Asia). If Keegan spends too little time on war in the twentieth century, his unusual design—a layering of material in chapters called "Stone," "Flesh," "Armies," "Iron" and so on—permits him to range across time and distance to brilliant comparative effect. He roams from the

Japanese suppression of firearms during the Tokugawa seclusion (an early success of gun control, unrepeatable and totalitarian) to the Aztec "Feast of the Flaying of Men"; from Sun Tzu to Clausewitz (he detests the latter as the ideological godfather of modern war-as-policy); and from the dark, irrational roots of Roman military violence to the question of why the horse nomads left the steppe to go marauding.

One of Keegan's charms has always been his independence, his sometimes brusque contempt for the merely academic: "How blinkered social scientists are to the importance of temperament," he remarks while discussing the attractions of warrior life and military culture. "I am tempted, after a lifetime's acquaintance with the British army, to argue that some men can be nothing but soldiers."

DECONSTRUCTING THE SUPER BOWL

January 18, 1999

INTELLECTUALS LOVE BASEBALL, AND THEY READ SWEET MEAN-ings into it. The game "has a mythic quality," Bernard Malamud thought—the myths being innocent democracy, recovered childhood, a harmless, universal cast of heroes (from Ruth and DiMaggio long ago to McGwire and Sosa in the memorable 1998 season) and a sentimental reconciliation, over peanuts and Cracker Jack, between the college-educated and the working class.

Overeducated fans turn baseball into "text." One historian sees the game as an American fertility rite. A professor of English at the University of Rochester, George Grella, has written that "while [baseball] radiates a spiritual transcendence, it also expresses a parallel paradoxical quality of sadness ... it instructs us in two crucial American concepts, the loneliness of space and the sadness of time."

I'm concerned that professional football has no such mythic dimension. I think that explains why football's television ratings have fallen off; ABC's *Monday Night Football,* for example, has in its 1998–1999 stretch just wound up the worst season in its twenty-nine years on the air. I have located the problem. Pro football remains in bad odor among thinkers. It needs a richer intellectual tradition.

Pro football's old reputation lingers: It runs on steroids and brute force; its model is militaristic (with a vocabulary of *aerial attack, offense* and *defense*), is aggressively over-male (*penetration*) and seems somehow stupider than baseball because its energy is raw and violent.

I was surprised several weeks ago at dinner when a friend of mine, the writer Ted Morgan, born French as Sanche de Gramont but years ago Americanized, launched into a rhapsody about professional football. Ted, whose Sundays are lost from September to Super Bowl, loves what he calls "the beauty" of pro football—its power, its grace, its intelligence. Ted explains that football is a symbolic reenactment of America's westward conquest of territory—while baseball is a "post-settlement" enterprise in which each team by turns pacifically yields the field to the other.

You don't run across this sort of profound reading of football every day. Ted inspired me to renew a lapsed relationship with the game and, eventually, as a favor to football, to cast about for an interpretive metaphysics.

I start by embroidering an obvious difference between baseball and football: the role of time. A baseball game may in theory go on forever: It ends only with the last out. Football binds itself to the existential tragedy of the clock. Did not Nietzsche write of "acting against time and thus on time, for the sake of a time one hopes will come?" Fleeting time aligns football in metaphysical parallel with life itself: All mortals play with the clock running. Football faces up to the pressure and poignance of its deadline, the official's fatal, final gunshot. Or something like that.

Surely the French deconstructionist Michel Foucault must be deployed. Football enacts the Foucaultian paradigm wherein all actions, even involuntary motions or fakes or failures (quarterback sacked), coalesce in meaning, and everything that the game organizes in the way of objects, rites, customs (the superstitious butt slapping, the narcissistically erotic Bob Fosse touchdown dances) constitutes a coherent whole—the game *lui-même*. Foucault saw pro football as the quintessential mutation of the Classical quadrilateral of language into the Modern anthropological quadrilateral. Actually, he didn't. But it amuses me to think he might have. Ha ha, Boomer Esiason!

What I mean is that a professional football game is the mutation of inert muscle (noun) into pure historicized act (verb), framed in a matrix (*gridiron*) of time and space. At the precise pencil-point of time, the quarterback's cogito presses urgently upon the possibilities of the unthought.

Let us improve upon the hermeneutics of chalk-talk pundits and initiate pro football in a richer obscurantism. The thoughtful spectator will see the players as nodes through which institutionalized power relations are transmitted. From the flip of the coin, the stark binary *either/or* (heads or tails) introduces us to a divided universe (kick off or receive? offense or defense?), a jockstrap yin-yang played out in a temporal dynamic of four quarters in a cycle of Sundays that recapitulates Vico . . . or is it Ibn Khaldun? I forget.

That's a start, anyway—football as text. Papers for future discussion: "The Huddle: *Gemeinschaft* or *Gesellschaft*?" "The Snap from Center: A Buried Semiotics of Homoeroticism?" "From Cosell to Madden: Pedants and Blowhards in the Booth."

End with a conundrum: A gain for one team is a loss for the other. One side's good, pari passu, is the other's evil. Such are the stakes. One side has "possession." Who, or what, then, is "possessed"? And with what satanic implications? This is a question that drives postmodern man to crush an empty beer can on his forehead—and even to open another one!

MOUNT SINAI

March 9, 1990

Elvis Presley's Graceland in Memphis has become a shrine, a sort of tackiness made sacred. Mount Sinai, where God came to earth, is about to become a sacred place made tacky.

A billboard on a road six miles north of Sinai's Monastery of St. Catherine says, "At this site will be 500 villas, a tourist village with 250 rooms, two hotels with 400 rooms, shopping center, school and hospital, supplied by all facilities." The "great and terrible wilderness" described by Deuteronomy is on its way to becoming a tourist trap.

The pilgrim will no longer have to make the 2½-hour climb from the monastery, on the steep steps carved in rock by Byzantine monks who began the task in the sixth century. Unless better angels intervene, there is to be a cable car to whisk the pilgrim up the volcanic rock. At the upper terminus, according to one plan, the visitor will find a restaurant, a casino (which in Egypt is not a gambling house but a non-alcoholic nightclub) and probably an asphalt walkway lighted at night to take the visitor to where Moses and God met.

"In other parts of Africa," the author Paul Bowles remarked, "you are aware of the earth beneath your feet, of the vegetation and the animals; all power seems concentrated in the earth. In North Africa the earth becomes the less important part of the landscape because you find yourself constantly raising your eyes to look at the sky. In the arid landscape the sky is the final arbiter." Is that the reason the three great monotheisms (Judaism, Christianity, Islam) were born in the desert, the reason that all the specialized deities left the earth and went into the upper air to coalesce into one invisible God?

The Lord "descended upon [Mount Sinai] in fire," Exodus records. The Lord gave the Law to Moses there: "And all the people saw the thunderings, and the lightnings, and the noise of the trumpet, and the mountain smoking." Today a visitor sees the massive granite front of Horeb that rises perpendicularly out of moonscape and that in the autumn and winter months may be surrounded by sudden clouds, thunder, lightning and lashing rains.

"Whosoever toucheth the mount shall surely be put to death," said the Lord. For over three thousand years, the occupiers of the Sinai peninsula, from Justinian to the Prophet Muhammad to Abdel Nasser and Golda Meir, took the site under their protection. Mount Sinai is enclosed in a convective divinity that is primitive and powerful. The mountain seems to gather thousands of years into a prismatic clarity. The Egyptian Ministry of Housing and Reconstruction, however, is not awed.

The tourist pressure has been building for years. Today some 30,000 visitors a year come to Mount Sinai. Most arrive in buses from Cairo or else take a twice-weekly Air Sinai flight that lands at an airstrip built by the Israelis during their occupation. If the Egyptian government's plans go according to projections, some 565,000 tourists—an almost 1,800 percent increase—will arrive every year. What is wrong with that? That part of the Sinai is a wilderness populated mostly by Bedouins and the seventeen Greek Orthodox monks at St. Catherine's monastery. Egypt urgently needs hard currency. The other tourist sites, the pyramids at Giza, the temples at Luxor, are overwhelmed by foreigners. Why not open up a sluice of tourism to the Sinai?

There are three irretrievable losses waiting here.

The first is to the monks of the Greek Orthodox monastery. St. Catherine's sits in a wadi at the foot of Mount Sinai. For fourteen continuous centuries, the monks have prayed there. Since the middle of the sixth century, they have placed the skulls and bones of dead monks in the monastery's charnel house. In one corner of the monastery, surrounded by a protective wall, is what tradition says is the Burning Bush, a large, dense bramble whose leaves have been coming out olive green for three thousand years. The monks' medieval tradition of hospitality to the wayfarer was never meant to accommodate tour buses. The volume of tourism is exhausting the monks. Increasing the load of visitors to an average of 1,500 a day would swamp the monastery. The monks might have to close down. Or perhaps the government could hire people to impersonate monks—a sort of Williamsburg pageantry. (Do prayers performed by impostors have any spiritual voltage?) Or the government might make the monastery a museum. Or a hotel. What would the ministry do with the skulls?

The second loss would be to the environment. There are 812 species of plants in the Sinai, half of them found in the high mountains around St. Catherine's. Of those, 27 are endemic, found nowhere else in the world, according to Joseph Hobbs, a University of Missouri geographer who has studied nature on the massif. Ibex browse and graze on Mount Sinai, virtually tame, because the Bedouins never hunt them, regarding the territory as sacred. The contemplated tourism would arrive in that nature like a neutron bomb.

The third catastrophe would be visited upon the idea of sanctity itself. No one would propose to raze the old city of Jerusalem, which contains some of the holiest sites of Christianity, Judaism and Islam, to make way for parking lots and discotheques. But because Mount Sinai is mere raw nature, somehow it is more vulnerable to the idea of *development*—a business word suggesting (ridiculously in this case) improvement.

Somewhere this bulldozing desanctification for money must end. If the attraction of Mount Sinai is its holy wilderness, and even the physical effort required to approach it, tourist development threatens to destroy the uniqueness and transcendence of the pilgrimage. The Egyptians are often haphazard about protecting their dead treasures. Now they seem ready to sacrifice a powerful, living mountain that is in their care. Perhaps they will make the cable cars in the shape of calves and gild them. Golden calves will slide up and down Mount Sinai.

FAITH AND THE GLOBAL CITY

March 15, 1993

THOSE WHO GLORIFY THE IDEA OF THE WORLD TURNING INTO a global village may not know much about the behavior of people in villages. Sometimes, as Cervantes understood, "there is more harm in a village than is dreamt of."

In any case, the global village—proliferating now into a planetary city, with a few luxurious districts, and many terrible slums, and some neighborhoods that are savage and very dangerous—has no police force. The people of Bosnia know this. What the global community does have is many churches. Sometimes it is the faithful of the churches, and the mosques, who need policing most of all.

If you scratch any aggressive tribalism, or nationalism, you usually find beneath its surface a religious core, some older binding energy of belief or superstition, previous to civic consciousness, previous almost to thought. Here is the paradox of God-love as a life force, the deepest well of compassion, that is capable of transforming itself into a death force, with the peculiar annihilating energies of belief. Faith, the sweetest refuge and consolation, may harden, by perverse miracle, into a sword—or anyway into a club or a torch or an assault rifle. Religious hatreds tend to be merciless and absolute. The mystery is now on view among the Hindus and Muslims of India, among the Islamic fundamentalists of Egypt or Algeria, and among Orthodox Serbs and Bosnian Muslims and Catholic Croats.

Religion is sometimes a fortress for the beleaguered tribe in the new-world disorder. Every cult is a kind of nation. The citadels bristle with intolerant clarities of doctrine—and with high-caliber weapons. Outside Waco, Texas, a cult called the Branch Davidians, apocalyptic and armed to the teeth, played out a siege drama that owed something to Jim Jones's last hours, when he and more than nine hundred members of his People's Temple cult died in Guyana, and to some older religious Americana, like Elmer Gantry, darkened with touches of the Road Warrior. The tragedy in Texas was self-contained, and seemed a familiar story of what happens when a group sealed away in paranoia succumbs to the influence of a sort of preacherly hypnotist.

Waco represented a microfanaticism. The week's other case suggested larger issues, a macrodrama. It may have involved religion in more political form. The arrest of a twenty-five-year-old Muslim named Mohammed Salameh raised the specter that the February 26, 1993 bombing of Manhattan's World Trade Center was perhaps a terrorist act of intense cultural symbolism, framed in religious context. And it brought serious terrorism across the American threshold for the first time.

When the Berlin Wall came down and the Soviet Union deconstructed and freedom swept across the old communist bloc, American foreign policy analyst Francis Fukuyama offered a much-discussed thesis about what he called "the end of history," wherein, with communism gone, the world's civilization would settle upon a kind of sun-splashed plateau of democratic pluralism and free-market rationalism. One of the worst dangers in the post-Fukuyama world might be boredom, a fitful cultural unease.

But obviously, "the end of history" has a dark side. The collapse of the binary cold war configuration produces an unstable, free-form arrangement of forces and impulses loose in the world, often traveling forward or backward at high historical speed. The world moves along a double track, tending toward one extreme or the other—toward economic internationalism and electronic interpenetrations, for example, and at the same time toward monomaniacal nationalisms. Toward intelligent tolerance on the one hand and toward irrational religious tribalisms on the other. The dark side tends to gain when fear and uncertainty are rising. That is, in fact, the entire working dynamic of terrorism.

When Muslims, millions of them living in deepening poverty, contemplate the materialist West, they experience a mixture of repugnance and envy that often resolves itself into militant fundamentalist anger.

On the other hand, the West and some of what comes with it (AIDS, drugs, pornography, the destruction of family and community, for example) are in many ways as dangerous and repulsive as a fundamentalist Muslim may believe.

The world is becoming both more religious and more secular simultaneously. In the United States, for example, respect for religion in areas of popular culture like music, books and television is as low as it has ever been (see Madonna, or Gore Vidal's elaborately blasphemous novel called *LIVE from Golgotha*). At the same time, both religious observance and the press of religious issues (questions of uncertainty, faith, anguish) are rising. Church leaders repeatedly condemn violence done in the name of religious tribalism—as Orthodox churchmen speak against "ethnic cleansing" in Bosnia and as some Muslim leaders criticize the bombing of the World Trade Center. But the zealots press on, shattering the silence, blasting the foundations.

MIRACLES

December 30, 1991

PEOPLE THOUGHT THE SUN WAS SPINNING IN THE SKY. SOME of them stared directly into the blazing light. They hoped to see the Virgin Mary there. A local housewife named Theresa Lopez had had visions of Mary and promised an apparition. Six thousand of the hopeful stared up at heaven near Lookout Mountain. T shirts (MOTHER CABRINI SHRINE and FEAST OF THE IMMACULATE CONCEPTION) sold for twenty dollars each. The bottles of HOLY WATER, MEANS OF SPIRITUAL HEALTH were free.

Theresa Lopez said she saw the Virgin "wearing a gold gown . . . surrounded by pink, sparkling lights." Everyone else saw blue sky and stabbing sunlight. When the day was over, a woman named Kathy left the Mother Cabrini Shrine near Denver disillusioned. She had brought her two-year-old son, who is mentally and physically disabled, because she thought the Virgin would help him.

Now yellow and green dots danced before her eyes. A doctor told her that when she had stared at the sun, she had burned both her retinas and damaged the central line of her vision. "I go up there to pray with one disabled member of my family and come home with two," she said bitterly. "I'm done praying. In a way, I'm angry with God."

Denver's Archbishop J. Francis Stafford advised Catholics to stop going to the shrine in the hope of visions. He warned about unreliable "private revelations" and appointed a committee to examine the Lopez case.

The realm of the miraculous lies just across the border from the fanatical or the tacky. Miracles may turn into roadside tourist traps, Fellini scenes. A revelation may go commercial and look like a snake farm beside the highway in north Florida. The transcendent moment falls from grace and spoils on the ground like rotten fruit. So the territory of the miraculous must be approached carefully, by stages, passing from the gaudiest, shabbiest outer display toward what may, occasionally, turn out to be a deeper truth.

Even the most accomplished soul may be ambivalent about miracles. The Buddha disapproved of them. Once, by the bank of a river, he met an ascetic who claimed that after practicing austerity for twenty-five years, he was at last able to cross the river by walking on the water. The Buddha said he was sorry that the man had wasted so much time and effort: The ferryboat would take him across for one penny.

Still, the Buddha understood the theatrical possibilities. In his native city of Kapilavastu, the Buddha rose in the air, emitted flames and streams of water from his body, and walked in the sky. In order to convince his relatives of his spiritual powers, he cut his body into pieces, let his head and limbs fall to the ground, and then joined them all together again before the astonished audience.

A miracle is a wonder, a beam of supernatural power injected into history. Up There descends Down Here for an instant. The world connects to a mystery—a happening that cannot be explained in the terms of ordinary life.

Is the miracle an external event occurring in the real, objective world? Or is it a sort of hallucination, an event of the imagination? During the 1960s, that hallucinatory decade, the writer Carlos Castaneda sought illumination with his teacher, Don Juan, through the use of peyote, jimsonweed and mushroom dust. Drug miracles: Castaneda found himself having conversations with a bilingual coyote and looking at a hundred-foot-tall gnat with spiky, tufted hair and drooling jaws.

The noblest miracles, arising not from drugs but from creativity, are events of the imagination. Yet skeptics dismiss miracles as being "merely" imaginary. Cicero argued doggedly, "Nothing happens without a cause, and nothing happens unless it can happen. When that which can happen does in fact happen, it cannot be considered a miracle. Hence, there are no miracles."

Elie Wiesel quotes a Hasidic rabbi's prayer, "I have but one request; may I never use my reason against truth." Wiesel's grandfather believed, "An objective Hasid is not a Hasid." The value of miracles hinges upon these distinctions. The subjective and objective flow into one another until the distinction between the two is meaningless, just as the distinction between God and human vanishes. Reason has its mechanical uses in an ordinary world but is counterproductive in the higher realms that miracles inhabit. So says the believer's mystic line.

The miraculous moves with a dreamy, dangerous ease across the boundaries of spiritual illumination, insanity and fiction. Miracles are like wonders of the storyteller's invention, full of surprise. They belong somehow to an oral tradition. They form pictures in the mind: living hieroglyphs, dramas of sanctity. This is work connected to the power of the supernatural, implicated with the business of creation.

Christ performed at least thirty-five miracles—walking on water, healing the sick, multiplying the loaves and fishes, turning water into wine, raising the dead. Why? Did he perform them to establish his identity, to persuade the people of his power? To solidify their faith? To show dramatically that God took such an interest in his creation? The Incarnation, as C. S. Lewis wrote, was the greatest of Christian miracles, the profound transaction in which the Word became flesh. God, the principle of eternity, becomes one with the human, earthly and mortal. The birth sanctified all human birth.

What is the use of traditional miracles now? Perhaps, as Elie Wiesel once suggested, people need reassurance that miracles are still possible, even for them: The dreariest fate may be reversed. The miracle is antidote to the despair that arises from sheer inevitability. The disintegration of Soviet communism, said to have been foretold at Fatima, has had a surreal quality of the miraculous reversal about it.

The traditional religious miracle—an apparition of the Virgin, say—occupies a problematic place in a technological world. Such a vision may not be the strongest card that divinity could play in the late twentieth century, when the globe is overstimulated by its extravagant secular wonders.

Is it a miracle when the heart of a man newly dead is lifted from his chest and installed in another man who is dying—whereupon the heart comes throbbing to life in the chest of the second man, who walks away and lives on for years? The event is repeated every day on medical assembly lines around the world. What is surgical plumbing today would have been a biblical masterpiece of wonder. Commonplace achievements of technology, like telephones, fax machines, television, communications satellites and computers, suffuse the earth with a sort of preternatural glow. The people of the industrialized world have become consumers of secularized miracles—and the people of the Third World yearn for such products with a kind of religious ardor. Show a developing Polaroid picture to a man in a remote forest of Africa or South America. The developing image (his own, perhaps) seems to him more astonishing and supernatural than the Shroud of Turin.

Whose work are such miracles? Are they wonders divine or human? Traditional miracles—for example, cures at Lourdes—have a certain quaintness about them, a period quality. Unlike secular technological wonders, traditional religious miracles do not have to top themselves from one year to the next. Secular miracles become obsolete: The first silent movies were miraculous. Then the talkies were miraculous. Then television. When miracles can be superseded by new miracles, they have descended from the realm of the absolute. Miracles become mortal.

Can miracles be programmed onto microchips and still belong to the category of the miraculous? Can the wonder of the other world, the hypothetical perfection, be dreamed up, designed and turned into products? A perfect digital reproduction of the Ninth Symphony owes its miraculousness not to the manufacturer of the sound system but to the divinity in Beethoven's music.

The supernatural has taken a thousand routes into the ordinary world. Sometimes the deed is the miracle. A candidate to become a Manchu shaman might put on a miraculous performance by cutting nine holes in the ice in winter—then diving into the first hole, emerging from the second hole, diving into the third and so on. Survival yields a shaman.

It is human nature to be awed by theatrical displays of God the Father. The deeper miracles are less garish. In any case, it is odd to look for healings, apparitions and other performance miracles when every bird's feather and fish's scale proclaims divinity. The miracle is creation itself.

Miracles take the form of lives. Abraham Lincoln was a miracle. Divinity poured almost spontaneously out of Mozart. Surely when it is time for the Catholic Church to canonize Mother Teresa, it will seem redundant for a panel of theologians in Rome to ask for proof of miracles she performed. She herself is the miracle.

A miracle makes an opening in the wall that separates this world and another. Divinity, another dimension, may flow through the aperture. A darker force could pass through the aperture as well. Or the whole thing may be only a magic trick.

The gaudier miracles are entertaining. A few of them may be authentic by Vatican standards. But a miracle without purpose is mostly a trick. Far from tourist trap and snake farm, there is the Ur-miracle from which all miracles derive. It is useful, simple, transforming and persuasive. It cannot be faked. It is love.

Hooray for Bill Gates . . . I Guess

January 13, 1997

It snowed almost two feet in upstate New York—wet, gluey snow that brought down trees across power lines and left our farmhouse in the dark and cold for three days and nights. We huddled under five blankets and a forty-pound dog and read by the light of oil lamps. The computer, of course, was dead. The Internet, an entire universe (bright leaping data, shooting stars, comets of information, meteor showers) shut down. We fumbled in the dark for match and wick; we watched our shadows on the wall.

That was weeks ago. Before the lights went out, I had been reading an article in *Time* ("Can Thor Make a Comeback?") that described how ancient religions have at last found their way to the Internet. There seemed something funny and very American about insisting that eternity must scramble to catch up with progress—God's obligation to gadgets. It is the Stout Cortez Syndrome, the new-world habit of needing a procession of new worlds, transformative revelations following upon one another like new-model cars.

The Pacific that John Keats's stout Cortez (actually, it was fat Balboa) beheld has become the Pacific Rim, and out over the horizon the Sandwich Islands have turned into an American state, Hawaii, where men may marry each other now. American fast food will gobble up China. The planet contracts to the size of a grape.

In *The Wind in the Willows,* Mr. Toad romances his gypsy cart until he is transformed by the sight of that splendid innovation, the motorcar. The gypsy cart is forgotten—is junk. We are all Toad. We need the sobering voice of Mr. Badger to talk us down from our manias.

Hooray for Bill Gates, I guess. Hooray (long ago) for Marconi's gypsy cart, the telegraph. The transcontinental railroad was a marvelous new cart (though you get an argument on that from remnant buffalo and

Sioux). The interstate highway system, brightest cultural blossom of the Eisenhower years, was a wonder. So were the electric carving knife, the fax machine and the splendid neckties and haircuts of the 1970s.

Overstimulation, hypergreed and a kind of idiocy—the three stooges—tumble into the room along with technological progress, which gives them respectability and theological cover. Mr. Badger makes these points: (1) each transformative moment will be superseded by another one, tomorrow or the next day—all marvels are disposable; (2) innovations are not always wonderful; (3) the world is round and time is circular; (4) human nature is constant, but may be damaged—or what is worse, humiliated—by novelties, which (like 1970s neckties or television in any decade) may have about them an aura of imbecility, leading to (5) the Paradox of Retrograde Progress. Television is a Faustian bargain (a technology that induces dullness and even moronism), and the Internet has the same tendencies. It is not a bad idea to mistrust the omnivorous vulgarity of innovation, even its (paradoxical) death instinct. Novelty, in its pointless ingenuity, keeps slaying itself.

Not that Mr. Badger is a Luddite. He merely points out that technology has a mixed record. CB radio was a Toad mania long ago. Technology is sometimes, in the end, a little stupid—as anything must be that was brilliant yesterday but was surpassed overnight—a phenomenon that lives on a hungry, dynamic need for its own obsolescence. The universe of Gutenberg should no more be an abandoned graveyard than, say, the American city, which, a generation after World War II, seemed to be in decline and headed toward extinction. Why did we need the cities when we had the new paradise of the suburbs?

It is a good rule to go where others are not. Go into books—not texts read in pixels on the screen, but read, rather, with their weight of thought held in the hand. Go to unread writers like Plutarch, whom I read during our blackout. They understood essentials that we have misplaced.

After three days, my computer sprang back to life, chipper, as if nothing had happened. I found myself wishing that a hard snow would fall on Seattle. Bill Gates and his geek brigades, I thought, need to sit in the dark for a while, or to light oil lamps and catch up on their reading.

I thought it, and nature responded with such overreaction (the heaviest weather in the Pacific Northwest in seventy years, days of snow, ice, thaw, rainstorms, flood, power failures) that I began to feel guilty.

The Pandaemonium of Men

February 14, 1994

After God cast Lucifer and his followers into darkness, all the fallen angels came straggling together on the plains of hell—to recriminate, to console themselves and to discuss their new identities as devils.

It may be time for men to hold a convention for the same purpose.

Let all men be summoned to a gathering of the masculine tribes, like a jamboree of the Indian nations in Montana long ago—a Pandaemonium of the patriarchy, a sweat lodge of the Granphalloon, Le Tout Guyim: as if the entire male audience of the Super Bowl had been vacuumed through 100 million television tubes (thuuuuppp!) and reassembled in one vast bass- and baritone- and tenor-buzzing hive.

In would gather young and old, warriors and elders, turbulent adolescents, the sleek and paunchy middle-aged, the venerable and wheezing. Lawyers and truckers, body builders, senators, good husbands and wife beaters, mouth breathers, waiters, neurosurgeons, garbage men and nerds, chauvinists beastly and Kennedys innumerable, sweet guys and pederast clerics, politicians, pillars of rectitude, forced-entry brutes, stockbrokers, philosophers, sales reps, homeless ruins, ex-wife-drained alimoners, gangsta rappers, J. Crew preppies and gun-rack bubbas, family-values Bobs and Herbs, whirlpooling cretins, introverts, fundamentalists, jocks, spazzes, fatboys and hunks and delicate blossoms, biologists, astronauts, alkies, Buddhist meditators, joggers, homeboys, bankers, skinheads, you libertarians, deer hunters, anchormen, bureaucrats, convicts, bleeding hearts, bikers, femsymps and sexual harassers, Rotarians and punks. Welcome, overmortgaged yuppie. Welcome, beery lout in the gimme hat (MY BEST FRIEND RAN OFF WITH MY WIFE—AND I MISS HIM). Welcome, chunky Limbaugh ranter. Welcome, Mr. Justice Thomas.

It is time to talk. We must make an examination of conscience. They are saying terrible things about us.

Are they true? Masculinity is in disrepute. Men have become the Germans of gender. Are we really as awful as they say we are?

[Uproar, cheers, gestures of fists upraised and twirling, chorus of "Har! Har! Har!," here and there a wagon master's drawn-out John Wayne "Yo-o-o-o-o-o!"]

[Gavel bangs.] Gentlemen: We meet at a moment when the prestige of maleness is in decline.

[Outbreak of mock sobbing, men sawing at imaginary violins.]

In a sidelong and subliminal way, men have become the Evil Empire, or, anyway, the ancien régime. We are "They," "Them," "the Enemy." The "manly" virtues (bravery, strength, discipline and, egad, machismo itself) remain admirable only by being quietly reassigned to women—to Hillary Clinton, say.

[Hiiiisssssssssss!]

Other manly traits, of the noxious-slob variety (emotional inaccessibility, sexual aggression, a lack of fastidiousness about lifting the seat) are ascribed to fraternity boys, the Senate Judiciary Committee and (guilt by association) males in general. People come in two models: Women (good, nice) and Men (the heavier, hairier life-form).

Perhaps I exaggerate. Anyway, we know the overt man-bashing of recent years has now refined itself into a certain atmospheric snideness—has settled down to a vague male aversion, as if masculinity were a bad smell in the room. Man-bashing is dispensed, so to speak, in aerosol spray (Man-Disss), which covers the male's nasty essence in a fine mist of shame.

All men have a dirty secret—bosses harassing, fathers incesting, priests abusing, ex-governors of Arkansas tomcatting. We have reached the point where the best a man can say for himself is that he is harmless.

What is the larger significance? Allan Carlson, president of the Rockford Institute, a conservative think tank in Illinois, offers this analysis: "We are at the tail end of the deconstruction of patriarchy, which has been going on since the turn of the century. The last acceptable villain is the prototypical white male."

[A surly silence in the hall.]

But they're going to miss us, boys. "I think matriarchies are always a sign of social disintegration," Carlson continues, selling wolf tickets in Oprah country. "In history there are no examples of sustained, vigorous matriarchal societies." Dire conclusion: "I think we're a society in decay and destruction."

[Men-devils nodding: Whud I tell you?]

Consider a text by Joyce Carol Oates, from her novel called *Foxfire, Confessions of a Girl Gang*. Oates, a writer with an instinct for the violent and gothic, invented the story of teenage girls banded together as secret female warriors in the 1950s in upstate New York. The narrator, called Maddy Monkey, describes the 1950s: "It was a time of violence against girls and women, but we didn't have the language to talk about it then." Her heroine, Legs Sadovsky, tells the gang, "It's all of them: men. It's a state of undeclared war, them hating us, men hating us no matter our age or who the hell we are." Every male who makes an appearance in Oates's 328 pages of female-empowerment myth is a slimy, sweating, smelly brute, a rapist, a feeler, a hitter, a fascist. Here is a casual sample, describing a couple of apparently harmless guys on the street: "The two of them beefy big-bodied men with smallish heads, fleshy faces and restless eyes."

That's the tone exactly: *Men-are-animals-I-don't-care-if-they're-not-doing-anything-at-the-moment-they're-thinking-about-it-and-they-will-when-they-have-the-chance*. What is expressed here is an aversion that is both aesthetic and intimate, a horripilation of the sexual reflex that is perfectly captured by the word *creep*. Maddy Monkey knows that women now have the language to talk about it. They are doing so. The war is not exactly undeclared.

But turn the picture inside out: If Legs Sadovsky (a charismatic gender-driven fanatic) were a man, he would say in the 1990s: "It's all of them: women. Them hating us, no matter our age or who the hell we are."

Before proceeding, a word about the media.

After the cold war ended, the war between the sexes had some potential to take its place, to fill the need for portentous conflict with seemingly enormous issues and irreconcilable differences. Men and women at one another's throats, or—in Lorena Bobbitt's famous cut to the chase in 1993—waving knives at one another's private parts, admirably fuse the dimensions of the intimate and the world-historical. Journalists and essayists have to make a living; men and women leading peaceful, productive lives with one another have to be dragged somehow into the combat. Accordingly: "You hear what she said about you? . . . You hear what he just did? Ain't he awful? Damn, she's awful! Let's you and her fight!"

Thus one interpretation of current gender sliming is that it is the work of the usual American overstimulation and culture-by-spin-and-tabloid—the commercialization of the id. Life on the ground continues, more or less as usual, while the sky is lit up with bright video games of rhetoric.

Maybe what we see is also just a swing of the pendulum—the man's turn to be "it." Or maybe the theme of garbage that has become American society's cultural motif has finally caught up with men and engulfed what they used to think of as their dignity. In a country where childhood and children go into Dumpsters, where women's bodies (and men's and children's too) are treated like garbage in the eight-billion-dollar-a-year pornography industry, and where popular culture itself, sluicing through the ever-efficient, stainless-steel First Amendment, is a Mississippi's inundation of septic personal garbage and out-of-control behavior), perhaps it is simply men's turn to be treated like garbage as well.

The war has escalated to a new stage of attack and counterattack at higher and higher frequencies. Men feel insulted. Women detect fresh assaults. The men-are-awful period has been going on for a while. There are signs that the oh-yeah-well-women-are-pretty-disgusting-too stage has arrived. For men and women, this is mostly a lose-lose combat. But it is entertaining for the crowds in the Coliseum.

Woman-dissing: During a period in the 1990s, retaliatory rounds were targeted at female ruthlessness at the office—for example, in the movie *Mrs. Doubtfire* (ruthless careerist mom keeps admirable father from his children); in Michael Crichton's novel *Disclosure* (ruthless careerist executive sexually harasses male subordinate and tries to destroy his career); in Ron Howard's movie *The Paper* (ruthless big-city tabloid editor played by Glenn Close).

But let us stick to exploring the proposition that it is the men who are swine. As Samuel Butler advised in the nineteenth century, "Wise men never say what they think of women."

Any honest male admits, in the privacy of his heart, that he considers men to be pretty awful sometimes. He has known guys who were so rotten that . . . Well, women don't know the half of it. If he were a woman, he knows, he would be disgusted by men's preoccupation with sex, which makes them alternately clumsy and dangerous; by their selfishness and egotism, by their bullying and insecurity, above all by their potential for violence. On the issue of rape, the man-trying-to-think-like-a-woman would go ballistic.

A few men take this breast beating too far. Some writers in the appease-the-sisters branch of men's-movement literature hold that masculinity is a destructive atavism and an encumbrance that a small planet could do without. John Stoltenberg, a radical feminist who wrote a book called *The End of Manhood,* divides men into misogynists and recovering misogynists. "Manhood," he writes, "is the paradigm of injustice. . . . Refusing to believe in manhood is the hot big bang of human freedom." Soft-core pamphleteering. Here we see the descendants of the ancient priests of Cybele, who as part of their initiation would castrate themselves and sling their testicles into the earth mother's pine tree.

A man who is still intact would repeat what James Joyce once said to his publisher when they were arguing about a manuscript change: I appreciate that there are two sides to this issue. But I cannot be on both sides at the same time.

In a culture of spin, attitudes churned up by mere hype may take on an enduring and powerful life of their own—in the economy, in the culture, in government and law, in people's lives. That is why the attitudes of one sex toward the other need to be looked at.

The market economy has found that man-bashing sells. Entrepreneurs have descended. Hallmark Cards' fast-selling line, Shoebox

Greetings, traffics in whimsical male-dissing. Another company marketed a card that said, "Hear you're looking for a man who's your intellectual equal . . . Does the expression Fat Chance mean anything to you?" Mild enough, but still: Would the company have sold a card that said, "Hear you're looking for a black who is your intellectual equal . . . Fat Chance"? The booksellers' shelves are heavy with volumes of the *Women-Who-Love-Men-Who-Hate-Women-Who-Are-Too-Good-for-the-Lousy-Jerks-Who-Snore-Anyway* variety. Simon & Schuster published *No Good Men*, one hundred pages of cartoons about what slobs and fools men are. *No Good Women* would not find a publisher.

An established genre of movies routinely assumes the awfulness of men, and portrays them in a way that would be judged bigoted and stereotyped if applied to blacks, Jews, Asians or, for that matter, women. In this genre, the good guys are women and children. The bad guys are adult white men—almost inevitably brutal, stupid, violent, seething with rage against women.

Tobias Wolff's subtle, vivid memoir, *This Boy's Life,* was converted into a one-track movie centered on the loutish, vicious behavior of Wolff's stepfather, played by Robert De Niro. *Fried Green Tomatoes,* released in 1991, was a masterpiece of artfully soft-edged propaganda, a regular *Birth of a Nation* of antimale bias: Almost all the male characters were brutes or fools or slobs except for a mute, guardian black giant, who was a sort of eunuch figure, and a sainted brother who died an awful death when young and innocent, and a little boy who has his arm severed by a passing train. In a climactic scene, one horrible man, a whip-mean, pockmarked little sheriff, literally eats another horrible man, the abusive husband, whom the ladies have barbecued and served up in their restaurant as an ingenious method of disposing of the corpse. Interesting fantasy: Render the heroic women crypto-sapphic, mutilate the men, or cook them, and reduce one man to unwitting cannibal. Let the one good male in the bunch be a sort of big black watchdog, faithful and sexually neutered, probably the great grandson of Big Sam in *Gone With the Wind.* White women loved the movie.

And so on. From the gay or transvestite side (or from both sides) come works that teach the superfluity of heterosexual maleness, indeed the gaucherie of it. These dramas, too, add to the atmosphere of contempt. They are fantasies of disassembled masculinity—movies, for example, like *M. Butterfly* or *The Crying Game*.

The assumption is that men are fair game. The insults are retributive: a payback for the years, the centuries, of male domination and oppression. And for the continuing Awfulness of Men.

In a similar way, of course, the bourgeoisie deserved every bashing it took under Soviet communism: After the revolution, the Zhivago family had to retreat to a corner of their Moscow mansion and submit to the insults of the proletariat who moved in to abuse the former masters and break up the furniture for firewood.

A man who objects to man-bashing must be antiwoman, a part of what is called the War Against Women—a war that is of course atrocious because women are . . . helpless? The War Against Men, on the other hand, is what men have coming to them, and high time. When women read complaints about "male-bashing," the words *give me a break* ticker-tape across their foreheads.

For most of history, men simply assumed their own importance, indeed their primacy. With masculinity under sustained assault, men have been slow to respond, to state their case, to articulate the rationale for something they regarded as self-evidently good—their manhood. This is the way that monarchs, bewildered and unshaven, are led out into the palace courtyard to be shot, thinking to themselves, "Oh, dear!" and "Maybe the people have a point."

Men should think more about their situation and their behavior. Women should as well. Both men and women have been oppressed by the other sex, in different ways. And both have been getting away with murder.

In her elegant, feminist cri de coeur, *A Room of One's Own*, written in 1928, Virginia Woolf wondered why men, who have so much power in the world, always seem to be so angry. She did not get it that in addition to men's natural male-beastly competitiveness, they get irritated about being such a disposable class of human beings in the world. If women are the victims, why is it the men who wind up dead? For example, not so long before Woolf wrote this book, World War I destroyed an entire generation of European men on the battlefield—8.5 million of them. Woolf and her sisters did not fight in that war. Similarly, the names of more than 58,000 men are on the wall of the Vietnam Veterans Memorial in Washington—and those of eight women.

Feminism's stated goal of real equality between the sexes will begin to be credible when females are required to register for the draft at eighteen, as males are, when 50 percent of combat units must be women—in short, when women are paying 50 percent of the real price, not only in war but also in society's other sacrificial exercises.

Why—aside from the fact that they are jerks—do men get angry? Does it have something to do with the fact that they die seven years earlier than women do, with rates of heart disease, ulcers, suicide, alcoholism and other stress diseases considerably higher than those of women? Are they angry because something in their conditioned or instinctive social roles as men revs them up in order to expose them to the worst dangers, like dying in war, or being killed in the line of duty as policemen and fire fighters, or otherwise doing the dirty, dangerous work? Of the people killed on the job, 93 percent are men. The more dangerous the job, the greater the percentage of men who are doing it. Federal, state and local governments spend hundreds of millions of dollars protecting women workers from sexual harassment, while millions of men are still left substantially unprotected from premature death by industrial hazard.

Actually, the real reason men get angry is not the danger of premature death. It is mostly because they feel unappreciated. Men are fairly simple creatures.

Warren Farrell made men's case admirably in a book called *The Myth of Male Power*. Farrell for some years was the country's leading male feminist advocate. But he came gradually to the conviction that the feminist take on men left out an important part of the story: the real powerlessness of most men. In any case: "Feminism suggested that God might be a 'she,' but not that the devil might also be a 'she.' Feminism articulated the shadow side of men and the light side of women. It neglected the shadow side of women and the light side of men."

The quarrel lies not with feminism per se, but with feminism incompletely or dishonestly or opportunistically pursued. Women must do their share, not just take the share they find attractive. Equality must be equality in all things, not just in the professional opportunities that white middle- and upper-middle-class women wish to exploit. Equality is a matter of real responsibility and risk, of accepting the liabilities as well as claiming the assets.

Women control the vast majority of consumer dollars in America—especially the discretionary dollars. If that is not power, and privilege, what is? An extraplanetary visitor might look at the evidence of their lives (the myriad labor-saving devices, the opulent food and shelter, the sheer abundance of choices that most of the rest of the world desperately envies) and come to the conclusion that white middle- and upper-middle-class American women—from whose ranks the majority of militant feminists arise, the ones who call themselves *womyn* to keep the hated syllable *men* out of their identity—are the most privileged people in the history of the planet. The alien would be stoned to death for saying it, however.

When will women take full responsibility, fifty-fifty with men, for initiating sexual contacts, thereby assuming the occasionally painful risks of rejection? That risk of rejection makes men, who usually must take the active part, not only look foolish many times, but also appear to be sexual harassers, when in fact they may be merely inept. A successful approach to a woman is called romance and courtship. An unsuccessful approach is called sexual harassment and may be a crime.

Feminist politics goes against the animal behaviorist's insight that females organize their lives around the getting of resources (food, shelter, nice things) while males organize themselves around the getting of females.

The collision produces a dishonest configuration. Women elaborately manipulate and exploit men's natural sexual attraction to the female body, and then deny the manipulation and prosecute men for the attraction—if the attraction draws in the wrong man. Women cannot for long combine fiery indignation and continuing passivity (attempting to have the best of both those worlds).

At the end of Ibsen's play *A Doll's House*, Nora walks out of her domestic prison and slams the door. When men try to behave decently and pay the bills and be good fathers, and then are informed for their trouble that they are not only unimportant in the scheme of things but also vicious and piggish, they may become sufficiently disillusioned to slam the door themselves—preemptively. They are warned off. A man begins to think that marriage is a very foolish choice, an overrated idea.

Let us proceed to the three mysteries (two violent, one benign) that lie at the heart of the matter: rape, judicial Bobbitt-lopping, and the Antioch rules.

More than any other factor, male violence against women animates the anger against men. That violence (murder, rape, battering) is in everyone's mind—an ambient viciousness that bewilders and angers and frightens men—though never as much as it terrifies women.

In the 1970s, the feminist polemicist Marilyn French wrote *The Women's Room*, in which she stated, "All men are rapists." Then with that inflammatory metaphorical extension that is typical of women's-movement rhetoric, she went on: "They rape us with their eyes, their laws, and their codes." The raping, in other words, is literal, figurative, pervasive. If we stick to the literal for a moment, it would be more logical to say, "All men are car thieves." Far more men are car thieves than are rapists. But it is women's vulnerability to rape that cries out. Rape is the ur-crime that unites women. Fine. But the charge that "all men are rapists" is a slander and an outrage. It is also not true—all men are not even potential rapists. All-men-are-rapists is a moral stupidity as well, since it annuls the distinction between a decent man, who does not rape, and a barbarian, who does. If there is no difference between the two men, then there is no meaning to civilization.

A borderless outrage at rape, wife battering, child abuse by men, and other enormities produces a kind of capillary effect: a seepage of disgust that merges the proposition "All men are rapists" with "All men are jerks" and makes the two offenses somehow coequal. Andrea Dworkin has simplified the discussion by asserting that every act of sex between a man and a woman, no matter what, is rape. (Some feminists edge nervously away from Dworkin and Catharine MacKinnon, extremists who are convenient targets for antifeminists.)

A kind of cultural-revolution zealotry has led some rape-crisis hysterics on college campuses to post photographs of male students, selected entirely at random, and labeled POTENTIAL RAPIST. Some women who have not been raped refer to themselves as "potential survivors"—a trope that takes American victim-wailing up to a higher octave. Asked by the *Washington Post* to define the "two kinds of people in the world," one reader responded, "Women and rapists." (What would the *Washington Post* have thought of someone who divided the world between "men and whores"?)

The psychology produces a technique of gender slur that might be called worst-case synecdoche: All men are assumed to be as bad as the very worst among them. The rapist is Everyman.

Men-are-monsters feminism is not quite proposing to send all men to the gas chambers, but it is a morally feckless and unhappy business to indulge oneself in this direction. It savors a little of the century's worst, most destructive political habit—condemning an entire category of individuals, such as intellectuals in Cambodia.

What explains male violence toward women? That men can get away with it so often? Some residual infantile anger at Mother? The inherent viciousness of men? Or an eruption of their sense of powerlessness? Cultural conditioning? Force of habit? Whatever the deeper cause, violence against women has become a habit (though most men do not indulge) and has taken on a dark life of its own.

That part of the male brain that is not fastidious about the U.S. Constitution and its phrase about "cruel and unusual punishment" produces this (typically male, violent) solution: a perfect retribution for the rapist, a condign mutilation. Let one-third of the instrument of his crime be removed surgically. If he rapes again, let one-third of what remains be removed. This is a sort of preemptive judicial Bobbitt-lopping. Let the justice system and its surgeons play Zeno's Paradox on the rapist's johnson and see how many offenses he is equipped for. (Zeno's Paradox, of course, states that a traveler going from, say, New York to San Francisco must first travel half the distance between the two cities, and then must go half the distance between that point and the destination, then half the distance again, so that, by this logic, he will never arrive where he wanted to go.) One-half, one-third, any fraction will do. At a guess, rape would drop by 90 percent if such a punishment were enforced.

The approach would not pass muster as law, of course, but it should be installed in the male psyche as attitude: American men should build a culture of profound intolerance for violence against women, an almost (no condescension intended) knightly solicitude for the sake of women's safety (we know, we know, they can take care of themselves) and men's honor. Every rape and every battering of women is, among other things, a dishonor to men, and men should see it as such.

Aside from dramatic mutilations, the problem probably must be solved by rebuilding in the young, both men and women, a structure of self-discipline and self-possession that collapsed years ago, during the youths of the baby boomers who are now the parents of college students.

The deconstructions that occurred in the 1960s have reverberations now. The baby boomers a quarter of a century ago assaulted the Fathers (Lyndon Johnson and the rest) and in doing so turned upside down the American idea of male power—that is, the idea of the legitimacy of male power. Vietnam was the funeral of the myth of admirable and legitimate male power.

When the Antioch rules went into effect in the early 1990s, they provoked a week or two of whooping and snorting among columnists. Sexual Stalinism! How ridiculous for Antioch College, that flawless little jewel of the correctness culture, to mandate that the boy must ask permission before touching the girl, and then before advancing to a further stage of intimacy (the buttons, say, and all that lies beyond).

But the rules are an intelligent idea—a necessary first step in the rebuilding of a sexual self-discipline that was hit by a nuclear device a generation ago, during the 1960s. The smoking ruins of the 1990s and beyond (the epidemic of date rape, for example) are the legacy of the "sexual revolution" years ago.

During the derided 1950s, any American past the age of thirteen was not automatically thought to be sexually active. A version of what have now become the Antioch rules was at that time a part of the adolescent's mental software. In the Pleistocene before the Pill and legal abortion (an era that most young feminists have been taught to consider barbaric), both boys and girls felt a terror that a mistake would lead to pregnancy, hence to unwanted, premature marriage or to an abortion nightmare. That terror enforced a certain discipline and formality. Everyone knew—as human beings understood from the dawn of time until the 1960s—that sex was powerful and that it had implications beyond the moment. The Antioch rules, which repeat that lesson, should be adopted on campuses throughout the country.

The only fault of the Antioch rules is they do not give first priority to the subject of alcohol. If a considerable amount of the current anger at men, especially on campus, arises from the high incidence of date rape, it is clear that an overwhelming proportion of date rapes occur when the couple have been drinking. Collegiate date rape could probably be reduced by 80 percent if alcohol could be removed from the picture. Camille Paglia, an intellectual gunslinger who frequently infuriates feminists, proposes common sense for young women on the subject of date rape: Don't get drunk; don't accompany boys to their rooms; realize that sexual freedom entails sexual risks; and take some responsibility for your behavior. Paglia blames male-bashing on what she calls the sincere but misguided path of current feminism. "I made all these errors about men when I was 12 or 14. I was confrontational with men, but I moved on. Feminism is stuck at that adolescent stage of resentment and blaming men." She believes, correctly, "white bourgeois yuppie women"—one of her phrases for feminists—are out of touch with the real world.

We must take into consideration the Virginia Woolf effect.

In *A Room of One's Own,* Woolf wrote, "Women have served all these centuries as looking-glasses possessing the magic and delicious power of reflecting the figure of man at twice its natural size." Because women would adoringly (or pseudo-adoringly) mirror men to themselves at twice their real stature and worth (thinks Woolf), the men, thus encouraged, felt wonderful and set forth to build empires. The inclination of American women today is not to mirror men at all, but to judge them at their true size at best—and sometimes to evaluate them at half-size or quarter-size. Perhaps women have always done that, but they kept their real opinions to themselves, or discussed them only with other women. Now women speak with aggressive, retaliatory candor.

The result is that men feel devastatingly diminished. They feel bashed. They feel unappreciated. *Wuzza, wuzza.*

But the Virginia Woolf effect has a twin. Men were similarly encouraged to overvalue and romanticize women. Women now profess to find that sort of idealization stultifying and ultimately imprisoning. Would so much be lost if each sex mirrored the other at twice the real size and stature?

Perhaps American men and women should accept that they are hopelessly at odds. Or anyway that they are a little sick of one another for the moment. Time to give gender a rest. Time to stop staring at life through the monomaniacal lens of gender politics. Put on the other lenses.

Or if that is not possible, let us split off into two separate republics: one for men, one for women. Their relations with each other would be formal and guarded, their contacts limited and chaperoned. Reproduction and child rearing would be conducted in a safe zone established on neutral territory. Only there would marriage be permitted: The privilege of mating and forming a family would have to be earned on both sides. Homosexuals would have their own separate republic. Bisexuals could apply for tourist visas from time to time.

These rules would, of course, reinstate a form of Edith Wharton's Age of Innocence, an elaborate gender diplomacy and de facto sexual apartheid.

But this is utopian dreaming. If we were to leave off argument and think kindly for a moment, on the premise that men and women will go on mixing with one another in the current mindless and anarchic way, we might spin the thought that good can come of each sex's thinking the best of the other, and might see the converse truth: that only bad can come of each one's thinking the worst. Tolerance and decency are creative, civilizing traits. A rising standard of expectation—a mutual hope, a sympathetic mingling of desires—will lift all boats. Quite a long time ago—remember?—we used to fall in love.

[Rising uproar from outside the hall, women's voices shouting "Take back the night!" "Viva Lorena!" and "We know you're in there, rapists!"]

That's it for now, boys. I was about to get sentimental. Time to break it up.

Remember Zeno's Paradox.

Go, and sin no more.

FORGIVENESS

January 9, 1984

USUALLY IT IS THE IMAGES OF THE IMMEDIATE AFTERMATH
that are imprinted on the mind, the fragments of a normality shattered
just a moment ago. The smoke from the bomb has scarcely cleared.
Bodies on stretchers are jounced frantically toward the ambulances,
and an arm waves at the camera to clear the way. Plaster clouds and
torn clothes everywhere, the neighborhood blown out of its shoes. All
in the same viewfinder: rescuers scramble in the chaos, a mother
screams as if in Guernica, the stunned survivors move off with a slow,
blank stare. The dead lie abruptly motionless wherever the latest outrage has deposited them.

Spectacles of terror and revenge occur so regularly that they seem to
be scheduled into the routines of the world. They have become a way
we punctuate our time. History unfolds as a sequence of detonations,
a portion of the nightly news given over to psychosis. The scenes define a distinct style of politics in the world today, politics in a ski mask,
violence dramatizing an unappeasable rage. Faceless, and morally
depthless, the zealots crash truck bombs into their targets in Beirut or
Tyre, go night riding with the Salvadoran death squads, or set the
timers for the I.R.A. One sees their work—the almost daily deposits of
bodies in the roads of Central America, for example. Or, in London,
the innocent blown up to make an awful noise for Irish unity—horses
of the Queen's Household Cavalry blasted while on parade, or
Christmas shoppers at Harrods department store.

The memory keeps one picture in particular: St. Peter's Square in
May 1981. It shows Pope John Paul II in white robes, capsized back-
ward on his seat, stricken, in a posture vaguely reminiscent of the
Pietà. There is an adrenal burst of motion in the scene as the security

men spring alive and the Pontiff's white Popemobile lurches off through the crowd.

Ordinarily, the spasm of savagery simply passes and recedes in time, an ugly, vivid memory. But last week, in an extraordinary moment of grace, the violence in St. Peter's Square was transformed. In a bare, white-walled cell in Rome's Rebibbia prison, John Paul tenderly held the hand that had held the gun that was meant to kill him. For 21 minutes, the Pope sat with his would-be assassin, Mehmet Ali Agca. The two talked softly. Once or twice, Agca laughed. The Pope forgave him for the shooting. At the end of the meeting, Agca either kissed the Pope's ring or pressed the Pope's hand to his forehead in a Muslim gesture of respect.

It was a startling drama of forgiveness and reconciliation. On one level, it was an intensely intimate transaction between two men. But if the Pope spoke in whispers, he also meant to proclaim a message to the world. The only other people in the cell with Agca and John Paul were the Pope's personal secretary, two security agents—and a Vatican photographer and television crew. The Roman Catholic Church for many centuries has used imagery—paintings, sculpture, architecture—to express its spiritual meanings. The Pope brought the photographer and the cameramen because he wanted the image in that cell to be shown around a world filled with nuclear arsenals and unforgiving hatreds, with hostile superpowers and smaller, implacable fanaticisms.

It is difficult to imagine a more perfect economy of drama. The Pope's deed spoke, not his words, and it spoke with the full authority of his mortal life and the danger to which Agca had subjected it. The meaning of John Paul's forgiveness was profoundly Christian. He embraced his enemy and pardoned him.

All during the past year, the 1,950th anniversary of Christ's death and hence of the Christian redemption, John Paul has preached the theme of reconciliation. The visit to Agca was his culminating gesture on the theme. The sermon that he preached with his visit to Rebibbia was an elaboration of what he had said in a town near Northern Ireland's border with Eire in 1979: "Violence is evil.

Violence is unacceptable as a solution to problems. Violence is unworthy of man. Violence is a lie, for it goes against the truth of our faith, the truth of our humanity."

John Paul meant, among other things, to demonstrate how the private and public dimensions of human activity may fuse in moral action. What he intended to show was a fundamental relationship between peace and the hearts of men and women, the crucial relevance of the turnings of the will and spirit. Seeing the largest possible meanings in the most intimate places of the soul, John Paul wanted to proclaim that great issues are determined, or at least informed, by the elemental impulses of the human breast—hatred or love. Wrote the Milan-based Catholic daily *Avvenire* last week: "In the midst of so many voices raised to ask for negotiations between the superpowers on the basis of pure equilibrium of strength, in the choir of pacifism which proclaims that only peace counts, all else is relative . . . a Pope has the courage to utter the ancient word—the responsibility for each evil rests in man as a sinner. There will be no escape from wars, from hunger, from misery, from racial discrimination, from denial of human rights, and not even from missiles, if our hearts are not changed." Said Italian Writer Carlo Bo: "The Pope intends to say, 'If we really want peace, we must make the first step, we must forget offenses and offer the bread of love and charity.' " The visit to Agca did not come as a surprise. It had been rumored for at least two weeks that John Paul intended to see his attacker during a Christmas-season visit to the more than 2,000 inmates of Rebibbia, on the northeastern outskirts of Rome.

Since his conviction on July 22, 1981, Agca has been serving part of a life sentence in the prison's maximum-security wing. When the Pope arrived in his cell, Agca was dressed in a blue crew-neck sweater, jeans and blue-and-white running shoes from which the laces had been removed. He was unshaved. Agca kissed John Paul's hand. "Do you speak Italian?" the Pope asked. Agca nodded. The two men seated themselves, close together, on molded-plastic chairs in a corner of the cell, out of earshot. At times it looked almost as if the Pope were hearing the confession of Agca, a Turkish Muslim. At those moments, John Paul leaned forward from the waist in a priestly posture, his head bowed and forehead tightly clasped in his hand as the younger man spoke.

Agca laughed briefly a few times, but the smile would then quickly fade from his face. In the first months after the assassination attempt, there had been in Agca's eyes a zealot's burning glare. But now his face wore a confused, uncertain expression, never hostile. The Pope clasped Agca's hands in his own from time to time. At other times he grasped the man's arm, as if in a gesture of support.

John Paul's words were intended for Agca alone. "What we talked about will have to remain a secret between him and me," the Pope said as he emerged from the cell. "I spoke to him as a brother whom I have pardoned, and who has my complete trust." As John Paul rose to leave, the two men shook hands. The Pope gave Agca, who will turn 26 next week, a small gift in a white box, a rosary in silver and mother-of-pearl. The Pope walked out. Agca was left standing alone, and the camera recorded a sudden look of uncertainty on his face. Perhaps he was thinking about the prospect of spending the rest of his life in jail for attempting to kill a man he did not know, a man who now came to him as a friend.

Later, John Paul spoke to the women inmates of the prison about what had happened on this "historic day." Said the Pontiff: "In the context of Christmas and the Holy Year of Redemption, I was able to meet with the person that you all know by name, Ali Agca, who in the year 1981 on the 13th of May made an attempt on my life. But Providence took things in its own hands, in what I would call an extraordinary way, so that today after two years I was able to meet my assailant and repeat to him the pardon I gave him immediately . . . The Lord gave us the grace to meet as men and brothers, because all the events of our lives must confirm that God is our father and all of us are His children in Jesus Christ, and thus we are all brothers."

Down in the murkier reaches of the affair, meantime, Italian authorities seemed ready to make a decision about whether to pursue the "Bulgarian connection." Agca has insisted that he had three Bulgarian accomplices in the assassination plot. One of them, said the gunman, was Sergei Ivanov Antonov, once the Rome manager of

Bulgaria's national airline. Agca has offered detailed but sometimes conflicting recollections of a labyrinthine plot involving the Bulgarians, right-wing Turks and, ultimately, the Soviet KGB. Agca claims that Antonov drove him to St. Peter's Square on the day of the shooting. Italian investigators are trying to decide whether to indict Antonov or dismiss the case.

The scene in Rebibbia had a symbolic splendor. It shone in lovely contrast to what the world has witnessed lately in the news. For some time, a suspicion has taken hold that the trajectory of history is descendant, that the world moves from disorder to greater disorder, toward darkness—or else toward the terminal global flash. The symbolism of the pictures from Rebibbia is precisely the Christian message, that people can be redeemed, that they are ascendant toward the light. In a less exalted sense, the scene may be important because it suggests that human beings can respond to inhuman acts by being sane and civilized and forbearing, more decent, perhaps, than the killers deserve.

The Pope obviously entertained high ambitions for the meeting as an example to the world of the healing powers of forgiveness. But the act of forgiveness is extraordinarily complex. It becomes especially intricate when the spirit of forgiveness is urged as a basis for public policy. John Paul's gesture proclaimed a larger exemplary message to the world. Is forgiveness a purely personal transaction, or can it be applied in a political way to reconcile enemies? What if Israeli Prime Minister Yitzhak Shamir and Palestine Liberation Organization Chairman Yasser Arafat forgave each other and came to some reconciliation, perhaps in the way Shamir's predecessor, Menachem Begin, and Egyptian President Anwar Sadat did in 1977 when Sadat made his dramatic journey to Jerusalem? If John Paul could forgive the man who shot him, could sit with him and hold his hands, could not Ronald Reagan and Soviet Leader Yuri Andropov have dinner some time? John Paul seemed to be suggesting that such acts could at least dampen some of the more murderous impulses that are loose in places like Lebanon and El Salvador. Is there a larger public and political application of John Paul's example?

The first complexity of forgiveness involves the question of justice. Personal or even divine magnanimity is not public justice, and it should not be permitted to override justice. The Pope forgave Agca, but Agca remains in jail, and should. President Gerald Ford did not seem to have the distinction clear in his mind when, using somewhat sacramental language, he pardoned Richard Nixon in 1974. Said Ford: "I do believe, with all my heart and mind and spirit, that I, not as President, but as a humble servant of God, will receive justice without mercy if I fail to show mercy."

It was one thing for Ford, as a human being, to forgive Nixon, but another for Ford, as President of the U.S., to grant a pardon, thus short-circuiting the judicial process. Says Father Robert Friday, professor of religion and religious education at the Catholic University of America: "Forgiveness doesn't mean that you become some sort of a wimp and forgive without some kind of demand. We are responsible for what we have done." Jesuit Theologian Avery Dulles agrees: "For the ordering of society, there should still be justice. Restraint and punishment are necessary even for forgiveness."

In public realms, there is very often a tension between justice and forgiveness. The Rev. Roger Shinn, professor of social ethics at New York City's Union Theological Seminary, emphasizes the difference between personal forgiveness and legal or social forgiveness. "Personal relations can be very spontaneous, almost oblivious to rules, to law and order," says he. "Society cannot be. That is the whole problem of Christian political ethics, how to translate the ultimate virtue of love into a social order that has stability, consistency."

There is a certain Panglossian spirit, sweet and fatuous, always at play in the margins of any discussion of forgiveness. Comedian Richard Pryor, in one of his routines, describes how he went to Arizona State Prison in order to make a 1980 movie called *Stir Crazy*. Before that experience, he said, he had recited a standard liberal line about the injustice of prisons. But after he met some of the homicidal brutes there and found out what crimes they had committed to earn their tuition, he said he was glad they had prisons with great big bars to hold people like that. In the real world, forgiveness sometimes makes sense as sentiment, but not as social policy.

That inconsistency can be resolved by assigning the two imperatives, justice and forgiveness, to different functional levels, to that of Caesar and that of God. Justice is a social question, while forgiveness introduces a transcendent element: love. Weighing the injunction in the Sermon on the Mount to turn the other cheek, Martin Luther concluded that an individual ought to obey the command, but a government should not. There are two orders, that of the law and that of the Gospel. One forgives in one's heart, in the sight of God, as the Pope did, but the criminal still serves his time in Caesar's jail. And yet if one assumes that the claims of God and Caesar are parallel lines, and do not connect with each other, then it is futile, or merely sentimental, to talk about how a spirit of forgiveness might come into politics and international affairs. It is in the realm of Caesar that the bombing goes on.

In any case, experience teaches that forgiveness runs somewhat against human nature. The corollary of "To err is human, to forgive divine" is that to forgive is not human, not entirely so. To forget is human, and that eventual fading of a grievance from memory, not direct forgiveness, is quite often the solution.

It is interesting to wonder how, nearly a decade later, the American people see the Nixon case, whether that forgetting, almost a form of pseudo forgiveness, has occurred. Repentance is said to be a precondition for forgiveness, and Nixon has shown no sign that he has ever repented the deeds that forced him to resign. He toughed it out. Now he is a comparatively prosperous man, pursuing his career, writing books, doing serious work.

Consider what has become of some of Nixon's enemies, the people who, over the years, thought that they had left him for dead. John Kennedy, for example, buried 20 years ago, has undergone some savage revisionism that held him to be a second-rate President and an indiscreet philanderer. Pat Brown, who won the 1962 California gubernatorial race that supposedly ended Nixon's career ("You won't have Nixon to kick around any more . . . this is my last press conference") was superseded by an ideological antithesis, Ronald Reagan, and eventually by Brown's son Jerry, who is now in political limbo.

The process of forgetting as a substitute for forgiving may occur most readily in societies with a high rate of change, of physical and social mobility. That could explain why Americans do not on the whole bear enduring grudges, and sometimes find it difficult to understand the profound and centuries-long hatreds that can grip, say, the Middle East, the Balkans or Northern Ireland.

Where ethnic identity remains strong and is fiercely perpetuated, the logic of the blood feud reigns, and it is infinitely harder to forgive or even think of forgiving. An old wrong, a kind of primal atrocity, sits in the tribal memory like a totem, an eternal reminder. For a man to forgive his enemy would mean betraying his father and grandfather and great-grandfather, dishonoring the sacrifices that they had made. It is treason to forgive, inexcusable to forget. So, between Armenians and Turks, Northern Irish Catholics and Protestants, between South Moluccans and Dutch, between Lebanese Maronites and Druze, between Hatfields and McCoys, between Montagues and Capulets, the ancient fury persists. The enemy is timeless. His very existence is unforgivable, but also indispensable.

Not all enmities are unreasonable, either. Timing obviously has much to do with whether or not forgiveness makes any sense. The deed, the source of the grievance, must be some time in the past, and the threat of further injury removed. If someone had taken a shot at a man and then ducked into the woods, still carrying a loaded gun, it would not be reasonable for the man to call after his assailant, "That's O.K.! I forgive you!"

Moreover, in all but the saintliest circles, forgiveness may be a luxury that depends upon a certain surrounding stability. It is more difficult to forgive when there is no protection against a recurrence, when there are no doors or windows on the house and one is at the mercy of every zealot and loon who cares to crawl in with a knife in his teeth. That is the barbarous condition of Beirut at the moment, a place that forgiveness deserted long ago.

There are in Catholic theology "the sins against the Holy Spirit." These include such offenses as despairing of salvation and obstinacy in sinning. As long as they persist, they are in some sense unforgivable. The doctrine raises interesting questions of unforgivability. If it had been 6 million Catholics who were exterminated in the Nazi death camps, would the Pope have forgiven Adolf Eichmann? Or would he have had Eichmann hunted down, taken to Rome for trial and executed, as the Jews brought Eichmann to Jerusalem for judgment and hanging?

The theme of the unforgivable offense reverberates up and down the 20th century, perhaps because such a crime is thought to be more against man—or more accurately, more against the tribe—than against God. Harold R. Isaacs, a journalist and political scientist, observed in his 1975 book *Idols of the Tribe*: "We are experiencing on a massively universal scale a convulsive ingathering of people in their numberless grouping of kinds—tribal, racial, linguistic, religious, national. It is a great clustering into separatenesses that will, it is thought, improve, assure, or extend each group's power or place, or keep it safe or safer from the power, threat, or hostility of others." But such fragmentation does not open people up through the offices of tolerance and forgiveness; instead it closes them in upon themselves and promotes the logic of revenge.

The 20th century has been one of enormous tribal slaughter, much of it distant from the world's eyes. As many as 200,000 Tutsi and Hutu tribesmen massacred one another during tribal warfare in Burundi in the early 1970s, for example. Some 3,000 Bengalis were murdered in Assam, India, last February. More than 100,000 Iranians and Iraqis have been killed in their war, which is now three years old. And each slaughter enforces upon the survivors in the tribe the imperative to take revenge.

Yet in a sense, the greater the sin, the more the forgiving is necessary—even indispensable. Consider the American South, the scene of an enormous historical wrong that persisted for centuries.

In 1982, when he was running for re-election for Governor of Alabama, George Wallace knew that he would need the black vote in order to win. He appeared before the Southern Christian Leadership

Conference and apologized for his behavior toward blacks in the past. He had once vowed that he would never be "out-niggered" again by a white opponent, and he had stood in the door of the University of Alabama to prevent two black students from enrolling. But after his apology, the black voters of Alabama forgave him, and voted for him in large numbers.

All over the South, in a remarkable display of grace, blacks forgave the injuries of the past. Says the Rev. Donald W. Shriver, a native Virginian who is president of Union Theological Seminary in New York City: "I think the decision by descendants of black slaves in this country to become citizens and active members of this society is a remarkable case of forgiveness. By and large, blacks have had a steadier sense of belonging to the United States and of being true citizens than many of those who have oppressed them." Says Atlanta Mayor Andrew Young: "We shared the burden of guilt for past racial abuses and we moved toward reconciliation. And we've grown together as brothers and sisters and we've prospered, mainly because of the ability to forgive and be reconciled."

Christ preached forgiveness, the loving of one's enemies.

It is at the center of the New Testament. Stated nakedly, superficially, the proposition sounds perverse and even self-destructive, an invitation to disaster. Those skeptical about the larger uses of forgiveness, in fact, tend to think of that principle as a little weak-minded. Rabbi Neil Gillman, assistant professor of philosophy at the Jewish Theological Seminary of America, does not believe that a private impulse toward forgiveness, symbolized by the Pope's visit to Agca, can be translated into a public policy of reconciliation. Jewish tradition, he says, links forgiveness to behavioral change. "There is a healthy amount of realism in the doctrine," says Gillman. "Forgiveness should be tied to the ability to see a real change in human—or national—action. An inner attitude of contrition on the part of the wrongdoer is not sufficient. Israel's stance [its refusal to reconcile with the P.L.O.] is based on the fact that the P.L.O., for all its verbalizing, still takes responsibility for destroying a bus. There is no evidence of real contrition."

Whatever the political maneuvers one makes with it, forgiveness is actually a profound transaction. It is the working model of the human relationship with God. It is not merely God who forgives man, but in some sense man who also forgives God, or forgives life, for its cruelties and injustices. The essence of the process is dynamic, for forgiveness makes change possible—spiritual change and, as the American South proves, social change.

The Old Testament view of forgiveness was contained in a verb that dominates its penitential literature, the Hebrew word *shuv*, meaning to turn, to return.

The doctrine implies that man has the power to turn from evil to good, to change, and the very act of turning will bring God's forgiveness.

Those who do not forgive are those who are least capable of changing the circumstances of their lives. In this sense, forgiveness is a shrewd and practical strategy for a person, or a nation, to pursue. It is the implacable, retributive tribes, like those of Northern Ireland or Lebanon, that find themselves back-watered, isolated, perishing in their own fury.

The psychological case for forgiveness is overwhelmingly persuasive. Not to forgive is to be imprisoned by the past, by old grievances that do not permit life to proceed with new business.

Not to forgive is to yield oneself to another's control. If one does not forgive, then one is controlled by the other's initiatives and is locked into a sequence of act and response, of outrage and revenge, tit for tat, escalating always. The present is endlessly overwhelmed and devoured by the past. Forgiveness frees the forgiver. It extracts the forgiver from someone else's nightmare. "Unless there is a breach with the evil past," says Donald Shriver, "all we get is this stuttering repetition of evil."

It is difficult to imagine a world willing to follow John Paul's example, ending that stuttering repetition any time in the near future. Too many societies are spiritually incapable of it. Marxism, the political doctrine under which about one-third of the world's population lives, is a stolidly unforgiving system. Stalin did not forgive the Kulaks for being a little too independent, but liquidated millions of them. The Chinese did not forgive their bourgeoisie after the 1949 revolution, but demoralized and decimated it. The Prophet taught that "God is with those who restrain themselves," but Ayatullah Khomeini's Shi'ite regime is in a state of religious intoxication and madness that is unlikely to be overtaken by tolerance.

Forgiveness is not an impulse that is in much favor. It is a mysterious and sublime idea in many ways. The prevalent style in the world runs more to the high-plains drifter, to the hard, cold eye of the avenger, to a numb remorselessness. Forgiveness does not look much like a tool for survival in a bad world. But that is what it is.